"Jung is an outstanding storyteller. Here he offers up an economic, transport, tourism and emigration history of Switzerland, well embedded in its context. The work is easy to read; Jung captivates the reader with his tales of the successes and failures of his pioneers."

Michael Kitzing, *Friedrich Naumann Foundation, Germany*

"This book presents the brilliant transformation of Switzerland in the 19th century, in which this country and its political system surpassed most other European nations in democratic progress."

Holger Böhning, *Jahrbuch für Kommunikationsgeschichte*

"An excellent, carefully illustrated and excitingly written panorama of an important chapter in Swiss history."

Jürg Müller, *Schweizer Revue*

The Laboratory of Progress

The Laboratory of Progress: Switzerland in the 19th Century tells the improbable story of how a small, backward, mountainous agricultural country with almost no raw materials became an industrial powerhouse, a hub of innovation, a touristic mecca and a pioneer in transportation – all in the course of a single century.

That a tiny landlocked country should become a dominant steamship builder for the rest of the world; that a country that had never seen a cotton plant should become the world's second-largest textile producer; that a country with hardly any level terrain should come to boast the world's most highly developed railway network; and that a country whose main export was impoverished emigrants should be transformed into one of the world's major financial centres – these astonishing developments, among many others, are explored and explained, both through the specific stories of individual innovators and through a prescient analysis of the political, economic, societal and cultural structures that formed the context in which Switzerland's astonishing transformation took place.

The book is a compelling read both for professional historians and for general readers with an interest in Switzerland; it highlights the roles of transport networks and individual pioneers in industrial and political development.

Joseph Jung is Professor Emeritus at the University of Fribourg and the author of bestselling biographies of the preeminent Swiss politician Alfred Escher and his daughter Lydia Welti-Escher, among many other works. He has received numerous awards for his pioneering research into 19th-century Swiss economic and cultural history.

Routledge Studies in Modern European History

89 **The End of Ottoman Rule in Bosnia**
Conflicting Agencies and Imperial Appropriations
Hannes Grandits

90 **Rethinking the History of Italian Fascism**
Edited by Giulia Albanese

91 **Deciphering the European Investment Bank**
History, Politics and Economics
Edited by Lucia Coppolaro and Helen Kavvadia

92 **European Integration and Disintegration**
Essays from the Next Generation of Europe's Thinkers
Edited by Nick Cohen and Ayana Dootalieva

93 **The Laboratory of Progress**
Switzerland in the Nineteenth Century, Volume 1
Joseph Jung

94 **Border Regimes in Twentieth Century Europe**
Péter Bencsik

95 **Catalonia: A New History**
Andrew Dowling

96 **The Laboratory of Progress**
Switzerland in the Nineteenth Century, Volume 2
Joseph Jung

For more information about this series, please visit: https://www.routledge.com/Routledge-Studies-in-Modern-European-History/book-series/SE0246

The Laboratory of Progress

Switzerland in the Nineteenth Century, Volume 2

Joseph Jung

Translated by Ashley Curtis

Routledge
Taylor & Francis Group
NEW YORK AND LONDON

First published in English 2023
by Routledge
605 Third Avenue, New York, NY 10158

and by Routledge
4 Park Square, Milton Park, Abingdon, Oxon, OX14 4RN

Routledge is an imprint of the Taylor & Francis Group, an informa business

2nd, revised edition published in German by Schwabe Verlagsgruppe AG 2020.

Library of Congress Cataloging-in-Publication Data
Names: Jung, Joseph, 1955- author. | Curtis, Ashley, translator.
Title: The laboratory of progress : Switzerland in the nineteenth century / Joseph Jung ; translated by Ashley Curtis.
Other titles: Laboratorium des Fortschritts. English
Description: New York, NY : Routledge, 2022. |
Series: Routledge studies in modern European history ; 93 | Includes bibliographical references and index. Identifiers: LCCN 2022005671 (print) | LCCN 2022005672 (ebook) |
Subjects: LCSH: Switzerland—Economic conditions—19th century. | Economic development—Switzerland—History—19th century.
Classification: LCC HC397 .J8613 2022 (print) | LCC HC397 (ebook) | DDC 330.9494—dc23/eng/20220330
LC record available at https://lccn.loc.gov/2022005671
LC ebook record available at https://lccn.loc.gov/2022005672

ISBN: 978-1-032-15227-1 (hbk)
ISBN: 978-1-032-15228-8 (pbk)
ISBN: 978-1-003-24314-4 (ebk)

DOI: 10.4324/9781003243144

Typeset in Sabon
by codeMantra

For my son, Benedict Jung (1994–2020)

Contents

Figures

Milestones

Preface

Like a traveller who pauses on the final hill before a city and looks back over his shoulder to regard his country one last time in its entirety, I have been moved to piece together into a whole the disparate insights I have gained, from different vantage points, over the course of decades. This book is composed of four main independent chapters. The reader can start in on any of them. They represent four narrative threads that all play out during the same period of time – the extended 19th century, which lasted until the outbreak of the First World War. The book does not present a systematic history of Switzerland, but rather a multidimensional panorama, intended to convey not just facts but rather a certain sense of life.

The writer who wishes to do justice to the brilliant transformation Switzerland underwent in the 19th century not only has to include certain happenings from the 18th century and earlier but also train his eye to distinguish the effects that this transformation is still having today. Many subjects are taken up in more than one chapter; this allows the same phenomenon to be examined, for example, in its political, industrial, cultural and touristic contexts. The reader who wishes to pursue a topic in all its various forms and iterations can refer to the extensive index at the end of the book. I have refrained from providing a summary of my most important insights, since conclusions about specific time periods and subjects are embedded in the text. Readers who would like to acquaint themselves with my most important stances from the start might begin with the overview presented in "Headlines," Chapter 3 in Volume 2.

It is clear to me that I could have emphasised different subjects and included many more. With all due respect to what I have omitted, I am here giving an account of what most interests me personally about 19th-century Switzerland and of those subjects to which I feel most drawn. This includes the first ascent of the Matterhorn, even though I myself have only ever viewed this mountain from below.

I have thus produced neither a systematic history nor a lexicon with a well-defined and numbered place for each of its entries. I wanted to be free to use space as I wished and to survey the broad field of my subject in my own manner. In fact, what I really want to do is to tell stories. If, in doing so, I here and there awaken some joy in reading, or communicate a valuable insight, my longstanding work on this project will have been of benefit to others – as it certainly has been to me.

Joseph Jung, November 2019

Acknowledgements

Every historical account, however objective it might endeavour to be, is inevitably influenced by its theoretical premises and thematic focuses. Historians must examine source materials and earlier research with a critical eye to determine which findings and ideas contribute most to the subject at hand. This means being selective; and the question of what to select – and what not – becomes especially important when, as in the present case, the historian sets out to describe the development of an entire country over an extended period of time.

I have allowed myself to be guided by my encounters with the historical figures who have most impressed me, and in particular, by the exceptional Alfred Escher, who contributed more significantly than any other person to the creation of modern Switzerland after 1848. Through Escher I imbibed the Spirit of '48, and he has taught me much, including how decisive the development of transport technology is for the fate of entire nations (-> Lifelines: Interconnecting Systems, Volume 2, Chapter 1).

As the former Managing Director of the Corporate History division at the bank Escher brought into existence, as his biographer, as the editor of an extensive collection of his letters and as the founding director of the Alfred Escher Foundation, I became ever better acquainted with Alfred Escher in all his many facets. This led me to settle on a theme: The importance of individual personalities – pioneers, entrepreneurs, scientists, visionaries – for the socio-political development of a country (-> Switzerland Unbound: Intrepid Progress, Volume 2, Chapter 2). My work at the Institute for Historical Research in Economics provided a framework for delving into this topic.

Through my activities on behalf of the Giovanni Segantini Foundation (Giovanni Segantini-Stiftung), I became acquainted with Alpine painting and the history of tourism and, through my own family background, with the history of the hospitality industry (-> The Discovery of the Mountains, Volume 1, Chapter 1).

The economic boom of the post-war years made a deep impression on me. Migrant workers were a part of everyday life. Thanks to Ulrico Hoepli, a successful Swiss emigrant for whose foundation I work as managing director, I was captured by the "Pull of the World" (-> New Beginnings, Volume 1, Chapter 2).

I would like to thank everyone I have encountered on my journey through the 19th century and all who have encouraged and supported me. My academic interest in the 19th century was fostered by courses I gave at the Universities of Fribourg and St Gallen, and I would like to thank all the students who critically commented on my arguments and approaches and especially those who have enriched my understanding through their own academic work.

Many friends and colleagues have been there for me throughout the process of writing this book. For their constant and motivating interest in my work, for their intelligent feedback and important suggestions, I would like to thank Professor Emeritus Urs Altermatt, Professor Emeritus Joerg Baumberger, Professor Emeritus Michael Böhler, Professor Emeritus Conradin Burga, Professor Urs Frauchiger, Professor Hildegard Elisabeth Keller, Professor Emeritus Franz Zelger and Dr Martin Meyer. I am particularly grateful to Privatdozent Jürg von Ins, who more than anyone else grappled with my ideas and texts and who gave me countless ideas for improvements. For the critical editing of individual chapters and for other productive suggestions, I thank Dr Klaus Anderegg, Daniel Anker, Mike Bacher, Hermann Biner, Dr Bruno Bohlhalter, Werner Bosshard, Diane Conrad-Daubrah, Anton Heer, Philip Hess, Dr Matthias Inderkum, Thomas Landolt, Dr jur. Valentin Roschacher, Professor Alexis Schwarzenbach, Dr Markus Somm, Dr Jürg Spiller, Gieri Venzin, Dr Peter Voegeli and Dr Roman Wild.

For small and large – but always appreciated – help and support of all kinds, I would like to thank: Peter Barth, Dr Franco Battel, Marc Baumann, Marianne Benz, Dr Georges Bindschedler, Romy Biner-Hauser, Nigel Buckley, Dr jur. Philipp Carlen, Sara Carnazzi Weber, Bernhard and Ulrike Clemenz, Martin Cordes, Maja Ebnöther, Markus Fischer, David P. Frick, Severin Gerber, Dr Andrea Grossi, Daniela Hardmeier, Jean-Claude Hayoz, Sandra Heim, Tarcisi Hendry, Daniel Hochstrasser, Corina Huber, Dr Rudolf W. Hug, Clemens Hunziker, Sister Marianne-Franziska Imhasly, Beat Jossen, Dr jur. Rochus Jossen, Sister Maria Andrea Käppeli, Sister Jennifer Kehrwald, Professor Peter Metz, Peter Michael-Caflisch, Dr Kurt Moser, Martin Nydegger, Benedikt Perren, Karin Rensch, the Reverend Stefan Roth, Edy Schmid, Dr Gerhard Schwarz, Dr Cordula Seger, Christian Seiler, Dr Mark Andreas Seiler, Stephan Seiler, Dr Gérard Seiterle, Barbara Stolba, Immanuel Senn, Dr Jürg Stüssi-Lauterburg, Dr Beat Stutzer, Jonas Taugwalder, Protodeacon Michel Vernaz, Julian Vomsattel, Patrick Waespi, André Weibel, Dr William Wirth, Andreas Züllig-Landolt and Hans Zumtaugwald.

In order to realise my "Project 2019" on time, I was dependent on colleagues who helped with academic research and provided logistical and administrative support. My thanks for research, analysis, sourcing of materials and compilation go to Mariel Baumann, who worked out a thematic system with me, and to my research assistant and doctoral student Fabian Henggeler. I thank Clemens Fässer, who grouped together and concisely categorised the Swiss pioneers; Basil Böhni, for the indices of persons and place names; Maud Fasel for her inquiries, and especially for clarifications at the Alpine Club in London; and Ida Maria Waltenspühl for the sourcing of images and for her manifold and resourceful support. I thank the institutions and private individuals who made available the illustrations; they are listed in the picture credits on p. xiii ff. I thank the libraries and archives that granted me access to their collections: the Alpine Club Library, London (Nigel Buckley); The City of Zurich Construction History Archive (Sara Pepe Fischer); Corporate Archives and History of Credit Suisse (Nicole Schenker, Tanja Neukom, Bruno Fischer); the St Moritz Library (Dora Filli); the Andelfingen Municipal Archive (Patrick Waespi); the Matterhorn Museum, Zermatt (Edy Schmid); the Parliamentary Services of the Federal Assembly, Bern (Diego Hättenschwiler); the Professor Beat Kleiner and Dorothee Kleiner-Frick Collection (Alfred Escher Foundation); the Saurer Museum, Arbon (Dr Rudolf Baer); SBB Historic, Windisch (Martin Cordes); the Swiss National Bank Archive (Christina Henss, Simone Epper); the Valais Cantonal Archives in Sion (Alain Dubois/Denis Reynard); the Zurich Cantonal Archives (Dr Beat Gnädinger); and the Zurich Central Library (Dr Jochen Hesse). My thanks go to Nina Baumgartner for the graphs and tables, to Claudia A. Trochsler for the creation of the railway maps, to my decades-long and untiring guide Edgar Haberthür for his conscientious copy-editing and proofreading of the German manuscript, and finally to the NZZ Libro publishing house for undertaking the original German-language publication of the book.

Finally, I would like to thank Ashley Curtis for the translation of my book into English. I was delighted to work with a translator who brought to the project his own cultural and historical knowledge about and personal interest in the phenomena I have depicted, which defined 19th-century Switzerland and still influence the Switzerland of today. I was also delighted that Ashley subsequently acted as my foreign rights agent in my collaboration with Routledge. He masterfully carried out the necessary adjustments to the German version, thanks to his deep familiarity both with the material and with the publication of English-language works. The emendations of the extensive and complex indices also bear his mark. I am especially grateful to him for our intensive and productive exchanges of ideas and for our constructive collaboration. I would also like to thank the Routledge Press for the inclusion of my work in its Studies in Modern European History series. Particular thanks go to my editor, Max Novick, who showed great understanding of the character and editorial particularities of my history of 19th-century Switzerland.

The publication of the original German-language editions of this book was made possible by generous financial contributions from the Bonny Foundation for Freedom, Bern; Professor Maria Bindschedler, Zurich;

the Ernst Göhner Foundation, Zug; the St Moritz Municipal Council, St Moritz; the Georg and Bertha Schwyzer-Winiker Foundation, Zurich; the Canton Schwyz Lotteriefonds, Schwyz; SBB Historic, Windisch; the Swiss Life Perspectives Foundation, Zurich; the Ulrico Hoepli Foundation, Zurich; the "200 Years Alfred Escher and Gottfried Keller" Association of the Canton Zurich Lotteriefonds; the Institute for Historical Research in Economics, Zurich; and a number of private individuals who wish to remain anonymous.

The English translation was made possible by generous contributions from the Heinrich Escher Family Foundation, Zurich; the Georg and Bertha Schwyzer-Winiker Foundation, Zurich; the Cultural Commission of the Municipality of Davos; the Canton of Zug; the Max Geilinger Foundation, Zurich; and the Willi Muntwyler Foundation, St Moritz.

1 Lifelines

Interconnecting Systems

Starting Points and Foundations

The Tracks of Progress

Up until the end of the 18th century, people travelled in rowboats, sailboats or flatboats, on horseback or in horse-drawn carriages, and, in winter, on horse-drawn sleighs – but primarily they travelled on foot, for which reason early travel guides listed travel times in walking hours. Advances in carriage design that allowed more space for passengers and baggage, along with the expansion of road networks, made travel more comfortable in the early 19th century. At the same time, transport on water was also evolving. In the 1820s, Switzerland's first mechanical means of transport, the steamboat, joined the more traditional boats plying the country's waterways. The capacity for both freight and passenger transport thereby increased substantially. Until the establishment of the railway in the 1850s, steamboats were the most comfortable and popular means of transport, and the most important for both goods and passenger traffic.

The introduction of steamboats made transport in Switzerland significantly easier. But investment in this infrastructure was not enough to bring the country up to date with contemporary standards. Swiss transport was suffering from a serious shortcoming: At the time of founding of the Federal State in 1848, the country boasted a grand total of 23 kilometres of railway track. Meanwhile, Great Britain, France and Germany had already laid thousands of kilometres of rails.[1] Given the political structures that characterised the pre-1848 Confederation, however, it was impossible for this infrastructural deficit to be remedied. Over the long term, this backwardness relative to other countries would not have been able to be compensated by stagecoaches or even steamboats.

In the middle of the 19th century, Switzerland found itself in a critical situation. This much is clear in hindsight. A look at how much the transport of goods and people increased after the 1850s and what a decisive role railway transport played in Switzerland's wider economic and socio-political development makes clear how inadequate the transport infrastructure was during the first half of the 19th century. The

DOI: 10.4324/9781003243144-1

obvious conclusion is that the transport conditions at the time of founding of the Federal State were significantly retarding Switzerland's development. Indeed, the transport infrastructure that existed in the Swiss Confederation before 1848 would have rendered impossible the rapid economic and social development that would take off in the early years of the Federal State. Without a well-developed infrastructure with the railway as its backbone, the transformation that the new Switzerland underwent after 1848 would not have been possible at the same rapid pace.

It must be said, however, that it was not only the selection of the right means of transport that would determine the country's future. Rather, it came down to the method of its implementation. The ground-breaking policy decision to invest in the development of the railway did not in itself solve the problem. The construction of tracks and train stations did not guarantee a successful and functional transport infrastructure. The question of who ought to build and operate the railways required equally prudent and prescient consideration.

An overview of the stages of modernisation that were accelerated or initiated by the expansion of the Swiss transport system reveals marked differences in different areas of the country. Not all regions were equally affected by the transformation that was launched in the second half of the 19th century. The cities and towns that knew how to position themselves advantageously became leading lights of progress, while those that failed to open themselves up to modernisation early enough, or even actively resisted the change, lost out – even if they had previously been relatively illustrious locations. Olten and Romanshorn were examples of the former, while Zofingen and Zurzach belonged to the latter category and therefore missed out. The fact that Zurich, and not Bern, became the economic centre of Switzerland, and that companies that would become global enterprises sprang up in Oerlikon, Kemptthal and Baden, can ultimately be explained by the layout of the railway lines.

Where a given town found itself in economic and socio-political terms might depend on its commercial and industrial framework, or on topographical and socio-cultural aspects, criteria which could be relevant either singly or in combination: The founding of companies, the development of tourist destinations, the establishment of winter tourism and the investment of activity and energy on the part of pioneers could be affected by a variety of changeable factors. Independently of these factors, however, progress was ultimately dependent on the railway, and to be precise, on where the tracks were laid, where train stations were built and whether a given region became connected to the railway network at an earlier or a later stage. Some places fought for access to the network and engaged themselves financially to achieve it. Others were demoted to a hinterland and passed over. The transport infrastructure that was reconfigured in the 1850s with the introduction of the railway was the key element in the fundamental transformation that, within a single generation, made an economically flourishing country out of a developing one.

Figure 1.1 "The construction of the Zurich Main Train Station," ca 1871. Photograph. Baugeschichtliches Archiv der Stadt Zürich (Architectural History Archive of the City of Zurich).

The Railway Act of 1852 set the course for the introduction of the new means of transport. In it the Swiss Parliament determined that the licensing of railway projects would lie in the hands of the cantons and agreed to leave the construction and running of the railway network to the private sector. Federalistic authority and private business were the two key elements of this landmark decision. The 1852 Act led to the onset of a two-decade-long historic era defined by economic liberalism – the only such period in Switzerland's history. The railway became the driver of progress. It transformed the economy and society to an extent that would previously have been unimaginable.

The pace and profundity of this transformation can be illustrated by a few key facts. As early as the 1860s, Switzerland was the most industrialised country in Europe, as well as the most visited by foreign tourists. The surge of modernisation that the railway gave rise to also extended to other areas, including research (the Polytechnic in Zurich, today ETH Zurich, 1854/1855), banking (the Schweizerische Kreditanstalt, today Credit Suisse, 1856) and insurance (the Rentenanstalt, today Swiss Life, 1857; Helvetia, the first transport insurer, 1858; the Rückversicherungs-Gesellschaft, today Swiss Re, 1863; Winterthur and Zurich, the first accident insurers, 1875) – and finally, to the entire economic, cultural and political landscape that would develop so successfully in Switzerland right up until the outbreak of the First World War. Rail transport was the lifeline of Switzerland.

Transport Systems on Waterways

Switzerland, the reservoir: A plethora of springs, streams, rivers and lakes characterise the country's landscape. Around 4.5 percent of Switzerland's surface is covered by lakes and rivers. Surrounding countries can lay claim to less than half this proportion. This high concentration of water was of great significance for transport before the arrival of the railway. There were around a thousand kilometres of navigable waterways in 18th-century Switzerland – a natural transport network. The rivers were used to transport goods from remote valleys (for example from Glarus) to the cities of the Swiss Central Plateau (Zurich) or abroad. Similarly, larger lakes connected the cities and towns of certain regions or tied a number of regions into a single economic area – as did, for example, Lake Constance. In Switzerland there are 13 lakes with a surface area of around 20 square kilometres or more. Within its present borders, Germany has 15 such lakes, though the country is almost nine times as large, while Austria, twice as large, has only four bodies of water of this size.[2]

Swiss transport history after the 1820s was characterised by the evolution of steamboat travel. This new technological capacity turned even larger lakes into hubs of transport – an impossibility back in the days of flatboats and freight boats. The transport of goods and passengers experienced a marked upswing as a result. In general, the waterways provided the most efficient mode of transport in the first half of the 19th century. The inland waters provided better transport links than the overland roads did. With the introduction of steamers, transport on Swiss lakes expanded significantly. Not only did the capacity to transport passengers and goods grow considerably but this growth also resulted in a substantial reduction of travel and transport time. That said, the speed of water travel was in itself no greater than that of travel on land; carriages and steamers were about equally fast. It was not the speed but the route that made the difference: A steamboat crossing a lake directly reached its goal well in advance of a carriage that had to drive around the lake.[3]

Speed, which was sometimes a crucial factor in economic performance, was not an equal priority for all who used the steamers. It is worth noting that foreign tourists did not always want their steamboat trips to be faster. The travellers who visited the country in the 19th century and in the years leading up to the First World War, and made up the majority of passengers on Swiss lakes, were not usually eager to make it from one lakeshore to the other as quickly as possible. Instead they wanted to enjoy the journey over the water and the scenic beauty of the landscape.

Certain destinations profited especially from the development of steamboat travel, especially harbour towns that became points of departure for or intermediary stops on popular tourist itineraries. On Lake Geneva, in addition to the city of Geneva itself, such places included Villeneuve –

which already had steamer service in 1828 – Nyon and Vevey, which followed in 1838 and 1853, respectively. On Lake Lucerne, Weggis and Brunnen were first serviced in 1837; Vitznau and Gersau followed later. On Lake Thun, Gunten and Spiez profited the most from the uptick in tourism, thanks to their steamer docks, which were first serviced in 1866 and 1870, respectively.

Steamboats were equally important for the transport of goods. The situation on Lake Constance provides an example: When Romanshorn – a small Thurgau fishing village that was not even accessible by road in the early 19th century and had only a small landing point for freight-bearing sailboats – became a steamboat harbour, it eclipsed the previously economically and culturally more important town of Rorschach in Canton St Gallen. Romanshorn's development occurred because its citizens – not least Johann Joachim Bachmann (1794–1878), the "Prince of Romanshorn" – recognised the significance of steamboats earlier than their St Gallen counterparts did and so built up their harbour facilities in the early 1840s.[4] Because paddle steamers required larger and more protected port facilities than barges, the towns that erected the infrastructure necessary to accommodate them came out on top. The authorities of Romanshorn had got to work while the other lakeside towns were still sleeping. In addition to requesting that a new road be built to Amriswil, they had entreated the Thurgau Cantonal Parliament to construct larger harbour facilities in their town. This investment would pay off a second time just a generation later – and on an even larger scale – when railway lines neared Lake Constance in the middle of the 1850s and the question of transport across the lake arose. Romanshorn then found itself once again in a far better position than other harbour towns, which did not have steamboat facilities. It was only logical that the transport of goods from Zurich towards southern Germany and Central Europe should now also pass through the already established hub of Romanshorn. Another factor was that, as far as Zurich was concerned, Romanshorn's location made it a cheaper Eastern Swiss transport junction on Lake Constance than Rorschach. This all shows how decisive it can be to recognise the onset of a historical trend and make the correct strategic decisions at an early stage. However, it also shows that it was effectively impossible to make up for previous neglect in the expansion of transport infrastructure and pull even with the competition, even when its lead had only been established over a single generation.

The era of steamboat travel on Swiss lakes was rung in on 18 June 1823, when the *Guillaume Tell* sailed away from the dock in Geneva. This was a premiere, not only for Swiss lakes but also for European waters in general. The impulse for it came from Edward Church (1769–1847), the American Consul in France. On a visit to Lake Geneva the previous year, Church had noted with astonishment that Switzerland – a free and spirited country situated in the middle of Europe and blessed with beautiful scenery – seemed unaware of the revolutionary development represented by steamboat travel. Built in the Mauriac shipyard in Bordeaux, the *Guillaume Tell* was assembled and fitted out with an English engine in Geneva. The steamer travelled daily between Geneva and Ouchy, taking six hours for the journey, a day-long trip by stagecoach.

The *Guillaume Tell* quickly inspired emulators. In 1824, the Genevan *Winkelried* took to the water, and in 1826, a Lausanne-based company launched the *Léman*. Thus continued the traditional rivalry between these two cantonal harbour towns on Lake Geneva. A number of different steamboat companies operated in the region before merging into the collective Lake Geneva General Navigation Company (Compagnie Générale de Navigation (CGN)). The steamboat was the primary means of transport until railway lines began springing up along the lakeshores. When this happened, the role of steamboats was reduced to taking tourists on excursions. In order to keep up with the inrush of tourists, the CGN was operating 11 lounge paddle steamers by 1896, 10 of which were built by the Sulzer company in Winterthur.

The development of Swiss waterways by the steamboat industry found widespread support in the industrial, commercial and tourism sectors. Innkeepers and manufacturers, with their vested interests in tourism and industry, respectively, were keen to support the improvement of water transport infrastructure. It should therefore come as no surprise that the Knechtenhofer hotelier brothers on Lake Thun and the chocolate manufacturer Suchard on Lake Neuchâtel were among the steamboat pioneers. As a consequence of this wide-ranging interest, steamboat transport soon came to dominate Swiss lakes.

Three years after the maiden voyage of the *Guillaume Tell* on Lake Geneva, the first steamers began operating on Lakes Neuchâtel and Murten and on Lake Maggiore. Steamboat travel experienced a powerful surge in the second half of the 1830s, with launches on Lake Zurich (1835), Lake Thun (1835), Lake Lucerne (1837), Lake Walen (1837) and Lake Brienz (1839). In the middle of the century, maiden journeys were made on Lake Lugano (1848), Lower Lake Constance (1850), the Rhein between Stein am Rhein and Schaffhausen (1851), Lake Zug (1852) and finally on Upper Lake Constance (1855). Within three decades, steamship travel had been introduced to the largest Swiss waters and those most significant for tourism; eventually, it also reached Lake Biel (1887) and Lake Hallwil (1888).

Thus, at the time of the founding of the Federal State, the most important Swiss waterways were all being trafficked by steamboats.[5] The young Swiss nation now had to decide whether it wanted to continue, or even increase, its reliance on this form of transport and whether the railway ought to be developed as an alternative or merely as a complement to water-based travel. These questions represented a crossroads, and their answers would have far-reaching consequences.

Conflicting Interests on Lake Lucerne

Until the first steamboat was launched on Lake Lucerne, freight boats known as "Nauen" transported wares and people across the lake towards the Gotthard. Navigation was traditionally organised by the guild-like mariners' associations in Cantons Lucerne, Schwyz and Uri. This all changed in 1837 with the launch of the *Stadt Luzern*, a steamboat owned by a public limited company founded by a 29-year-old banker, Casimir Friedrich Knörr (1808–1882), and his business partner, Josef Maria Ronca (1781–1871). The *Stadt Luzern* could carry ten tonnes of freight and 300 passengers and travel at a speed of up to 18 kilometres per hour. This apparently overwhelming competition from Lucerne inspired apocalyptic sentiment in Brunnen (Schwyz): The new conveyance threatening their livelihoods was seen as a "curse on mariners" and a "wailing of women."[6] Resistance against the steamboat operators of Lucerne was not long coming in Uri, either. Numerous arbitration sessions were held, facilitated by Cantons Lucerne and Ticino and attended by representatives of the cantons affected by the novel form of transport. The negotiations collapsed, however, and the matter proceeded to a trial. The result was that the *Stadt Luzern* was allowed to dock in Flüelen (Canton Uri) but had to pay a fee to do so.

In 1843, Knörr launched another steamboat. In the same year, the Chief Magistrate of Canton Uri, Karl Emmanuel Müller (1804–1869), founded the Postal Steamboat Company (Postdampfschiffgesellschaft), unmistakably conceived as a competitor to Knörr's enterprise. Both the ships that Müller commissioned, the *Waldstätter* and the *Rigi*, were built by Ditchburn & Mare in London, as Escher Wyss in Zurich had an exclusive contract with Knörr. The transport of the boats took place piece by piece, first by water to Strasbourg, then by train to Basel and then by 18-wheeled horse-drawn carriages to Lucerne. A state of war prevailed between the Uri- and Lucerne-based businesses, with no end in sight to its escalation. The embittered rivalry was not based solely on business competition but had political undertones as well: Knörr and his company were Liberal, Müller and his crew Conservative. The battle was only resolved by federal legislation passed on 30 May 1849 that regulated transport on the lake between Lucerne and Flüelen and compelled the two parties to come to an agreement.

A new competitor threatened to enter the scene at the end of the 1860s: the Swiss Central Railway (Centralbahn). This line, which connected Basel to Lucerne by train, was behind the 1870 founding of the Steamboat Company of Lucerne (Dampfschifffahrtsgesellschaft Luzern), which operated two steamers. In the very same year, the steamers were sold on to the United Steamboat Company (Vereinigte Dampfschiffsfahrtsgesellschaft). The tactic of eliminating the competition by buying their boats or by merging companies was not unique to Lake Lucerne.

These kinds of entrepreneurial strategies were also employed in the competitive rivalries that would later emerge between private railway companies. Under considerable pressure, Knörr's and Müller's companies merged on 1 January 1870 to become the United Steamboat Company of Lake Lucerne (Vereinigte Dampfschiffgesellschaft auf dem Vierwaldstättersee). The larger merger of the United Steamboat Company of Lake Lucerne and the Steamboat Company of Lucerne followed just six months later. Knörr's ambition was not satisfied, however. He soon founded the Luxury Steamboat Company of Lake Lucerne (Salon-Dampfschifffahrtsgesellschaft des Vierwaldstättersees), which was based in Gersau and launched two new boats, the *Italia* and the *Germania*. But Knörr was not able to withstand the competitive pressures for long. He sold his steamboats and exited the industry. He even made a commitment to refrain from establishing any further competing companies.

Steamboat travel on Lake Lucerne kept pace with rapidly increasing tourism. The decrease in passenger numbers caused by the opening of the Gotthard Railway in 1882 was only temporary: While the numbers of through-travellers diminished for a time, the Belle Époque brought in a new and continual stream of international guests to Lucerne and other tourist hotspots in Central Switzerland. As a result, the number of passengers on Lake Lucerne increased markedly at the end of the 1880s. The steamboats were now both a tourist attraction in their own right and a shuttle service to the lower stations of an increasing number of new mountain railways. A connection between boat and railway transport was established in 1891 in the form of train ferries; the train ferry on Lake Lucerne was managed by the United Steamboat Company of Lake Lucerne up until 1920. That said, this interlinking of transport systems never attained the same importance on Lake Lucerne as it did on Lake Constance.

An examination of steamboat travel on Lake Lucerne reveals both parallels and fundamental differences between the development of steamboat and railway transport:

- Traditional means of transport were eclipsed by technological innovation. The progress that steamboats spearheaded in Brunnen on Lake Uri could not have been held off over the long term, even by an armada of rowboats and freight boats, nor could complaints about noise-sensitive and jumpy horses and declining milk production prevent the iron horse from speeding past farms near a train line.
- Steamer travel was naturally tied to certain areas, while the railway could develop across the whole country.
- Routes on Swiss lakes and rivers were in principle open to all boats. Problems did arise before 1848, however, as the levying of tolls at the harbours of foreign cantons sometimes degenerated into a kind of harassment. The railway, however, was only realisable thanks to compulsory purchase laws. Certainly, permission for a railway line had

to be granted by cantonal authorities, but once that had happened, the construction and management of the lines were guided by purely economic considerations. By contrast, the disagreements on Lake Uri, which involved not only Cantons Uri, Schwyz and Lucerne but also Canton Ticino, had cantonal and party-political undertones.

- As was later the case with locomotives and rolling stock, steamboats were produced by the Swiss engineering industry and were soon among its flagship products.
- The operation of a steamboat company involved less capital expenditure than that of a railway company. This explains why the steamboat companies of the 1830s and 1840s could be financed by a single individual or family, while only commercial banks structured as public limited companies had the capacity to make available the necessary investment and risk capital needed for the construction and operation of the railways from the 1850s onwards.
- The establishment and management of both steamboat and railway companies were in the domain of the private sector. This accounts for the speed with which infrastructure was made available for public use and suggests how difficult and protracted the realisation of transport projects would have been, had it been in the remit of the public sector. In other words, the speed with which Swiss waterways

Figure 1.2 Carl August Schöll (1810–1878), *Die Eisenbahn als Bauernschreck* (*The Train, Horror of Farmers*), 1858, Lithograph, 24.8 cm × 32.6 cm. Swiss Museum of Transport, Lucerne.

and the Swiss countryside became accessible by boat and railway – a precondition for the economic upturn the country would experience – was only possible because responsibility for this development was assumed by private business.

- Steamboat travel triggered the economic development of individual regions but not on the same scale as the railway, which significantly influenced all areas of Swiss society.

Figure 1.3 Johann Caspar Dikenmann (1823–1861). *Zurich prise du pont de la Cathédrale, vers la chaîne des Montagnes*, before 1844. Coloured aquatint, partly varnished, 12.9 cm × 18.6 cm. Sturzenegger Stiftung, Schaffhausen.

In Zurich too, the modernisation of the transport system in the 19th century first played out on the water. In 1835, the first steamboat sailed on Lake Zurich. During its maiden voyage on 19 July, the townships along the lake still had no suitable landing docks. Barges carried passengers from the steamer to the docks to land at some locations; passengers had to change vessels while still far out on the lake. In 1838, several smaller companies merged to form the Zurich-Wallensee Company (Zürichsee-Wallensee-Gesellschaft). Its fleet comprised 12 steamboats. The growing importance of steamboat travel on Lake Zurich is reflected in statistics: While the Zurich-Wallensee Company transported around 80,000 passengers on its 13 steamboats in 1840, in 1870 the newly formed Steamboat Company for Lake Zurich (Dampfbootgesellschaft für den Zürichsee) transported around a million passengers on its 17 boats. In the 1850s, as the railroad network in the Greater Zurich area expanded, it became necessary to synchronise train and steamboat schedules. As the more prevalent mode of transport, steamboats determined the timetables. This, however, would soon change.

The Interlinking of Transport Systems

It Was a Light-Hearted Journey: Parliamentarians on Their Way Home, 1853

While steamboat traffic rapidly established itself as the most important form of transport on the Swiss Central Plateau, its significance for the overall economy could only be optimally realised through its interlinking with other forms of transport. Restricted by the natural boundaries of the waterways, its transport of goods and people relied on incoming and outgoing connections. Correctly timed and structured, steamboat traffic became astonishingly important, and this importance extended beyond the flatlands to affect Alpine passes and the Jura.

The way in which different modes of transport complemented each other is illustrated in an 1853 diary entry by a member of the Council of States, Arnold Otto Aepli (1816–1897). The account takes on historical significance when one realises just who was in Aepli's travel party, making its way home towards Eastern Switzerland via Thun, Brünig and Beckenried after the conclusion of the June session of the Swiss Parliament in Bern. The group of political heavyweights included, among others, the Zurich National Councillors Alfred Escher (1819–1882) and Jakob Dubs (1822–1879), the Thurgau member of the Council of States Johann Karl Kappeler (1816–1888) and the Graubünden National Councillor Andreas Rudolf von Planta (1819–1889). The fact that Federal Councillor Wilhelm Matthias Näff (1802–1881) of St Gallen, at the time the Head of the Political Department, had arranged for a large government-owned post carriage to bring the party as far as Thun – with the expectation that they would visit the quarters of the St Gallen troops there – gave the journey a special start. Aepli wrote:

> Next, we took the boat over both lakes. On Lake Brienz we were surprised by a heavy thunderstorm and a torrential downpour that was accompanied by severe winds. Lightning hit the lake not far from us. We had three oarsmen, one of whom had his oar torn away by the waves. It was not a comfortable situation and we discussed amongst ourselves whether we shouldn't try to reach the shore somehow. However, this wasn't possible as the boat would have been in danger of being struck abeam, as the storm winds were blowing in the direction of travel. We managed, however, though thoroughly soaked, to arrive in Brienz, where we stayed the night. The next day we journeyed over the Brünig Pass. Escher and I reached the pass on horseback, while the others travelled on foot. A steady rain set in in Lungern as we ate lunch, forcing us to hire coaches and ride to Beckenried, where we spent the night in the nice guesthouse by the lake. It was a light-hearted journey, full of jokes, both good

> and bad. The next morning Planta and I set off without the others, travelling via Brunnen and Schwyz to Lachen, from where Planta took the post carriage to Chur, while I journeyed home via Uznach and Toggenburg.[7]

Apparently these parliamentarians were not concerned about taking the most direct route home. And in fact, the choices both of the route and of the methods of transport suggest not a speedy homeward journey but rather an entertaining little cultural tour. National Councillor Escher, for example, could have taken a stagecoach from Bern across the Swiss Central Plateau to Zurich. Changing horses would not have taken much time, and for the final 23 kilometres from Baden to Zurich, he could even have taken the train – especially since he was the President of the railway company's Board of Directors. With this itinerary, Escher's door-to-door journey – from the Swiss Parliament in Bern to his Belvoir estate – would only have taken around seven hours.

Starting in 1848, when Escher began to travel to Bern several times per year for parliamentary sessions, he usually opted for the shorter route. The considerable tasks and obligations that awaited him both in Bern and Zurich required him not only to travel as quickly as possible but also to use his journeys to prepare for parliamentary sessions. In 1858, the railway line between Zurich and Bern was completed, enabling him to live out his work ethic in a more efficient and goal-oriented way than when he had had to travel in noisy stagecoaches. Not primarily because of the time required for the trip – the railway was not much faster than the horses – but rather because a reserved train car now awaited the good doctor in the Zurich train station, inside of which, on a custom-built desk of his own design, he could tend to his affairs while underway. The schedule of his Swiss Northeastern Railway Company (Schweizerische Nordostbahn) was required to serve the working rhythms of its president; in Zurich, the train left when Escher arrived. In the other train stations of his empire, he also used his influence as and when needed, staying trains past their scheduled departure times as he waited for the appearance of one or the other travel companion.

Connecting Railways and Waterways

It might initially seem paradoxical that steamboat travel experienced an upswing at the start of the railway era. This was due to the fact that, early on, important railway lines only went as far as the shores of lakes, at which point further travel was by water. This explains why some railway companies founded in the 1850s operated their own boats on Lakes Geneva and Lucerne, or even – as was the case on Lake Constance and Lake Zurich – took almost complete control of the steamboat industries. The interlinking of steamer and train transport caught on; for example, the steamboat company operating on Lakes Thun and Brienz was purchased in 1913 by the Bern-Lötschberg-Simplon Railway.

The situation took a turn for the worse, as far as steamboats were concerned, when railway companies began to extend their rail networks along the lakeshores. At this point, the transport of goods and passengers largely shifted to the rails. This change occurred across the board, in both national and international transport. The steamboat companies had to make do with local transport, the ferrying of tourists to specific destinations and the allure of their luxury steamers. This was the case around Lake Lucerne in Central Switzerland, Lake Thun and Lake Brienz in the Bernese Oberland and the lakes of Ticino in Italian-speaking Switzerland. Within these particular topographies, steamboat travel remained important. Not every shore was suitable for a train line, and in any case, railway travel could not compete with direct lake crossings. This is why the Zurich Steamboat Company, for example, contrary to expectations, had around 1.6 million passengers in 1913 – 100,000 more than in 1875, before the opening of the Zurich-Ziegelbrücke-Näfels railway line.

Ideas for combining boat and railway operations were frequently discussed in the Switzerland of the 1840s and sometimes even progressed to the planning stage. However, because the railway had yet to develop, they never came to anything. A notable discussion took place in Schaffhausen in 1852/1853 between the initiators of the Rheinfall Railway (Rheinfallbahn) over the question of the location of a new train station. After a trial period with a provisional station, one of the main shareholders, Heinrich Moser (1805–1874), advocated siting the station near the Rhein bridge to Feuerthalen. He thought that a station in this location would position Schaffhausen as an international hub, a junction of the Baden Railway (Badische Bahn) from the north, the Rheinfall Railway with its onward connection to Zurich, and the steamboat on the Rhine, with its direct connection to Lake Constance. In his opinion, this would have facilitated "enhanced trade and transport via Schaffhausen, as the iron road would have been connected to the waterways."[8] Moser was, however, in the minority, and the train station was erected in its present location. In hindsight, this was a good decision, since the Schaffhausen train station was constructed within a reasonable distance of the neighbouring town of Neuhausen. This paid off later, for example, with the establishment of Schweizerische Waggonfabrik (Swiss Wagon Works, today SIG). Yet what failed to occur in Schaffhausen and on the Rhine was realised shortly afterwards in Romanshorn on Lake Constance, and on a much larger scale.

Train Ferries

That steamboats and railways were not inherently rivals, but rather could together form an increasingly optimised transport system through seamless structural intertwining, was illustrated by so-called ferry transport – the swimming train – which assumed particular significance on Lake Constance. There, steamboat travel played a key role at the start of the railway era; not only did it connect a number of railway lines but it actually became a part of the railway network itself. From 1869 onwards, the train ferry made it possible for railway carriages to cross the lake, rendering the manual reloading of freight onto tugboats unnecessary.

Romanshorn, which became a transport hub on the Swiss side of Lake Constance thanks to its steamboat harbour facilities, experienced another prodigious phase of development thanks to the Northeastern Railway. It was initially connected by train to Zurich via Winterthur, but soon there were train lines to Romanshorn from Konstanz (Germany), Rorschach and, later, St Gallen.[9] The one-time fishing village had become a veritable transport centre. Yet Romanshorn was even more than just a railway junction like Olten; its harbour became a centre of international traffic, and thereby a gateway from Switzerland to the wider world.

In the beginning, railway lines ended at Lake Constance: in Lindau and Friedrichshafen on the German side and in Romanshorn and Rorschach on the Swiss side. Between the two shores there was only steamboat transport. This meant railway companies had to venture onto the water so that their terminus stations were not dead ends. Thus, lakeside destinations with harbours, and especially ones on bodies of water between two countries, assumed strategic importance for certain railway companies. This explains why the Zurich-based Northeastern Railway made the construction of train tracks towards Lake Constance – rather than towards Bern or western Switzerland – its first priority in the years after its founding. It built the necessary facilities in the Thurgau harbour town of Romanshorn and was soon operating its own steamboat line from Romanshorn to Lindau and Friedrichshafen on the German side of the lake.

Even before the railway line between Zurich and Romanshorn opened in 1856, the Northeastern Railway operated two steamers, the *Thurgau* and the *Stadt Zurich*, whose construction they had commissioned themselves. The boats were intended for the transport of both passengers and goods and were named for the catchment areas of the railway company. The *Stadt Zurich*, unfortunately, soon became an object of anxiety and dread, as it was repeatedly involved in massive collisions. These accidents led locals to call it the "devil's ship."[10] Nevertheless, trains and boats were now connected, and transfers from one to the other were guaranteed. That said, between the terminus stations in Romanshorn and Friedrichshafen in the Kingdom of Württemberg there were 12 kilometres of water, and between Romanshorn and Lindau in Bavaria, 23 kilometres. While these distances were no great obstacle for passenger transport, they were a serious problem for freight, especially as Lake Constance was immensely important as a hub of international traffic. Large amounts of highly diverse wares and goods were transported across the lake, including grain, wood and cattle and many kinds of natural resources and industrial products. Brought in from Hungary and Austria, Bavaria and Württemberg, these goods made their way over the water to Switzerland and then onwards: southwards and to the west in the direction of France or northwards to the provinces along the Rhine. Meanwhile, steel and iron goods, railway tracks and steam engines and industrial and commercial wares – especially from France, Belgium and Switzerland – were transported in the other direction over Lake Constance to the north and east. In 1876, for example, on a total of 342 days of traffic between Lindau and Romanshorn, 1,014 train ferry crossings were made (in both directions), transporting 29,211 carriages with 132,863 tonnes of freight.[11]

When Northeastern Railway trains began arriving in Romanshorn in 1855, the once insignificant fishing port was gradually expanded into the largest harbour on the Swiss shore of Lake Constance, and the flow of goods was entirely re-routed: Instead of going via Konstanz and Schaffhausen, freight intended for Zurich and Basel – including that which would subsequently travel onwards – was now diverted to the train line from Romanshorn to Zurich. Once this change had been made, freight transport to Switzerland across Lake Constance increased dramatically, and this would have far-reaching effects on Romanshorn. The goods had to be reloaded onto boats there. Then, when the boats arrived at the harbours on the other side of the lake, they were unloaded again and sent onwards once more by train. This process was time-intensive, costly and harboured risks, including potential damage to the freight. The system of transferring the wares from the railway to the boat had other negative consequences as well, as the railway cars unloaded at the terminus stations either had to continue on empty or wait in place to be loaded again.

The fact that railway lines carrying heavily laden freight trains ended in Romanshorn and Friedrichshafen presented an economic and logistical challenge. As the problem became increasingly acute, the directors of the Zurich-based Northeastern Railway met with the administration of the Württemberg Railway in Stuttgart to look for solutions. Various plans were examined, and alternatives tested. A project involving a large fleet of small barges reached an advanced stage. The rail carriages were to be mechanically lifted onto barges, and a powerful steamboat would pull the whole fleet across the lake. This plan was ultimately found wanting. Instead, the idea of making the waterway navigable for trains came to fruition: Lake Constance was to be a railway line. This idea would only work, though, if it were possible for trains arriving in the harbour to make their way across the lake without delay and to immediately continue onwards from the opposite shore. An infrastructure of this kind would transform the 12-kilometre-long waterway between Romanshorn and Friedrichshafen into a 12-kilometre-long railway line. The project managers therefore directed their attention to the place where essential industrial developments were being launched: Great Britain. There, the idea of train ferries had already been considered in the 1830s. It was only in 1850, however, that history was made by the maiden journey of the first railway ferry, over the Firth of Forth (near Edinburgh).[12]

The planning of the train ferry on Lake Constance was assigned to no less impressive a figure than the Scottish engineer and architect John Scott Russell (1808–1882). Russell was one of the foremost pioneers of shipbuilding; his so-called wave-line theory had led to innovations in ship design. The Institution of Naval Architects, co-founded by Russell in 1859, was responsible for England's world-leading role in the development and construction of trade- and warships. The fact that Emperor William II of Germany (1859–1941) looked to the English example offered by the Naval Institution when he founded the German Technical Ship Construction Company (Schiffbautechnischen Gesellschaft) testifies to Russell's influence. Russell made a name for himself as an engineer by relocating the Crystal Palace in London (1854) and designing the rotunda at the 1873 Vienna World's Fair. He won the attention of the scientific community through his discovery of solitary waves, whose true importance was only recognised after his death.

Russell made history in the field of ship design with his innovative steamboats, which he sketched, planned and constructed, first in Glasgow and later in London. The showcase project that established him as a first-rate designer was the *Great Britannia* (originally called the *Great Eastern*), which was the largest ship in the world for half a century and was said to be far ahead of its time. Conceptualised as a sailing steamship, it was not initially profitable; later, however, repurposed as a platform for laying the transatlantic telegraph cables, it gained legendary status. Among the projects that recommended Russell as the designer of the great train ferry on Lake Constance was the paddle steamer *Stadt Schaffhausen*, which was built in 1851 in a shipyard in Millwall (present-day London) and was the first steamer to operate on the Rhine and Lake Constance.

The train ferry itself was commissioned by the Northeastern Railway and the Württemberg Railway administration. At the same time, plans were drawn up for the reconstruction of harbour facilities in Romanshorn and Friedrichshafen. The train ferry, to be made of iron, was built by the Zurich-based company Escher Wyss, which was awarded the commission after a careful scrutiny of competing offers. Constructed and assembled in the workshops on the Stampfenbach, the train ferry was then disassembled; its parts were brought to Romanshorn by railway and reconstructed in the Northeastern Railway stockyard. Massive new facilities and interventions in the harbour landscape were required to enable train cars to travel directly onto the boat. Even the laying of the tracks along the piers, which were built as tongue-like quays on the sloping lake floor, presented a technical challenge.[13]

The first train ferry built by Escher Wyss, which could accommodate up to 16 train cars, was launched in October 1868. Already in 1882, however, it was decommissioned, as it had proved to be a coal guzzler. Three years later it was purchased by a Zurich-based scrap-iron trader and shredded.

Regular train ferry transport between Friedrichshafen and Romanshorn began on 11 February 1869. Almost simultaneously, the state railway of the Kingdom of Bavaria opened a ferry service between Lindau and Romanshorn, for which it initially used train barges. These smaller, engineless boats could be towed by either steam ferries or passenger steamboats. They could each carry around eight railway cars. In 1874, the Kingdom of Bavaria's state railway began using a motorised train ferry, also built by Escher Wyss. It became a showcase project for the Swiss engineering industry and remained in operation until 1923. When the Arlberg Railway (Arlbergbahn) connected Bregenz to its railway network in 1884, an Austrian steamboat company was founded that took over train ferry operations between Bregenz and Romanshorn.

Of the new train ferry lines, the route between Lindau and Romanshorn had the greatest volume of traffic. Already in its first year of operation, 1868/1869, more than 12,000 railway carriages were transported, more than half of which were laden with freight. In the following years, the numbers continued to grow. The transport of goods between Romanshorn and Lindau increased by no less than 171 percent within eight years (1869–1876), while passenger transport tripled. The Franco-Prussian War (1870/1871) led to a brief collapse in the transport of goods, but by 1875, new records were already being set. In 1880, for example, around 43,000 rail carriages made the trip between Lindau and Romanshorn, almost four times as many as were transported between Romanshorn and Friedrichshafen. Figures for the volume of freight transported confirm this trend.[14]

Train ferries on Lake Constance satisfied transport needs for a long time. Even after the integration of the Northeastern Railway into the Swiss Federal Railways (Schweizerische Bundesbahnen, SBB) in 1902, the ferries continued to operate. Even the increasingly developed transport infrastructure in the area – for example, the lakeshore railway lines and the Vorarlberg Railway – was not able to supplant the train ferries. In 1939, however, following the annexation of Austria by Hitler's Germany, the final days of the train ferry seemed to have arrived. At this point the railway of the German Reich had reached the Swiss border station of St Margrethen and was thus connected directly to the SBB network.[15] However, after the Second World War, the train ferry on Lake Constance experienced a kind of rebirth. In 1966, the SBB acquired its last train ferry, the *Rorschach*. It was decommissioned in 1976, remodelled as a car ferry in 1983 and sold to the German Federal Railway (Deutsche Bundesbahn) in 1983. This ferry is still in operation today, under the name *Friedrichshafen*.

The train ferry on Lake Constance was a pioneering achievement by the Northeastern Railway and the railways of Bavaria and Württemberg. And there was no real reason not to implement this system on other Swiss waterways. Especially on the larger lakes – those exceeding 50 kilometres in length – train ferries seemed a forward-looking solution. Lake Thun (1873/1893), Lake Zurich (1885/1894) and Lake Lucerne (1891/1920) also developed train ferry transport. Ferry operations on Lake Constance, however, remained unmatched, both in terms of quality and quantity.

Connecting Boats and Stagecoaches, Through-Trains and Mountain Railways: The Gotthard Route and the Rigi

Ever since the Middle Ages, a classic north-south route has crossed the Gotthard Pass. The approach from the north meets with a natural obstacle in the form of Lake Uri, and until the construction of the Axenstrasse in the 1860s, travel between Brunnen and Flüelen was by boat. From Flüelen, travellers arrived at the pass via a thin and rocky mule track. Goods were transported on mules driven by sumpters. Everyone – lone travellers and groups alike – had to take this dangerous route. The section over the churning Reuss, with the gigantic Schöllenen Gorge and its imposing Devil's Bridge, presented a particularly impressive natural spectacle. The new bridge was inaugurated in 1830.

As early as the 1810s, Canton Ticino began work to make the Gotthard Pass accessible by coach. The construction on the Tremola – the section between Airolo and the pass – presented a particular challenge. Canton Uri followed suit from the northern side. The stretch from Hospental to the pass proved to be almost as difficult as the section through the Schöllenen. Significant portions of the road had been completed by 1830, and by 1831, the Gotthard road was trafficable for smaller coaches. By 1835, it could be used by postal stagecoaches. Stagecoach operations between Flüelen and Altdorf had begun even earlier. From 1844 onwards, a postal stagecoach travelled daily in both directions between Altdorf and Milan.[16]

The case of the Rigi illustrates yet again the diverse ways in which technological advances affected transport systems, as well as the importance of interlinked systems connecting various forms of transport infrastructure in a single location. As on the Gotthard, it would have been impossible to manage the huge volume of passenger traffic on the Rigi without this interplay of systems.

The booming era of Rigi hotels only became possible once tourists could reach the summit by mountain railways. These mountain railways, in turn, depended on the transport systems that brought people to the bottom of the mountain. Steamboat travel on Lake Lucerne played an important role in this, but the primary shuttle service was provided by the railway lines that led to the foot of the Rigi from various directions. The gateway to the Rigi was not in fact found in Goldau or Vitznau but rather in the train stations of Basel, Lucerne and Zurich. From there arrived the international tourists who made up the majority of visitors. Even the journey to the foot of the mountain was marketed as an excursion – for example, the approach by train from Zurich to Zug via Affoltern. From there, the journey continued across Lake Zug to Arth on the luxury steamer *Helvetia*. The next leg to Oberarth was by adhesion railway, on the so-called Arther Trämli, which was initially pulled by locomotives from the valley. Travellers then took the cog railway up the Rigi, via Goldau, with mountain locomotives pushing the passenger coaches from behind.

After the construction of the Gotthard Railway, the tracks were extended to Goldau, where a new train station was built. From 1891 onwards, the Southeastern Railway (Südostbahn) led from Lake Zurich through Pfäffikon and Biberbrugg to Goldau; from 1897 onwards, one could also travel by train from Zug to Goldau via Walchwil. The approach from the Lucerne side via steamboat was also sold as a tourist experience, with Lucerne as the principal point of departure.[17]

Alpine Roads and Stagecoaches

The improvement of Alpine roads to make them suitable for four-wheeled carriages and coaches took place in three phases.

The two primary routes of north-south transport, the roads over the Simplon (1805) and Gotthard (1830) Passes, were designed in the early 19th century. The San-Bernardino route first became trafficable in 1821, the Splügen road followed in 1822, and the construction of the Julier road – which began in 1820 – was completed in 1826. For economic and political reasons, an effort was made to keep these passes open even in winter.

In contrast to the construction of roads on the Swiss Central Plateau, which took place in short bursts of activity in individual cantons in the 1830s, the construction of Alpine roads – the second phase of road construction – only occurred in the early years of the Swiss Federal State. Plans for this cantonal infrastructure repeatedly appeared on the agenda of the Swiss Parliament, which primarily had to determine which Alpine roads were of national significance and which had only cantonal relevance. To answer this question, consideration was first given to considerations of national security. This was the case in 1860, when the Federal Council was charged with investigating the "construction or improvement of military connecting-roads in the Alps."[18] Based on expert opinions, it reached the conclusion that the existing bridle paths were in no way sufficient for military operations, for during the winter months it was difficult, if not impossible, for troops – not to mention war vehicles – to cross certain passes. The Federal Council painted a grim picture of what would happen if passes or Alpine regions were to fall into enemy hands: If this were to happen to the St Luzisteig Pass, for example, Graubünden would be cut off from the rest of Switzerland, and with a single blow the whole canton would be lost. St-Maurice presented a similar scenario: If it were taken, Canton Valais would be separated from the rest of the country. In order to prevent such disasters, the Swiss Parliament decided that the planned cantonal pass roads deserved financial support from the state. Political and economic factors also affected the decision; it was important for Switzerland, as a small country, to have all of its regions connected, not only by a Federal Constitution but also by a transport infrastructure. While the railways – so the assessment at the time – had linked the regions of the Central Plateau in a way that "could hardly be more comprehensive," roads over the Alpine passes would especially benefit the Alpine valleys.[19] In addition to these military, cultural and political demands on the transport infrastructure, there were also those made by the international tourists who began to visit Switzerland in the summer seasons and whose numbers increased rapidly from the mid-19th century onwards. And so, with the passes of Graubünden as their hinge, east-west connections were created in the 1860s, with the Oberalp (1862/1863), Furka (1863/1866), Albula (1865), Bernina (1866) and Flüela (1867) Passes.

The third phase of road building, which involved the Ofen (1872), Lukmanier (1877), Jaun (1872/1878), Grimsel (1891/1894), Great St Bernhard (1893) and Klausen (1899) Passes, took place over the course of the last quarter of the 19th century. The importance of maintaining Alpine roads increased with the onset of winter tourism. International guests expected even the highest and most remote locations to be comfortably accessible, even in the snow and the cold.

The construction of the pass roads brought about a new state of affairs. In contrast to the mostly privately run steamboat and railway systems, the Alpine roads were publicly financed and remained in the remit of the public sector. It did happen, though, that individual roads were realised through private funding in the early years of the Federal State, when public funds were insufficient for the task at hand. This was the case, for example, with the construction of the spectacular Axenstrasse.

During the course of the 19th century, Canton Bern fell behind Cantons Graubünden, Uri and Valais in the construction of Alpine roads. The roads over the Pillon and the Grimsel, which were not of central importance to the canton, were only upgraded in 1890 and 1894, respectively. Around the same time, roads were built in the Bernese Jura. In 1870, the road from Biel up to Magglingen was improved; in 1877, the *Grand-Hotel Kurhaus* opened in Magglingen. In the same year, a funicular reached Magglingen, and it became an important tourist destination. These investments in transport were a necessary condition for Magglingen's further development. Through the construction of further

Figure 1.4 "Die Hotelanlage in Territet," ca. 1890. Copperplate engraving. Gesellschaft für Schweizerische Kunstgeschichte (Society for Swiss Art History). Boat, railway and funicular connections were present at the hotel facilities in Territet.

infrastructure, such as tennis courts, it would make a name for itself in the international sporting world. The fact that the innkeeper of the *Krone* built an Anglican chapel in 1900 is evidence of a significant presence of British tourists at the time.

In sum, the development of road transport was a necessary precondition for progress in Switzerland in the 19th century, even though roads played a smaller role in modernising the country than the railway did.

The Development of Railway Tourism

All Aboard!

> There is a fork in the railway line in Saint-Maurice, and those travellers who wish to take the Western Switzerland Railways (Schweizerische Westbahn) to Bex, Villeneuve, Vevey and Lausanne should leave the carriage there. The train of the Compagnie de la Ligne d'Italie travels to Monthey. The terminus of the railway line is Bouveret, the port for all Savoy traders' goods headed for Italy.

This announcement, which did not sound out of a loudspeaker, but rather could be read in these or similar words in travel guides of the late

1860s, highlights a couple of notable aspects of the pioneering age of Swiss railways.[20]

At the time, private railway companies were engaged in fierce competition. In 1866, three trains travelled daily from St-Maurice to Bouveret, where there was a connection to the steamboats of the Compagnie d'Italie to and from Geneva. The line had been inaugurated in 1859; it was later extended, one section at a time, towards the Simplon. By 1860 it had reached Sion, and in 1868 it reached Sierre and Brig.

The construction of railways in Valais did not run smoothly. In Saxon, for example, farmers revolted against the expropriation of their land – a phenomenon that occurred in a number of other places in Switzerland as well. In 1860, after the annexation of Savoy by France under Napoleon III, fears arose that the French-owned Ligne d'Italie might point France's territorial desires in the direction of Valais as well. The fact that most private railway companies were controlled by foreign capital was also not unique to Valais but a nationwide phenomenon. When the tracks had been laid as far as Sion, the accomplishment was celebrated with pomp and circumstance at the Saxon Casino after the usual fashion. The empty champagne bottles were barely disposed of, however, when the Compagnie d'Italie went bankrupt – as had a number of other railways before it. The shareholders had to write off millions in investments. At this, the original initiator of the project, Adriene de La Valette (1813–1886), took the opportunity to buy back the company for a song. This became common practice as the railway project overheated and the market bubble burst.

The second company in Valais, the Western Switzerland Railways (Compagnie de l'Ouest-Suisse), expanded its line from Villeneuve to Bex (completed in 1857) and in the direction of St-Maurice. In 1873, the line from Geneva to Lausanne and Villeneuve was completed. St-Maurice continued to serve as a transfer station on the main line from Bouveret to Sion.

Railways in Valais made history with their mountain lines. The line from Visp to Zermatt, which opened in 1891, was the highest railway in Europe and offered spectacular panoramic views. At 19.803 kilometres, the Simplon Tunnel (1906) was the longest tunnel of its time, and the Simplon line was the first electric main line in Switzerland. The Lötschberg line opened in 1913. The construction of the Furka-Oberalp line began in 1911. In the summer of 1916, the company tasked with its construction had to temporarily suspend work for financial reasons, but thanks to public funding, the operation was kept afloat. In 1923, the company was forced into liquidation. Valais and Graubünden took over a large part of the existing infrastructure, including the rolling stock, and in 1925, the Furka-Oberalp Railway (Furka-Overalp-Bahn) was founded. This line was extended to Brig the following year. The construction of the Furka-Oberalp Railway was an unhappy chapter in the history of Swiss Alpine railways. In comparison to the north-south route over the Gotthard, the interconnection of Valais and Graubünden through the Urseren Valley was of little significance in terms of strategy or transport policy.

A Complex Network, Climbing Ever Higher into the Tributary Valleys

Without the vigorous development of its railways, Switzerland would never have become a tourist destination. Its allure grew tremendously in the second half of the 19th century, culminating in the Belle Époque. The hundreds of thousands of travellers from all over the world who visited the country year after year relied on a functional railway network that connected the Central Plateau with the Alps. The major gateways for passenger transport were Basel, Geneva, Schaffhausen and St Gallen. From these starting points, tourists had to be transported to the portals of the High Alps – to Bern/Interlaken, Martigny/Sion and Chur.

The Swiss Central Plateau was the first area to be developed by private railway companies, and within a short period of time Switzerland, once a blank spot on the railway map of the continent, had been transformed into the country with the densest railway network in Europe. By 1860, it was already possible to travel from Lake Constance to Lake Geneva by train, which just ten years earlier would have seemed incredible. One would, however, have to change between railway companies several times when making this journey across the Swiss Central Plateau.

Switzerland's east-west axis had thus been very rapidly developed. Further expansion in the 1870s had two aims: first, to increase the number of offshoots from the main lines, and second, to bring the railway as close as possible to the High Alps. Sion, which was connected to the network in 1860, and Sierre, which was connected in 1868, were points of departure for secondary lines that led into Upper Valais towards Leuk (1877) and Brig (1878); Interlaken played the same role for Lauterbrunnen (1890), as did Glarus for Linthal (1879) and Lucerne for Alpnachstad (1889). During this phase, the landmark project of a transalpine rail link was already being realised. The opening of the Gotthard Railway in 1882 was the high point of the successful era of privately owned Swiss railways – not only because from then on Cantons Ticino and Uri, and therefore northern and southern Switzerland, were joined but also because, with the transalpine rail link, Switzerland had created a global route connecting Northern Europe to India. With the Gotthard Railway, all obstacles seemed to have been overcome. Even high mountains could no longer stand in the way of the railway's progress.

There now arose the need to make conceptual and technical changes, as the infrastructure on the Central Plateau had been designed for standard-gauge trains, while the topographical conditions in

Graubünden, the Bernese Oberland and Valais required narrow-gauge networks. The railway was now winding its way higher and higher up the valleys, in a triumph of engineering over nature; in 1890, the network was extended to Lauterbrunnen (802 metres), Grindelwald (1034 metres) and Davos (1560 metres); in 1891, it reached Zermatt (1608 metres) and Mürren (1650 metres); and in 1904, it finally arrived in St Moritz (1822 metres). As a result, those places which were already established tourist destinations became markedly more attractive, while other places, which had until this point remained untouched by tourism but were now accessible, underwent rapid and profound changes. Thanks to narrow-gauge track, the iron horse was able to find its way into remote valleys. The consequences were striking, even where tourism did not take root. The increasingly frequented tourist hubs in the mountains, which were soon drawing guests in the winter season as well as in the summer, provided work for the local populations, and even people who were not from tourist hotspots benefited. But with the railway, a modern, urbane lifestyle also found its way into the villages. Through their interactions with tourists, locals came into contact with a previously unknown world. Directly exposed to the pulse of high society, hotel workers developed a new identity. The age of the sheltered village community was over, and seclusion was no more. And not only did the railways bring modernisation to the High Alps; the process also worked in reverse, bringing mountain villagers down to the Central Plateau.

The narrow-gauge railways connected the main lines with local tourist transport infrastructure like cog, adhesion and funicular railways. By the turn of the century, the Swiss railway infrastructure, which had been developed rapidly and ambitiously since the 1850s, was essentially complete. Switzerland was now covered by a branching network of roads and passes; bridges and tunnels; standard-gauge, narrow-gauge and mountain railways; steamboats and train ferries. This interlinked transport system, which reached from Lake Constance to Lakes Geneva and Lugano, became foundational for the development of both summer and winter tourism. It effortlessly carried guests to the most scenic places in the country, where a rapidly growing tourist industry was waiting to fulfil their every wish.

Mountain Railways

Swiss cog railways made history. The Rigi Railway, whose principal line between Vitznau and Rigi Staffelhöhe began operations in 1871 and was subsequently extended, was considered a marvel of engineering. It remained one of a kind until the railway on Pilatus opened in 1889. This too – the steepest cog railway in the world – was primarily designed as a means to reach a vantage point on a mountaintop. The Pilatus railway inspired the construction of more railways of this kind, with Central Switzerland markedly ahead of other tourist regions in this respect. There were also railways that served as shuttle services to hotels, as was the case on the Bürgenstock. The economic destinies of railways and hotels were often inextricably linked. In these cases, when the hotel flourished, so did the railway; when the hotel closed, the railway also disappeared. The Brunnen-Morschach-Axenstein railway was built in 1905 to serve the two prestigious hotels in Morschach, the *Axenfels* and the *Axenstein*. It ceased operations in 1968 after the *Axenstein* was demolished (1965); the *Axenfels* had shut down in 1947.

However, railways held their own when they were able to emancipate themselves from the hotel business by becoming excursion railways.

In 1888, the Brünig Railway (Brünigbahn) became the first railway company to lay tracks over a pass. With this, the traditional route between Central Switzerland and the area around Thun and Interlaken became a tourist attraction in itself. In the early 1890s, it seemed as though Switzerland had been seized by "mountain railway fever." Tourist hotspots developed in quick succession: Monte Generoso (1890), Mürren (1891), Rochers de Naye (1892), Brienz Rothorn (1892), Schynige Platte (1893) and Kleine Scheidegg (1893). At the turn of the century, amidst the overblown glitz and glamour of the Belle Époque, the construction of mountain railways was also in its heyday. Highlights included the opening of the first electric cog railway in Switzerland, from Zermatt up to the Gornergrat (station at 3090 metres), in 1898, as well as that of the highest railway station in Europe, the Jungfraujoch (3454 metres), in 1912.

Figure 1.5 "Inauguration of the Pilatus railway on 4 June 1889." Photograph. PilatusBahnen AG.

Foreign tourists reached Alpine destinations on standard and narrow-gauge trains and then made their way up to spectacular vantage points on cog and adhesion railways. Finally, funiculars took them up among the highest summits. It is notable that the first funiculars were not constructed for the High Alps but rather to make hotel facilities in elevated parts of cities more easily accessible. This was the case for the line from the Lausanne train station down to Ouchy on Lake Geneva, which began operation in 1877, and for the connection from the steamboat dock on Lake Brienz to the *Hotel Giessbach* (1879) – the oldest surviving railway in Europe designed exclusively for foreign travellers. Later than both Central and western Switzerland, but then with even greater vigour, the Bernese Oberland was also seized by a railway fever; it broke out in the 1880s and 1890s and lasted until the beginning of the First World War. The particular intensity of this phase is evidenced by the fact that, in the decades that followed, no further mountain railways were built – with the exceptions of the Gelmerbahn (1926) and the Chapfbahn (1939). Only beginning in the 1950s did the construction of mountain transport, driven by increased tourism, experience a further upswing – this time on an even greater scale than during the Belle Époque.

Railway Access and the Development of Tourism: Cantonal and Regional Differences

In the first half of the 19th century, tourism was still rudimentary in Canton Graubünden. So-called commercial roads (Kommerzialstrassen) were the first forms of tourist infrastructure and led even to out-of-the-way towns. After the construction of the Albula road, tourist inns were built in Bergün and elsewhere along the road. The commercial road over the Julier Pass brought winter tourism to the Engadin. That said, decisive surges in development were generally precipitated by a town's connection to the railway network. This is shown in the following examples, which are grouped by canton or region.

Graubünden: St Moritz could only become the "Top of the World" once it had been connected to Chur by the railway. Before 1904, the travel time from Chur to St Moritz was 12 hours. By train, the journey only took four hours. The improved accessibility afforded by the railway triggered a construction boom in St Moritz and the Upper Engadin. Additional luxury hotels were built, and other infrastructure was expanded. As a result, St Moritz, which had 58 hotels before it was connected to the railway (1900), a decade later had 74 (1911). Alternatively, one can look at the number of available beds, which rose from 3,160 in 1902 to 4,547 in 1911. The transformation from farming village to international tourist destination is also evidenced by the number of St Moritz residents, which rose from 183 in 1803 to 200 in 1830 – before the completion of the Julier road – to 228 in 1850, and by 1900 had

Figure 1.6 Robert Miller. "The Stanserhorn Railway and the Stanserhorn Hotel." 1893. Photograph. In *Der Hotelberg: Geschichte und Geschichten vom Bürgenstock Resort: 1871 bis heute*, by Romano Cuonz. Basel: NZZ Libro, 2018, 136.

The area around Lakes Thun and Brienz, including the Lütschinen valleys, became the region in Switzerland most densely connected by mountain railways: Funiculars carried travellers to Beatenberg (1889), Grütschalp (1891), the Reichenbach waterfall (1899), the Heimwehfluh (1906), the Harder (1908) and the Niesen (1910), and there were cog railways to Schynige Platte (1893) and Wengernalp (1893). The region around Lake Lucerne was also home to a number of mountain railroads. Here, however, it was primarily a matter of smaller and less spectacular funiculars, for example, to Gütsch (1884) and Sonnenberg (1902). The first one-track electric funicular with a passing loop was the Bürgenstock Railway, (1888), and the first such funicular without a gear rack brake was the Stanserhorn Railway (1893), shown in a photograph taken in 1893. Franz Josef Bucher (1834–1906) and his brother-in-law Josef Durrer (1841–1919) built the funicular and the summit hotel at the same time.

Mountain railroads were also built in Valais; the Gornergrat Railway, for example, was inaugurated in 1898. Reluctantly, the township of Zermatt was forced to give in and grant the Seiler hotel family a way leave for a tram track from the Hotel Riffelalp through the forest to the Gornergrat Railway. In 1899, the highest electric tram in Europe (2209–2222 metres) began operations. After a fire at the hotel in 1961, operation of the tram line was suspended; it has since been taken up again.

reached 1,603. In 1910, after the opening of the railroad, St Moritz had a population of 3,197. The number of its mostly foreign visitors rose in parallel. The transport of so many tourists to the Upper Engadin valley would not have been possible with the traditional form of transport, the stagecoach. The inrush could only be accommodated thanks to the Albula Railway (Albulabahn), which opened in 1903 and was extended to reach St Moritz in 1904.

A similar transformation took place in Pontresina, which in 1850 could still pride itself on having a larger population than St Moritz. By 1888, the population had almost doubled, from 270 to just under 510. In the 1880s, Pontresina already boasted more than 800 guest beds. The English doctor and meteorologist William Marcet (1828–1900) stated in 1882 that the beds in the hotels *Roseg* and *Kronenhof* alone accommodated more than 300 guests per day, "of whom at least half are English."[21] Then the railway reached Pontresina, and the expansion of hotel and leisure facilities continued.[22]

Davos would not have been able to play its role as Europe's sanatorium if not for the railway line to Landquart. After the middle of the century, the town gradually developed into a climatic health resort, but it was only with the introduction of the railway that the village became known across Europe as the first port of call for people with lung disease. The increase in the number of hotels is astounding: from 8 in 1870 to 43 in 1880; in 1890, the year of the inauguration of the railway station, there were 65; then 98 in 1900, and 128 in 1910. The same trend was evident in Arosa. The town had a total of 56 full-time residents in 1850. By 1900, that number had risen to 1,071, and in 1910 – before the construction of the railway line – to 1,643, of whom 705 were immigrants. The transformation of this small farming village into a hotspot of tourism was initiated by the construction of the road through the Shanfigg in 1890. The road was soon being used to its capacity, however, and a railway was planned; it began operating in 1914.

These well-known Graubünden destinations, which developed rapidly thanks to railway transport, stand in stark contrast to Disentis and Ilanz in the Graubünden highlands. Both recorded only a slight increase in population during the same time period: Between 1850 and 1900, the population of Disentis rose from 1,260 to 1,359, and that of Ilanz from 663 to 981. That these two towns did not benefit from the upswing in tourism that touched other places in the canton was due partly to topographical reasons but mostly to the fact that Disentis was only connected to the railway network in 1912. Ilanz had a railway station beginning in 1903 but was not yet able to play its later role as a transport hub – in contrast to, say, Spiez in the Bernese Oberland. Neither Lugnez nor Surselva had the tourism infrastructure to compete with top destinations like St Moritz, Arosa and Davos.

Valais: Travel guides of the 18th and early 19th centuries featured three highly recommended destinations in Valais: the Pissevache waterfall, which cascades down between Martigny and St-Maurice, was lyrically praised by Goethe and was considered a competitor to the Staubbach waterfall in the Bernese Oberland; the Rhône Glacier, which was touted as particularly worth seeing; and finally Leukerbad, one of the best-known travel destinations in Switzerland, reachable over the Gemmi Pass from Bern – an important factor in its development.[23]

For a long time, the Matterhorn was not considered a signature symbol of Valais or Switzerland. This can be explained by the history of Zermatt and its transport routes. It was the railway connection between Visp and Zermatt, inaugurated in 1891 as the highest railway line in Europe, that catapulted the storybook village at the foot of the Matterhorn into the touristic stratosphere. Once the railway opened, the number of guest beds in Zermatt increased rapidly. By the outbreak of the First World War, Zermatt had become the most important tourist hotspot in the Valais Alps and was Europe's second-most-famous Alpine tourist destination after St Moritz.

Bernese Oberland: The access road from Interlaken to Grindelwald, which was built in the 1860s, triggered hotel development in the region. In 1873, there were three hotels in Grindelwald. In 1914, there were already 33 hotels and pensions with a combined capacity of 1,900 beds, of which 1,275 were in first-class hotels. Grindelwald's transformation illustrates the enormous increase in tourism around the turn of the century. In fact, the six decades after the Belle Époque saw comparatively little development: In the 1960s, Grindelwald had around 40 hotels and larger pensions and 2,000 guest beds.

Meiringen in the Haslital, on the other hand, owed its importance to the Brünig Railway (1888). Thanks to the railway, the town became a starting point for travellers journeying to the newly built hotels in surrounding high-altitude tourist locations. The Brünig Railway not only improved the transport connections between the Bernese Oberland and Central Switzerland but also gave Canton Obwalden a touristic boost, facilitating, among other things, an increase in the number of pilgrims visiting the memorial of Brother Klaus in Flüeli-Ranft.

The first hotel in Mürren was built in 1857, and by 1878 there was already an Anglican church in the village. Despite only being accessible by mule path, the fascination with this town in the middle of High Alpine peaks was so great that by 1888 it already had 310 guest beds. In 1891, Mürren was connected by rail to Lauterbrunnen and thus to the valley. By the end of the 19th century, Wengen had also become a high-altitude tourist destination in the Jungfrau region, thanks to its transport connections. A hotel boom then ensued in Wengen and Mürren, two sunny locations that lay across the valley from each other. In 1909, Wengen became a destination for winter travel, but only after the Wengernalp Railway (Wengernalpbahn), urged on by hoteliers, began to operate throughout the winter.

The Kander Valley also experienced an upswing in tourism after it was connected to the railway network. Foreign travel to Adelboden increased markedly in the mid-1880s, after the extension of the road from Frutigen. Spiez became a tourist destination around the turn of the century, thanks to its role as a transport junction. Gstaad provides a clear example of how connection to a rail line could help modest farming villages become international tourist destinations. Throughout the entire 19th century, Gstaad was a small village, made up of just a few farmhouses. The Montreux-Oberland Bernois Railway was originally planned to bypass Gstaad. The politician Karl Reichenbach (1846–1916) strongly advocated for a change to the railway's planned route, and in the end Gstaad was conceded a station. This allowed for the development that would transform the town into a glamorous meeting point of international celebrities after the turn of the century. Thanks be to Reichenbach. In Reichenbach's honour, a curve in the railway line was named after him. Gstaad's development occurred as a result of its inclusion on the Montreux-Oberland Bernois line, which connected the Bernese Oberland to Lake Geneva and the wider world.[24]

Appenzell: Appenzell Innerrhoden remained an agricultural region throughout the course of the 19th century and up until the outbreak of the First World War, and agriculture remained its most important economic sector well into the 20th century. The textile industry developed into a second mainstay of the Innerrhoden economy. The transition from linen production to hand embroidery as the primary cottage industry took place in the early 19th century, and hand embroidery retained its economic importance until 1914. When the hand embroidery industry experienced a crisis around 1870, the first industrial operations began, but they did not lead to further development. Instead, tourism took on new importance.

The transport network was fundamental for the canton's development. The tourists who sought out Appenzell came to Gais (Ausserrhoden) for whey cures. The Weissbad whey cure establishment opened its doors at the end of the 18th century. Spas, hotels and mountain inns developed in parallel to the construction of roads and railways. In 1809, the first road suitable for carriages was completed between Gais and Appenzell, and new roads from Appenzell to Gonton and to Wasserauen followed in the early 1860s.

Appenzell was connected to the railway network relatively late. In 1889, the line between St Gallen and Gais opened. Around the turn of the century, various projects foundered for financial reasons. In 1911/1912, an attempt was made to build a feeder railway from Appenzell to Wasserauen via Weissbad. But here too, because of collapsing tourist numbers after 1914, the means to finish the project were not available. The aerial tramway Schwägalp-Säntis was only built in 1935 – again, relatively late – and as a result, the touristic development of Säntis trailed behind that of other mountains. This is evident when one compares the situation to that on Pilatus, which also had the advantage of being accessible by steamboat.

Central Switzerland: Frenzied development set in in the towns along the Bay of Küssnacht after it was connected to the transport system by steamboat and railway. Weggis established itself as a harbour town in the 1830s. Vitznau, on the other hand, profited in the last quarter of the 19th century from the steadily expanding Rigi Railway. This expansion triggered a surge of tourism on the Rigi itself and led to the construction of large hotels. By 1860, there were several hotels on the Rigi, with a combined capacity of around 500 beds, as well as dozens of inns. In 1871, a cog railway began operations between Vitznau and Rigi Staffelhöhe, and by 1873 it had been extended to the summit. In 1874, the line between Kaltbad and Unterstetten was opened; it was extended to Scheidegg in the following year. Rigi Kaltbad became the mountain's railway junction.[25] The Rigi became one of the best-known mountains in Switzerland – at least judging by the extensive descriptions of it in contemporary travel guides. In 1870, around 40,000 people visited the Rigi on foot, on horseback or by sedan chair.

The opening of the cog railway rang in an era of vigorous construction. In 1871, the railway transported 100,000 guests up its first section. Soon day tourism on the Rigi knew no bounds. And in 1875, when the railway from Arth in Schwyz began operating, the tremendous growth in visitor numbers led to a kind of gold rush. While the two railways were competing, new inns were springing up like mushrooms. In the early 1880s, the Rigi could accommodate around 2,000 overnight guests. This Rigi euphoria not only attracted tourists but also drew speculators to the

Figure 1.7 Johann Rudolf Dikenmann (1793–1883), *Axenstrasse, Blick aus der Tunnelgalerie in Richtung Flüelen* (Axenstrasse, View from the Tunnel Gallery towards Flüelen). Zurich, Zentralbibliothek Zürich.

mountain, leading to takeovers and the building of yet more infrastructure. This speculation reached its peak with the *Hotel Schreiber*, which became famous for its palatial design. Most of the buildings constructed during this tumultuous period of development are now long gone.

For centuries, the transport of goods and passengers along Lake Uri was only possible by water. In 1865, however, the spectacular Axenstrasse, with its many tunnels and galleries carved out of the cliff, made the way passable for carriages. Subsequently, the first hotels and inns appeared along the lake. In the 1860s, a number of tourist attractions emerged at higher elevations – for example, on the Seelisberg, one of the region's best-known locations.

Ticino: Travellers made their way over the Simplon road to the southern Lake Maggiore region, to Baveno, Stresa and Arona. These places, which have long ceased being top tourist destinations, are described in Swiss travel guides from the mid-19th century onwards. The Borromean Islands were also tourist attractions. But for a long time, tourism in Ticino remained in the shadow of the flourishing industries in the Bernese Oberland and Central Switzerland. Through-traffic on the road over the Gotthard, which had become suitable for carriages in 1831, failed to spark a surge of tourism, though some previously isolated towns between Airolo and Bellinzona – such as Faldo and Biasca – did become respectable tourist spots. It was only in 1882, with the transalpine rail link through the Gotthard Tunnel, that Ticino achieved the fundamental infrastructure necessary for its growth as a tourist destination.

Despite the opening of the *Hôtel du Parc* (later *Palace*) in 1850, Lugano only developed in fits and starts. As in Lucerne and Geneva, quays were built up between the city centre and Paradiso in the 1860s. With the Gotthard Railway under construction, a train line from Lugano to Chiasso began operations in 1874. The transalpine rail link was the catalyst for the breakthrough in tourism that took place beginning in the 1880s. On the initiative of Bucher-Durrer, Lugano became the fourth Swiss city – after Zurich, Geneva and Basel – to operate an electric tramline. The tram led to the lower station of the funicular that brought people to the peak of Monte San Salvatore from 1890 onwards. The most important hotels were constructed in the area around the train station and the tramline. The *Continental Parkhotel* (1870) was joined by the *Victoria au Lac* (1885), the *Splendide Royale* (1870/1887) and the *De la Paix* (1905).

After Lugano, Locarno was the second-most-important tourist destination in Ticino. It, too, had been touristically unimportant until the mid-19th century. At that time, Magadino – across the lake from Locarno – was the economically more important of the two towns; freight was transported by water, and transshipment took place not in Locarno but in Magadino. There, goods brought over the Gotthard by horse-drawn carriage were loaded onto boats and sent southwards. Only in the 1860s did Locarno begin to develop. And here, too, it was the connection to the railway network – in this case through the 1874 opening of the line to Bellinzona – that brought a touristic influx and provided the impetus for the construction of more impressive hotels.

Mass Tourism and Technological Development: The Rigi

The technological marvels realised in Switzerland in the second half of the 19th century set new international standards. The construction of mountain railways was one such marvel and accounted for one superlative achievement after the other. The consequences for tourism cannot be overstated: The Belle Époque and railway transport are inextricably linked. The hotels and inns that were constructed in growing numbers in increasingly extreme locations had to be comfortably accessible. This paved the way for a first phase of mass tourism, which began in the Belle Époque and lasted until the First World War. The construction of the Vitznau-Rigi Railway line, the first passenger cog railway in Europe, set the course for this new kind of Swiss tourism. Once the economic crisis of the 1870s had been overcome, mountain railway construction experienced a boom. Following the model of the Rigi Railway, no fewer than 170 cog railways were constructed. These initially employed the Riggenbach system and then, after 1885, the Abt, Staub or Locher systems.

The Rigi Railway was not the first cog railway in the world, however. Its predecessors were introduced at the beginning of the 19th century in early industrial Great Britain. At this early stage, no thought was given to using cog railways to transport passengers, though this would later become their main function as an essential part of tourism infrastructure. In 1811, John Blenkinsop (1783–1831), the owner of a coal mine in Middleton, patented his design for a gear rack along which a cog was to turn. The mechanical engineer Matthew Murray (1765–1826) was then tasked with building a model according to Blenkinsop's blueprints. This first steam-engine cog railway was used in a mine in Leeds in 1812; it replaced the horse-drawn tram that had been employed since 1758. In the 1830s, the USA took the lead in the development of the new technology. The first American cog railway, which ran between Madison and Indianapolis (Indiana), began operating in 1848; the train cars were pulled by a locomotive. In order to reach the elevated bank of the Ohio River, it had to overcome a gradient of up to 60 per mille for more than two kilometres.

The inventor and machine designer William Hoyt of the DuPont locomotive factory in Indiana suggested designing a gear rack based on Blenkinsop's design. Andrew Cathcart (1808–1871), a machinist at the Madison & Indianapolis Railroad Company, bought the blueprints from Hoyt. Among other modifications, he shifted the gear rack from the side to the middle of the track. Based on the blueprints, Cathcart ordered two locomotives from Baldwin in Philadelphia, which were delivered in 1847. These had separate engines for their cog and adhesion systems, but their climbing power was only modest.

Eight years later, in 1855, Sylvester Marsh (1804–1884) of Chicago suggested building a cog railway up Mount Washington in New Hampshire. He was granted a concession by the relevant authorities. He patented his gear rack design in 1858, and construction began in 1866. The railway began operating in 1869. The Swiss General Consul in Washington, John Hitz (1828–1908), reported this advance in railway technology to the Swiss government. Niklaus Riggenbach (1817–1899) was personally sought out by Hitz in Olten in 1867.

There is much to suggest that it was this news from the USA that prompted Riggenbach to build a cog railway in Switzerland. The choice of the Rigi for this project comes as no surprise; Riggenbach, as a machinist and head of the principal workshop of the Central Railway – whose main line connected Basel with Lucerne – knew Central Switzerland and recognised its importance for tourism. In his autobiography, Riggenbach wrote that he had already received a French patent for his invention in 1863 and that he tested the prototype of his cog railway in a stone quarry in Ostermundigen. The debate about who owned the patent of the cog system that would soon make Riggenbach world famous would escalate in the 1880s.[26]

It remains uncontested, however, that Riggenbach was only able to successfully implement the Rigi project on the basis of Marsh's exact plans, and the question of when Riggenbach tested his first prototype in the stone quarry is ultimately not relevant to the engineering of the cog railway on the Rigi. The decisive impulse, as well as the exact blueprints, did not result from the trial runs in the quarry. Rather, it was Marsh's Mount Washington project that showed Riggenbach the way. As news of the US cog railway became known in pertinent Swiss circles, the engineer Otto Grüninger (1847–1888) travelled to the USA – probably at the behest of Riggenbach and his associates – where he observed and documented the pioneering venture first-hand. [27] Based on this input from the USA, Riggenbach changed and improved his system, which was then employed on the Rigi Railway. Riggenbach was supported by notable engineers, including Olivier Zschokke (1826–1898) of Aargau and Adolf Naeff (1809–1899) of St Gallen.

The success on the Lucerne side of the Rigi motivated its neighbours in Schwyz to follow suit. In 1871, the Arth-Rigi Railway Company (Arth-Rigibahn-Gesellschaft) was founded in Goldau. Two years later, Riggenbach and Zschokke were tasked with designing a railway from the Goldau side. It began operating in 1875. It made history as a pioneering railway for a second time in 1907, when it was re-engineered as an electric cog railway.

It was necessary for the transport of passengers and goods that the railway infrastructure in Switzerland be compatible with foreign systems. The first train journey to the Swiss border took place in 1839, from Alsace right up to the gates of the city of Basel. In 1844, Basel itself was connected to the network. No more happened until the Swiss Central Plateau was gripped by the boom in railway construction of the 1850s. At this point, Swiss border stations assumed new significance for transport to and from the southern German regions and France. This can be seen, besides in the example provided by Basel, in the changing circumstances in Romanshorn.

In the Belle Époque, luxury trains began to carry the international elite to Swiss tourist destinations. Among them were the trains of the International Sleeping-Car and European Great Expresses Company (Compagnie Internationale des Wagons-Lits et des Grands Express Europeens), with their legendary teak-wood wagons. Exclusive destinations were also marketed to the international elite, including certain locations in Valais. Beginning in 1859, a train to the infamous casino in Saxon began to meet the steamboat that arrived in Bouveret from Geneva; the first part of the route, terminating in St-Maurice, was operated by the Ligne d'Italie.

The Western Switzerland Railway's line through Lausanne was completed in 1873. On this route, the train stopped directly in front of the *Hôtel des Alpes* in Territet. In 1895, the (London-) Calais-Interlaken/Engadin-Express began operating. Because Alsace-Lothringen had been annexed by Germany in 1871, the train had to be routed through France to Pruntrut-Delsberg. From there, some coaches continued into the Bernese Oberland along the lines operated by the Jura Railway and the Central Railway, while the others went on to Chur. The Chur contingent travelled further along track belonging to the United Swiss Railways (Vereinigte Schweizerbahnen). After an interruption of service during the First World War, the express from Calais began operating again. The luxury train reached speeds of up to 120 kilometres per hour. It left London at 11 a.m. and reached Interlaken at 8.23 a.m. and Chur at 10.05 a.m. A marked shortening of travel time on this route was only achieved 100 years later by high-speed lines and the Eurotunnel (1994).

Transport Infrastructure and Industrialisation

What was true for tourism was also true for other areas of the economy: Wherever tracks were laid, industrial development got started or accelerated. Where train stations were built, industry and commerce were established. When economic centres grew on the Central Plateau, this facilitated the development of local and regional infrastructure in the Alpine valleys. The railway project redrew the social and economic landscape of Switzerland and determined which locations would be central and which peripheral.

In his autobiography, Alfred Escher explained why he was for private railways and therefore against the construction of railways by the state:

Figure 1.8 "The railway between Passhöhe and Meiringen, Brunig, Bernese Oberland, Switzerland," between ca. 1890 and ca. 1900. Coloured postcard. Library of Congress, Prints & Photographs Division, LC-DIG-ppmsc-06849.

In addition to the mountain railways that served as shuttle services to hotels or took tourists to scenic outposts on mountaintops, there were others that covered far larger areas. Among these was the Stansstad Engelberg Railway (Stansstad-Engelberg-Bahn), which connected the valley (Stansstad) to the spa and holiday town (Engelberg) in 1898. In the same year, the *Bellevue-Terminus* was built in Engelberg; it was expanded into an elegant and winter-hardy Grand Hotel after the turn of the century.

The Brünig Railway, inaugurated in 1888 by the Jura-Bern-Lucerne Railway, was of great importance. It initially went from Alpnachstad (steamboat connection) to Brienz (steamboat connection) via Meiringen. In 1889, the line was extended to Lucerne. Also in 1889, the hotel king Franz Joseph Bucher-Durrer opened the *Grand-Hotel Brünig* above the train station on the Brünig Pass. In 1890, the railway was taken over by the Jura-Simplon Railway.

He expressed his particular concern that state construction would have neglected Eastern Switzerland.[28] And in fact, private railway companies did quickly develop railway networks in Eastern Switzerland. This was because the railroad routes were determined by economic criteria. Tracks were laid where economic prospects were good. The Northeastern Railway, for example, prioritised connecting Zurich to Romanshorn rather than Frauenfeld, the political centre of Thurgau. The same was true of the train line leading from Zurich to Affoltern and towards Central Switzerland: Cham was more important for the Northeastern Railway than was the political capital, Zug. With its strategic focus on business interests, the Swiss railway project fundamentally distinguished itself, even in its early days, from the railways in the Kingdoms of Sachsen and Württemberg, in the Duchy of Baden and in France, where the focus was on connecting cultural and political centres.

The fact that the railway network in Eastern Switzerland was particularly dense was, as Escher pointed out, due to the region's industrial importance. He was also correct in his assessment that towns with their own train stations and with connections to business centres would benefit from development spurred on by the railway. Industry that would not otherwise have existed in these towns sprang up along the railway lines.[29]

In 1850, for example, Neuhausen was still a small and unassuming village of 992 inhabitants by the Rhine Falls in Canton Schaffhausen. In 1853, however, the Schweizerische Waggonfabrik was established there; it would later become the Schweizerische Industrie Gesellschaft (SIG). The decision to base the factory in Neuhausen was taken by promoters with an eye to the projected Rheinfall Railway (Rheinfallbahn), which they were themselves simultaneously planning. Put simply, when a company was founded, the choice of its location depended largely on its accessibility by rail. When Neuhausen was connected to Zurich via Winterthur in 1857, its population grew explosively. In 1888, the town had 2,023 residents. By 1900, the population had grown to 3,905 – more than doubling within a single decade. Other locations where industry was established on account of planned or existing transport infrastructure experienced similar growth. This was true of Baden in Canton Aargau, for example, after Brown Boveri (BBC) was established there in 1891; of Valais after the founding of Lonza in 1897; of Arbon in Canton Thurgau after the founding of Saurer in 1853; of Schönenwerd in Canton Solothurn after the founding of Bally in 1851; and of Cham in Canton Zug after the establishment of the Anglo-Swiss Condensed Milk Company in 1866.[30]

While the traditional centres of watch manufacturing that became connected to the railway network in the last quarter of the 19th century expanded, the sites of the proto-industrial textile industry were passed by. This illustrates the basic economic insight that the industrial progress brought about by the railway touched economic sectors that were not tied to natural features such as waterways. Or, to put it slightly differently, the proto-industrial textile industry did not profit from the expansion of the railway network to the same extent as did its successor, the engineering industry or, later, the chemical industry. With this in mind, it becomes understandable why regions characterised by a traditional textile industry experienced no marked population growth, and even sometimes saw their populations shrink, in pronounced contrast to the areas dominated by the chemical and machine industries. Wattwil, with its muslin weaving roots in the 18th century and its later cotton factories, provides an example of this downward trend. Its railway station was only built in 1870. Neuthal, the location of the Guyer spinning factory since 1826, also struggled with depopulation. The town did not have its own railway station for a long time and was only connected to the Uerikon-Bauma line, via Bäretwil, in 1901.

The Swiss Railway Project

A Modest Track Record Before 1848

England played the pioneering role in railway construction, as it did in many other industrial sectors. It all began with the transport of coal. In 1818, businessmen in Stockton began building a canal from the river Tees to their city in order to bring in coal. Their competition in Darlington reacted by planning the construction of a tramway between its coal mines in Bishop Auckland and the city of Stockton-on-Tees. It was to be a simple, horse-drawn conveyance, pulled along a track. Even before construction had begun, however, the engineer George Stephenson (1781–1848) designed a railway, this one pulled by a locomotive. The design was a success, and so, in 1825, the world's first railway was inaugurated on the route from Stockton to Darlington. In this early phase of railroad history, attempts to connect mines to tracks on which coal would be transported were also made in other countries. The Austrian Empire, for example, did just this in 1824.

Stephenson made history as the first commercially successful builder of locomotives and railway cars. Earlier steam locomotives did exist, but they were too heavy and unsuited for regular operations – this was true, for example, of the model designed by Richard Trevithick (1771–1833) in 1802. Neither the steam-operated cog railway that John Blenkinsop (1783–1831) developed in 1812, nor the steam engine known as Puffing Billy, built a year earlier by William Hedley (1779–1843), was serviceable. Especially during the 1830s, countries besides England also began to construct railway lines: In 1830, the Baltimore & Ohio Railroad began operations in the USA. In France, the St Etienne-Lyon line opened in 1832. In the Grand Duchy of Baden, discussions were already underway in 1833 about a transalpine north-south connection from Mainz and Frankfurt to Northern Italy, passing through Basel and Chur, while in 1835, the Nürnberg-Fürth line was inaugurated in Bavaria.[31]

Switzerland had no part in this early railway fever.[32] In 1844, however, a train began to operate between St Louis in Alsace and Basel. With this, the city of Basel became connected to the French line from Strasbourg, which had almost reached the Swiss border in 1840. In 1845, after national security concerns had been given extensive consideration, the French railway station in Basel was allowed to open. But this still did not spur railway development in Switzerland. The opening of the Swiss Northern Railway (Schweizerische Nordbahn) route from Zurich to Baden in 1847 – the legendary "Spanish bun railway" – also failed to trigger further development. In comparison to its neighbours', Switzerland's railway project had not come into its own, and the country was being left further and further behind. Switzerland was a blank space in the middle of an increasingly dense European rail network.

This fact is surprising, because ideas for railways had been discussed in various regions of Switzerland as early as the 1830s – for example, in 1836, when railway enthusiasts in St Gallen set their sights on a line between Rorschach and St Gallen, or when the Zurich Chamber of Commerce established a railway commission. This commission toyed with the idea of using share capital to build a train line along Lake Constance, from Basel to Zurich and Winterthur. The plan was, for the most part, deemed a good one. It fell apart, however, because of bickering over cantonal party-political special interests. The proceedings of the Zurich railway commission did, in any case, result in the design of a route. In 1837, the Zurich Chamber of Commerce hosted a railway conference in the Zurich Town Hall, in which the representatives of six cantons took part. They founded an inter-cantonal committee tasked with planning a railway line from Basel to Zurich. In 1838, the Basel-Zurich Railway Company (Basel-Zurich-Eisenbahngesellschaft) was founded, but it had to be liquidated in 1841: Unresolvable questions about expropriation and the route of the track – among other things – had brought the plans to nought. In Lucerne, Geneva and Bern, too, railways were discussed, and possibilities for train lines mapped out.

Events in Schaffhausen provide telling insights into this early phase of the Swiss railway project. In 1839, numerous residents of Schaffhausen met to discuss matters related to shipping on the Rhine. At this meeting, the then 22-year-old Friedrich Peyer im Hof (1817–1900) drew attention to planned transcontinental railway lines. This did not inspire much discussion. A public debate on the issue did occur in 1841, however, triggered by a letter published in a newspaper calling on the authorities "to not merely [sit back] and watch, with [their] hands idly in [their] laps."[33] No resources should be spared – so the letter – to convince the Grand Duchy of Baden to extend the train line on the German side of the Rhine from Basel to Schaffhausen. From there, steamboats could travel upriver on the Rhine towards Lake Constance.

On 6 June 1841, a further meeting of parties interested in the railway took place. Again, Peyer im Hof called on his peers to take action, and in particular to send a delegation to Karlsruhe to convince the authorities there to pursue the Basel-Schaffhausen project. His opponents did not stand idly by. In newspaper articles, they called into question the economic usefulness of the railway and the financial strength of Schaffhausen. The conflict went on like this for years. In 1844, Peyer im Hof appealed to the Schaffhausen government to finally press ahead with planning and to budget accordingly. He feared that if a competing project that aimed to build a train line from Basel to Zurich was realised, Schaffhausen would be left isolated. The government of Schaffhausen finally acknowledged the seriousness of the situation and declared itself ready to invest in a private company. It also supported efforts to send a delegation from Schaffhausen to London, where it hoped to round up the capital necessary for the construction of the railway. The mission had to be aborted, however: The internal political situation in Switzerland had heated up as anti-clerical rebels attempted to topple the Conservative government of Lucerne (Freischarenzüge), and this forced the government of Schaffhausen to reset its priorities. The railway project was once again put off indefinitely.[34] It remained on hold until 1853, when the Rheinfall Railway was founded in what had, in the meantime, become a very different political environment. The goal was now no longer to build a line to Basel but rather to Zurich.

In 1842, a Zurich-based group bought the plans for the liquidated Basel-Zurich Railway Company that had been put up for auction by Martin Escher-Hess (1788–1870). They intended to reboot the project under new circumstances. However, another four years passed before the founding of the Swiss Northern Railway in 1846. The delay was primarily caused by competing ideas about the layout of the line. Despite all the adverse circumstances, the section between Zurich and Baden was opened for transport on 7 August 1847. It was the first train line to run exclusively on Swiss territory. After a promising start, the Northern Railway ran into financial difficulties and had to relinquish its further plans. It is striking that the continuation of this line, under completely different circumstances, only went ahead in 1852. The originally intended extension of the line from Baden to Basel was at first dropped. Instead, northeastern Switzerland and the economically significant region around Lake Constance became the first priority. The railway line from Zurich to Winterthur and Romanshorn was rapidly constructed, and the connection to Schaffhausen soon followed.

Plans for a transalpine rail link were being considered as early as the 1830s. Richard La Nicca (1797–1883), an engineer and road inspector from Graubünden, argued that, in addition to the Splügen Pass, the Lukmanier Pass would serve especially well as a north-south connection. In 1838, an Italian, Zanino Volta (1795–1869), designed a railway line from Lake Walen to Lombardy via Chur and sought permission for the construction of a tunnel under the Splügen Pass. He estimated that construction of the line would take 30 years. Yet all these projects for train lines through or over the Alps broke down, as did all other attempts to build a railroad in Switzerland before 1848.[35]

Figure 1.9 "Hammetschwandlift," ca. 1900. Coloured postcard. Private collection.

Switzerland is a country of pioneering railways and pioneering facilities. After the Vitznau-Rigi Railway (1871/1873) – the first cog railway in Europe – came the Bödeli Railway (Bödelibahn) (1872/1874) with its double-decker carriages. Providing a connection between the steamboats on Lakes Thun and Brienz, it was the first standard-gauge train line in Switzerland to be built in a valley for touristic purposes. In the Belle Époque, one distinction followed the next: The Giessbach Railway (1879) and the Territet-Glion Railway (1883), both water-ballast funiculars designed by Niklaus Riggenbach, were the first funiculars in Switzerland; the Grütschalp-Mürren Railway (1891) – alongside the later Albula Railway – was the highest adhesion railway in Switzerland (metre gauge, electric); the Jungfrau Railway (1896 and 1912), which carried passengers to the Jungfraujoch (3457 metres) via the Kleine Scheidegg (2064 metres), became the highest cog railway in Switzerland (metre gauge, electric). And a mountain station partway up the Wetterhorn was the destination of Switzerland's first cable car.

A number of important hotels of the Belle Époque were built at remarkable vantage points, high above lakes and cities, and were seamlessly connected to the transport network by trains of all kinds. There was the water-ballast funicular that ran from the steamboat dock on Lake Brienz to the *Hotel Giessbach*, for example (1879); another ran from Lucerne to the *Hotel Château Gütsch* (1884), and yet another from Biel to the *Grand-Hotel Magglingen* (1887). In Zurich, too, a funicular was soon operating, this one between the Römerhof and the *Grand-Hotel Dolder* (1899).

The Federal Diet concerned itself only fleetingly with the question of developing a railway before declaring that this task was not in its remit. Nor did it consider itself responsible when, in 1846, the Bernese delegation requested that it standardise railway gauges across the country. The parliamentarians didn't even open a debate, as they had not discussed the matter in their cantonal committees and thus had not received instructions on how to proceed. The old Confederation was evidently not structured to meet and overcome challenges such as those presented by the construction of the railway.

To say the achievements of this first epoch of Swiss railway history were meagre would be an understatement. The reasons for this are evident and are telling for the later success story of the railway. That no meaningful results had been achieved by the end of the 1840s was due neither to the differing interests of individual regions nor to rivalries and diverging ideas about the laying of the train lines: Later, such competition would arise on a much larger scale. The fact that Switzerland was unable to begin its railway project until 1848 was due to insufficient, or entirely non-existent, political and economic preconditions. The structural make-up of the Confederation made high-flying railway plans impossible to realise. The prevailing conditions presented obstacles of all kinds – from the confusion created by different measuring units and currencies to the restrictions created by tolls, sluggish licensing procedures and the impossibility of expropriating land: a corset fastened too tightly and an insufficiently high-flying spirit! It took the Federal State of 1848 to create a political framework that fundamentally improved the prospects for railway construction in Switzerland. But even with the birth of the Federal State, Switzerland still had not been launched as a railway country. It required an intelligent, far-sighted railway policy, like the one introduced in 1852, to divvy up authority and responsibilities between national institutions and private businesses. And it required personalities, pioneers and entrepreneurs who were willing and able to optimally exploit the unfolding opportunities.

The Railway Project Finds Political Expression in 1849

The new Federal State offered an incomparably better structural and economic foundation for a nationwide railway project than the pre-1848 Confederation had. It may thus come as a surprise that the Constitution of 1848, in which the architecture of the modern Swiss state was laid out, was silent about the construction and operation of railways. The word "railroad" appeared only a single time in the entire constitutional text, in a discussion of contracts regarding transit fees and tolls. That was it. No conception of a railway policy; no fundamental mapping of a way forward. This is especially striking when compared to other issues that were discussed extensively in the Constitution, such as a ban on Jesuits (Art. 58) or the regulation of the production and sale of gunpowder (Art. 38). One might even be tempted to accuse the writers of the Constitution of having failed to understand the significance of the railway. In hindsight, however, leaving the railway out of the Constitution turned out to be the best thing they could have done for the future development of their country. It was because of this omission that the opportunity arose to approach the task under the general terms of Article 21, which dealt with public works; in this way, it remained the responsibility of the future Parliament to create relevant legislation.

In fact, when the Constitution was being worked on in 1848, the conceptual, economic and technical foundations necessary to tackle the question of the railroad as a nation were lacking. The discussions that were held in the early days of the Federal State leave room for no other possible conclusion: Had the Constitution been explicit about the railway, the railway would not have been a success. The gun smoke from the recent Sonderbund War would have clouded judgement, obscuring the priorities of the economic and societal policy agenda, making impossible the clear-sightedness that was necessary to realise the railway project.

It took the parliamentarians of the nation's first hour to realise the existential importance of the railway for the country. The very structure of proceedings in the old Federal Diet had skewed perceptions of the issue. The new form of government that came into being in 1848, with its two councils and their commissions, laid the institutional foundation for making decisions about the railway that did justice to its complexity. Now, however, a visionary mover and shaker was required to lead the iron horse onto the right track. This role was assumed by Alfred Escher. He recognised the seminal importance of railway transport for the development of Switzerland.

Like almost no other business, the matter of building the railway brought cantonal and local political outlooks into conflict. Only when the Federal Council and the Swiss Parliament addressed the great infrastructural questions facing the new Federal State – in such a way that critical discussions had to be conducted about the responsibilities of the state versus those of the cantons, the roles of the public purse versus those of private businesses – had the right time come to build a railroad. For years, the railroad was the most discussed matter in the Federal Parliament Building, and it became prominently associated with Escher's name. The railway project soon seemed to be personified by him. The building and financing of the Swiss railway network marked the beginning of Escher's political ascent. Later, it would be the arena in which he suffered his greatest defeat and probably the most painful disappointment of his life. In numerous and fateful ways, Escher's career became interwoven with the early history of the Swiss railroad.

In 1849, Swiss industrialists and bankers submitted a petition to the Federal Council in which they called on it to lay the groundwork for the construction of the railway.[36] This initiative was taken up by Escher, then President of the National Council, who, along with 13 other councillors, put forward a motion on the issue on 11 December 1849. It called on the Federal Council to work together with experts to draw up a plan for a Swiss railway network, to submit proposals for its realisation and, especially, to prepare the necessary legislation. In order not to lose time, and to underline the importance of the motion, the National Council put together an 11-person railway commission a week later. This commission was to examine the Federal Council's report immediately after its completion and introduce a motion in the National Council. Alfred Escher was elected to this committee with the greatest number of votes and assumed the chairmanship.

The last day of the 1849 session of the National Council fell on 22 December. In his closing address, Escher reflected on the business that had been attended to in the session. Inevitably, he addressed the railway issue, which was now awaiting further action by the Federal Council. Despite "investigations and assessments of all kinds," Escher noted tersely, not a single piece of track had yet been laid. Finally, Escher touched on the decisive question that would occupy the political committees for years and decades to come. Who ought to be the competent authority for the railway? Should it be the cantons, as in the old Confederation, or should it be the federal government? By the end of 1849, the question had still now been answered.

At its core, the increasingly entrenched political debate around the construction and operation of Swiss railways was at first a continuation of earlier discussions regarding the Federal Constitution. Put simply, it first dealt with the question of whether the railway project should be approached from a centralised or federalised perspective. In this respect, the question of the railway was not significantly different from other infrastructural issues for which a framework existed in the new Constitution, and which now had to be translated into practice, under either cantonal or national leadership. In light of the basic architecture of the new Federal State and the reigning zeitgeist in the first Swiss Parliament, it was assumed that responsibility for the railroad would be taken on by the state. It seemed impossible that a solution reliant on private business would enjoy majority support. In the German states, inter-regional train transport by national and provincial railways was largely organised by the state; in the Austro-Hungarian Empire, a phase of railway nationalisation had taken over an industry originally run by private companies. In Great Britain, by contrast, railways were exclusively privately run throughout the 19th century – but circumstances were very different there, and the British practice would not necessarily serve as a model for Switzerland. The practice in Denmark, however, did appear to present an interesting possibility. In 1835, the Royal Railway Commission had been founded, and in 1840, Danish railway operations began. The proprietor was a public limited company in which the state held a majority interest. The further expansion of the railway network, though facilitated by the state, was propelled for the most part by private businesses and entrepreneurs. A national structure was eventually developed in 1865, in the form of the Danske Statsbaner, which bought the railway back from the private companies piece by piece.[37]

So it was that when leading politicians in 1849 critically examined railway construction in neighbouring countries, they assumed that the solution in Switzerland, too, would be based on state management. Also important was the radical spirit that pulsed in the young Federal State and called out for centralised structures. Proponents of privately run construction were few and far between. The matter seemed decided before it had even been discussed.

It might have been expected that, after 1849, Escher would have expressed his stance on the railroad issue in terms equally as uncompromising as he used for other matters. Instead, he felt his way carefully. The speech he gave about the railroad on 12 November 1849 was limited to a discussion on the level of general infrastructural considerations. It should nevertheless be noted that in the motion he submitted to the Federal Council, he gave serious consideration to the alternative of private construction. The political and technological conditions that would allow Escher to cut to the chase were not yet ripe. His hesitancy might also be explained by the fact that, in 1849, he still lacked practical expertise on railway matters. Without this expertise, he apparently did not want to go out on a limb. Perhaps, however, Escher was also aware that the centre of power in the area of railway policy did not lie in Zurich but rather in Basel, where many decisive infrastructural plans in the young Federal State originated.

The Federal Council took up the task that the National Council had given it at the end of 1849 and set to work. A Federal Railway Office was set up in the Post and Construction Department and put under the leadership of the engineer Gottlieb Koller (1823–1900). Koller was tasked with putting together basic documentation, gathering fundamental publications about railway matters and conducting detailed studies. The Federal Council prepared legislation on expropriation that was enacted by the Federal Assembly on 1 May 1850. The Federal Council also conducted an all-encompassing survey of existing railway technology. It found that many cantons were still stuck in the same old disputes that had characterised the hapless 1830s and 1840s. Based on this unpromising finding, the Federal Council attempted to find experts to design a plan for a nationwide railway network. It hoped to form two separate expert committees: One would deal with technical questions, while the second would be responsible for the project's economic and financial aspects.

The Stephenson/Swinburne Expert Assessment of 1850

The Federal Council's first choice of technical expert was the English engineer Robert Stephenson (1803–1859), the son of George Stephenson (1781–1848).[38] Stephenson was invited to travel throughout Switzerland

and then issue a report about what would be the most practicable layout for the railway lines. The Post and Construction Department of the Federal Council was informed on 1 May 1850, to its irritation, that Stephenson would only be able to travel to Switzerland in August. As a Conservative MP in Britain, he first had to see out the ongoing parliamentary session. In order not to lose time – and at Stephenson's recommendation – the department asked the English engineer Thomas Longridge Gooch (1808–1882) if he would be willing to serve as an expert. For health reasons, Gooch was unable to accept the offer. The 29-year-old English engineer Henry Swinburne (1821–1855) stepped in to help out in this moment of need. He started off on an exploratory trip from Geneva. Stephenson arrived in Switzerland somewhat later, as had been planned. The two British engineers were accompanied by numerous Swiss experts. In Gottlieb Koller, who provided them with necessary materials and documents, they had a point of contact and a direct connection to the Federal Council.

On 7 June 1850, the Federal Council had presented a report to Parliament in which it set out its instructions to Stephenson and Swinburne. The two experts were first to comprehensively assess all of the train lines which might figure in the network and present their thoughts and estimates about financial and managerial matters. Second, they were to travel along the proposed routes and assess the situation on site, identifying any obstacles. The primary goal was for the two Englishmen to identify the main lines on which the Swiss railway network could most advantageously operate, always taking into account considerations of national security. Further, they were to determine the priority that should be assigned to the construction of each section of the railway. And finally, Stephenson and Swinburne were to clarify the feasibility and profitability of a transalpine rail link, evaluate advantageous routes and specifically look into the Lukmanier project.

Stephenson and Swinburne's assessment was presented on 12 October 1850. It proposed the laying of the rail lines principally along the water courses, connecting rather than replacing shipping routes. The railway lines should follow the banks of rivers and lakes and connect to the existing Alpine roads. This would allow for the integration of railways, steamboats and roads into a linked transport system. The two experts were of the opinion, however, that steamboat operations offered greater advantages than the railway. The network they proposed comprised 659 kilometres, at an estimated cost of 100 million French francs. Stephenson and Swinburne designated five main lines that were to serve as the backbone of the Swiss railway network.

The final part of their assignment – the assessment of a Lukmanier railway in relation to other possible transalpine rail links – was not given due consideration by Stephenson and Swinburne. It is possible that they lacked the necessary knowledge. Still, both experts stated that, while they thought a Lukmanier railway was technically feasible, they did not think that the trade benefits of such a line would justify it. A railway over or through the Alps did not necessarily have to be a part of the Swiss railway network, since the German states and the Kingdom of Piedmont-Sardinia would be its primary beneficiaries. It should therefore be planned in collaboration with these neighbouring countries. They identified the Splügen and Gotthard Passes as possible options for a north-south connection.

The experts also delivered their opinion on the question of whether a competitive situation would be beneficial for railway operations and whether the layout of the lines should be made along the shortest routes possible, without considering topography or population density. They recommended that Switzerland consider the experiences made in England and attempt an "even-handed" distribution of railway lines. Contrary to the practice in England, towns might not necessarily be connected by the shortest possible route. Despite their criticisms of the structure and condition of English railway companies, Stephenson and Swinburne made no explicit recommendation for or against private or state railway construction.

7 April 1851: The Federal Council Takes a Stand

The Federal Council chose the Basel alderman Carl Geigy (1798–1861), the Winterthur engineer Jakob Melchior Ziegler (1801–1883) and the Basel secondary-school teacher Wilhelm Schmidlin (1810–1872) to provide the expert opinion on how the railway could most efficiently be constructed from a financial perspective.[39] These experts estimated a return of 2.67 percent on the entire railway network. On the question of whether the construction of the railway ought to be financed by the state or by private interests, their opinions diverged. Geigy's opinion was striking. He believed that state involvement was vital; financing by private equity would mean that no trains would travel through Switzerland for years. However, he was aware that the state was not in a position to provide the entire necessary capital on its own. As a result, he believed that cantons ought to assume the financial risk. In any case, he believed the federal government should be in charge of the railway. It should decide the layout of the lines as well as the order in which different sections were to be constructed. This position was opposed by Ziegler, who favoured privately managed construction, though he did think the federal government should be afforded the power of oversight and a right of repurchase. Neither of these positions ultimately won out. In any case, it is clear that neither of their suggestions would have provided the railway project with the necessary momentum.

Based on the various expert opinions, the Federal Council presented its stance on the issue to the Swiss Parliament on 7 April 1851. It proposed a system that combined private financing, a state interest rate guarantee and publicly managed construction. Every main line of the railway network would be a joint venture between the national government and the relevant canton. This would allow the parties involved to unite numerous main lines into a single enterprise, whose executive leadership would fall to a board of directors. The directors, along with other officials, would share in any profits. The Federal Council accepted Geigy's financial proposal: Securities worth 500 new Swiss francs were to be offered at a minimum interest rate of 3.5 percent. In the event that the revenues failed to cover the interest, the federal government would guarantee one third of the interest, and the cantons two thirds. How the interest guarantees would be divvied up between cantons was left up to them. The federal government and the cantons would be entitled to redeem their securities for their nominal value after 50 years. Finally, the state should build and operate the railroad through a private-law organisation, while the public would finance construction and thus receive a state guarantee on interest.

While the expert recommendations had already kindled strong emotions at the end of 1850, the Federal Council's announcement now added fuel to the fire, and the railway project was sucked into the maelstrom of local political interests. When the Federal Council set out its concrete proposals about the layout of the railway network, cities, towns and regions realised that the fate of their connection to the railroad would be decided in Bern. They began to market their locations, lobbying and forging political alliances. The idea of the railroad as a means of transport that connected cities, cantons and countries, and simplified the transport of goods and passengers, was lost in the tunnel vision of local politics.

Yet another key element spoke against a railway run by the federal government, and it had to do with the fair distribution of national resources among the cantons. If because of their geographical location and their economic structure some cantons required a significantly more comprehensive railroad network than others, while a third group could not be accessed by rail at all due to its topography, the federal government would be giving funds for railroad construction – money that had been contributed proportionally by all the nation's cantons – in large amounts to some cantons, in lesser amounts to others and not at all to the third group. This, however, would be unfair. Or the government could have given all cantons the same amount for the construction of railways – which would have been more fair but have made little sense.

State Railway or Private Railway?

If one dissects the multi-layered task of formulating a railway policy in the young Federal State, two fundamental questions emerge: First, should the construction of the railway be executed by the state or by private companies? And second, who should be responsible for concessions? If the railway project were made the responsibility of the state, one would have to take the next step and decide between national and cantonal responsibility. Only once these questions had been answered could the routes of train lines be decided on, and the order of their construction prioritised. If one were to decide to leave the construction and operation to private companies, there would also remain the question of how the licensing procedure was to work: Concessions might, in this case, be granted by both the national government and the cantons. Based on the experts' assessments, the Federal Council presented a proposal to the Federal Assembly on 7 April 1851 that, in line with the proposal made by Geigy, envisioned a combination of state and privately managed construction. The responsibility for the construction and operation of the railway lines would be granted to the state, and public funds would play the dominant role in the development of the railroad.

The National Council's railway commission, under Escher's leadership, could not reach a consensus regarding the Federal Council's proposal.[40] There were disputes about the layouts of the train lines suggested by the Federal Council. In the end, the railway commission saw no other way forward than to propose that the National Council postpone its decision.

In March 1852, the railway commission again turned its attention to the question of who should own and operate the railway. In the meantime, news and rumours about huge losses actually or allegedly suffered by foreign railway companies had sparked fears that the Federal State might overextend itself. As a result, the merry-go-round of local patriotic interests began spinning even faster. Not only at the federal but also at the cantonal level, there was a shift towards a preference for private management. Within the 11-member railway commission, a narrow majority of six voted in favour of public construction, but the committee did not formulate a definitive motion to be put before Parliament.

There now reigned such general confusion in Parliament about the way forward that individual voices began to advocate postponing the question for years. In this climate of general disquiet and irritability, the idea of private management increasingly gained approval. Foreign investors also showed growing interest in the Swiss railway and began applying for concessions from cantonal authorities. The situation was becoming so unclear that here and there – without awaiting the outcome of the stalemate in Bern – railway lines were being planned every which way at the local level. In St Gallen, for example, a public subscription raised 2 million Swiss francs in a very short time, making possible the start of construction on the Wil-Rorschach Railway on a private basis. In Canton Thurgau, National Councillor Johann Conrad Kern (1808–1888) assumed leadership of a railway committee and began laying the groundwork for the Zurich-Lake Constance Railway, which he founded with interested parties from Canton Zurich at the end of 1852.

The Railway Act of 1852 and the Question of Higher Education

The die had apparently been cast, despite the fact that Parliament had still not made up its mind. Escher must have been sure of this, for on 14 April 1852 he reported in a letter to his friend Johann Jakob Rüttimann (1813–1876) that the majority of the Higher Education Commission's members only wanted to submit their proposals for the establishment of a federal institute of higher education to the National Council after the railway question had been resolved.[41] The timing of this motion, put forward by Escher himself, was thereby cleverly and tactically determined. Escher, who became a member of the Federal Council's Higher Education Commission in May 1851, found himself in a difficult political position with regard to these two infrastructural matters of crucial importance for the young Swiss nation. At the time, many could not understand why he vehemently and uncompromisingly advocated a federalist and private-sector solution to the railway dilemma while at the same time staunchly supporting a centralised approach to higher education. Escher had to find a balance. The fact that these two bills were being discussed at the same time was a formidable challenge both for Escher personally and for the entire political system.

In 1851/1852, the focal point of the political debate regarding the railroad and the federal higher education institution became the question of how to finance them both. The idea of having to pay for both undertakings simultaneously was downright frightening. It was in this context that a number of tactical voting scenarios played out. In a letter to Escher, Peyer im Hof asked the decisive question:

> Have you also thought about which matter, the railway question or the university question, should be prioritised? This is not unimportant, because if the principle of state involvement in the railway is legally enshrined, then the means at our disposal will be tied up; and if, on the other hand, higher education is decided for, then we will have no funds available for the railroads.

Similarly, Jonas Furrer (1805–1861) wrote to Escher and expressed regret "that these two important things have to be dealt with at the same time."[42]

The final round of the railway debate took place in May 1852, with the release of the reports of the National Council commission. For the proponents of state construction, it was a fiasco. They had become deeply committed to their public-sector model and would not give up their position despite the about-face in public opinion and the abundance of proposals motivated by local patriotism. These Radicals overlooked the fact that time had not stopped in the year 1848. The vote in the National Council on 8 July 1852 was decisive: The minority motion brought forward by Escher in favour of private construction received 68 votes, while that for state construction only received 22. On 21 July, the Council of States voted in the same sense. Finally, the Railway Act was enacted on 28 July 1852 by the two councils.[43]

The consequence of this decision was that, for all intents and purposes, the federal government was excluded from the railway project and had no legal leverage in the matter. It did not even have the authority to oversee railway companies and could only influence the layout of the railway lines when national security questions were involved. The construction and operation of the railway were left entirely in the hands of the markets. The federal government was not to concern itself with these matters and was to leave decisions to private business executives and, ultimately, to company shareholders.

The result of the vote highlights the political coherence of the young Federal State. It especially illustrates the condition of the Radical-Liberal camp, which had presented a unified front before the founding of the Federal State, bound together in a common fight for progress and modernisation, doctrinally opposed to everything Conservative. But now there were matters at hand that could no longer be answered in religious or denominational terms. As a result, the camps of the Radical-Liberals and of both the Catholic and Protestant Conservatives began to dissolve. Their followers began to form new factions made up of both federalists and centralists: Catholic Conservative Central Swiss could band together on political proposals with both Liberal Protestants from Zurich (endorsement of privatised railway construction, rejection of an expansionist foreign policy) as well as with Protestant Radicals from Vaud (opposition to a federal institute of higher education in Zurich). This too is evidence of the difference between the time before 1848 and the time after it: Interest groups that had been cantonally oriented up until 1848 now joined together to form inter-cantonal constellations that advocated for the concerns of entire regions. This was evident during the railway debate, when – with the exception of two National Councillors – every single member of the National Council from Eastern Switzerland voted for private construction. The fact that the Zurich delegation – with the exception of the socialist Johann Jakob Treichler (1822–1906) – followed Escher's lead is therefore not surprising. From this perspective, it is remarkable that Escher's opposite number, the Bernese Radical Jakob Stämpfli (1820–1879), was not able to win over the majority of Bernese National Councillors for his proposal in favour of state construction.

The inter-cantonal perspective is also expressed in Escher's autobiography:

> In the matter of the railway, I was for private construction and against construction by the federal government. I took this stance

> because I feared that if the Swiss railway network was designed by the state, Eastern Switzerland might be treated like a stepchild, despite the fact that, based on its industry and traffic, it was entitled to stake the greatest claim.[44]

The Success Story of the Railway

The Vital Importance of Railroad Construction for Switzerland

That railway projects could be of vital importance to a region is illustrated by the example of Canton Schaffhausen. In the spring of 1850, the authorities of Schaffhausen had submitted a request to the Swiss Post Department for permission to construct a railway line from Schaffhausen to Zurich via Winterthur. Because of its geographical location on the Swiss border, north of the Rhine and only connected to the rest of Switzerland by two bridges – one in Schaffhausen, the other in Stein am Rhein – Canton Schaffhausen was almost entirely surrounded by the Grand Duchy of Baden. Up until the 1830s, its location had not been a hindrance to trade and transport, since the border with its northern neighbours was highly permeable. After the Grand Duchy of Baden had been integrated into the German tariff union in 1835, however, the transport of goods from Schaffhausen to the north became subject to an import tax. As a result, the Canton was at a serious disadvantage in its vital trade with the Grand Duchy of Baden, yet still had little access to the Swiss markets on the other side of the Rhine.

The future National Councillor Johann Friedrich Peyer im Hof was especially aware of the danger this situation posed to his canton. Passionately and urgently, he called for Switzerland to set new political priorities. Specifically, he advocated setting aside denominational and religious disputes and instead dedicating energy to creating a forward-looking economic policy. He regarded the approach of European railway lines from the north with mixed emotions. He pointed out the tremendous potential that the construction of railway lines presented but feared that Canton Schaffhausen, and Switzerland in general, could be forced to the periphery if what he saw as an urgently needed expansion of transport routes – especially railway and steamboat connections – was not finally taken in hand. He saw danger in the German railway's plans to establish routes from Karlsruhe and Stuttgart eastwards to Venice via Bolzano. On such a line, transalpine rail traffic from the North Sea to the Mediterranean would pass Switzerland by.

> **The Railroad**
>
> My friend, what does the railroad give?
> I'll tell you, as well as I can.

Not mountains of gold, not bags of money,
As you might be imagining;
Not golden days in the lap of luxury,
Not Saint Monday or castle banquets.
Yes, perhaps it will even render meat and eggs
A few centimes too dear for you.
But, you ask, what good will it bring?
This I'll say to comfort you:
Work, and fresh life,
Early waking, diligent effort,
Thrift with time and strength,
Courage and zeal in business.

My friend, what will the railroad take?
I'll tell you, as well as I can.
It will take no earnings from the hard worker,
Nor profit from the good innkeeper,
Not the friendly countenance from the city,
Nor the quiet citizen's peace,
But laziness and idleness
And the comfort of old refrains:
"If I don't come today, I'll come tomorrow!"
And the anxious complaining and worry,
The overflowing glass too many,
That you drink while playing cards
Without profit or reward –
Oh, all this it will take![45]

Railways began to be mentioned in newspaper articles in Switzerland in the 1830s. After the Railway Act of 1852 was passed, they were mentioned with significantly greater frequency. The inaugurations of new lines were an especially popular topic. Occasional poems like "The Railroad" also took on the subject. In contrast to Germany – which had authors such as Heinrich Heine (1797–1856) – the Switzerland of the first half of the 19th century could claim no well-known writers whose reflections on the railroad deserve literary recognition. The yield of the second half of the 19th century was also disappointing. While it is true that, in addition to Gottfried Keller (1819–1890), there were other Swiss authors who wrote in various ways about diverse aspects of the railroad – including the societal changes it brought about, its economic significance and financial instruments (stocks) – a contemporary critical reflection on the age and its culture does not exist. This is so despite the fact that these authors were eyewitnesses to the opening of the first railroad line in Switzerland, that tracks were soon being laid across the entire country and that the railway was a topic of daily discussion. Heine, meanwhile, was in Paris to follow the opening of the train line to Orléans and Rouen. He did much more than depict the technical advances involved in the new means of transport. He also recognised that with the emergence of the railroad, a new chapter of world history was being rung in, one in which fundamental ideas like space and time would become inoperative. Heine looked far beyond French cities and predicted a continental interconnectedness: "To me it is as though the mountains and forests of all countries have been brought closer to Paris. I can already smell the scent of German lime trees; the North Sea is surging against my door."[46]

In his brilliant speech to the Cantonal Parliament of Zurich on 28 September 1852, Alfred Escher described the construction of railways as a necessity of life, particularly for industrial countries, and as a precondition for the self-preservation of Switzerland and particularly of Canton Zurich. Through its considerable acceleration of passenger and goods transport, through an increase in the productivity of all echelons of society and an improvement of commercial opportunities, the railroad would contribute to the health of the Swiss domestic economy and ease transport between Switzerland and nearby foreign countries. Escher emphatically pointed to the real disadvantages afflicting Swiss industry compared to its foreign competition, disadvantages that the expansion of the Swiss railway network would go some way to alleviate. Because of the country's geography, Swiss industry had to overcome obstacles not faced by foreign competitors. It had to import resources from far away and was reliant on remote markets. Escher resolutely defended the decision made by the Swiss Parliament in the summer of 1852 to realise the railway project on a private basis. He called on all people of means and good faith to support the construction of the railway, especially since the outlook for investments was so positive.

After this introduction, Escher came to the actual purpose of his speech: The Cantonal Parliament of Zurich should declare itself ready to support private construction with public funds. If the railroad brought the country the advantages he had just named, was it not obviously justified that the canton and affected townships should contribute to the down payment? Escher compared the railroad with road transport and argued that if the cantons assumed all the costs for the construction of roads, why should they not be held to account for discharging their responsibilities with regard to that most consummate of roads: the railroad?[47]

In Escher's speech opening the winter session of the Cantonal Parliament, he underlined the fact that the railway project had become the most important domestic policy issue for the entire country. He attributed the fact that work had progressed with such speed to favourable economic circumstances. He also warned that these circumstances could change at any moment due to the unstable international situation, which could bring the construction of the railway in Switzerland to a standstill.

However, should the favourable economic conditions prevail for a while longer, and should the authorities and private entities alike act decisively and prudently, then the goal could be attained. Escher painted a picture of a Canton Zurich that was at the centre of a comprehensive railway network – a vision that only a few weeks ago would have appeared utopian to the parliamentarians he was addressing.

MILESTONE 1.1

28 July 1852

The Railway Act of 1852: A Landmark Decision

The construction and operation of railway lines and stations were left to the private sector, cantons were granted the authority to issue concessions and the federal government assumed a passive role. Part of the idea was that public entities could invest in private railway companies, an opportunity that cantons and municipalities made use of in a variety of ways. This support from the public sector provided private companies with a solid foundation that allowed them a certain self-confidence when dealing with other investors. But the most prominent feature of the landmark decision taken in the summer of 1852 was that private companies were to build and operate the railway. With this decision, a new era of Swiss history was rung in.[48] When one considers Heinrich Heine's reflections on the importance of railroad construction in world history, this claim does not seem overstated.

One might ask whether it would have been better for the effective omnipotence of private railroad companies codified in 1852 to have been curbed somewhat at the legal level. It is true that passengers and the transport of goods would have benefitted had the private companies been better coordinated and certain procedures made more uniform. But such speculation is futile, and the answer ultimately irrelevant. The private sector proved itself capable of leading the railway project to success. And it is incontestable that the potential for railway construction in Switzerland was well and truly unleashed by the decision made in the summer of 1852. The speed at which railway lines were subsequently built and the dynamism with which railway construction accelerated industrial development and revitalised the national economy confirm that the position taken by Alfred Escher in the middle of the 19th century was the correct one.

The financial turmoil in which railway companies became embroiled in the last quarter of the 19th century, the numerous takeover battles fought between them and the fact that the majority

(*Continued*)

of most companies' shares were in foreign hands from the start, all do nothing to change this assessment. Nor does the fact that the large railway companies were nationalised at the beginning of the 20th century dim the success story of the private railway. Thanks to the private companies, Switzerland was able to very quickly make up its deficit relative to neighbouring countries. Within a few years, private rail transport was in a position to provide the necessary transport capacity for the domestic market and to secure international rail connections. Despite blunders and embarrassing developments, mistakes and malicious schemes, bankruptcies of both individuals and entire railway companies, the 1852 decision of the Swiss Parliament in favour of private railroad construction and cantonal authority over its licensing proved to be the key to success. This success is principally to be seen in the record-breaking speed with which the main transport axes were developed and in Switzerland's consequent connection to international transport routes. From today's perspective, one can state conclusively that there was no promising alternative to private construction in the middle of the 19th century. Switzerland lagged about 20 years behind other countries in terms of railway development at the time. Just a few years later, thanks to the tireless activity of the private railway companies, the country had caught up with its neighbours.

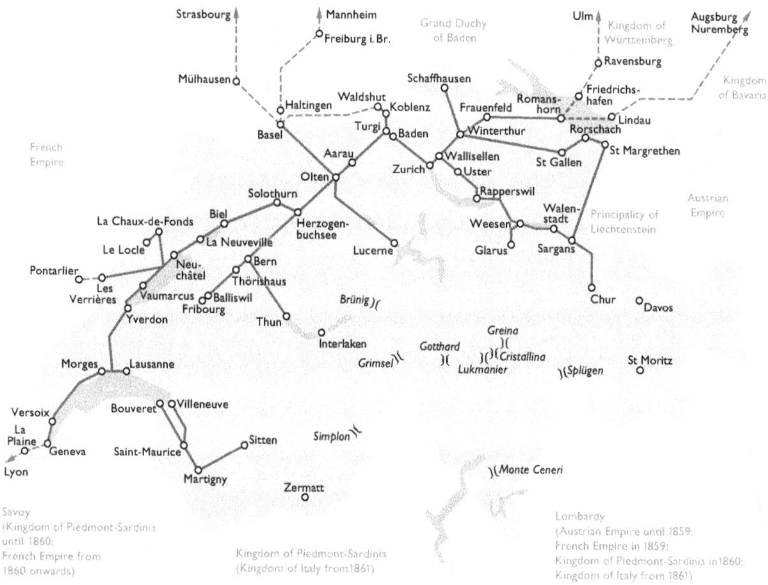

Figure 1.10 The Swiss Railway Network in 1860. Map by Claudia A. Trochsler.

How, except through private construction, could Switzerland have pulled even? The years of disputes between cantons and municipalities that had made the construction of railway lines effectively impossible before 1848 hardly provided a good reference for a state railway project.

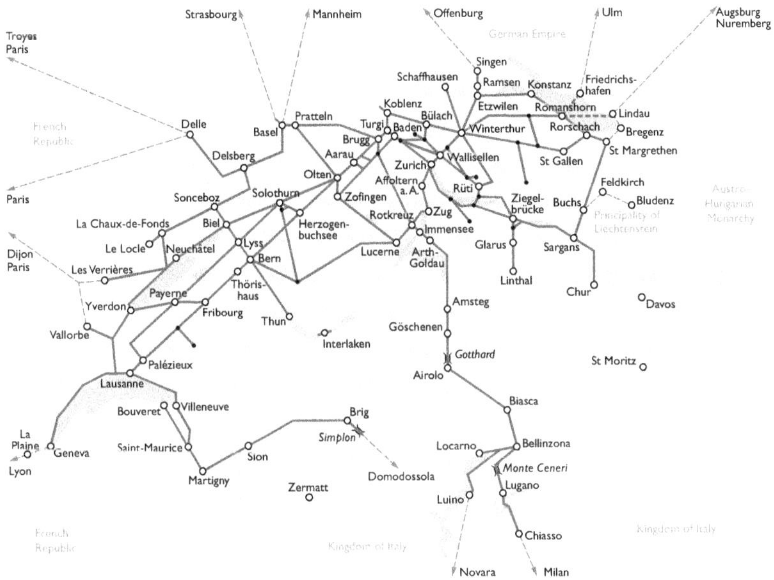

Figure 1.11 The Swiss Railway Network in 1882. Map by Claudia A. Trochsler.

The Railway Redefines Power Dynamics

Both the construction sites and the operational centres of railway companies created new jobs. And while traditional businesses along the train lines, for example, stagecoach operations, would eventually suffer because of the railway, even they initially benefitted from the new means of transport; deliveries to railroad stations, and transport through regions that were not accessible by rail, depended on horses and carriages. The same was true for steamboat transport, which was not eliminated by the rise of the railway but instead repositioned.

The American entrepreneur Charles Page (1838–1873) travelled to various locations in Switzerland looking for the ideal site for his planned milk factory, and his choice, tellingly, depended on transport links. During the US Civil War (1861–1865), which Page had reported on as a war correspondent for the *New York Tribune*, he had learned about a newly discovered process for producing condensed milk. In 1865, he arrived in Zurich as the US Vice-Consul. He soon recognised the considerable economic potential of high-quality Swiss milk, which he saw as a plentiful resource just waiting to be exploited, particularly as condensed milk was unknown in Europe at the time. He quickly applied for and received the necessary permission and, in early 1866, founded the Anglo-Swiss Condensed Milk Company in Zurich.

That summer, Page began looking for a location for his factory. His main criteria were the availability of high-quality milk as the primary raw material, a sufficient labour force, a stable economic and political environment and, especially, a connection to railway infrastructure. The towns of Wald in the Zurich highlands and Cham on Lake Zug were

Figure 1.12 Claude Monet (1840–1926). *La gare St Lazare* (*The St. Lazare Train Station*), 1877. Oil on canvas, 54.3 cm × 73.6 cm. © The National Gallery, London.

The railroad was the key to economic and societal modernisation in the 19th century. Thanks to the introduction of the new means of transport, processes of change were far more profound and rapid than they had ever been before. Not only the tracks on which the new trains steamed by but also the train stations where the locomotives hissed to a halt symbolised faith in progress. At this point, no area of life could remain isolated from the effects of technological progress. But exactly this inevitability of change – for example, in the experience of space and time – gave rise to opposing forces around the middle of the century, predominantly in artistic circles. The tensions between technology and nature, acceleration and leisure, proved not to be fixed and frozen but rather became the subject of a many-layered critical dialogue.

his two final candidates. Because of its textile industry, Wald had extensive and well-built roads and was indirectly connected to the railroad network via Rüti; only in 1876, however, would a train station be built in Wald itself. Page chose Cham, and its position on the railway line between Zurich and Lucerne was the decisive factor.

At this point, Charles Page's older brother George Page (1836–1899), then a secretary in the US War Department, became involved in the enterprise. He was tasked with purchasing the machines necessary for the production of condensed milk in the USA. This he did, having learned the basics of the trade from the condensed-milk pioneer Gail Borden (1808–1874). In July 1866, George Page arrived in Zurich with the machines. He was promptly named General Director of the planned production plant. The construction of the factory in Cham began in the late summer of 1866, and condensed milk was being produced by November of the same year. Because Page's company merged with Nestlé S.A. in 1905, Nestlé has ever since been legally based in both Henri Nestlé's Vevey and in George Page's Cham.[49]

A connection to the railway was also the key criterion in the choice of location for Maggi, another foodstuffs company that later merged with Nestlé. Julius Maggi (1846–1912) took over his father's mills in Kemptthal and Frauenfeld. He sold the Frauenfeld operation in 1867 and expanded the one in Kemptthal, a village in the municipality of Lindau. At the time, Kemptthal was no more than a collection of individual farmsteads and mills, despite being on the railway line between Zurich and Winterthur and having had its own train station since 1855/1856. When Maggi began processing legumes and producing soup concentrates in the early 1880s, he expanded his Kemptthal operation into a factory. Its success motivated him to build a second factory, in Singen in the Duchy of Baden, adjacent to Ramsen in Canton Schaffhausen. He chose Singen because it was directly connected to Kemptthal by rail, ensuring the easy transport of goods between the two locations. The growth of Maggi increasingly attracted workers to Kemptthal. In 1896, Maggi constructed overnight quarters for no fewer than 200 employees. The increase of the resident population in Lindau from 1850 (1,051 residents) to 1900 (1,627 residents) can largely be credited to Maggi's expansion in the 1890s.

The railway determined the power dynamics between the cities of Zurich and Winterthur. It could hardly have been predicted during the death throes of the Old Confederation in the years leading up to 1848 that the city of Zurich would become the economic capital of Switzerland. This role could just as easily have been assumed by Winterthur. Winterthur lost out when Bern, and not Zurich, was named the federal capital, and Zurich was therefore owed some recompense. This effectively decided for Zurich and against Winterthur as the site of the first federal university. Yet the most decisive factor in determining the power dynamics between the cities was the railway. It was Zurich rather than

Winterthur that became a transport hub, though locomotives would later be built in the latter city. And consequently, it was in Zurich that the decisive institutions were established – the Polytechnic (later ETH), the Kreditanstalt and the insurance companies connected to the Kreditanstalt – that would make the city the research, banking and insurance centre of Switzerland. To be sure, Winterthur did make its own advances by founding the Technikum, an important platform for Swiss education. By then, however, Zurich had already established itself as the Swiss metropolis.

Stock prices and dividends quickly assumed new importance. Soon after their founding, many companies experienced great financial difficulties; some avoided collapse through mergers, only to see the newly merged company itself teeter on the brink of ruin. There were also worries and misgivings about the domineering influence that foreign financial circles exerted on Swiss railway companies. It had not escaped the notice of the general public that these companies paid for foreign capital by offering the representatives of banks – primarily French banks – seats on their governing boards. Many formerly enthusiastic shareholders now worriedly noted how quickly the influence of foreign banks on the Swiss railroad was growing.[50]

Initially, it was primarily patriotic pride that was injured by foreign influence on the construction of the Swiss railway. Soon, however, the worries took on political dimensions. There were concerns about Switzerland's military preparedness and how Swiss soldiers were to do battle if foreign speculators controlled the ways and means of transport. In the lustre of the brilliant advances of the railway since 1852, such considerations were being thoroughly neglected. Yet every critical observer could see that the Swiss railway network was not being built according to a systematic and centralised plan and that national political interests were not being taken into account. The private railway companies instead had their eyes on their balance books and built according to purely economic criteria.

It would have been practically impossible for the 22 cantons and the federal government to have suddenly come to an agreement about the layout and prioritisation of train lines in the middle of the 19th century. And in any case, the young Federal State did not have at hand the enormous resources necessary for the construction of the railroad. Even contemporary commentaries expressed the view that state construction would have led to tracks being laid on paper rather than on Swiss soil.[51] Private construction led to a completely different story.

The railway companies were subject to the forces of the market. Ultimately, there was only a single aim: to be successful and to prevail over the competition. The speed with which a company could construct and inaugurate a line became the decisive criterion for its success. So began the race for railway kilometres, for topographical advantages and for concessions. Takeovers and mergers followed hard on one another.

The constant drumming up of capital was a laborious and tedious activity. For many companies this was a rocky road, one often paved with prices that were far too high. Many a hopeful prospect, drafted in the exuberance of initial enthusiasm, soon came to nought. Not infrequently, this was the precursor to complete submission to foreign financial domination. And still, the challenge had to be taken on. Despite all the dangers and snares which could turn the dealings with possible financial backers into an obstacle course, neither railway stations nor tracks could be built without risk and investment capital. And so the railway pioneers made a virtue of necessity: They themselves founded commercial banks that became the financial vehicles of their companies. It is striking that during the construction of financial and railway infrastructure, important Swiss politicians led the way, including James Fazy (1794–1878) in Geneva, Daniel Wirth-Sand (1815–1901) in St Gallen and later Jakob Stämpfli (1820–1879) in Bern. They illustrate the complex interwovenness of politics and business at the time.[52]

But no one was as successful or as influential in this respect as Alfred Escher of Zurich. Not only did he lead the Northeastern Railway out of the danger zone with a grandiose gambit and elegantly and enduringly solve the problem of raising investment capital by founding the Schweizerische Kreditanstalt. As a politician, captain of industry and businessman, Escher was altogether an exceptional phenomenon in Swiss history.[53] His interlinking of politics, economics, and science and technology was unprecedented in scale and became a veritable system. The Radical Vaudois politician and future Federal Councillor, Louis Ruchonnet (1834–1893), wrote in 1866 that the Swiss Parliament found itself in the hands of a number of "great beasts," led by Alfred Escher of Zurich. "These people are not in the Federal Council, but rather rule over it – with no accountability." Escher's Conservative adversary, Philip Anton von Segesser (1817–1888) of Lucerne, described the power dynamics after 1848 in a similarly biting and ironic tone:

> There soon formed a tighter circle of men, who presided over all public initiatives; they were called, in jest, the "federal barons", as they were mostly well off, or on their way to being so, and moved with exceptional self-confidence. Around them orbited stars of the second-degree, the aspirants, the parasites, of whom only a few succeeded, over time, in gaining entry to the higher and ever-more exclusive category. This prestigious, representative-democratic, industrial liberalism most resembles an aristocracy in its promotion of a stable party leadership, the creation of subordinate coteries, and a compartmentalised association of interests.[54]

In fact, Alfred Escher did build up a centre of political power in Zurich and purposefully promoted the city. The interweaving of politics, economics, and science and technology was his formula for success. That he was titled the Princeps, the Tsar of Zurich and King Alfred I testifies to his power and influence. These were also dramatically illustrated in a contract signed in 1853, pertaining to the construction and operation of the railway line from Zurich to Dietikon.[55] Escher signed his name four times at the bottom of the document – each time in a different political or commercial function. And precisely this four-fold aggregation of roles epitomises the kind of broadly conceived and interlinking networks that characterised representative democracy in the young Federal State and led to its success.

The Swiss Railway Network up to 1902

The development of the Swiss railway network from the middle of the 19th century up until the founding of the SBB in 1902 can meaningfully be divided into two phases. Neither Basel's inclusion on the French train line that led from Strasbourg to the Swiss border via St Louis in Alsace in 1844 nor the route from Zurich to Baden that opened in 1847 was of any real significance for the development of railway infrastructure in Switzerland. One can therefore view these as isolated events. The real launch of the railroad project in Switzerland began in 1852. The first phase lasted until 1872. The second phase ended in 1902 with the nationalisation of the large private railway companies and the onset of the era of the SBB.[56]

The first phase began with the 1852 decision of the Swiss Parliament that railway construction would be in private hands. It was initially characterised by intensive preparation and planning and then by the breathtaking speed with which the plans were implemented. A first high point was achieved in 1855, when 170 kilometres of track were laid in Switzerland. The main railway network, as it was conceived at the time, had three principle axes: the first between Lake Constance and Lake Geneva, the second running from north to south from Lake Constance to Chur and on to the passes of Graubünden, and the third, also running from north to south, from Basel to Lucerne with connections in the direction of the Gotthard and Ticino. In 1857, the Central Railway surpassed the Northeastern Railway in number of kilometres of track and became the leading company of the day. Beginning in the 1850s, the Northeastern Railway, the Central Railway, the United Swiss Railway and the Western Switzerland Railway would dominate the Swiss railway network. These four alternately led the pack in terms of kilometres of track.

The 1850s were characterised by railway-related conflicts. In Eastern Switzerland, for example, two competing railway companies were working on the line from Lake Constance to Zurich via Winterthur. There was dogged competition between the Northeastern Railway, which aimed to reach Romanshorn, and the St Gallisch-Appenzell Railway, which sought to reach Rorschach, as both endeavoured to optimally connect northeastern Switzerland to southern Germany in order to open up economic channels. Despite their competition, the two companies had a shared interest in the possibility of a north-south line over the Lukmanier Pass. For both companies, though, there was a further pivotal question to answer: How were their main networks to be connected to the west? Both were therefore interested in the development of the railway network in western Switzerland. But there, too, a bitter fight broke out between various companies with rival main lines. History books designate this disagreement the Western Railway Conflict (Westbahnkonflikt). It was ignited by the question of whether the line from Geneva to Bern ought to go via Yverdon and Murten, as wished by Canton Vaud, or via Lausanne and Fribourg, as wished by Cantons Fribourg and Geneva. The decision taken in 1856 fell in favour of the so-called Oron railway that ran via Fribourg. As a consequence, the Morges-Yverdon railway line, inaugurated by the Western Railway in July 1855, lost out in importance compared to the Bern-Fribourg-Lausanne-Geneva line.

Figure 1.13 The main building of the Schweizerische Kreditanstalt with a horse-drawn tram and carriages. Photograph from ca 1900. Credit Suisse collection.

Added to the mix in the 1850s were the unrelenting conflicts that played out between two French financial powerhouses – Crédit Mobilier and the Rothschild banking house's Réunion Financière – on the battlefield of the Swiss railway market, a situation that led to continual pressure for companies to merge. These conflicts reveal the dependence of Swiss railway companies on foreign capital at the time. With the founding of the Schweizerische Kreditanstalt in the 1850s, a new financial powerhouse emerged, one that participated confidently in negotiations with foreign investors and strengthened the backbone of the Northeastern Railway and other companies.

At the end of the turbulent 1850s, the track belonging to the top four railway companies totalled around 800 kilometres. It was during this period that the question of building a transalpine rail link was raised once again. The two projects on the Lukmanier and the Gotthard Passes sidelined other possible routes, such as the Splügen, Grimsel and Simplon variants.[57]

The 1860s were a time of consolidation. The Northeastern Railway, which had fallen to fourth place in terms of kilometres of track, rapidly began to catch with its competition. At the end of 1865, with 292 kilometres, it almost surpassed the leader, the United Swiss Railway, which boasted 295 kilometres. At the end of the 1860s, the combined length of the track built by the four largest companies was around 1,100 kilometres. The most important event of this time period, however, was not the extension of the network by around 300 kilometres but rather the beginning of construction on the north-south transalpine rail link through the Gotthard.

The Railway Act of 1872 rang in the second phase of the railway era. In 1875, the Northeastern Railway's network was extended by 107 kilometres, from 292 to just under 400, through the opening of the Bözberg line and the line along the left banks of Lake Zurich and Upper Lake Constance to Näfels. During this period, the National Railway (Nationalbahn) was also laying down track, seeking a direct confrontation with Escher's Northeastern Railway. The plans of this "democratic" railway company from Winterthur had slid from the sphere of political ideology into that of economic fantasy. The result was its quick demise and a financial debacle. Ironically, the liquidation of the National Railway ended up bestowing yet more track on the Northeastern Railway. In 1882, the year of Alfred Escher's death, the railway network of the four major companies had reached a combined length of 1,625 kilometres. In this second phase, efforts to nationalise the railway gained in momentum.

When the four private railway companies became the SBB on 1 January 1902, the standard-gauge railway network in Switzerland totalled 3,215 kilometres. In 1856, around 10 percent of this track had been laid; by 1880, 75 percent. For comparison, in 2018 the SBB operated on 3,228 kilometres of track.

An Overview of Opportunities and Risks

The length of track laid per year by the four largest private companies is not the only relevant statistic. Train stations also represented expenditures. Take, for example, the Northeastern Railway: This company, headquartered in Zurich, possessed 38 stations in 1860. By 1870, the number had increased only negligibly, to 43. By 1880, largely because of successful takeovers, the company owned 144 stations. The length of track operated by the Northeastern Railway grew correspondingly, from 178 kilometres in 1860 to 607 kilometres in 1880. In 1860, the company had 30 locomotives in its service, as well as 114 passenger coaches and 401 freight cars. By 1880, it was operating 155 locomotives, 559 passenger coaches and 2,718 freight cars. At this point, the Northeastern Railway was the best positioned among the four large railway companies as far as rolling stock was concerned. It had outstripped the second-place Western Switzerland Railways by more than a third.

In addition to its railway operations, the Northeastern Railway also had a fleet of steamboats. In 1860, the company's five steamboats and four barges provided transport on Lake Constance and the Rhine. By the end of the 1870s, these boats had been joined by another barge and three ferry-barges, which the Northeastern Railway Company jointly owned and operated with Württemberg and Bavaria. In 1880, there were six steamboats and four tugboats, a steam-ferry jointly operated with Württemberg, and a steam-ferry and a barge jointly operated with Bavaria. In the meantime, with the acquisition of the Lake Zurich Steamboat Company (Dampfschiff-Gesellschaft für den Zürichsee) in 1874, the Northeastern Railway was running a second steamboat operation. This included one luxury steamboat, eight paddle steamers, and three screw steamers, as well as seven iron and twenty-six wooden tug and coal boats.

By the end of the 1860s, the Northeastern Railway already had more than 1,000 employees. By 1880, that figure had reached 3,718. In 1857, the first complete year of operation of the Lake Constance rail line, the railway transported around 940,000 people on a network stretching 134 kilometres. In 1880, its passengers numbered just under 5.5 million, and the track length was 607 kilometres. In 1860, the company transported 1,634 tonnes of freight per kilometre of track; by 1870, this number had risen to 3,493 tonnes per kilometre; in 1880, it was 2,726. In 1860, the Northeastern Railway also operated 16 telegraph offices with 22 telegraph machines.

The aggressiveness of the expansion strategies of the competing railway companies depended on whether the construction and operation of a new stretch of track could be financed. Not only did an enormous amount of capital have to be raised but continuing investment capital also had to be secured. As the latter was dependent on the liquidity of the capital market, terms were necessarily subject to fluctuations. Managerial questions took a back seat, and other factors became decisive instead: Companies had to proceed as quickly as possible, both in choosing which locations to connect to the network and in actually building the train lines. The capital required for the construction of a new railway line was gargantuan for the time: Huge sums had to be raised to cover the purchase of land, the costs of civil engineering, of railway stations, rolling stock and much more. And not only this: Investment capital had to be procured on terms favourable enough to allow the railway company to run a profitable operation. The operative leadership of a railway company, therefore, faced a two-fold challenge: first, to make optimal use of opportunities for expansion, and second, to finance this expansion. Especially in the early stages of private railway construction, it was of vital importance for individual companies to position themselves strategically.

The pressure that foreign financial institutions exerted on railway companies with respect to the layout and operation of train lines, strategic goals and especially mergers could place the leadership of a company in a difficult position. The financial resources offered by the foreign institution were indispensable, yet in accepting them, companies wanted to avoid becoming unnecessarily dependent on the foreign banks. In this context, the financing of an expansion strategy could become a difficult balancing act, in which the loss of independence always loomed large.

In order to understand the intentions of these foreign banks, and in particular of the French ones, one has to realise that their interests were narrowly focused on the founding of companies. They were not particularly interested in supporting the economic development of Switzerland by financing its railroad. Rather, they wanted to gain control over private railroad companies in order to dictate their strategies and business policies, with the sole goal of maximising profits. The Parisian banks wanted as much information as possible about the business operations of their clients and, among other things, reserved the right to send representatives to board meetings. If the banks gained influence over numerous railway companies at once, they tried to consolidate the market through mergers. They thereby brought about a situation in which the merged companies were only able to meet their needs for capital through these very banks – that is, through the market-dominating French financial institutions. The primary goal of these banks was to increase the profits of the companies they financed as quickly as possible so that high dividends could be paid out and stock prices rise. Once this goal was achieved, the securities would be sold on at the highest possible price. Then the banks would invest the profits in a new project.

It was against this backdrop that the directors of the railway companies had to make their decisions. In the domestic competition for track and railway stations, the Northeastern Railway initially grew at an above-average rate. But this success was qualified by the obligations and terms on which the concessions for new lines had been conditioned.

The profitability of the Northeastern Railway also collapsed, in part because cost estimates for new stretches of track were, in some cases, too optimistic, and the profits from the new lines therefore less than originally expected. This led to the company's failure in the second half of the 1870s. In 1877, the company had to announce to the public that it could no longer raise the funds needed to complete all of its contracted construction projects on the capital market.[58]

The Question of Capital: The Kreditanstalt as an Engine of Progress

These events make clear the extent to which the young and capital-hungry railway companies were at the mercy of foreign financial consortiums and how much this restricted their freedom to act. Given this situation, it is understandable that Alfred Escher began to contemplate ways and means by which he could further develop the Northeastern Railway as an independent Swiss company. The solution he came up with was to found a bank himself, one that would protect the railroad from foreign diktats and takeover attempts.[59]

The founding of a Swiss financial institution that was in a position to mobilise Swiss capital for the railroad was so eminently important precisely because French bankers were leaving no stone unturned in their attempts to use their market-leading position to influence the development of the Swiss railway to promote their own interests. In March 1856, for example, the Réunion Financière intended to merge the Northeastern Railway, the Southeastern Railway and the St Gallen-Appenzell Railway in an attempt to improve profitability by achieving economies of scale and fostering other synergies. In addition, the necessarily greater financial needs of the larger company that would have resulted from the merger could have been covered by very few banks – among them Rothschild's Réunion Financière. Mergers therefore represented a way for the banks to exclude their own competition and place themselves in a strategically superior position.

Escher found himself in a dilemma. On the one hand, he clearly recognised the negative consequences of dependence on French financial institutions. On the other hand, he also knew that mergers represented an effective path to rapid growth. He therefore first had to carefully analyse the Réunion Financière proposal. But something decisive had changed since the beginning of negotiations between the Northeastern Railway and the Réunion Financière about the contested sale of shares and the merger plans that had been presented in the spring of 1856. Now, the founding of a credit institution in Zurich was not merely a vague idea but had become a tangible possibility. Escher's principal motive for founding a Zurich-centred credit institution was to liberate Zurich-based railway operations from foreign capital. Escher was planning his bank precisely in order to end the influence of the Rothschild banking house and its Réunion Financière on Swiss railroad companies, and in particular on the Northeastern Railway.

Just how crucial raising capital was for success in the initial phase of private railroad construction is evidenced by the explosive expansion of the Swiss railway network from around 300 kilometres in the year 1856 to around 1,300 kilometres ten years later. It was mainly the Kreditanstalt that raised the capital for this expansion. Its essential contribution was to mobilise the Swiss capital market. Benefitting from the overlap of personnel between the Kreditanstalt and the Northeastern Railway, the bank promoted the development of the railroad by purchasing substantial numbers of securities, thereby decisively influencing the share values.

One of the first business decisions made by the Kreditanstalt related to the purchase of shares in the Northeastern Railway. Though the bank had barely begun operations, by the summer of 1856, it already owned 1,176 shares in the railway company. In the following months, it made further purchases, and by the end of 1857, it held a total of 1,909 Northeastern Railway shares with a net asset value of around 920,000 Swiss francs. By the end of 1859, the Kreditanstalt owned over 5,700 shares, worth just under 3 million francs. By the end of 1860, the net asset value of Northeastern Railway shares and bonds owned by the Kreditanstalt had risen to around 4.4 million francs and, by 1865, to around 8 million. According to the Kreditanstalt's 1865 annual report, Northeastern Railway shares and bonds made up 52 percent of the bank's holdings of Swiss securities and 14.2 percent of its total assets.

As early as 1857, the Kreditanstalt, in collaboration with two German banks, issued over 10 million francs in bonds for the Northeastern Railway. By 1865, the Kreditanstalt had issued Northeastern Railway bonds four more times, for a combined value of over 20 million francs. Of the Northeastern Railway bonds that were issued from 1856 until the mid-1860s, 99 percent were either issued by the Kreditanstalt itself or else under its lead. This clearly shows that the Kreditanstalt, which was founded as a financial vehicle for the Northeastern Railway, did in fact indisputably become its house bank.

The Ups and Downs of the Northeastern Railway

The founding and development of private railway companies took place in a very competitive market environment. There was a ruthless struggle for new construction concessions, as companies attempted to extend their lines as quickly as possible. In hindsight it is clear that, in their bids for concessions, the executive committees of the individual companies were primarily motivated by strategic and tactical considerations, often neglecting questions of profitability. In the fight to strengthen their market positions, they were consumed by a desire for growth. They did not hesitate in the face of high initial costs and, no less consequentially, did not shrink from continually committing themselves to massive construction projects.[60] Workers' salaries and, especially, investments in rolling stock added to the costs. Between the mid-1850s and 1870, railway companies acquired around 150 locomotives and 900 passenger carriages; by 1890, they owned no fewer than 510 locomotives and 1,200 coaches. The number of people employed by the companies – almost 20,000 in 1890 – is also striking.

The Northeastern Railway provides a good illustration. By 1873, the construction commitments it had taken on amounted to around 83 million francs. The company only had around 20 million francs in subsidised loans from participating regions. To fulfil its commitments, then, it needed another 63 million francs. The entire capital (private and borrowed) of the Northeastern Railway at the end of 1873 amounted to no more than 96 million francs, so an astronomical need for financing had arisen. Because other railway companies were also in significant need of capital and the capacity of the Swiss capital market was still limited, issuing new bonds became increasingly difficult. This, in turn, diminished the trust of the Northeastern Railway's investors, and shares ultimately came under enormous pressure. In order to proceed with its considerable participation in the Gotthard and other projects, the Northeastern Railway was forced to search for new sources of financing. Thus, in 1875, it approached the German capital market. But it could not drum up the necessary backing there, either, since the Austrian financial crisis had by now also gripped Germany. It thereby became clear that the realisation of its already contracted construction projects was in danger. Finally, in 1877, the value of Northeastern Railway shares collapsed. While the lowest value of the standard shares in the early 1870s had been 600 francs, it now slid to 470 in 1875, 255 in 1876 and just 70 francs in 1877. In 1878, it reached a deplorable low of 53 francs.

The unfavourable ratio of the Northeastern Railway's own assets to its debt was an important factor in its financial crisis. In 1853, the company's inaugural year, there were a total of 7.1 million francs in paid-up share capital, compared to borrowed capital totalling around 818,000 francs. Ten years later, in 1863, the paid-up share capital had reached around 29 million francs. The borrowed capital had, however, increased by a significantly greater amount: By 1863, it amounted to 30 times more than it had a decade earlier, totalling around 26 million francs. The paid-up share capital at the time was still larger than all the debt combined, by around 10 percent. Already by 1864, however, the scale had tipped: While the share capital remained the same, the borrowed capital had increased to around 31 million. The following years were characterised by an increase in debt that ever more egregiously outstripped the company's net worth. The development of this imbalance was especially striking between 1868 and 1875. In 1868, the value of the company's assets was still around 75 percent of its debt, but by 1875, this figure had decreased to 37 percent. Initially, the decrease in the equity ratio brought the shareholders thoroughly positive results – at least in terms of the size of their dividends. And as long as the returns on invested capital surpassed the average interest on the debt, consistently high dividends were paid out.

A further factor that led to the increasing debt of the Northeastern Railway was the appalling inaccuracy of the cost estimates for the construction of new railway lines. The bill of costs for 1876 demonstrates just how massively estimates were overrun: The projected costs for five sections of track were exceeded by no fewer than 71 million francs. The cost overruns were thus a solid 94.4 percent of the original quotes. And while the cost estimates were too low, the projected revenues were also far too high. The insufficient oversight of company spending came about because, until 1877, the Northeastern Railway did not draw up a budget. In a commission report on the operating conditions of the railway in 1877, it was emphatically recommended that this grave shortcoming be put to rights as soon as possible.

Viewed from the perspective of the crisis year of 1877, the dividend policy that the Northeastern Railway had practised up until then was also problematic. Until 1875, the company paid very generous dividends, generally around 8 percent – far more than its competitors. In doing so, the leadership wanted to demonstrate the company's solidity and prosperity to its investors. Problems with the distribution of dividends began to arise when the financial situation of the Northeastern Railway worsened dramatically after 1877. The year 1876 was the last one that a dividend (3 percent) could be paid, thanks to reserve funds and profits carried forward. After that, a distribution no longer came into question.

The main culprit in the financial downturn into which the Northeastern Railway had gradually manoeuvred itself after 1872 was Johann Friedrich Peyer im Hof, the company's operating director and a former National Councillor from Schaffhausen. Alongside the business crisis, Peyer im Hof was also experiencing a personal disaster: He was the victim of an ongoing scam and had lost almost his entire fortune, which he had recklessly invested in a questionable enterprise in Hungary. He had also overstepped his authority in commitments he had made as director of the Northeast Railway. Alfred Escher, who, as President of the Board of the Gotthard Railway Company (Gotthardbahn-Gesellschaft) was already under extreme pressure, took action. Peyer im Hof had to go. In 1880, the Northeastern Railway once again paid a dividend, this time of 5.78 percent.

The Transalpine Rail Link and the Railway Act of 1872: On the Way to a Nationalised Railway

Not all opponents of private construction considered their cause lost after the decision taken in the summer of 1852. Jakob Stämpfli, a Bernese National Councillor and future Federal Councillor, became the leading voice of advocates for a state railway. He relentlessly used every opportunity given to him as a parliamentarian and then as a Federal Councillor to derail private construction. The question of state repurchase of private rail operations was continually on his mind. A motion he drew up in 1862 became a novelty in Swiss politics. Stämpfli, then the President of the Federal Council, bypassed both the Federal Council and the Parliament by making public in print his own position on railway policy. In doing this, the strident Bernese politician provoked a passionate national debate. Politicians and the media criticised the new, sensational political culture and condemned Stämpfli's breach of the political rules of play. Discussion about nationalisation of the railroad also found its way into letters exchanged between Jakob Stämpfli and Alfred Escher. Stämpfli argued that if a "railway monarchy" was inevitable, then he would prefer it were a "national railway monarchy" rather than a "private railway monarchy." Escher countered by saying that such an important issue ought not to be resolved with catchwords.[61]

At the end of the 1860s, the situation confronting railroad policymakers was different from the one they had faced in 1852. The construction of the transalpine rail link was imminent. Its realisation, however, had turned out to be hardly possible without the financial support of Prussia and Italy. The Swiss government now faced the problem that, according to the Railway Act of 1852, it had no authority over the railway. It quickly became clear to the Federal Council, however, that the state had to find a way to negotiate about railway matters with foreign powers on the diplomatic and political level. The constitutionally fraught path that the Federal Council was minded to take awakened hope in the proponents of nationalisation – hope that they might achieve their objective through the back door of the Gotthard project. For Escher and like-minded Liberal partisans, the issue had become a double-edged sword. They had to try to win the support of Stämpfli and his fellow Radicals for the Gotthard enterprise, but at the same time to take care that it retained its private form.

MILESTONE 1.2

1 June 1882

The Inauguration of the Gotthard Railway

No other construction project changed Switzerland as fundamentally as the Gotthard Railway. Despite the fact that trains only began operating on the line in the final quarter of the 19th century, the project indisputably had its roots in the early years of the Federal State. It was during those years, when the country was characterised by visionary thinking and a daring, pioneering spirit, that a transalpine rail link was conceptualised. It was within this larger

(Continued)

framework that plans and institutions matured. The Gotthard Railway project was possible thanks to the powerful spirit of economic liberalism that drove forward the breaking of new ground in Switzerland with a vigour that had not been seen previously and has not been seen since. What luck that its construction could no longer be halted in the following era, when grandiose ideas were trimmed back with the clippers of direct democracy.

On 1 June 1882, the Gotthard Railway began operations. It was more than a local connection between Cantons Ticino and Uri and more than a Swiss Alpine railway. The Gotthard Railway was internationally oriented, became the lifeblood of the Swiss export economy and opened up new dimensions for the economic and cultural relationships between Switzerland, Italy and Germany. But it was even more than that. By piercing through the barrier of the Alps, it became a global railway, tying Northern Europe to the Suez Canal and the Far East – through Switzerland, which became the eye of the needle. The Gotthard train line was the Swiss world wonder of the 19th century.

The Swiss railway network was built at a breathtaking pace during the 1850s and 1860s, and this dynamic growth fuelled scientific and industrial development. Only because of this progress did the Gotthard Railway assume the contours of a realisable project. Hindsight validates the stance taken by Alfred Escher. Whether one likes it or not, it was the rapid development of the Central Plateau by private railway companies that brought the prospect of a transalpine rail link to the cusp of technical possibility in the early 1870s. Although it was necessarily the federal government that negotiated and signed the political agreements with Germany and Italy, successful state leadership of the project would have been inconceivable. Up-to-date planning for and effective execution of the enormous endeavour could only have been shouldered by the management of a private company. One can only imagine the temporal confusion and domestic policy errors that a publicly directed Gotthard Railway project would have given rise to. And besides, the Federal State could never have financed the undertaking. Moreover, had it been a public project, this would have precluded the financial backing provided by Germany and Italy. And Italy's role was not confined to financial support. Most of the workmen on the enormous construction sites on the Gotthard were Italian migrant workers. Their lodgings were often catastrophically unhygienic, and inside the tunnel itself, fresh air was in short supply. As a result, many returned to their southern homes suffering from silicosis.

If the line had been built by the state, Gotthard Railway trains would not have passed through the Alps anywhere near the end of the 19th century. And the following economic crises and wars would likely have pushed the project's realisation back even further! Thanks to Alfred Escher, Switzerland was spared such nightmare scenarios.

Figure 1.14 The southern entrance of the Gotthard Tunnel. Credit Suisse collection. The Latin inscription refers to the financial involvement of Germany, Italy and Switzerland in the Gotthard project. It fails to note, however, that most of the project's funding was sourced on the capital market.

In early 1869, the Federal Council had unanimously rejected state-financed construction of the Gotthard rail link – in accordance with the words and spirit of Alfred Escher's position on the matter. This did not prevent advocates of a state railway from once again raising the idea of government-managed construction. But even supporters of private construction understood the need for action, as the legal framework determined in 1852 would not suffice for realising the complex and enormous Gotthard. Federal Councillor Emil Welti (1825–1899), who alongside Stämpfli dominated the railway debate in the Federal Council, suggested amending the Railway Act of 1852 to fit the present circumstances. He especially wanted the authority for granting concessions to be transferred from the cantons to the federal government.

On 30 April 1869, the Federal Council adopted an important position. Though it took no formal decision, it was of the majority opinion that the Federal State should not negotiate with foreign powers as a mediator but rather in its own right. Even though the majority of the Federal Council did not support state construction, it recognised that the Railway Act of 1852 had to be modified to facilitate the large-scale Gotthard project. In particular, the existing legislation was insufficient to allow for negotiations with other nations. In order to effect the international treaties that would be necessary for the realisation of the Gotthard Railway, the federal government's authority would have to be expanded. The federal government insisted on its legislative authority and made clear that any international treaties not based on that authority would be invalid. Escher was left no other choice than to concede on this point. As a jurist, and as a result of his contact with leading political figures in Germany and Italy, he was experienced enough to recognise that the prevailing circumstances and the landmark Gotthard project required a modified legal structure. And so, the new Railway Act of 23 December 1872 was passed. Its constitutional basis was to be found, after the fact, in the revised Constitution of 1874, which retroactively allocated to the federal government the authority to legislate on railway matters.

The differences between the Railway Acts of 1852 and 1872 jump from the page and are more far-reaching than one might initially think. To be sure, the new Act essentially stayed faithful to the doctrine of private ownership, but the various clauses addressing the construction and operation of railways in Switzerland – addressing everything from scheduling and pricing to rolling stock and railroad track beds – set a new course: The railway companies were forced to become more uniform. It was clear that the rail transport system would be made less cumbersome as a result. Understandably, critical voices were raised. The decisive difference between the two Acts, however, was that in the new legislation of 1872, the granting of building and operating concessions no longer fell under the authority of the cantons. Sovereignty over the railroad had been transferred to the federal government. This sovereignty was also enshrined in later legislation. In this respect, the Railway Act of 1872 mirrored the political development that Switzerland had undergone since 1848.

Nationalisation

The question of the repurchase of the railways by the state became topical in 1883, when the possibility first arose to revoke the concessions of most railway companies.[62] The federal government now had to officially engage with the issue. To be sure, the question of nationalisation had remained an issue throughout the years, both behind the scenes and on the public political stage. The reanimation of the discussion in the 1880s had to do with the fact that the great promoter of the private railway, Alfred Escher, was increasingly disappearing from the political scene. Old and ill, he no longer possessed the vigorous potency with which he had once nipped in the bud attacks that threatened the success of the private railway. It is not surprising that, with Escher's death in 1882, the fate of private railway companies was finally sealed. Resistance to nationalisation did still exist, and there were also – as would soon appear – party-political considerations that led to the adoption of tactical positions. The spokesperson for and leading figure among the proponents of nationalisation was Federal Councillor Emil Welti. It seems that during Escher's lifetime he had not been keen to express his opinion on the matter all too clearly. The same was true of Johann Friedrich Peyer im Hof, who had become important in Escher's business and political orbit and had assumed leading roles in the Rheinfall and Northeastern Railways but who later took up with the proponents of nationalisation. And there were others in the same position as Welti and Peyer. It appears that they had all been waiting for Escher's death to dare to say that they had in fact believed in a state railway all along.

The Federal Council reached the decision that a repurchase of concessions did not initially come into question. It considered the capital assets of all the railways to be overvalued. Concretely, it would have had to demand an 85-million franc reduction of these assets. It also expressed the opinion that, for years, the dividends paid out had been far too high. Even though the time was not yet ripe for repurchase, the Federal Council argued that the railway companies should at least be placed under the financial oversight of the state. In 1883, Parliament passed a law on the financial accounting of railway companies, which supported the policy pursued by the Federal Council. The now codified obligation to systemise bookkeeping practices put an end to the lack of transparency that had often been complained about in the financial reporting of the railway companies. In placing the financial management of the railroad companies under state supervision, Parliament had effected an important precondition for the looming process of nationalisation. Still, the path to a state railway would prove a difficult one. In 1888, Federal Councillor Welti's attempt to take over the Northeastern Railway by means of a contract with its shareholders, instead of according to the terms of its concession, met with no success.

The voices advocating the transfer of the railway companies to the public sector did not die away. The question of repurchase was also persistently discussed in the media. In the Swiss Parliament, the proponents of nationalisation grew still louder. Opponents feared that the state would have to pay too much for the railway companies. The Federal Council initially continued with its share purchase programme, in an attempt to gain majority holdings in the companies. In 1891, Welti made a further attempt to purchase a railway on a contractual basis – this time the Central Railway. Though Parliament approved his motion, the Swiss electorate rejected it in a national referendum on 6 December 1891. On the same day, Welti announced his resignation from the Federal Council, effective at the end of the year. This decision was undoubtedly related to the bitter loss he had suffered with the rejection of the repurchase of the Central Railway, despite the urgent recommendations of the Federal Council to approve it. It was a difficult setback for Welti, personally as well as politically. It was not only the dispute about railway policy, though, that led to his resignation. Family difficulties also played a role. It was at this time that a scandalous drama unfolded in the marriage between his son, Friedrich Emil (1857–1940), and Alfred Escher's daughter Lydia.[63] The rejection of his nationalisation proposal meant that Welti, who had stood in Alfred Escher's shadow throughout the course of the entire 19th-century rail project, and who had had to grant precedence to Escher with regards to the transalpine rail link even after Escher's death, had definitively failed to leave a legacy of his own in the area of railroad policy.[64]

The result of the 6 December 1891 referendum was also a defeat of the Liberal Party's strategists and a victory for the Economic-Liberal camp in its alliance with the Protestant Conservatives of western Switzerland and the Catholic Conservatives of Central Switzerland; all in all, it was a victory for federalists over centralists. Despite its rejection of the proposal, the vote had far-reaching and important consequences for Swiss domestic politics. It marked a caesura in the history of Swiss politics and provided a ticket into the Federal Council for the Catholic-Conservative camp. In the new post-1891 political constellation, and against the background of the changed political climate that developed with a Catholic-Conservative seat on the Federal Council, the Federal Council on 15 March 1897 published a draft of legislation that would nationalise the five largest Swiss railway companies: the Central Railway, the Northeastern Railway, the Jura-Simplon Railway, the United Swiss Railway and the Gotthard Railway. The latter was eventually struck from the list, as its repurchase was contractually excluded prior to 1909. On 20 February 1891, the legislation was decisively approved by the Swiss electorate after an emotional campaign, with 386,634 votes in favour and 182,718 against. With this, the foundations were laid for the Swiss Federal Railways to begin operations on 1 January 1902, with a staff of 61 civil servants.

Notes

1 Examples from 1850: Prussia, 2,842 kilometres; Saxony, 471 kilometres; France, 2,758 kilometres; Austria, 1,315 kilometres; Great Britain, 10,653 kilometres; USA, 14,515 kilometres. See *Statistisches Jahrbuch der Schweiz 1905*, (Bern: A. Francke Verlag, 1906), 147.

2

> There are around 1,500 lakes in Switzerland. The largest of them are at the foot of the Jura (Lake Geneva, Lake Neuchâtel, Lake Biel), on the Swiss Central Plateau (Lake Constance, Lake Zurich), in the Prealps and on the northern flank of the Alps (Lake Thun, Lake Brienz, Lake Zug, Lake Lucerne) and on the southern flank of the Alps (Lake Lugano, Lake Maggiore). In addition, there are hundreds of smaller natural lakes and reservoirs, especially in the Alps.

"Lakes and Rivers," Federal Department of Foreign Affairs, accessed 13 September 2019, https://www.eda.admin.ch/aboutswitzerland/en/home/umwelt/geografie/seen-und-fluesse.html.

3

> From today's point of view, with our trains and automobiles, postal stagecoaches were slow. A study of the postal stagecoach network around 1850, based on contemporary schedules, reveals the factors that made the journeys faster: good roads, frequent change of teams, and above all efficient connections. A comparison of the ticket prices with average salaries also demonstrates that only the very wealthy could even afford this rapid means of transport.

HansUlrich Scheidt, "Postkutschen im Spiegel ihrer Fahrpläne: Relaisstationen, Tempobolzen und Hafermotoren," in *Wege und Geschichte: Zeitschrift des Inventars Historischer Verkehrswege der Schweiz IVS* (2007): 12.

4 *St. Galler Tagblatt*, 3 February 2014.

5 "In contrast to today, at their beginnings the boats did not serve touristic purposes, but were rather an important means of transport for travelers and freight." Bernhard Ruetz, foreword in Jürg Meister, *Transport und Tourismus: Pioniere der Dampfschifffahrt*, vol. 89 of *Schweizer Pioniere der Wirtschaft und Technik*, ed. Verein für wirtschaftshistorische Studien (Zurich, 2009), 7.

6 Theophil Fritz Wiget, *Der "Waldstätterhof" in Brunnen: Geschichte eines berühmten Hotels* (Schwyz, 1975), 12.

7 Jürg Düblin, *Die Anfänge der schweizerischen Bundesversammlung: Untersuchungen zur politischen Praxis der eidgenössischen Räte in den zwei ersten Legislaturperioden (1848–1854)* (Bern: A. Francke Verlag, 1978), note 124.

8 Jürg Zimmermann, "Heinrich Moser als Eisenbahnpionier," in *Schaffhauser Magazin*, no. 3 (September 2005): 35.

9 I am grateful to Anton Heer for his suggestions and critical discussions.

10 "The English shipwright John Scott Russell built the gigantic ferry-steamboat, later dubbed the 'coal-guzzler', for the Romanshorn-Friedrichshafen route. Towed ferry barges were initially used for transport to Lindau." Anton Heer, "Wie die Bahn am See ins Rollen kam," in *Ostschweiz* (1 May 2019): 142.

11 "From 1856 to 1868, Swiss goods traffic on Lake Constance increased from 15,541 tonnes to 123,945 tonnes. During the same period, the volume of passenger traffic tripled." Klaus Kramer, "John Scott Russell und der 'Kohlenfresser' – oder: Was das Friedrichshafener Trajekt mit der Great Eastern verbindet," in *Friedrichshafener Jahrbuch für Geschichte und Kultur*, no.1 (2007): 142.

12 "The ferry facilities were a great success. The train ferry made four or five round trips each day, and transported more than 75,000 carriages annually." Klaus Kramer, "John Scott Russell und der 'Kohlenfresser' – oder:

Was das Friedrichshafener Trajekt mit der Great Eastern verbindet," in *Friedrichshafener Jahrbuch für Geschichte und Kultur*, no. 1 (2007): 142.

13 When building the tracks, the varying level of the surface of the lake had to be taken into account. They were laid in such a way that they could be raised or lowered according to the water level so that they would always remain level with the ship. To accomplish this, so-called Schwimmanleger were constructed in both Romanshorn and Friedrichshafen. These docks, which floated on pontoons in order to always remain at the same level as the boats, were connected to the fixed track by joints. Both on the ferry and on the dock, two tracks were laid in parallel. This enabled two trains to simultaneously board or leave the boat. For details see: Anton Heer, ed., *Seelinie und Trajekt: Visionen, Meilensteine und Episoden* (Flawil, 2019).

14 Annual report of the Royal Bavarian State Transport Association (Königlich-Bayerische Verkehrsanstalten), 1876.

15 In the 1930s, in addition to the Lake Constance ferries, there were train ferries on the Baltic Sea and the Mediterranean.

16

> After the Gotthard and the Furka, the Graubünden passes were the most important routes towards the south. The hub of the postal transport system was in Chur, centre of an important postal district. It was equipped with modern facilities for the postal carriages and sledges.

Furger, Andres, *In der Kutsche durch die Schweiz: Fahrkultur und Wagenbau um 1900* (Zurich: NZZ Libro, 2006), 47f.

> Steamboat traffic brought new destinations around Lake Lucerne to the attention of travellers, who had previously tended to visit only the Rigi and Lucerne. It allowed passengers to comfortably enjoy the scenic charm of the lake, and quickly access historical sites, such as the Rütli and the Tell Chapel.

Erika Flückiger Strebel/ViaStoria, *Tourismusgeschichte Zentralschweiz: Detailprojekt* (Bern: University of Bern, 2013).

17 *Bundesblatt* 1860, no. 3/63, accessed 26 October 2019, https://www.amtsdruckschriften.bar.admin.ch/viewOrigDoc.do?id=10003287.

18 *Bundesblatt* 1860, no. 3/63, accessed 26 October 2019, https://www.amtsdruckschriften.bar.admin.ch/viewOrigDoc.do?id=10003287.

19 I have published several studies of the political deals made concerning the railways, as well as the takeover attempts and mergers of the railway companies. See for example: Joseph Jung, *Alfred Escher 1819–1882: Der Aufbruch zur modernen Schweiz*, 4 volumes (Zurich: NZZ Libro, 2006), 466ff.

20 See Diane Conrad-Daubrah, notes accompanying the exhibition "Britische Gäste im 19. Jahrhundert und ihre Kirche in Pontresina: Persönlichkeiten, Tradition und Architektur 1860–1900," at the Museum Alpin in Pontresina, 2016. My thanks to Diane Conrad-Daubrah for providing me with valuable information.

21 My thanks to Annemarie Brülisauer, Director of the Museum Alpin in Pontresina, for her helpful suggestions.

22 "From a great height, a powerful stream shoots out of a narrow cleft in the rock and blazes down into a pool, where foam and mist are blown about every which way by the wind." Uwe Hentschel, "Der Staubbachfall in den Berner Alpen," in *Landschaft um 1800: Aspekte der Wahrnehmung in Kunst, Literatur, Musik und Naturwissenschaft*, ed. Thomas Noll, Ute Stobbe and Christian Scholl (Regensburg: Wallstein Verlag, 2012), 89.

23 "After the Montreux-Oberland-Bernois line had secured a connection to the rest of the world with the Gstaad loop (Reichenbach Contour) in 1905, conditions were in place for favourable development as a resort, spa, and vacation town." Gstaad Tourismus, accessed 26 October 2019, https://www.gstaad.ch/fileadmin/user_upload/Dokumente/PDF/jubilaeums_broschuere_2052812_mail.pdf.

24 Before the cog railway was constructed, wealthy guests were often carried to vantage points in sedan chairs. Queen Victoria made this experience when she was "carried down the steepest part from Seelisberg." "It is a demeaning procedure," the Queen reported. See Peter Arengo-Jones, *Queen Victoria in der Schweiz*, ed. Christoph Lichtin, trans. Nikolaus G. Schneider (Baden: Hier und Jetzt: 2018), 226f.

25 "To summarise, the Riggenbach cog system – like most other inventions – had a prehistory. This does not detract from Riggenbach's merits: He helped the cog railway achieve its breakthrough in Europe." Werner Latscha, Hans G. Wägli, Hans Wismann and Alfred Waldis, *Sieben bergbahnenpioniere*, vol. 81 of *Schweizer Pioniere der Wirtschaft und Technik*, ed. Verein für wirtschaftshistorische Studien (Zurich, 2005), 20. In 2016, Lorenz Degen wrote a Master's thesis on Niklaus Riggenbach: *Niklaus Riggenbach: ein Leben für die Eisenbahn* (master's thesis, University of Freiburg). He is currently doing further work on the subject.

26 The 30-page report by Otto Grüninger is in the collection of the Swiss Museum of Transport in Lucerne; a transcription of it can be viewed there: VA-57000: "Beschienung des Mount Washington" (Track-laying on Mount Washington).

27

> I was in favour of private construction and against state construction for the railway. This was partly due to my fear that, should the layout of the railway network be determined by the federal authorities, Eastern Switzerland would be treated as a stepchild, when in fact, considering its industry and traffic, it was entitled to make the largest claim.

Joseph Jung, *Alfred Escher 1819–1882: Der Aufbruch zur modernen Schweiz*, 4 volumes (Zurich: NZZ Libro, 2006), 1017.

28 "Along the great transit routes a series of industries will be established that otherwise would not be there." Joseph Jung, *Alfred Escher: Visionär, Grossbürger, Wirtschaftsführer*, vol. 114 of *Schweizer Pioniere der Wirtschaft und Technik*, ed. Verein für wirtschaftshistorische Studien (Zurich, 2019), 8.

29 Resident populations: Baden: 1850, 3,159; 1900, 6,489; Gampel: 1900, 531; 1910, 2,086; Arbon: 1850, 927; 1870, 1,919; Schönenwerd: 1850, 556; 1900; 1,812; Cham: 1850, 1,321; 1888: 3,140. A description:

> At the end of the 19th century, Neuhausen experienced a veritable population explosion. Between 1888 and 1910, the number of inhabitants increased from 2,023 to 5,524. This 273 percent growth was greater than that of most other Swiss municipalities during the same period. The small farming village on the Rhine Falls had become the second-largest industrial town in Canton Schaffhausen...Connection to the railway network...led to the...burgeoning of the Rhine Falls hotel business.

Urs Conrad, *Die Realschule Neuhausen 1900–1950* (licentiate thesis, University of Freiburg, 1999).

30 I have published multiple works on the development of the Swiss railway system, most extensively in Volume Two of my four-volume biography of

Alfred Escher, which first appeared in 2000: Joseph Jung, *Alfred Escher 1819–1882: Der Aufbruch zur modernen Schweiz*, 4 volumes (Zurich: NZZ Libro, 2006). A shorter version appeared in my one-volume biography of Alfred Escher: Joseph Jung, *Alfred Escher 1819–1882: Aufstieg, Macht, Tragik*, 6th ed. (Zurich: NZZ Libro, 2017). The present text is based on these two earlier works. Some of the content has been updated, and some passages reworded. My most recent discussion of the railway project appeared in 2019: Joseph Jung, *Alfred Escher: Visionär, Grossbürger, Wirtschaftsführer*, vol. 114 of *Schwiezer Pioniere der Wirtschaft und Technik*, ed. Verein für wirtschaftshistorische Studien (Zurich, 2019).

31 Joseph Jung, *Alfred Escher 1819–1882: Aufstieg, Macht, Tragik*, 6th ed. (Zurich: NZZ Libro, 2017), 162.

32 Max Ruh, "Schaffhausens Bestreben um einen Eisenbahnanschluss," in *Schaffhauser Mappe Magazin*, 5 April 2007, 18.

33 "The missing capital was to be sought with the help of Johann Conran Im Thurn, a Schaffhausen businessman living in London. The mission did not succeed." Max Ruh, "Schaffhausens Bestreben um einen Eisenbahnanschluss," in *Schaffhauser Mappe Magazin*, 5 April 2007, 19.

34 Joseph Jung, *Alfred Escher 1819–1882: Aufstieg, Macht, Tragik*, 6th ed. (Zurich: NZZ Libro, 2017), 367.

35 Joseph Jung, *Alfred Escher 1819–1882: Aufstieg, Macht, Tragik*, 6th ed. (Zurich: NZZ Libro, 2017), 166.

36 Johann Jakob Rüttimann to Alfred Escher, Zurich, Wednesday, March 1850, Alfred Escher Foundation, accessed 13 September 2019, https://www.briefedition.alfred-escher.ch/briefe/B0861/.

37 I have published several studies on the founding history of the Swiss railway and the expert opinion of Stephenson and Swinburne, for example: Joseph Jung, *Alfred Escher 1819–1882: Aufstieg, Macht, Tragik*, 6th ed. (Zurich: NZZ Libro, 2017), 169ff. The present discussion draws on my earlier work. Some of the content has been abridged, and some reworded.

38 "Botschaft des Bundesrates vom 7. April 1851," *Schweizerisches Bundesblatt* III/1, no. 19, 358.

39 See Joseph Jung, *Alfred Escher 1819–1882: Der Aufbruch zur modernen Schweiz*, 4 volumes (Zurich: NZZ Libro, 2006), 373ff.

40 See letter from Alfred Escher to Johann Jakob Rüttimann, Bern, Wednesday 14 April 1852, Alfred Escher Foundation, https://www.briefedition.alfred-escher.ch/briefe/B1018/.

41 See the Letter from Johann Friedrich Peyer im Hof to Alfred Escher ca 1851, accessed 13 September 2019, https://www.briefedition.alfred.escher.ch/briefe/B1018/; and also, the letter from Jonas Furrer to Alfred Escher, Bern, Wednesday, 19 February 1851, accessed 13 September 2019, https://www.briefedition.alfred-escher.ch/briefe/B0856/.

42 For more details, see Joseph Jung, *Alfred Escher 1819–1882: Aufstieg, Macht, Tragik*, 6th ed. (Zurich: NZZ Libro, 2017), 174f.

43 Joseph Jung, *Alfred Escher 1819–1882: Der Aufbruch zur modernen Schweiz*, 4 volumes (Zurich: NZZ Libro, 2006), 1017.

44 Flyers from 1855 concerning the future location of the Schaffhausen train station.

45 Heinrich Heine, 5 May 1843. Quoted from "Heinrich Heine – Lutetia," accessed 13 September, 2019, https://heinrich-heine-denkmal.de/heine-texte/lutetia57.shtml.

46 Minority Report of the Commission of the National Council, 23 July 1861.

47 I have published much on this landmark decision and have always emphasised that it was the foundation on which modern Switzerland was built in the 1850s and 1860s.

48 "George Page died on 20 April 1899. Five weeks later, Nestlé declared itself ready to negotiate a merger with the Anglo-Swiss. During George Page's lifetime this would have been unthinkable." Michael van Orsouw, Judith Stadlin and Monika Imboden, ed., *George Page: Der Milchpionier* (Zurich: NZZ Verlag, 2005).

49 I have published several studies about the influence of foreign financial institutions on the Swiss railways. See, for example, Joseph Jung, *Alfred Escher 1819–1882: Aufstieg, Macht, Tragik*, 6th ed. (Zurich: NZZ Libro, 2017), 97ff.

50 Much was published in this vein in the press as well, for example, in the *Neue Zürcher Zeitung*, which referenced the *Solothurnerblatt* of 17 March 1852:

> No railways will grow from federal protocols, and if the only tracks the Swiss get are those built by the federal government with state funds, no innkeeper will have to close his inn, or budge from his location. Our railways will only flourish as private companies...

51 "Politicians Are Also Pioneers" is the chapter title of a study about businesses, innovation and networks in the young Federal State: Jung Joseph, ed., *Schweizer Erfolgsgeschichten: Pioniere, Unternehmen, Innovationen*, vol. 100 of *Schweizer Pioniere der Wirtschaft und Technik* (Jubiläumsausgabe), ed. Verein für wirtschaftshistorische Studien (Zurich, 2013), 52f.

52 Letter from Luis Ruchonnet to François-Louis Ruchonnet, 7 December 1866, in Felix Bonjour, ed., *Louis Ruchonnet: Sa vie; Son œuvre* (Lausanne: Impremerie Vaudoise, 1936), 204.

53 Philipp Anton von Segesser, *Sammlung kleiner Schriften: Reden im Schweiz. Nationalrathe und staatsrechtliche Abhandlungen 1848–78*, vol. 3 (Bern, 1879), 8.

54 "Yet Escher's wish was to take on responsibility and to create. He felt that he was responsible for the emergence of modern Switzerland. His power met with criticism." Joseph Jung, "Der Aufstieg der Schweiz hat einen Namen," *Neue Zürcher Zeitung*, online, no. 45, 23 February 2019, 4–5.

55 The history of the development of the private railway companies in Switzerland from 1844 or 1847 up until nationalisation in 1902 has been divided into different phases by historians and railway experts. Depending on the approach taken in the research, this classification takes different forms. I myself have in the past differentiated between four phases in the period before Escher's death in 1882: I. 1847–1852; II. 1852–1859; III. 1859–1874; and IV. 1875–1882. For this book three caesurae are of relevance: 1852 (Railway Act), 1872 (Revision of the Railway Act), and 1898/1902 (decision of the Swiss electorate to nationalise the large railway companies/beginning of SBB operations).

56 Joseph Jung, *Alfred Escher 1819–1882: Aufstieg, Macht, Tragik*, 6th ed. (Zurich: NZZ Libro, 2017), 370ff.

57 The reasons for the worsening of the financial situation were diverse, yet all had to do with aggressive strategies for growth. In the face of a very competitive market environment, the companies had paid a high price to ensure the rapid expansion of their lines. As long as the revenue per kilometre of track could be maintained at a high level, this business policy could be financed, one way or the other. When at the beginning of the 1870s, however, the profitability of all the Swiss railway companies began to decline, while operational considerations were not given the necessary priority despite the unpromising market horizons, it became ever more difficult for the Northeast Railway to find financing for the construction of new lines. An additional burden was that it had increasingly financed its growth through borrowed

capital and thus became ever more dependent on the moods of the capital market.

58 I have published numerous works on the history of Switzerland as a banking centre, and especially on the Schweizerische Kreditanstalt (Credit Suisse Group). A comprehensive work appeared in 2000. See Joseph Jung, *From Schweizerische Kreditanstalt to Credit Suisse Group* (Zurich: NZZ Verlag, 2000). Volume 3 of my four-volume biography of Alfred Escher contains an in-depth examination of the bank's founding history. See Joseph Jung, *Alfred Escher 1819–1882: Der Aufbruch zur modernen Schweiz*, 4 volumes (Zurich: NZZ Libro, 2006), 733ff. The present text draws on both of these works. The content of certain passages has been modified, and the text has been reworded.

59 How dramatically the competition between the railway companies escalated in the 1870s is suggested by the following remark from the report of the governing board of the Northeastern Railway of 21 June 1877:

> Either it (the Northeastern Railway) stood by while the most dangerous competitive lines emerged next to its own lines, and sucked the life blood out of them, or it built the lines itself, suffering damage in the here and now but rescuing the company for the future.

Quoted from Joseph Jung, *Alfred Escher 1819–1882: Der Aufbruch zur modernen Schweiz*, 4 volumes (Zurich: NZZ Libro, 2006).

60 Letters: Jakob Stämpfli to Alfred Escher, Bern, Saturday, 20 December 1862, Alfred Escher Foundation, accessed 13 September 2019, https://www.briefedition.alfred-escher.ch/briefe/B1966/digitalisat/; Alfred Escher to Jakob Stämpfli, Zurich, Thursday 25 December 1862, accessed 13 September 2019, https://www.briefedition.alfred-escher.ch/briefe/B1968/.

61 I have published many studies about the context of the nationalisation. See, for example, Joseph Jung, *Alfred Escher 1819–1882: Der Aufbruch zur modernen Schweiz*, 4 volumes (Zurich: NZZ Libro, 2006), 408ff.

62 For more about the tragedy that befell Alfred Escher's daughter Lydia, see Joseph Jung, *Lydia Welti-Escher 1858–1891* (Zurich: NZZ Libro, 2016).

63 This is also evidenced by the fact that Escher's monument stands symbolically in front of the Zurich Main Station, while Welti's is found in front of the Zurzach train station.

2 Switzerland Unbound

Intrepid Progress

Get to Know This Pioneering People

Switzerland is a country of pioneers. For many years, to take an example, it sat at the top of global rankings for per capita patent applications.[1] Only in 2017 was it overtaken by China and relegated to second place. The impressive number of new businesses launched annually, which has plateaued at around 40,000 (39,125 in 2016), also attests to Switzerland's pioneering character.

Switzerland boasts many companies with histories that go back for decades, or even centuries. Impressive examples include the Rüetschi bell foundry in Aarau, which was established in 1367 and is probably the oldest surviving company in Switzerland; the paper mill on the Werd island near Zurich, which was founded in 1471; the Schwabe publishing house, whose first books date back to 1488 and which is considered the oldest publisher in the world; and the Schuler St Jakob winery in Seewen, which sprang from the Castell trading firm founded in 1694.

Pioneers have shaped Switzerland. Their activities have extended well beyond industry, trade and business. They have been influential in culture and technology, tourism and alpinism, research and development – in sum, they have contributed to all aspects of civilisation. And while there have surely always been people who have founded, developed, tested and explored, the extraordinary intensity of the pioneering era that erupted in Switzerland in the 19th century is exceptional.

On examining the period more closely, it becomes clear that the second half of the century was especially fruitful in terms of pioneering work. Many of the firms founded then are still in existence today and have developed into national or even international leaders in their sectors. Of the 20 companies in the Swiss Market Index (SMI), for example, ten have their roots in the period from 1852 to 1878, five were established in the 1890s and only five were founded in the 20th century.[2] There are various reasons for this. The political, economic and academic institutions that provided post-1848 Switzerland with a modern foundation were of decisive importance. The founding of the Federal State set off a powerful dynamic. Belief in progress and the push towards new

DOI: 10.4324/9781003243144-2

frontiers became part of the programme. The "Spirit of '48" propelled a profound transformation.[3]

But this transformation cannot be attributed solely to a burning enthusiasm for progress. The spirit of an age can create history only in a dialogue with naturally given circumstances. And these circumstances can be seen in different lights at different times. Such was the case with the topographical particularities of Switzerland, whose social significance changed from one epoch to the next. The Alps, for example, went from being seen as obstructions to traffic and obstacles to the construction of roads, tunnels and bridges to being viewed as a source of water power, a place of rest and relaxation and a playground for alpinists. The opportunities offered by the latter point of view were first exploited by the pioneers of tourism in the 19th century.

External factors determined by international circumstances could also facilitate or impede the activities of pioneers in Switzerland. So it was for Henry Dunant (1828–1910). A failing businessman, Dunant travelled to a Northern Italian war zone in 1859 to ask Napoleon III (1808–1873) to support his ailing company in Algeria.[4] His traumatic experience of the horrific slaughter at the Battle of Solferino inspired him to found the Red Cross.

Nations also are dependent on luck, for war and peace are not only self-determined. Disasters, emergencies and misery may drive people to flee their circumstances. For a long time, many Swiss sought out better lives in the world beyond their country's borders. In the 19th century, emigration intensified, but the reverse also occurred: Increasing numbers of foreigners, especially politically persecuted refugees, came to Switzerland and brought new ideas with them. Some of these ideas were of seminal importance in the era of great pioneering achievements in Switzerland.

Switzerland's post-1848 transformation from a developing country to an economically successful nation was a consequence of widely differing conditions and events. The fundamental political transformation, which made a modern federal state of a backward confederation, provided a necessary foundation for this progress. But the Swiss metamorphosis from an agrarian nation to a country of world-class industry, research and services was due to more than just a new constitution, even if that constitution was the most progressive one in Europe. The clever division of responsibilities between the state and private business, as between the federal government and the cantons, was also pivotal for the change.

Yet all of these channels, foundations and frameworks were not enough, on their own, to bring modern Switzerland into being. This required visionary individuals who launched projects, founded businesses and pursued research. It took pioneers! It was pioneers who covered Switzerland with roads and rails, built bridges across rivers and valleys, tunnelled through mountains, manufactured innovative products, drafted daring plans, ran risks and had faith in their ideas. Many of the companies they founded remained small- or medium-sized enterprises, but others achieved leading positions in international and even global markets. These pioneers launched the development of their country in the 19th century and bequeathed it its success. They shaped the brand known as Switzerland, and, thanks to this achievement, they are still with us today.

Highlights: From the Helvetic Republic to the Industrialised Welfare State

The success of pioneers stems from more than their own abilities. Spirit and vigour emerge from a cultural framework and depend on institutional conditions. The craft of watchmaking in Switzerland, for example, benefitted from the fact that in the rural-agrarian Jura of the 17th and 18th centuries, business practices were not constrained by the regulatory corset that constricted trades in the cities. Similarly, at the end of the 19th century, the absence of patent protection regulations in Switzerland gave the Swiss chemical industry a decisive advantage over its competitors.

Switzerland found itself in an unusual situation in the first years of the 19th century. The Helvetic Republic (1798–1803) brought with it certain economic innovations, such as freedom of trade and the abolition of cantonal customs duties. The Helvetic model of governance, however, was too centralised to provide a durable foundation for a national economy in a number of respects. In terms of political economy, the positive effect of the Helvetic Republic lay mainly in its breaking up of the confining structures of the Ancien Régime that had preceded it. It was not suitable, however, as a model for the Federal State of 1848. In the end, however paradoxical it might sound, the French boycott of Great Britain, which Emperor Napoleon I required all continental European states to participate in, was far more important for the economic development of Switzerland than were the few short years of the Helvetic Republic. Napoleon's so-called Continental Blockade, which was in effect until 1813, proved a windfall for several areas of the Swiss economy, which profited from the elimination of British competition. Swiss firms exploited this favourable opportunity, broke into new markets and diversified into other economic areas, in which their know-how soon caught up to that of the previously market-leading British companies. This was particularly true of the textile industry. Having operated in the shadow of British producers up until the beginning of the 19th century, the Swiss now became market leaders themselves. And because they were no longer able to access spare parts from across the English Channel, they began to build textile-manufacturing machines themselves – thereby laying the foundation of the Swiss engineering industry, which would quickly become a significant branch of the national economy.

Between 1808 and 1835, a number of volcanoes erupted in Southeast Asia, and the atmosphere and oceans subsequently cooled. The most important eruption was that of Tambora in Indonesia in 1815, which affected even Switzerland. Agriculture especially suffered under the unusual temperatures and meteorological conditions, and crop yields declined. The consequences were dramatic and affected not only the peasantry but cottage industries as well. The crisis lasted for about two years. Then the Swiss economy recovered, and the lot of homeworkers improved.

Yet prospects soon dimmed again. Like the watch industry, the textile industry was traditionally oriented entirely towards exports, and the pressures of international competition led to decreasing salaries towards the end of the 1820s. The profits of small manufacturers also collapsed. In order to address this situation, the Zurich Cantonal Parliament introduced a voluntary tax to support impoverished municipalities in the crisis areas in the southeastern part of the canton (Fischenthal, Bäretswil and Wald). Among the beneficiaries of this support would also be manufacturers, who were to use the funds to hire unemployed spinners and weavers. Private collections were also carried out, and aid organisations formed in certain municipalities in Canton Zurich.

In the 18th century, the businesses of Zurich-based silk merchants and manufacturers were primarily oriented towards Europe. These companies initially sourced the majority of their supplies from Northern Italy and sold their products in the Netherlands, England and the German cities on the Rhine. Gradually, French cities and parts of Eastern Europe also developed into markets. At this point, the cotton spinning and weaving business began to boom in Zurich, growing even more quickly than the silk trade. The raw material was delivered through the Italian ports of Genoa and Leghorn and the French ports of Marseille, Bordeaux and Nantes.

In other areas of Switzerland, trade was already changing course in the 18th century, increasingly seeking out overseas markets. Merchants from Geneva, Neuchâtel and Vaud in particular, but also from Basel and St Gallen, built up commercial relationships with North and South America, as well as with Asian countries like China and India. Cotton and dyes were imported from these countries, while watches were exported to them. Over the course of the 18th century, trade between Europe, America and Africa took on new dimensions, and a transoceanic orientation left an enduring mark on the Swiss export economy in the 19th century. Meanwhile, to the extent that Swiss merchants played an important role in world trade, Switzerland became a hub of global commerce in raw materials.[5] Triangular trade flourished. Textiles and other goods were shipped from Europe to Africa and traded for slaves, who were then sold in America. From there, European merchants brought home colonial goods such as sugar and coffee. As actors in this global commerce, Swiss trading houses, too, were complicit in the slave trade.[6]

Figure 2.1 Johann Jakob Aschmann (1747–1809). *Freiheit durch Aufstand.* Coloured engraving. Zurich, Zentralbibliothek Zürich.

During the period of the Helvetic Republic (1798–1803), Switzerland became a stage for violent conflicts between the major European powers. After the peace accords of 1800 and 1801, French troops pulled out of most of the areas of modern-day Switzerland. Barely had they left, however, than the Swiss began fighting among themselves. Eventually, the Helvetic regime was driven out. In 1802, Napoleon again had French soldiers march into Switzerland, and gave the country a new federal constitution (Acts of Mediation, 1803–1815). Conditions of subservience were to be abolished, and equality was to be established between the cities and rural areas. But such reforms were more easily written down than realised. In many areas, living conditions changed for the worse, and social wrongs increased. Torture, corporal punishment and press censorship were introduced again, and the population of the countryside, shaken by the many years of war, was oppressed by the urban aristocracy. This led to numerous uprisings across Switzerland. The Zurich Cantonal Parliament added fuel to the fire by reintroducing the Act of Homage (Huldigungsakt) in 1803. Resistance grew in the countryside, and protests escalated to revolts. In various townships on Lake Zurich, rebels – initially from the impoverished underclass – banded together under the leadership of the cobbler Johan Jakob Willi (1772–1804) of Horgen and took up the fight against the city of Zurich. They were disappointed by Napoleon. He had brought neither democracy nor equality to Switzerland, as Willi and the others had erroneously hoped he would: Even their most powerful neighbour could not be counted on. This experience was a bitter one. The rebels set fire to the castle of Wädenswil in one of the last slightings in Swiss history. In 1804, the Bocken War broke out – named for a skirmish at Bocken on the Horgenberg. The rebels did not stand a chance against the superior forces of the Swiss Confederation. Willi was executed on 25 April 1804 in Zurich. The conflict is sometimes played down today as merely a regional affair, or a mini-revolution, but in its time it received international attention.

The July Revolution of 1830 in France increased pressure on the urban ruling classes in Switzerland. The population in the countryside sensed that change was afoot, and was no longer content with empty promises. On 22 November 1830, a popular assembly was held in Uster in Canton Zurich to demand equality between the city and the countryside. Immediately afterwards, the government of Zurich resigned: The ruling elite capitulated without a fight, and the rule of city over countryside was effectively ended. As early as 6 December of the same year, new elections were held for the Cantonal Parliament, and rural areas were assured two-thirds of the seats. This was not yet equal representation, given that the city accounted for only 5 percent of the population. But the process of democratisation introduced by the new Zurich Constitution of 1831 proved decisive. With its ratification, Zurich joined ten other cantons in the Liberal camp in taking steps towards a modern Switzerland, even before 1848. The dissolution of the Ancien Régime did not always occur as peacefully as it did in Zurich; in Basel, for example, it involved a civil war, which ultimately led to the division of the canton.

In the early 1830s, sporadic unrest broke out when it became known that manufacturers were experimenting with mechanical looms. In the midst of these tensions, a celebration in remembrance of the Uster assembly of 1830 took place on 22 November 1832. The approximately 10,000 participants were mostly small manufacturers and homeworkers who had fallen into economic hardship; some were so badly off that they were anxious about their very survival. Hardly any factory workers were present. At first the assembly proceeded peacefully under the leadership of its Liberal initiators, as constitutional questions were discussed. The crowd began to get unruly, however, when the focus turned to education, press freedom, the separation of powers and tax relief. Finally, a call for the abolition of weaving machines was voiced. The atmosphere was already highly charged. Nevertheless, the assembly was peacefully brought to an end, and further economic issues, like the redemption of agricultural tithes, found their way into the minutes.

An edict of the Cantonal Parliament of 1830 had called on the citizens of the canton to submit their proposals for change to the constitutional commission. Many of the petitions demanded the abolition of weaving and silk-spinning machines. This wish was doubtless expressive of the tense and sometimes desperate financial situation of the homeworkers and small manufacturers who were most affected by mechanisation. They hoped that the proposed prohibition would halt in its tracks, or even roll back, what they considered a sinister form of progress. Many small manufacturers and homeworkers were thus disappointed with the result of the 1832 assembly. In its wake, windows were smashed at the Corrodi & Pfister factory. Burning pieces of wood were then thrown into the building. In the end the factory, which had begun operating in 1816, burned to the ground. The arsonists and their accomplices were apprehended, and violent scenes ensued. The authorities reacted severely. In the course of restoring order, nine municipalities were occupied by the army. Seventy-three men were charged with crimes – homeworkers, craftsmen and tradesmen. Forty-five of them were from Bäretswil; only one of them was a factory worker. What they had in common was their poverty.

The court punished the principal offender, Hans Felix Egli (1783–1841), to no fewer than 24 years in chains; the prosecution had argued for the death penalty. Egli was granted amnesty after serving seven years. Others were also condemned to years in chains or in prison. The trial against Egli is marked by a particular historical curiosity, in that the counsel for the defence was Jonas Furrer (1805–1861), who would later serve as the first President of the Federal Council.

The Uster fire of 1832, the Uster Assembly of 1830 and the Bocken War of 1804 were interconnected historical events that affected both Zurich and Switzerland as a whole. The fire represented an important step towards the attainment of political equality between city and countryside. The social misery of factory workers, often identified as its cause, was not actually a factor at all. The fire became a symbol. The flames that blazed out of the factory building in Uster had been intended to incinerate the path of progress: Mechanical means of production were to be destroyed. The fire was a protest against a future characterised by continual increases in productivity. The incident illustrates that the "Industrial Revolution," so often used as a blanket term for the first half of the 19th century, does not suffice to explain the complexity of the epochal transformation that was underway.[7]

If by progress one means innovations that contribute to solutions to social, economic or political problems, one ought to be discriminating enough to add that not all social classes, professions and parties in a given epoch have the same problems. While the streamlining of production processes in the first half of the 19th century certainly solved a problem for manufacturers, who could now operate more profitably and become internationally competitive, for many working people the shift from cottage industry to factory work signalled a decline in social standing. Multi-layered processes were thus interfused. Social restructuring and political reorientation accompanied the economic boom. The picture of a uniform trend in this transformation is deceptive. The hope of weavers and small manufactures that the industrialisation of textile production could be halted by their protests and demands also proved illusory. To be sure, the process of mechanisation was delayed. Yet even if the situation of home-weavers improved somewhat in the 1830s, it deteriorated again in the 1840s, by which point the mechanisation of production had become unstoppable.

The 11 cantons that adopted liberal constitutions in 1830/1831 took a significant step towards building a modern economic system.[8]

These constitutions, besides introducing universal male suffrage and the separation of powers in government, also established a significant number of individual rights, among them property rights and the right to inter-cantonal free trade and free enterprise. This political progress was dynamically interconnected with the economic boom. In the 1830s, a strikingly large number of young pioneers founded their own companies, and many existing small firms began to grow or to reorient themselves. Just as striking is that several companies were founded that later became powerful players in the Swiss economy or even took on international dimensions. There are several reasons for this. The engineering industry especially profited from economic liberalisation. It developed out of artisanal business enterprises and workshops downstream from textile operations.

The watch and textile industries were already flourishing in the middle of the 19th century; the engineering industry was still awaiting the important impulses that were to propel its breakthrough onto the world stage. Yet it was precisely the demand for textile machinery that would turn Swiss textile enterprises and artisan operations into global machine-manufacturing firms. Soon not only mechanical looms but also turbines and steam engines would be manufactured, while the expansion of steamer traffic on Swiss lakes would help fill the order books. When railway companies began springing out of the ground like mushrooms in the 1850s, the Swiss engineering industry was there to supply them with steam locomotives. The number of locomotive and carriage builders increased quickly to keep pace with demand; the economic regulation of railroad construction thus turned out to be of epochal significance. In 1852, after heated discussions between proponents of a centrally organised national railroad and advocates of private train lines, the Swiss Parliament decided in favour of the latter. With this decision, the way was cleared for exceptionally rapid economic growth and modernisation.

MILESTONE 2.1

1 January 1878

The Swiss Factory Act Lays the Foundation for a Public Welfare System

Neither at the popular assembly in Uster in 1830 nor at the ceremony commemorating it in 1832 was there an outcry over the working conditions in factories, the long hours – through both day and night – the hardships of child labour, or the general societal misery of the time. Although social initiatives and charitable projects were launched here and there in Switzerland during the first half of the 19th century – mainly by private organisations and the church – no significant socio-political reforms were introduced. In Canton Zurich, regulations addressing the employment of minors on spinning machines and a ban on night and factory work for children under nine were enacted in 1815 but went unenforced.[9]

Canton Glarus became known as a pioneer in socio-political legislation. Factory work shaped the everyday life of many Glarus residents, and industry was omnipresent in the Glarus countryside. In the mid-1840s, the first laws were passed restricting children's working hours in mechanical spinning mills. In 1856, this legislation was expanded to include all factories, and in 1858, work on Sunday was also prohibited. Finally, in 1864, Canton Glarus made history by enacting regulations on factory work that were among the most progressive and comprehensive in Europe.

At the federal level, however, discussions dragged on. It was not until 1877 that the (male) electorate narrowly accepted a federal law that came into force on 1 January 1878 and represented a socio-political turning point. It limited adults to 11 working hours per day, prohibited night work and work on Sundays, and banned child labour. Federal inspectors were required to carry out factory inspections to ensure compliance. This first Swiss Factory Act (Schweizer Fabrikgesetz) was subsequently amended several times, and completely revised in 1914. In addition to setting a limit on working hours, the law brought about another essential socio-political advance in its recognition of causal liability. From then on, factory owners were liable for industrial accidents. In taking this step, the legislature recognised that the accelerated production afforded by mechanisation during the 19th century had significantly increased the demands on factory workers and that this had led to an increasing number of industrial accidents, sometimes with serious consequences. And it was not just about personal injuries due to accidents and occupational health hazards. The financial consequences of the death or disability of a breadwinner could hit a whole family hard.

Though the law initially only regulated factory work, with it the state had committed itself to a new social policy. With the legal obligation for employers to insure employees against industrial accidents, a pivotal moment had come for private non-life insurance companies. A discussion about state insurance was quickly taken up, but its implementation through the referendum process (1890,

(*Continued*)

1900) took decades. Finally, after a passionate referendum battle, the Swiss electorate approved the Health and Accident Insurance Act (Kranken- und Unfallversicherungsgesetz) on 4 February 1912. Since preparations for setting up the Swiss Accident Insurance Fund (Suva) fell during the First World War, the law did not come into force until 1 April 1918. With this law, Switzerland became one of the last European countries to establish a public social welfare system.

Figure 2.2 Construction site in Zurich, 1910. Photograph. Baugeschichtliches Archiv der Stadt Zürich (Architectural History Archive of the City of Zurich). Excavation was done by hand.

Because of this landmark decision, the year 1852 marks a crucial turning point. Just as the textile industry had triggered the development of new business sectors 50 years earlier, in the middle of the 19th century the railways steamed in, bringing progress along with them. The transformation they gave rise to left all that had come before in the dust. In contrast to earlier developments, the evolving transport networks took in all of Switzerland. Modernisation was now unstoppable and reached even the most remote regions of the country. Thanks to the railways, not only did Switzerland develop as a tourist destination and a location for research and industry but commercial intercourse and the credit business also evolved, and with them the modern banking and insurance industries. Prosperity increased, making possible further pioneering achievements in economic sectors that had previously not even existed in Switzerland.

This dynamic affected employment and social structures across the entire population and recast the Swiss national economy. The transformation was especially evident in agriculture. The expansion of the transport infrastructure revolutionised the entire agricultural sector by connecting Switzerland to the international railway network. Goods from countries near and far could be imported more easily and at a lower cost, while the possibilities for exporting Swiss products expanded. This connection to the global economy fundamentally transformed agricultural production in Switzerland.

Even before 1850, Swiss farms were not capable of feeding the entire Swiss population; imports of essential goods such as grain were indispensable. Accelerated population growth in the 19th century exacerbated this problem. The imbalance between agricultural production and demand increased markedly in the early years of the Federal State. New tourism facilities, which were expanded first for summer and later for winter tourism, created needs that had to be satisfied – the tens of thousands of tourists flowing into Switzerland had to be fed. An imbalance was also evident in the relationship between the area of cultivated land and the number of farms: Many farming operations were simply too small. This problem became more acute when farming was mechanised in the course of the second half of the 19th century, and fields had to be large enough to accommodate the agricultural machines. While most farmers on the Swiss Central Plateau were not engaged in a struggle for survival, others, farming on higher ground, barely got by on the yields of their operations. Often there were few prospects for a fundamental improvement of this situation, and, especially in Alpine regions like Valais and Ticino, life-threatening shortages arose.

The industrialisation of Switzerland also led to a decrease in the amount of arable land, due to the increasing amount of space required for infrastructure such as residential buildings, factories, commercial enterprises, hotels, and roads and railway lines. The price of land correspondingly went up. This development led to changes in the Swiss banking sector, for example in financial services and forms of financing, which in turn affected farmers. To the extent that investment and venture capital flowed into industry, it was not available for agricultural purposes. This, in turn, explains why, in addition to the new industrial and commercial banks that financed the breakthrough of modern Switzerland, new institutions were also necessary to satisfy the changed needs of agriculture: rural mortgage banks and cantonal banks.

Farmers had various options for dealing with these many-layered processes of change and the challenges they gave rise to. They could switch to a job in a growing industrial concern or, alongside their farming, take up a form of cottage industry, for example textile work. Or they could emigrate. Beginning in the 1850s, when mercenary service was no longer an option, a striking number of young Swiss from farming families emigrated to the Americas. And while the USA became an increasingly popular destination for emigrating Swiss farmers – the Civil War (1861–1865) caused only a temporary decrease in emigration – other countries in the Americas, such as Argentina, were also alluring destinations. In many cases, entire families emigrated; in others, single young dairymen sought their professional and personal fortunes in California or elsewhere. Seen from an overarching perspective, the young Swiss Federal State – remarkably – depended on immigration for the expansion of its material infrastructure and for its economic development. Thus, while Swiss industry increasingly absorbed foreign labour after the mid-19th century, Swiss natives from agricultural milieus were emigrating abroad.

As early as the 1830s, and increasingly from the middle of the century onwards, a fundamental structural change took place in Swiss agriculture. Generally, sectors in which imported products were less expensive than domestic ones saw a decline. By contrast, those areas in which Swiss products were competitive or filled a specialised niche expanded. This meant concretely, on the one hand, a decrease in grain cultivation, and on the other an intensification of dairy farming. While it is true that over half of Swiss farmers grew grain even into the 21st century, this grain was primarily for their own use, both at home and as feed for their livestock.

The shift in agricultural emphasis did not occur from one day to the next, and its harbingers can be seen in earlier processes and phenomena. As early as the 1830s, cheese production in some regions moved from Alpine areas into the valleys. Up until this time, with the exception of certain large-scale seigneurial farms, cheese had been produced on the Alps. But then village cheeseries began to crop up; in contrast to the alpine cheese operations, these could produce cheese all year long. And when it was realised that the quality of valley-produced cheeses was in no wise inferior to that of cheese produced on the alp, previously unknown possibilities opened up for increased production. Canton Bern led the way. Jeremias Gotthelf (1797–1854) wrote about this development in his novel *Käserei in der Vehfreude*. Mercilessly and delightfully, he describes how a sleepy village pursues modernisation and what happens when, instead of building a school, it commits its resources to commercial activities.[10]

Canton Lucerne followed the example set by Canton Bern, and from the 1860s onwards village cheeseries increasingly opened in Eastern

Switzerland as well. This had the further consequence that, in addition to local cheeseries and dairies, industrial milk-processing plants were built. In the course of this displacement of production, the cowherds and cheesemakers on the Alps, who had substantially shaped the image of Switzerland in the 18th century, increasingly became cheesemakers and farmers down in the valleys. In addition, from the mid-19th century onwards, new technologies – such as fodder shredders, threshers and other harvesting machines – affected agriculture, leading to an increased emphasis on grass-based farming that would turn out, on the whole, to be a stroke of good fortune for Swiss agriculture and ultimately for Switzerland as a whole. Thanks to this structural transformation, foodstuffs such as chocolate and cheese developed into Swiss export products of the first rank – as they still are today – joining the luxury products produced by the watchmaking industry. If Swiss agriculture had continued to focus on grain production, it would have been eclipsed in a very short time by the far more efficient production abroad.

This fundamental structural transformation, from grain to milk, was followed by other changes: Those farmers who had specialised in meat, vegetable or fruit production also had to contend with imports that cost less than their homegrown Swiss products. In the end, all Swiss agricultural products – even potatoes and eggs – suffered in the face of international competition. And farmers were faced with the same strategic choices as the producers of goods in other sectors: They could specialise and focus on niche products, improve the quality of their goods or produce them more cheaply.

On top of all this, from the mid-19th century onwards technical progress – from mechanisation to synthetic fertiliser – swept across the entire spectrum of Swiss agriculture. And while Swiss farming continued to play a role in providing for the food security of the population even after all these structural changes, its character had changed: Now, like other branches of the economy, it was dependent on exports. The structural transformation can be seen in the shrinking amount of cultivated land. While up until the mid-19th century Switzerland boasted more than 500,000 hectares of cultivated land, making up about half of all agricultural land, by 1914 this number had shrunk to 200,000. Viticulture in Eastern Switzerland also declined, and fruit and vegetable farmers increasingly produced their goods for urban markets, and soon for the canning industry.

With the founding of the Eidgenössische Polytechnische Schule (known as the Polytechnic; today's ETH) in Zurich in 1854/1855, and of the Technikum Winterthur in 1874, the greater Zurich area gained momentum as a centre of technical industry. Beginning in the 1830s, Zurich and Winterthur had gradually developed into the hub of the Swiss engineering industry, boasting firms such as Sulzer, Rieter and Escher Wyss. The

Maschinenfabrik Oerlikon (Oerlikon Machine Works, MFO) and the Schweizerische Lokomotiv- und Maschinenfabrik (Swiss Locomotive and Machine Works, SLM) in Winterthur began operating in the second half of the 19th century. Schaffhausen, where Johann Conrad Fischer's (1773–1854) foundry had already kicked off industrialisation in the early years of the century, became part of the hub as well. The foundry only really attained heavyweight status in the 1850s, under the name Georg Fischer, concurrently with the Schweizerische Industriegesellschaft (Swiss Industrial Company, SIG) in Neuhausen am Rheinfall. The Maschinenfabrik Rüti (Rüti Machine Works), the Maschinenfabrik Gebrüder Bühler (Bühler Brothers Machine Works) in Uzwil and the Mascheninenfabrik Saurer (Saurer Machine Works) in Arbon also distinguished themselves as internationally competitive machine-makers in the Zurich/Eastern Switzerland region. This "Greater Area" of machine manufacturing, which was already an important industrial location due to its traditional textile businesses, expanded further westwards at the end of the 19th century with the founding of Brown Boveri in Baden. Thanks especially to Brown Boveri and the Maschinenfabrik Oerlikon, electrical engineering developed into a key new industry in Switzerland. The importance of the larger industrial region around Zurich can be seen in statistics: In Canton Zurich alone, the number of employees in the industrial sector jumped from 69,559 to 133,352 in the 50 years from 1860 to 1910.

The engineering industry dominated the Swiss economy for more than 100 years. Hydraulic turbines and steamships made by Escher Wyss, steam engines and diesel motors by Sulzer, looms by Honegger, electric motors and steam turbines by Brown Boveri, textile machines by Rieter – top-quality Swiss products served the world market up until the last quarter of the 20th century. Afterwards, driven by liberalisation and the cost pressure it gave rise to, a rapid process of consolidation set in. Locally and nationally anchored enterprises fused with international conglomerates. Of the traditional Swiss companies mentioned above, only Rieter has remained an independent actor.

The Swiss economy of the 19th century was in part shaped by so-called linkage, a common process in the history of international industry.[11] Linkage usually happens in one of two ways: when a side-business of a company (for example, machine repair) grows to become its main operation, or when a supplier (for example, of machines) of a key industry sector (for example, the textile sector) closes ranks with it and supplants it as the leading sector. Such linkages occurred at Escher Wyss and at Rieter, for example. There is also a third kind of linkage: the friendly and ingenious cooperation of two different personality types. The cooperation between Charles Brown Sr and Johann Jakob Sulzer, and between Charles Brown Jr and Walter Boveri, provide examples of this kind of linkage.

The fact that we speak of a Greater Zurich Area existing as early as the 19th century points to a characteristic aspect of Swiss industrial history: In contrast to industry in countries like Germany and England, Swiss industry did not conglomerate in factory cities but rather in clusters. Although the city of Zurich was defined by its textile and machine industries, its population remained modest in comparison with other European industrial cities: It grew from 42,000 in 1850 to 104,000 in 1888. In Leeds, by contrast, population growth took on dimensions of another order, increasing from 72,000 in 1850 to 368,000 in 1890. And while Zurich's growth after the turn of the century, to 215,000 in 1910, may seem impressive by Swiss standards, it was in part a consequence of the city's incorporation of other towns. In any case, the increase in Zurich's population did not have the colossal dimensions of that of British and German industrial cities. Between 1890 and 1910, Glasgow, for example, grew by around 450,000 inhabitants, becoming a city with a population of over a million, while in the Ruhr region, Bochem grew from 47,000 inhabitants in 1890 to 137,000 in 1910.

The formation of sector-specific industrial regions is a typical feature of Swiss economic and industrial history. The cluster of textile and machine industries in and around Zurich can be likened to the agglomeration of the watch industry along the arc of the Jura, the concentration of the chemical and pharmaceutical industries in the Basel area, and that of thc food and beverage industry between Bern and Lake Geneva. The branch-specific characters of the clusters later became less pronounced as the original industries attracted delivery firms, construction firms, transporters and other companies to their areas. Increasingly better transport connections due to the growth of the railways beginning in the 1850s also soon allowed the clusters to extend beyond their narrower areas of concentration so that they became intermixed. In this sense, practically all of Switzerland offered favourable conditions for strong networks to develop between companies, and the country continued to profit from this phenomenon long after the 19th century. Thanks to good rail connections, it was possible even for companies in outlying regions to deliver goods to clients all around the nation. Examples are the Valais chemical firm Lonza, located in Visp, and the instrument manufacturer Kühni in Basel-Landschaft. Kühni produced goods not only for the chemical industry in nearby Basel but also and extensively for the just-mentioned Lonza in Valais. A further example is provided by Berneli and Merz, a Bernese producer of luminescent materials, and later of glues, which made a name for itself as a supplier of the Genevan watch industry.

The development of the Swiss banking industry was decisive for industrial construction and for other large-scale infrastructural projects that led to the emergence of modern Switzerland.[12] In the first half of the 19th century, banking was characterised by the parallel existence of two separate frameworks. A predominantly rural banking system consisting of local banks – especially savings banks – principally served farmers, artisans and tradesmen. The other system, shaped by urban elites and committed to the tradition of private banking, was internationally oriented from the start. Since the early industrialists largely financed their own enterprises, the capital accumulated by private bankers, in Switzerland and abroad, was hardly ever made available to Swiss businesses.

The Federal State of 1848, however, fundamentally altered Swiss political and economic structures. Growing industries created new demands. In the face of industrialisation, private bankers saw themselves confronted with difficult-to-assess risks on an unprecedented scale and were not ready to take them on. Nor were the savings banks in a position to cover the rising demand for capital and the specific financial needs of industry. The same was true of the so-called note-issuing banks (Notenbanken), which had been founded as joint-stock banks in the 1830s, and would not approve, for example, the awarding of large open credits. There were thus no institutions functioning as commercial banks oriented towards business, and in particular towards the founding of and investment in companies. The idea of founding such banks arose of necessity at a time when Swiss industry was increasingly in danger of coming under the sway of foreign institutions of high finance, and in particular that of the Rothschild Bank. In the 1850s, the Crédit Mobilier, founded in France, became a model for company start-up and underwriting banks in Switzerland as well.[13] Such banks were established in Geneva in 1853 (Banque Générale Suisse de Crédit International Mobilier et Foncier), in St Gallen (Deutsch-Schweizerische Kreditbank) and Zurich (Schweizerischer Kreditanstalt) in 1856, in Winterthur (Bank in Winterthur) and Basel (Basler Handelsbank) in 1862, and in Bern (Eidgenössischer Bank) in 1863. The banks founded in Geneva and St Gallen, after successful starts, soon ran into difficulties and vanished from the scene, while those in Basel and Bern struggled and found a stable business footing only after several mergers. The Schweizerische Kreditanstalt (today's Credit Suisse) led the pack when it came to driving industrialisation forward and building up Switzerland's economic infrastructure. It, too, was a privately structured commercial bank on the model of the Crédit Mobilier. Founded specifically to support the Swiss Northeastern Railway (Schweizerische Nordostbahn), it soon became involved with other railway companies, expanded its business scope and began to serve all parts of the country. It was heavily involved in the founding of businesses, placed venture capital at the disposal of companies and developed into the true engine of the Swiss economy.[14]

Alongside this institutional expansion, two additional financial instruments were indispensable for the enormously increased investment needs that existed in Switzerland from the mid-19th century onwards: the bearer share and the bond issue. These not only made possible the acquisition of capital by commercial banks but also paved the way for the creation of stock exchanges. In the last quarter of the 19th century and in the years up until 1914, a large number of mostly smaller banks were founded, such as the Raiffeisen banks (rural credit banks), but in the end the most influential development – besides the founding of the Swiss National Bank – was the establishment of finance companies. The latter, which included the Schweizerische Eisenbahnbank (Swiss Railway Bank) in Basel (1879), were originally founded to serve railway companies. They can be understood as a kind of hinge that connected banks and large industrial concerns; their purpose was to meet the swelling demand for capital, which they supplied – in this case to the railway companies – by selling their own shares or bonds to other banks. Similar structures were later created for the electricity industry after a boom in the sector triggered a new wave of investment in the 1890s. The Bank für elektrische Unternehmungen (Bank for Electrical Companies), for example, was founded in 1895 and later became the Electrowatt. By 1910, there existed no fewer than 20 such financing companies.

The turn of the century and the years up until 1914 were a time marked both by the establishment of banks and by movements towards concentration. Here the mergers that created the Schweizerische Bankverein (Swiss Bank Corporation) in 1895/1896 and the Schweizerische Bankgesellschaft (Union Bank of Switzerland) in 1912 are particularly notable. The large number of Swiss institutions, however, ought not to deceive: Swiss banking in the 19th century was a minor affair compared with its international banking competition. Until 1914, a Parisian, Berliner or Londoner would have noted that the biggest Swiss banks operated on a scale comparable to that of large regional banks in their own countries.[15] Still, in the last quarter of the 19th century, the Swiss financial centre had grown into a unified whole and had gained in international stature. Most importantly, a banking structure had evolved in the second half of the 19th century that was capable of satisfying the demands of business and society, which had increased massively compared to pre-1848 times, thereby making possible Switzerland's transformation from a developing country to a nation of research and industry.

Before the middle of the 19th century, the conditions necessary for the flourishing of a Swiss insurance industry did not exist.[16] In the pre-1848 Confederation, there were a large number of provident societies in the form of regional or company-based cooperative health funds and widows and orphans funds, some of whose origins dated back to the 16th century. The financial resources of these funds largely stemmed from legacies and gifts, with some money also coming from public subscription. Yet these institutions were more a late form of Medieval welfare foundations than private-sector insurance companies.

It is easy to see that the small size of the economic areas circumscribed by cantonal borders and the labile political conditions that increased the fragmentation of power formed decisive obstacles to the establishment of modern Swiss insurance companies. The lack of access to the sea made keeping up with developments in transport and foreign trade occurring in coastal nations difficult, while demographic imbalances and differences in mentality between the various cantons were detrimental to concepts of insurance and obstructed inter-cantonal business dealings. An understanding of the balancing of risks is a fundamental condition for the concept of insurance, and such an understanding did not develop in Switzerland before 1848.

The first private insurers to take up the business in Switzerland were foreign contents insurance companies in the 1820s. From 1830 onwards, French companies began to offer life insurance. The first Swiss private insurer was the Bernischer Hagel-Versicherungs-Verein (Bernese Hail Insurance Association), which was founded in 1825. Up until 1857, only three other private insurance companies were founded in Switzerland, two of which – like the Hagel-Versicherungs-Verein itself – had to be liquidated soon after their establishment. The Schweizerische Mobiliar-Versicherungs-Gesellschaft (Swiss Contents Insurance Company, commonly known as the "Mobiliar"), founded in 1826, represents the exception and is still in business today.

From the 1850s onwards, the new industrial society with its leading textile and machine-building sectors triggered a rapid increase in the demand for insurance. While large-scale manufacturers, factory owners and tradesmen were the initial focus of the quickly evolving insurance market, soon the labour force and social welfare issues excited its interest. Insurance coverage for factory workers was a fundamental concern of large-scale industry and led to the introduction of measures to prevent accidents. Many industrialists saw themselves as their workers' patrons and as such considered themselves responsible for their well-being. The powerful development of tourism and the growth of the middle class in the last quarter of the 19th century also produced a situation conducive to the evolution of new forms of insurance in Switzerland.

The political, economic and social factors that made possible the brilliant development of the young Federal State went hand in hand with a rising demand for insurance benefits. Yet despite these favourable conditions, the insurance industry in Switzerland was not yet fully established. Two points appear of central importance here: the first, that incisive events could be influential for the shaping of the insurance sector and insurance products; and second, that the impulses of pioneers in the field were indispensable for progress. Catastrophes like the Great Fire of Glarus in 1861 opened the way for new ideas. This firestorm triggered important progress in the insurance business and led to the founding of numerous private companies, as well as to improvements in the insurance already offered by existing cantonal agencies. Personalities like Johann Conrad Widmer (1818–1903) (Rentenanstalt),

Moritz Grossmann (1830–1910) (Helvetia, Swiss Re), Heinrich Rieter (1814–1889) (Winterthur), and John Syz-Landis (1822–1883) and Carl Abegg-Arter (1836–1912) (Zurich) played pioneering roles in the development of the industry. Alongside Alfred Escher (1819–1882), who recognised the importance of the Swiss insurance industry for the independence of the country as hardly any other politician did, these pioneers shaped the founding histories of their institutions and thereby contributed to their development into international leaders in the insurance business.[17] And in contrast to the commercial banks that have since become the major banks of our time, the large Swiss insurance companies were founded without substantial foreign participation.

The development of modern public limited companies and well-funded businesses would not have been conceivable without a well-developed financial sector. While the banks primarily served as suppliers of the capital necessary for the establishment and operation of businesses, the insurance companies delivered a less tangible but equally important commodity: security. Without the possibility of hedging against the most various business risks, many a pioneer of the founding generation would probably not have dared to take the decisive step towards the founding of his business, or else would have gone bankrupt in its early days.

The local embeddedness of the original pioneer businesses is remarkable. Despite their changing palette of products, and in some cases enormous growth, many companies remained largely loyal to their original locations. This tenacity, which contrasts sharply with the rapid changes in headquarters that take place today, was not the result of considerations of short-term profit. This essential feature of Swiss economic history is seen not only among the giants of the financial, pharmaceutical and watchmaking industries but among niche players as well – for example, the Schnorf brothers' vitriol factory, founded in 1818, which today belongs to Chemie+Papier Holding AG. In contrast to the chemical firms in Basel, which concentrated on premium specialty products, the Chemische Fabrik Uetikon (Uetikon Chemical Factory) – so called after its incorporation in 1899 – continued to produce basic chemicals. It maintained its position as the largest – and soon the only – producer of vitriol in Switzerland up until the turn of the millennium. It maintained continuity, in part, by remaining based in Uetikon. From a purely economic point of view, this location was disadvantageous, at least in the latter half of the company's history. After the company had stuck it out for over a century, however, it was no longer able to buck the tide; rising cost pressures due to international competition and the necessity of inexpensive production conditions led to the closing of operations at the firm's original location.

The shifting of authority and responsibilities between the federal government and the cantons and between the state and private business occurred in a number of sectors. Post and telegraph services were already in the remit of the public sector during the early days of the Federal State, while the authority to grant railroad concessions lay with the cantons, as per the Railway Act of 1852. The building and operation of train lines were in the hands of private enterprise. This changed in 1872 with the new Railway Act, which, in accordance with the spirit of the times, transferred licensing authority to the federal government. Then, in 1902, implementing a decision taken by the Swiss electorate in 1898, the four major private railways became the Schweizerische Bundesbahnen (Swiss Federal Railways, SBB). In a single blow, 2,375 kilometres of rail lines were nationalised. Subsequently, most of the previously privately run standard- and narrow-gauge lines, as well as the tram lines, were either transferred to the remit of the public sector or were placed indirectly under its control. Today, with a few exceptions like jubilee and heritage lines, private industry only operates mountain railways and cable cars.

The nationalisation process reflected the political and structural development of the Federal State from the middle of the 19th century to the outbreak of the First World War and thus illustrates the zeitgeists of successive periods. First came the awakening, characterised in the young Federal State by dynamism and a belief in progress, a "Spirit of '48" that inspired economically liberal forces to take on risks in order to accelerate development. Next, from the 1870s onwards, there occurred a balancing out between political forces, the vitalisation of popular sovereignty, democratisation, and the emergence of political parties, associations and interest groups. The federal government was now firmly established, able to cope with large-scale projects and responsibilities. It was financially healthy, important infrastructure had been built, the railway network had been developed and a rail link through the Alps had been realised. The time was ripe for centralisation and nationalisation.

These processes also affected the finance industry. It is true that certain cantons had already established publicly controlled savings banks and mortgage banks in the 1830s. These laid the foundations for the earliest cantonal banks, which were established in Bern (1834) and Vaud (1845). From the 1850s onwards, this trend intensified: In response to the founding of industrial and commercial banks, new (semi-) public-sector banks and cooperatively organised savings and loan institutions were founded in many cantons. Between 1850 and 1858, there was a first wave of new cantonal banks, and by 1914 no other country, with the exception of Germany, boasted as many state-run credit institutions. These were typically founded with the goal of advancing land credit and creating inexpensive mortgage opportunities, thereby aiding both farmers and the commercial and mercantile middle classes. Nationalising tendencies were temporarily halted when the project of a central note-issuing bank was scrapped in 1897. In 1907, a semi-public national bank was founded. By 1918, due to increasingly close ties to the Federal Council that developed during the war years, this national bank had become nothing more or less than the central bank that, a few years previously, had been considered a nightmarish option and rejected in a referendum. It became the central reservoir of money in Switzerland and is responsible for bank rate policy.[18]

With the creation of the Federal State, a phase of development began that led to private insurers taking on important insurance branches: fire, life, transport, reinsurance and finally also accident and liability insurance. The most important type of insurance in the first half of the 19th century was fire insurance. Interestingly, the decisive impulse for the creation of a systematic arrangement came from the Frick Valley, which had become part of Switzerland in 1803. Before then, under Austrian rule, residents had been insured against fire by a public fire insurance organisation. Now, in the new Canton Aargau, they pushed for the establishment of a compulsory state building insurance institution, which was realised in 1805. By 1812, similar institutions had arisen in 13 other cantons. These public service providers limited themselves to the insurance of buildings, leaving the more difficult insurance of contents to private enterprise. Coverage for natural disasters was initially not even up for discussion. These public fire insurance agencies were compulsory monopolies: All buildings were required to be insured by them under legally prescribed terms, conditions and rates. In contrast to the later practice of private insurers, these public institutions usually worked with a system of flat premiums. It is notable that these cantonal fire insurance institutions became models for insurance institutions in a number of US states.

Like private fire insurance, contents insurance in Switzerland was originally offered by foreign companies. In the mid-1820s, almost a dozen companies – most of them French – insured Swiss household possessions and movables. The cantons at first refrained from offering fire insurance for contents, as doing so would have served more a private than a public interest. In the 19th century, in fact, only two public contents insurance institutions were founded, one in Vaud (1849) and the other in Glarus (1895). The Schweizerische Mobiliar-Versicherung, founded in Bern in 1826 and the oldest surviving private insurance company in Switzerland, offered insurance for household possessions. It was organised as a co-operative, or, as one said at the time, as a "mutual institution with joint liability among members" (gegenseitige Anstalt mit Nachschusspflicht).

In the night from 10 to 11 May 1861, Glarus, the capital city of Canton Glarus, was reduced to ashes and rubble by a huge conflagration. The damages amounted to some 10 million francs. The cantonal building insurance was hit with claims totalling 3 million francs but had only half a million in its reserves and was thus incapable of covering all the damages. The state had to step in. The Great Fire of Glarus provided the stimulus for the foundation of a number of private contents insurance companies that operated across cantonal borders and focused on fire damage. Due to the difficulty of calculating the risks involved, these usually took on the then-novel form of public limited companies. The transport insurer Helvetia, founded in St Gallen in 1858, would have been able to provide fire insurance according to its statutes but left this line to its sister company, Helvetia Fire Insurance, which was founded in 1861, also in St Gallen. In 1863, a fire insurance company was founded in Basel, also as a public limited company. Subsequently, other fire insurance companies were founded, some with regional orientations. The only cantonal building insurance institution that was dissolved in the 19th century was the one in Geneva (1865). In 1900, there were a total of 17 cantonal monopolies. Efforts to establish a contents insurance institution at the federal level at the start of the 20th century came to naught.

While building insurance was publicly regulated and based on monopolies and compulsory participation, contents insurance remained in private hands. Several attempts to nationalise fire insurance for contents were unsuccessful. Transportation insurance and reinsurance, fields that began to emerge in the mid-19th century, were also left to the private sector. The companies active in these areas, along with those offering fire insurance, dominated the Swiss market in the non-life sector.

In the last quarter of the century, pioneering companies like Zurich and Winterthur made a name for themselves with novel products in the areas of accident and liability insurance. By 1900, these two insurers had become market leaders in the non-life sector, surpassing the contents insurers. In 1910, for example, more than half of the premiums for non-life insurance paid in Switzerland were for accident and liability products. Winterthur and Zurich also provide examples of Swiss insurance companies that expanded into foreign markets at an early stage. They were soon earning more than half of their non-life insurance premiums outside of Switzerland – by 1910, as much as two thirds.

Even though discussions of public accident insurance took place somewhat later in Switzerland than in Germany and other countries, they were well underway by the 1880s. In the new political climate of direct democracy – which had been established by the Federal Constitution of 1874 – and with nationalised insurance systems prevalent in neighbouring countries, private insurers feared that they would be increasingly supplanted by public agencies and soon rendered superfluous. The situation came to a head for the flourishing private companies in 1885. The federal government was then in the process of developing a national authority to oversee the insurance industry, the Federal Insurance Office (Eidgenössisches Versicherungsamt). Moreover, the Federal Council had been charged with examining the possibility of introducing a generalised workers' insurance. Soon concrete plans were on the table that horrified the executives of private insurance companies. But things did not develop as quickly as they had feared. While the Swiss electorate approved the anchoring of obligatory health and accident insurance in the

Federal Constitution in 1890, in 1900 they rejected the corresponding law (Lex Forrer). Thus, the actualisation of the constitutional obligation was delayed. This allowed the private insurance companies to seek out new areas of business. Finally, in 1912, after heated discussions that had lasted more than a quarter of a century, the new health and accident insurance law was approved in a referendum. Switzerland thus became one of the last countries in Europe to ratify a public social welfare system – a system that would subsequently become one of its signature features. Still, with the establishment of the Schweizerische Unfallvericherungsanstalt (Swiss National Accident Insurance Fund, Suva) in Luzern in 1918, accident insurance was largely taken out of the hands of private insurers. That they were later able to make up for their substantial losses through the gradual expansion of their foreign operations and through individual accident insurance was but cold comfort.

Alongside fire and accident insurance, the federal government also attempted to develop public pension schemes during the second half of the 19th century. Motions aimed at establishing a pension fund for federal employees came to naught in Parliament in 1866/1867 and in a referendum in 1891, but in the end SBB and government employees did obtain pension funds, in 1907 and 1921, respectively.

Between 1848 and 1914, the state's entrepreneurial activities were modest. Canton Vaud owned a salt mine in Bex, and the other cantons co-owned the Vereinigte Schweizerische Rheinsalinen (United Swiss Rhine Saltworks). The manufacture and sale of gunpowder was made a federal business by Article 38 of the 1848 Constitution. As a consequence, a number of private powder mills were nationalised. This process developed into a bizarre and long-drawn-out affair in the case of the powder mill in Chur, which had been founded in 1842 by Peter Theodor Marin (1818–1864). Marin left no stone unturned in defending his business against nationalisation. In 1849, his complaint even reached the Federal Council. But in 1858, he was forced to admit defeat. His business became a national production site and, like many other powder mills, was greatly expanded during the First World War.

The state's role in forestry was more significant. Around two thirds of the forested area in Switzerland had for centuries been owned by municipalities and corporations, just under 30 percent was privately owned, and the small remainder – the so-called national forest – belonged to the cantons. The Federal Constitution of 1848 did not mention the management of forests. In the 1874 Constitution, however, the federal government was granted the right to supervise the forestry authorities in the high mountains, and this led to the creation of a federal supervisory forest inspectorate. The state was also involved in agriculture, as the proprietor of agricultural schools, prisons and individual foundations, and as the owner of cantonal and municipal vineyards. Although it possessed a commercial monopoly in the Alcohol Board, the federal government did not act in an entrepreneurial capacity. It is striking that the budgets of the early Federal State did not include any outlays on behalf of agriculture. The first items of this kind came in 1860 and totalled 6,120 francs; after this, the amount continued to increase until 1883, when, in connection with the National Exhibition, an interim maximum of 278,000 francs was paid out. The average outlay between 1860 and 1884 was around 57,000 francs per year. In the last decade of the 19th century, the outlays increased further and quickly approached a million francs. These were the circumstances in which the Federal Resolution of 21 August 1878 was issued, establishing a federal trade and agriculture department within the Federal Council.

The provision of electricity at first lay almost completely in the hands of private businesses. This was especially the case in Ticino, in western Switzerland and in other regions that were supplied by the Centralschweizerische Kraftwerke ("Central Swiss Power Plants"). The rest of Switzerland was provided its electricity by public operations or hybrid firms. In 1910, three fourths of the electricity supply was still entrusted to private operations.

Cultural policy was a secondary concern in the early Federal State. While in other countries support for the arts was used as a means to promote state interests, a comparable practice hardly existed in Switzerland.[19] Federal support for the arts was negligible. In 1860, as one of the first measures taken to support the arts, the federal government awarded an annual contribution of 2,000 francs to the Swiss Arts Association (Schweizerische Kunstverein). In the 1820s and 1830s, it was said that the nation had neither the inclination, the desire, nor the financial means to support the arts, and this attitude did not change with the advent of the Federal State. The Federal Constitution only marginally touched on cultural matters.

This may at first glance seem surprising, since the modernising impulses of progressive forces might have been expected to extend to this area as well. In principle, the Constitution offered certain possibilities for federal support of the arts: Article 2 addressed the fostering of communal welfare, and Article 21 empowered the Federal Council to establish and support public works. The head of the Department of Home Affairs, Stefano Franscini (1796–1857), made reference to these articles when, in 1849, he attempted to promote artistic exhibitions. He proposed to his colleagues on the Federal Council that they budget an outlay for the arts and sciences. The Department of Finance, however, forestalled the move, pointing to the sovereignty of the cantons in cultural matters. Cultural policies could not be priorities of the young Federal State – so the Department – because its monies were all tied up in economic, military and university-related commitments. The proposal would fragment the state's financial capacities and would, in particular, endanger the realisation of the planned federal university. Besides, a cultural politics at the federal level would invert the idea of federalistic power-sharing. Nor did the 1870s bring a climate ripe for federal cultural policies, as the so-called cultural battle (Kulturkampf) between Catholic-Conservative and Liberal-Radical camps was reopening old wounds.

Against this background, it is understandable why federal support for the arts was extremely modest for more than three decades following the founding of the Federal State. The fact that the building of the Polytechnic was itself a daring artistic project does not alter this fact. In its support – or lack thereof – for cultural activities, the Federal Council acted without a clear policy. In 1859, it held firm to the idea that it would not support the arts and sciences by subsidising artists and scholars. Yet the following year it helped finance the acquisition of various works of art, effecting exactly the opposite policy. Its cultural policies were also not well thought through when it supported the erection of monuments or the hosting of national or international exhibitions, without having established any general principles to govern such support. In short, the federal government's cultural policies were characterised by sporadic individual measures and actions taken without a conceptual basis.

Support for the arts at the cantonal level was a different story. Here, a model developed that is still effective today, involving a synergy of private and public support. This model was exemplified in the 19th century by private individuals who financed the establishment of museums, like Jeanne-Françoise Rath (1772–1856) and Jean-Henriette Rath (1773–1856), the daughters of a watch merchant who bequeathed to the public a mansion in Geneva to be used for exhibitions; Gustave Revilliod (1817–1890), who founded the Ariana Museum, also in Geneva; the painter Marc-Louis Arlaud (1772–1845), who paid for the construction of a museum in Lausanne with his private fortune; and the architect Gottlieb Hebler (1817–1875), who endowed a museum in Bern. Private engagement for public museum operations took on other forms as well, such as contributions to public art collections, for example through the donation of works of art or through financial gifts for the purpose of acquisitions. At the end of the 19th century, a further form of public engagement on behalf of the arts emerged: the establishment of non-profit foundations. Among the pioneers in this area was Lydia Welti-Escher (1858–1891), who placed the Gottfried Keller Foundation at the disposal of the federal government in 1890. This well-endowed instrument might have been used to expand the national art collection, as well as to enhance federal policies in support of the arts. But the chance went unexploited. The federal government squandered the opportunity offered by the foundation through a lack of strategic orientation, mismanagement and political horse-trading.

The 1880s were the decisive decade for cultural policies in 19th-century Switzerland. Essential decisions were taken in this decade that provided a foundation for federal support of cultural activities. The Federal Resolution on the Support and Elevation of Swiss Art (1887) established a state credit for acquisitions, made possible national art exhibitions and founded the Swiss Art Commission. This phase was concluded in 1891 with the decision to establish a national museum in Zurich.

The "founding epoch" (Gründerjahre) in Swiss economic history was characterised by the presence and influence both of entrepreneurial pioneers and of family businesses with roots that in some cases went back generations. Never before in Swiss history, however, had such a comprehensive, profoundly structured and delicate interplay of politics, trade, industry, transport, banking and insurance developed as during the early years of the Federal State. In the 1850s and 1860s, under the conditions created by representative democracy, an epochal dynamic built up that unleashed the emergence of modern Switzerland. The socio-economic and political elite, which had become wealthy in trade or in the engineering or textile sectors, now began to exploit the economic opportunities that arose in the 1850s – for example, by investing in railroad companies, banks and insurance firms, or through sitting on their administrative boards. Beyond this, by taking on operational leadership roles, they drove the system towards peak performance. In the young Federal State, a small number of individuals, mostly from the greater Zurich area, brought important areas of the economy under their control while simultaneously occupying the corridors of political power. Their influence was immense. To be sure, the great railway lines built in the 1850s and thereafter, which were financed both by the newly formed Swiss commercial banks and by foreign capital, facilitated the import of raw materials and the export of industrial products and were indispensable for Switzerland's infrastructural awakening. But the individual contributions of industrialists, investors and capitalists to this economic success were also significant. To illustrate: The owner of a trading company or an entrepreneur in the field of engineering who contributed with his own capital to the building of a railway line or the founding of a bank at first profited from the expansion of the transport network. Now he used the bank he had invested in for financial transactions conducted by his own business. In order to guarantee the insurance protection that had become necessary for trade and industrial production, he invested in the founding of a transport insurance company through his bank. He then insured the transport activities of his company through this insurance company. In order to close any gaps, representatives of the thus-formed network of trading or engineering companies and banks and transport insurance companies founded a reinsurance company, to which the transport insurance company could turn for backing. In this way, all of the affected entrepreneurs, institutes and companies profited from the rapidly unfolding potential for synergy. At the same time, the continually intensifying transfer of knowledge drove further economic development. And finally, the small circle of founders, thanks to its political contacts and offices, was in a position to influence the framework within which commercial activities took place so that, for example, legislation was more liberally oriented, customs barriers were set aside and favourable trade agreements were signed.

Figure 2.3 Landesmuseum Zürich, ca 1900. Photograph. Zurich, Baugeschichtliches Archiv der Stadt Zürich (Architectural History Archive of the City of Zurich).

From the 18th century onwards, Switzerland developed into a stomping ground for art hunters of all kinds. Old art was a particular focus. Important Swiss glass paintings crossed the border and found their way to the manors and castles of English, Scottish and German nobles. Whole collections, as well as innumerable individual panes, were snatched up by art brokers. Not only private individuals but also public institutions and even state bodies failed to recognise the worth of their treasures and often sold them at give-away prices: porcelain, relics, choir stalls, world maps, broadsheets – even entire staterooms. This selling off of art began to be increasingly criticised in the early 1880s, and a Federal Resolution was promulgated in 1886. The Federal Council had recognised the need for measures to curb the incessant sale of antiquities and artworks. Yet it refrained from setting out a workable concept and instead only addressed peripheral issues. National Councillor Salomon Vögelin's (1837–1888) proposed national museum thus seemed to be off the table. But then, in an early 1888 editorial published in the *Neue Zürcher Zeitung*, Heinrich Angst (1847–1922) made the case for constructing a museum in Zurich.[20] Angst had correctly assessed the political situation; he argued that whichever city could present a suitable facility would have the artistic treasures that had been acquired by the federal government bestowed on it. And soon, Bern, Basel-Stadt, Lucerne and Zurich had thrown their hats into the ring. A phase of manoeuvres and intrigue followed, in the vein of "Give us a seat on the Federal Council, and we will let you have the national museum." Such was the political horse-trading in which Catholic-Conservative parliamentarians from Central Switzerland and lobbyists from Zurich engaged. Out of this wrangling, the City of Zurich emerged victorious in 1891 – precisely the year in which Josef Zemp (1834–1908) of Lucerne took a seat on the Federal Council as the very first representative of Catholic-Conservative Switzerland. The opening of the museum, whose location was tellingly only a stone's throw from the newly built Catholic Liebfrauen church, followed in 1898.

The Social Profile of the Pioneers

The pioneers were a diverse cast of characters, and the typical pioneer cannot be painted with a few broad brushstrokes. This is not surprising, when one considers their widespread and multifaceted areas of activity.[21]

The pioneers came from all social classes. The idea that the overwhelming majority of them were men does not entirely correspond to reality and is partially due to stereotypes and research bias. That pioneers were well educated may be generally true but was not always the case. Practical knowledge often stood in for formal education. The question of religious denomination is a dicey one; the pioneers were not all Protestant, and deficiencies in education cannot be attributed solely to religious practice but are more deeply rooted. Though some pioneers had military careers, their number is small. The number of pioneers who were immigrants, however, is striking. The pioneers of the second half of the 19th century tended to be active in politics, where they were principally involved with economic policymaking. As politicians, they shaped the framework of their own business environments. They were politically engaged at the municipal, cantonal and federal levels. The interweaving of business and politics was an essential factor in the success of the young Federal State.

In the first half of the 19th century, pioneers in the textile and engineering industries were able to develop their businesses especially well in the Greater Zurich Area. But it is not the case that Zurich was predestined by an especially important economic history or a particularly favourable location on centuries-old trading routes to become Switzerland's leading research and finance centre nor, indeed, to become the economic engine of the entire country. Rather, the economic and political cards were dealt anew after 1848. Zurich became the most important hub of the new means of transport, the railway. Then, a couple of decades after the founding of the university, the Polytechnic opened its doors. Industry, commerce and trade were more quickly and efficiently served on the banks of the Limmat than elsewhere due to Zurich's modern banking and insurance institutions. That Zurich's infrastructure developed in this way was a result of decisions that were taken after 1848, and in which Alfred Escher played a leading role.

Many pioneers founded businesses. Often they were not lone warriors but worked together congenially. That certain pioneers once or even repeatedly met with failure in their firms and products is just as often attested to as are unbroken success stories. That some pioneers understood how to learn from foreign enterprises or role models, and tested out already proven practices under Swiss conditions, should not diminish their accomplishments in expanding their horizons and optimising imported products, goods and services.

That many pioneer enterprises survived for generations is an astonishing phenomenon. Problems of succession often arise both in family businesses and in corporations and can lead to tailspins during generational changes within a firm. Alongside such internal obstacles, external factors in the economic and political environment can be existentially threatening. The durability and stability of many of the pioneering firms founded in the 19th century are all the more impressive when compared with current statistics: Of the 37,317 companies founded in Switzerland in 2013, for example, only 61.7 percent were still in existence in 2016.[22]

That the 19th-century pioneers were predominantly men has to do with the gender roles of the time, and how they played out in politics, business and the wider society. The patriarchal order in Switzerland as a whole was especially tenacious. Accordingly, no women left their mark among the pioneering founders of the key watchmaking, textile, engineering, metal and finance industries. The tourism sector, however, was an exception. As much as men are generally celebrated as pioneers in this branch – for example, as hoteliers – it is clear that their wives were also involved in their businesses. This is because reception, accommodation and service were compatible with the female gender roles of the time. That these female pioneers were not recognised as such, either by their society or, for a long time, by later researchers, is partly due to the fact that women were constrained to work in the background. Based on how the hotels were actually run, Katharina Seiler née Cathrein (1834–1895) and Marie-Louise Ritz née Beck (1867–1961) should have found admission to the ranks of renowned Swiss pioneers alongside their husbands, the hoteliers and businessmen Alexander Seiler (1819–1891) and Cäsar Ritz (1850–1918).

And yet there were also female pioneers who emerged as personalities in their own right, and are recorded as such in contemporary documents. For example, Gertrud Riggenbach-Landerer (1792–1855), the mother of the railway pioneer Niklaus Riggenbach, was the founder and proprietor of the colonial goods shop "Riggenbach zum Arm" in Basel; Anna Pestalozzi née Schultheiss (1738–1827), who was largely responsible for the financial investments and bookkeeping of her husband Johann Heinrich Pestalozzi (1746–1827), single-handedly cared for institutionalised children and was director of the school in Neuhof in Canton Aargau. Other women made their pioneering contributions in fields of activity thought more appropriate for their gender. Rosette Niederer-Kasthofer (1779–1857) was a teacher and the director of Pestalozzi's School for Daughters, while Elise Rupp (1790–1873) was a patron of women's and women teachers' education and the founder of a girls' school in Sarmenstorf. Emma Stämpfli-Studer (1848–1930) is remembered as a patron of day-nurseries. Susanna Orelli-Rinderknecht's (1845–1939) influence is still felt today; in 1894, together with a group of other women, she founded the Zurich Women's Association for Temperance and Public Welfare (Zürcher Frauenverein für Mässigkeit und Volkswohl), which became a flourishing enterprise. Marie Sollberger (1846–1917) was active in a similar field. In Herzogenbuchsee, she founded a Blue Cross association and a treatment centre for women with addiction. In 1868, Marie Heim-Vögtlin (1845–1916) became the first Swiss woman to enrol in a Swiss university; she earned her doctorate in 1874 from the Medical Department of the University of Zurich. Together with Anna Heer (1863–1918), she founded the first women's clinic in Switzerland, with an affiliated school for female nurses. These enterprises were at first managed exclusively by women. The career path of Emilie Kempin-Spyri (1853–1901), the first woman to earn a law degree at the University of Zurich, was also pioneering. Since she was not allowed to practise law in Switzerland, she emigrated and founded her own law school in New York, at which she also taught. The University of Zurich was the first university in Europe to admit women to regular courses of study; as a result, many foreign women, especially Russians, came to Zurich to study. Kempin-Spyri is representative of other Swiss women who made history abroad but have mostly been forgotten in Switzerland.

Lydia Welti-Escher (1858–1891), who grew up in a man's world, also played a pioneering role. After the death of her formidable father, Alfred Escher (1819–1882), she attempted to live out her passion for the arts but met with failure. Out of the ruins of her tragic life, however, an arts foundation emerged, and Lydia Welti-Escher included among its purposes the support of further education and independence for women. In doing so, she propagated her understanding of the equal rights of men and women, which she had experienced as a matter of course in her dealings with business leaders, politicians and artists in her youth. What had worked in her earlier life, however, completely miscarried in her relationship with her husband and in her contacts with the Federal Council. Neither met her as an equal; instead, they tore to shreds the "ideas of a woman."[23] Yet even intrigue and power politics could not stop Lydia Welti-Escher from making history as a pioneer of Swiss support for the arts; in 1891, she founded the Gottfried Keller Foundation.

That the pioneers were largely Protestant is often divorced from all context and asserted as axiomatic. In fact, however, the issue of religious denomination was deeply connected with processes that transformed the economy and the wider society in the 19th century. The railways defined anew which areas would be central and which peripheral. It was the rail routes that determined where industry would set roots and where local commerce would boom. Because of this, the Protestant city of Zurich became the Swiss economic metropolis in the second half of the 19th century. Other cities in Eastern Switzerland also profited from industrial development, particularly in the engineering and textile industries. Winterthur, Schaffhausen and the rural Zurich Oberland were Protestant home territory, or at least shaped by Protestantism. Seen in this light, it is not surprising that most industry pioneers were Protestant – not because the Catholic population had fewer talents and competencies or a different work ethic but because a significant Catholic population simply did not exist in the Greater Zurich Area until well past the middle of the 19th century. The financial sector presents a similar situation: The commercial banks, which began to be founded around the middle of the century and were indispensable for the economic development of Switzerland, were located especially in the predominantly Protestant cities of the Swiss Central Plateau. Where railway stations were built and trains ran, and where banks and insurance companies were founded, there industry, trade and commerce flourished. And the governing boards of these public limited companies always recruited new members from the same circles.

That there were Catholic as well as Protestant pioneers is evident from the development of tourism infrastructure. For if the local hotel pioneers in the Bernese Oberland were, of course, Protestant, so those in Central Switzerland and Valais were Catholic. Who was more successful as a pioneer in the hospitality industry of the 19th century than Alexander Seiler and Cäsar Ritz, both Valais Catholics? Or let us consider health tourism: The pioneers in Leukerbad were, as could be expected, Catholic, while in Stachelberg in Canton Glarus and in Scuol in the Engadine, they were Protestant. And if in Heiden, in Canton Appenzell Ausserrhoden, they were Protestant, so were they Catholic in Weissbad in Canton Appenzell Innerrhoden.

The theory that pioneering activity is somehow a Protestant virtue was given the lie early on by the enterprising Valais clergymen who authored their own chapter of Swiss tourism history. Among these pioneers was Josef Imseng (1806–1869) of Saas Grund. The naturalists and alpinists who arrived in the Saas Valley in increasing numbers in the first half of the 19th century took their lodgings in Imseng's parish house.[24] Imseng soon recognised a business opportunity. He attempted to create a bond between the foreign visitors and his valley and became a pioneer of tourism. On his initiative, the residence of Franz Andenmatten in Saas Grund was rebuilt; it opened in 1850 as the *Hotel Monte Rosa*. The mayor and Imseng's fellow clergymen, for whom the profane activities of the tourism-priest were a thorn in the eye, attempted to have him relocated by the bishop. But Imseng stuck to his course. In 1857, he built the *Berggasthof Mattmark* and initiated work on the *Hotel Monte Moro* in Saas Grund, as well as on an inn at Huteggen.

Imseng died in 1869. The circumstances surrounding his death have not been completely cleared up to this day, although they were the subject of contemporary judicial proceedings. What seems sure is that Imseng fell into Lake Mattmark while returning from the *Gasthaus Mattmark* to Saas Grund. The locals wondered whether this accident was due to a heart attack or whether Pastor Imseng was the victim of a crime.

In Zermatt, too, the parish house offered the only lodgings for foreign visitors up until the early 1850s. In 1854, the Zermatt parish priest, Joseph Ruden (1817–1882), had no qualms about realising his innovative ideas in the sphere of worldly commerce: He built a 17-bed inn on the Riffelberg. The onslaught of British visitors soon overwhelmed the inn's capacity. As nature-lovers of all kinds increasingly joined alpinists in the village, the priest began to showcase herbariums, minerals and beetle collections, and to lead botanical excursions.

The discrepancy in educational levels between the denominations was also largely a matter of location. While in several Protestant cities of the Central Plateau universities and universities of applied science were already operating by the middle of the 19th century, there were no such institutions in the predominantly rural and Alpine Catholic regions. The first university in a Catholic canton opened in Fribourg in 1889. Still, even in knowledge-intensive branches of the economy, there was no lack of Catholic pioneers. The civil engineer Karl Emanuel Müller (1804–1869) of Uri made transport history with his roads and bridges and attracted international attention with his road over the Gotthard Pass in 1830, the Catholic pioneers Richard Theiler (1841–1923) and Adelrich Gyr (1843–1928) of Einsiedeln founded the future multinational company Landis & Gyr in Zug in 1896, and the Old Catholic Carl Franz Bally (1821–1899) was the founder of the eponymous footwear factory in Schönenwerd. The pioneers, then, were not exclusively Protestant.

The young Federal State of 1848 was dominated by Liberals and Radicals. The presence of business heavyweights in the Swiss Parliament meant that conditions favourable to industry, trade and commerce would remain in place. In view of this interweaving of business and politics, it is natural that most of the pioneers in the Greater Zurich Area in the second half of the 19th century were economic liberals. Yet it is not difficult to locate conservatively oriented pioneers in other regions. Hoteliers again provide a case in point. The idea that innkeepers generally thought and acted in line with a Liberal or Radical politics is incorrect. Examples of hoteliers from Conservative milieus include Melchior Britschgi (1830–1904), who ran the *Hotel Pilatus* in Alpnach and was a member of the Cantonal Parliament and the Government Council of Canton Obwalden, and Michael Truttmann (1833–1905), innkeeper of the *Sonnenberg* at Seelisberg, who was a member of the Cantonal Parliament and the Government Council of Canton Uri. Julius Eberle (1839–1907) presents an interesting case: son of the Conservative Axenstein hotelier Ambros Eberle (1820–1883), he married Anna Fassbind (1853–1892), daughter of the Liberal hotelier Fridolin Fassbind (1821–1893) of the *Walstätterhof* in Brunnen. His father Ambros was a member of the Cantonal Parliament and the Government Council of Canton Schwyz, as well as a National Councillor.

The permeable social structures of the liberal Federal State present a characteristic that still distinguishes Switzerland today. Swiss bourgeois society was significantly more egalitarian than those of the neighbouring monarchies with their hierarchies of nobles and officers. The educational policies of the liberal cantons, too, with their comprehensive compulsory schooling and the vocational training opportunities they offered to relatively broad segments of the population, paid little heed to students' origins, even in the 1830s. In addition, censorship, professional prohibitions and other governmental obstacles were little known in Switzerland, and what did exist in this vein was largely eliminated in 1848. All of this meant that brilliant minds could more easily develop business ideas and put them into practice in Switzerland than elsewhere in Europe. One did not necessarily have to come from a "reputable household" or even a "good family" to succeed in life. Movement up the social ladder might still founder on societal barriers in certain locations, particularly in cities shaped by patrician traditions such as Bern, Lucerne, Fribourg, Solothurn and Basel, where a socially well-defined group of rich bourgeois families made up the upper class. It was generally true, however, that pioneers could come from all social classes. Some big businessmen and industrialists came from wealthy families, while others were born into modest circumstances or even poverty.

Alfred Escher, for example, came from a highly influential and once-respected Old Zurich family, which had, however, fallen from grace. When Robert Schwarzenbach (1839–1904) took over his father's silk-weaving mill, it already boasted over 100 employees and a history of pronounced growth – a comfortable starting point from which to develop the business into one of the world's largest textile companies after the turn of the century.

Among the pioneers with less privileged beginnings was Gustav Adolf Hasler (1830–1900). Without any financial means of his own, he began his career as an assistant at the Federal Telegraph Workshop (Eidgenössische Telegraphenwerkstätte), only to lead the Workshop, in a few years' time, to worldwide prominence as a private company. Hasler's telephones became the measure of all things. He was granted an honorary doctorate from the University of Bern in recognition of his telegraphic water gauge, and Hasler speedometers were standard equipment on the fleet of SBB trains for decades and are still used by the SBB today.

Bernhard Simon (1816–1900) also belongs in this category. He came from a Glarus shoemaking and small-farming family. He attended school irregularly, and for no more than six years. As a 19-year-old, he left home to work as an apprentice painter and plasterer with his uncle in Lausanne. He used the small amount of money he was able to save to study mathematics and geometry. He then realised his dream: After a stint in Paris, he arrived in St Petersburg and enrolled in the St Petersburg Academy of Arts. Simon became an architect. His sketch of a new bridge over the Neva awakened the interest of Count Tatischev, who hired him to enlarge his residence. Other aristocratic clients followed. Simon became a star.[25]

Due to health problems, Simon returned to Switzerland after 15 years abroad. In the mid-1850s, he was involved in the take-off phase of the private railways. First, he worked on the railway project in Eastern Switzerland, especially the line from Rorschach over St Gallen to Winterthur.

On failing to achieve his goal of being appointed operative director of the United Swiss Railway (Vereinigte Schweizerbahnen), he turned to entrepreneurship and investment. He built a residential area near the St Gallen train station (1859–1862) that still bears his name today, and with the *Quellenhof* hotel (1869) and other facilities he transformed the small farming village of Ragaz into an internationally renowned spa. After the horrific conflagration in Glarus (1861), Simon was involved in planning the reconstruction of the city. His contributions there, as well as a number of other architectural works in Switzerland, still attest to his talent today.

Foreigners who sought refuge in Switzerland for economic, political or religious reasons could also count on the openness of Swiss society. Immigration of this kind peaked in several different periods. In the 1830s, when certain cantons adopted liberal constitutions, many political refugees settled in Switzerland. Among them were two German authors who came to occupy very different places in literary history. The first was Georg Büchner (1813–1837), who found refuge in Zurich, where he conducted research in comparative anatomy and worked on his play *Woyzeck*. In 1836, he received his doctorate for his study of the nervous system of the common barbel. He died young, in 1837, leaving *Woyzeck* unfinished. The second author, Georg Herwegh (1817–1875), studied theology and law. He was a colourful figure whose poems about class warfare in emotive and martial language survived in socialist milieus for a time and experienced a revival in East Germany. Today, however, he is no longer well known. He is buried in Canton Basel-Landschaft.

Figure 2.4 Albert Anker (1831–1910), *Dorfschule von 1848* (*The Village School in 1848*), 1895/1896, oil on canvas, 104 cm × 175.5 cm. Private collection, Switzerland. Reproduction with courtesy of the owner.

Figure 2.5 "The old gymnasium in Zurich," ca 1850. Coloured engraving. Zurich, Zentralbibliothek Zürich.

The old gymnasium (upper-secondary school) of Zurich served as the school building of the Polytechnic from 1855 until it moved into its new facilities in 1864. The University of Zurich was located at the Fröschengraben from 1833 until 1864. From the beginning, it was staffed primarily by foreign – primarily German – professors, who made up more than half the faculty up until the 1870s. Its first director was Lorenz Oken (1779–1851), a scientist from Bohlsbach in Baden. A comparable development took place at the University of Bern, whose first director, the colourful legal scholar Georg Wilhelm Snell (1789–1851), was from Hessen. Important German scholars were active in Switzerland even prior to 1848, among them the physician Johann Lucas Schönlein (1793–1864), who contributed significantly to the construction of the new cantonal hospital in Zurich (1842). The trend became more pronounced in the 1850s, however, because of the series of failed revolutions (1848/1849) and the founding of the Polytechnic (1854/1855). Although the new wave included scholars of all disciplines, an increasing number of professors of mathematical, technical and scientific subjects now came to Switzerland to work at the Polytechnic, where they promoted new directions in research. In this way the academy made an essential contribution to the awakening of Switzerland after 1848. For while Theodor Mommsen (1817–1903), a great scholar of Roman archaeology, did not feel at home in Zurich and characterised the "Athens on the Limmat" as a nest of owls – and soon left the University – there were also a series of personalities who stayed on: from Rudolf Clausius (1822–1888), one of the founders of thermodynamics, to Pompejus Alexander Bolley (1812–1870), whose research on textile dying, textile printing and yarn spinning technology was of outstanding service to the Swiss textile industry, to Georg Lunge (1839–1923), whose work was valuable for the soda industry and tar processing. There were also many other notable professors who instructed the legion of engineers, architects and geologists that the country so desperately needed in the course of its modernisation.

Foreign pioneers in Switzerland, like the Frenchman Alexander Clavel (1805–1890), the Pole Norbert de Patek (1812–1877) and the German Heinrich Nestlé (1814–1890), laid the foundations for future global companies. Towards the end of the 1840s, a wave of political refugees entered Switzerland. Among the thousands of German immigrants were artists and academics – such as Richard Wagner (1813–1883) and Gottfried Semper (1803–1879) – as well as entrepreneurs and other colourful figures who would leave their marks on Switzerland. Conrad von Rappard (1805–1881) belongs to the latter category. He purchased the Mariafeld estate on the right-hand shore of Lake Zurich, founded microscopical institutes in Zurich and Bern, and ran the *Kurhaus Jungfraublick* in Interlaken and the *Hotel Giessbach* on Lake Brienz, as well as a screw steamer to provide access to the latter. Von Rappard is an example of a political refugee who has a place in Swiss tourism history.

It would be easy to gain the false impression that immigration to Switzerland in the 19th century was purely a matter for international revolutionaries. But in fact foreigners came to Switzerland in all periods and for various reasons: Georg Wander (1841–1897) of Osthofen, Germany, worked as a research assistant in the chemistry department at the University of Bern; he went on to transform a mineral-water plant into a chemical and analytical laboratory, thereby laying the groundwork for Wander AG and its most successful product, Ovomaltine. Charles Page (1838–1873) and his brother George Page (1836–1899) of Palmyra, USA, settled in Switzerland in 1865/1866 and found conditions ripe for building up their Condensed Milk Company. Charles Brown was one of many English engineers who settled in Switzerland in the course of the 19th century and contributed to the boom in the engineering and electrical industries. Academics, too, showed growing interest in Switzerland, as is evidenced by the large numbers of foreign professors at Swiss universities and at the Polytechnic. Among these were great names in a variety of disciplines. They founded academic schools with their research, developed landmark theories and sometimes even became Nobel Prize winners. Other immigrants worked in the fields of education and training or were active in business or politics.[26]

The immigration of professionals from the most varied countries suggests how attractive Switzerland had become on the international stage. Its transformation from a backward agricultural country to an important locus of industry, service and research was in fact possible largely due to the know-how and initiative of immigrants. Yet the awakening of Switzerland after 1848 is not only the result of the work of specialists, brilliant intellectuals and creative entrepreneurial pioneers. The innumerable private and public buildings and especially the large-scale infrastructural projects that became symbols of modern Switzerland – such as the Gotthard train line –would not have been possible without foreign construction workers.

Figure 2.6 Albert Anker (1831–1910), *Der Geometer* (*The Surveyor*), 1885. Oil on canvas, 67.5 cm × 97 cm. Private collection.

The Nation Needs Topographers

In the beginning were the topographers. The construction of road and rail networks, bridges and tunnels, cog and cable railways required exact measurement of the mountainous Swiss landscape. Dependable measurements of altitudes and distances formed the foundation for the expansion of infrastructure; without the precise surveying of the country, there could have been no progress. In 1854, the Swiss mathematician and astronomer Jakob Amsler-Laffon (1823–1912) invented the polar planimeter for the measuring and plotting of surfaces. In 1857, he introduced another invention, the pivoting spirit level, for the measurement of altitude differences. Together with his son Alfred Amsler (1857–1940), he invented other measuring instruments that allowed for the most varied and refined calculations – measurement parameters that were indispensable for the formation of industrial Switzerland and the development of a modern society.

Looking back, we can see that Switzerland boasts a long cartographic tradition. The first Swiss maps, the work of the Zurich city doctor Conrad Türst (1450–1503) and the Glarus historian and statesman Aegidius Tschudi (1505–1572), were based on estimates and drawn without technical measuring procedures. A 1667 map created by Hans Conrad Gyger (1599–1674) and his Zurich surveying school became the standard for almost 200 years. Only with the work of Guillaume-Henri Dufour

(1787–1875) and his school was Gyger's map surpassed in precision. Surveying and cartography developed further in the 18th century. In 1785, Johann Georg Tralles (1763–1822) initiated his geodesic work as professor of mathematics and physics in Bern. A foundation for further work was laid in 1798, when weights and measures were standardised in Paris. Tralles was at hand. When he returned to Bern, he carried prototypes of the metre and the kilogram in his luggage. Ferdinand Rudolf Hassler (1770–1843), one of Tralles's students, began increasingly independent work in the field. The times were ripe: The Helvetic Republic (1798–1803), which was driven by a mania for documentation, promoted the collection of data, maps and all available topographical documents. The country was to be measured to its most remote corners. But the Republic expired after only five years, and Hassler emigrated to the USA with his family. He became a professor at West Point Military Academy and made his name as a pioneer of coastal measurement.

As soon as the country had been surveyed, construction could begin. Roads were among the first public works projects. Franz Ludwig Pfyffer (1716–1802), who rose to fame and fortune as a lieutenant general for the French military, was tasked with the reorganisation of the street system in Lucerne. His chief topographical work, completed in 1786, was a large-scale relief of Central Switzerland, which can be found today at the Glacier Garden in Lucerne. The Frenchman Nicolas Céard (1745–1821) engineered the construction of the Napoleonic road over the Simplon Pass. Other public infrastructure construction depended heavily on preceding topographic work: for example, the Linth Canal, which was based on the plans of Hans Conrad Escher von der Linth (1767–1823), or the correction of the Jura waters, which was based on the overview map drawn by Johannes Oppikofer (1782–1864), one of the best surveyors of his time.

It was not only new maps that advanced the development of topography – drawings and reliefs also did their part. Marc-Théodore Bourrit (1739–1819) crafted a horizontal circular panorama for de Saussure's *Voyages dans les Alpes*. Escher von der Linth's drawings of Alpine mountain landscapes represent another topographical highlight. Joachim Eugen Müller (1752–1833) left a legacy of over 1,000 panoramas and mountain drawings, as well as innumerable reliefs. Heinrich Keller (1778–1862) made Swiss topographical history with his map of Switzerland (1799), his early panoramas (e.g. from the Rigi, 1804) and his travel map of Switzerland (1813).

The works of the *Kleinmeister* also contributed to the development of a national topography. Jean-Antoine Linck (1766–1843) stands out from the crowd in this respect. His coloured outline etchings of the area around Geneva and his Alpine vistas of the Simplon, Jura and Gotthard regions are impressive for their geological precision. Caspar Wolf (1735–1783) left his unmistakable artistic mark somewhat earlier. The photographic precision of his mountain motifs is astounding. Wolf's work fulfils documentary purposes even today, aiding in the comparison of 18th-century landscapes with current ones. Wolf serves as a reliable witness, especially as regards the growth and shrinking of glaciers. The next step in the development of landscape and Alpine painting, the use of elevated perspective, led to a new artistic surveying of Switzerland. François Diday (1802–1877) gained international recognition in this area.

Johann Rudolf Meyer (1739–1813) was a man of many and diverse commitments: He was President of the Helvetic Society (Helvetische Gesellschaft), initiated the correction of the Linth River and launched the first survey of the Alps, which he financed with his own means. He commissioned a relief of the Swiss Alps (1790/1798) and the "Carte Générale de la Suisse" (1802), which was one of the best cartographical representations until the Dufour map became available. Meyer's patronage extended to Swiss traditional costumes, which he commissioned the painter Joseph Reinhart (1749–1824) to document in drawings. His pioneering spirit was inherited by his two sons. Following in their father's footsteps, they became notable alpinists.

Jean-Frédéric d'Ostervald (1773–1850) also supported cultural projects, for example the large-scale, 35-panel album *Voyage pittoresque de Genève à Milan par le Simplon* (Picturesque Journey from Geneva to Milan via the Simplon, 1811). This became famous not least due to the true-to-life drawings of Lory *pére* and *fils*. D'Ostervald was a colourful figure who began his career as a merchant, became an engineering topographer and later held the rank of major general. With the first topographical depiction of Neuchâtel (1801/1806), he even aroused international attention. He was emulated by others, like Johann Rudolf Amstein (1777–1862), who produced the first map of Graubünden in 1806.

Natural history research also formed a basis for the development of a national topography. Significant topical networks sprang up, and these led to the formation of new organisations across the country. In the 18th century, physical and natural history societies were already being formed in various locations in Switzerland, among them Zurich in 1746. Henri-Albert Gosse (1753–1816) was involved in the Geneva Association, which was founded in 1791. He was the driving force behind the 1815 founding of the Swiss Society of Natural Sciences (Schweizerische Naturforschende Gesellschaft), which was the first of its kind in Europe and a unique platform for exchange among naturalists.

In terms of academic study, however, Switzerland suffered from a certain deficit. Because up-to-date opportunities for training and research leading to a degree did not exist for many disciplines – particularly in the area of the natural sciences and mathematics and technology – the only option was to study abroad. While it is true that, for example, natural history was already being taught at the Academy in Bern in 1805, it was only in 1818, in Basel, that a Swiss university chair in natural history also gave instruction in chemistry and physics. Its founding professors were Peter Merian (1795–1883) and Christoph Bernouilli (1782–1863).

Swiss researchers already enjoyed international recognition in the 17th and 18th centuries, as their memberships in foreign academies and court circles attest to. How can this be explained, given that Switzerland had no research institutions at the time? The answer is to be found in the above-mentioned societies, which began to be established in Switzerland in the mid-18th century. Since they were open to everyone who was passionate about their subjects, these associations brought together interested laypeople and specialised researchers. Around the turn of the 19th century, other important scientific institutions were established, in the form of botanical gardens and natural history museums at various locations in Switzerland. These took as their models the oldest Swiss botanical garden, which was established in Basel in 1589; the natural history collections of the Benedictine monasteries, which dated back to the Late Middle Ages; and later collections in the Jesuit colleges.

The initiatives of Augustin-Pyrame de Candolle (1778–1841) set the course for the establishment of future scientific infrastructure. In 1817, de Candolle opened an academic museum in Geneva, as well as a botanical garden that set new standards with its plants from around the world. Natural history collections were subsequently assembled in both large and small towns in Switzerland. They existed not only to provide leisure activities for wealthy circles but also to promote the study of the natural world. As was true of the botanical gardens that were laid out in several cities before the mid-19th century, such collections were privately owned but open to the public.

These developments in the field of the natural sciences assumed a remarkable direction in the last quarter of the century. To please tourists, botanical gardens were created in locations outside of cities: the Botanical Garden of Canton Ticino on San Pancrazio Island (1885); the La Linnea Alpine Garden on the north side of the Saint Bernhard Pass, at 1689 metres' elevation – the oldest Alpine garden in the Western Alps; the La Thomasia Alpine Garden at the foot of the imposing rock face of the 3000-metre-high Grand Muveran (1891) in Canton Vaud; La Rambertia (1892) above Caux, named for the writer Eugène Rambert (1830–1886); and the Alpineum on Schatzalp (1907). Enclosures for wild animals were also built in the second half of the 19th century, such as the Langenberg Animal Park (1869) and the Basel Zoo (1874).

Developments in topography called for ever more precise measurement procedures, and technological innovation was required to provide them. The Frenchman Jacques Paul (1733–1796), who settled in Geneva and became a Genevan citizen, constructed the first Swiss theodolite. His workshop also produced high-precision scales. Others followed in his footsteps, building devices such as hair hygrometers, wind gauges and altimeters. Among the commissioners of these instruments in the late 18th and early 19th centuries were the most important scientific alpinists, including de Saussure.

The name Kern is associated with an impressive manufacturing workshop. Jakob Kern (1790–1867) at first mainly produced drawing instruments, following in the footsteps of Louis Esser (1772–1826), the founder of the Aarau Drafting Instruments company (Aarauer Reisszeugfabrikation). Kern worked as an apprentice for Esser. In 1819, he established his own modest workshop in Aarau and worked there with a single assistant. In addition to drafting instruments, Kern soon developed other tools: water gauges, scales, air pumps and camera obscuras. The surveys that were carried out all over Switzerland starting in the mid-1820s were decisive for the growth of Kern's company. The theodolite that Kern built for a survey carried out in Thurgau was especially important. With it, the firm made a name for itself far beyond the Aarau cantonal borders. Dufour, who ordered several of Kern's theodolites, heaped praise on his instruments.

The collaboration with Dufour, the quartermaster-general of Switzerland who was responsible for the trigonometric survey of the country, began in the early 1830s. Kern's company was commissioned to repair an instrument that had been destroyed by lightning on Säntis. At the same time, he was to replace its sexagesimal scale with a centesimal one. It was a particular honour for Kern that Dufour also ordered a 12-inch theodolite for the Swiss Topographical Bureau (Eidgenössische Topographische Bureau). In the 1850s, Kern's sons, Adolf (1826–1896) and Emil (1830–1898), joined the business. A new factory was built, and the number of employees increased to 148. Kern instruments were in demand as never before, for without them the railway lines could not be built. The same was true of the small- and large-scale tunnel constructions that were being initiated throughout the country. Kern instruments were used in the Mont-Cenis, Gotthard, Simplon and Lötschberg Tunnel projects.

There is no doubt that progress was underway on various fronts in the field of topography in Switzerland. The considerable number of topographers who emerged over the years ought not to disguise the fact, however, that their work was neither systematic nor nationally coordinated – the only exception being during the brief intermezzo of the Helvetic Republic. Not much changed in this respect in the early 19th century, despite the fact that individual cantons created departments that oversaw specific kinds of infrastructure, and larger cities had chief builders and municipal architects who supervised the construction and maintenance of public buildings. Only in the 1830s did a concerted topographical effort get underway, notably in those cantons that had adopted modern constitutions. Now streets were built, rivers channelled, water sources exploited and swamps drained. For these public works projects, state institutions were conceived, and corresponding jobs created. At this point, topography again became a prominent field. In Zurich, for example,

Heinrich Pestalozzi (1790–1857) was appointed street and waterworks inspector and director of the topographical survey of the canton. In Canton Aargau, the East Prussian Ernst Heinrich Michaelis (1794–1873) was appointed director of surveying. Michaelis had developed his skills as a graphic artist working under Alexander von Humboldt (1769–1859). In 1826/1827, he travelled through the Swiss Alps making barometric altitude measurements. The Michaelis map (1849) of Canton Aargau would serve as a basis for the Dufour map.

That the Swiss Society of Engineers and Architects (Schweizerische Ingenieur- und Architekturverein, SIA) was founded in Zurich in 1837, and that Pestalozzi was its first president, appears a logical consequence of the liberal phase of modernisation occurring at the time. It is similarly unsurprising that one of the most prominent engineers in the field of public infrastructure, the Graubünden native Richard La Nicca (1794–1883), was among the society's founders. La Nicca, who had been the chief cantonal engineer of Graubünden since 1823, campaigned for the channelling of rivers, supervised the upgrading of the Graubünden pass roads and would soon make a name for himself with plans for a transalpine rail link. That trigonometric surveys became increasingly important in Switzerland in the 1830s, and that Hans Conrad Finsler (1765–1839) energetically initiated the surveying of Eastern Switzerland, also corresponded to the zeitgeist and the structural needs of the time.

In 1838, the Swiss Topographical Bureau was established by Major Dufour, who hired Johann Jakob Goll (1809–1861) as its first employee. This national organisation was an exception in the pre-1848 Confederation. The explanation for the early date of its founding lies in the Swiss policy of neutrality, which was recognised by the great powers at the Congress of Vienna (1815). In order to cement this policy, a federal army composed of cantonal contingents was created in 1817. In 1832, Dufour became quartermaster-general of the Confederation. It was in this military-political context that he initiated the triangulation of Switzerland – a massive undertaking carrying with it the most varied challenges: technical, logistical, financial, physical and psychical. Equipped with expensive instruments, the surveyors made long and taxing journeys through Switzerland. Even in pathless terrain, they had to find suitable positions from which to make their measurements. Dependent on the support of locals with knowledge of their areas, they experienced diverse and wide-ranging receptions, which often revealed much about the cultures and mentalities they were working among. Particularly in isolated mountainous areas, the appearance of a surveyor was not necessarily met with in a welcoming manner. New technology was suspect, and activities on behalf of the centralised state were often less than appreciated.

The topography itself was also a source of great difficulty. Reaching the triangulation points, which by their very nature were at the highest and most exposed locations, required wearisome and difficult climbing on the part of the surveyors. Besides technical competence and a fine touch for dealing with the local populations, they also had to have mountaineering skills at their command when at work in the High Alps. They had to carry their heavy instruments to hard-to-reach locations in all kinds of weather. Particularly in winter, in conditions marked by cold, snow and storms, the work was extremely challenging.

An accident that occurred at the beginning of July 1832 triggered a powerful response in the media. The surveyor Anton Joseph Buchwalder (1792–1883) and his assistant, Pierre Gobat, had been occupied with triangulation work in the Säntis area for several days. On the morning of 5 July 1832, the weather quickly took a turn for the worse, and the two found themselves exposed to an approaching thunderstorm without any shelter. Gobat was struck by lightning and died. Buchwalder was injured but succeeded in pulling himself together and descending to Gamplüt in Toggenburg, where he was helped by herdsmen. Such occurrences further exacerbated the already dubious image of surveyors.

The triangulation work was concluded in 1837. Dufour subsequently founded a private topographical office in Carouge in Canton Geneva, which was taken over by the Confederation the following year. The first sheets of the so-called Dufour map bore the numbers XVI and XVII and depicted Vevey/Sion and Geneva/Lausanne. When they were first sold in the 1840s, they were met with astonishment. At the 1855 Exposition Universelle in Paris, the Dufour map was awarded a gold medal of honour. In 1864, the prominent German cartographer August Petermann (1822–1878) dubbed it "the most exquisite map in the world."[27] The Dufour map truly set new standards.

The same is true of the *Topographical Atlas of Switzerland* (Topographischer Atlas der Schweiz), which was published in 604 sheets between 1870 and 1926. Dufour's successor Hermann Siegfried (1819–1879) was responsible for the drawing of the maps. The Atlas's contour lines were a novelty; they depicted altitude differences and features of the terrain more precisely than the hachures of the Dufour map. The representations of cliffs became world-famous for their geological precision.

Leonz Held (1844–1925) also won acclaim as a topographer and cemented the position of Swiss cartography at the top of world rankings. Having worked as a topographer for the Swiss Topographical Bureau since 1872, he became its provisional director in 1901. From 1903 to 1920, he was the Director of the newly founded Department of National Topography (Abteilung für Landestopographie). He is known as a pioneer in the field of precision altitude measurement and had wall maps produced for schools – in particular, a new 1:100,000 scale map of Switzerland that was completed in 1914. Held is also remembered as the creator of a hiking map of Flims Waldhaus that is considered a tour de force.

The tourism industry, too, took up the new maps. In order to be useful for travellers and hikers, maps had to be available in suitable forms, and map-publishers now began to crop up to provide them. In Switzerland, Gottfried Kümmerly (1822–1884) and his studio became well known for printing the Siegfried map. Gottfried's son Hermann Kümmerly (1857–1905) continued the studio's work and was widely recognised for his relief map of Evolena/Zermatt/Monte Rosa, a trailblazing work that, thanks to its rich colour spectrum, accentuated contrasts in the terrain particularly clearly. Starting in the 1890s, street maps, particularly for bicyclists, became available in many places. Some of these provided indications of distances and changes in altitude. The Men's Bicycle Club of Zurich (Männer-Radfahrerverein Zürich) published a street map in 1890 and was among the pioneers in this field. Kümmerly+Frey developed street maps for the Touring Club Suisse (TCS) that were designed for both motorists and bicyclists. After the turn of the century, automobile maps became products in their own right. Kümmerly+Frey became known to another, even larger audience with its 1:200,000-scale school wall map of Switzerland, a fixture in Swiss schoolrooms for generations. Kümmerly+Frey still publishes maps today, as a division of Hallwag AG.

Engineers: Switzerland as Construction Site

Political and institutional conditions fundamentally changed with the establishment of the Federal State, and Switzerland set off on an undreamt-of new beginning. Buildings large and small were soon shooting out of the ground like mushrooms. The new infrastructure transformed the country in a very short time; indeed, in the second half of the 19th century, Switzerland was built anew. This rapid transformation would have been unthinkable without the foundation provided by topographical work. Yet Switzerland was not built on the basis of cartography alone. Additional competencies and materials were required.

The new start was astonishing. The colossal building activity that began in the new Federal State lasted into the Belle Epoque and up until the outbreak of the First World War. Over 3,000 kilometres of standard-gauge and 1,000 of narrow-gauge track were laid during these years. Additional track was laid for seasonal mountain railways, cable railways and trains of the most diverse sorts serving local and tourist traffic, as well as for streetcars in the larger cities. The building of roads, which had experienced a pronounced upswing in the 1830s – particularly in the liberally oriented cantons – accelerated after 1848. By 1914, thousands of kilometres of streets and paths had been expanded or newly built, from large Alpine roads to cantonal and municipal streets to access roads for new neighbourhoods and hiking and walking trails.

These two large transport systems – roads and rails – could only function thanks to hundreds of tunnels, bridges and viaducts. The face of the country was also changed by innumerable private and public buildings, residences, magnificent villas and workers' quarters, factories and commercial buildings, banking and insurance palaces, schoolhouses, slaughterhouses and museums, hospitals and homes, asylums and prisons, gas and electricity works, barracks and sewage systems. The volume of construction is reflected by the total value of insured buildings, which more than tripled between 1850 and 1880. In Canton St Gallen, for example, the total value came to around 105 million francs in 1851 and some 325 million in 1878. The increase in the number of hotels and inns was equally impressive. There were about 1,000 hotels and restaurants in 1880; in 1913, there were no fewer than 3,600. The number of beds climbed correspondingly, from 58,000 to over 170,000. The number of overnight stays varied from one location to the next, sometimes rising continuously and sometimes increasing in leaps and bounds. In Lucerne, for example, overnight stays rose from 308,000 in 1895 to over 575,000 in 1910. Peak values like these, typical of the fin de siècle, were not reached again in many locations until the 1950s. And all these visitors, who were soon arriving from all over the world, not only generated employment in Swiss holiday destinations but also demanded a wide variety of platforms and facilities for cultural and athletic free-time activities.

An unprecedented amount of money was invested in public and private building in Switzerland from the middle of the 19th century until the outbreak of the First World War. This amount of construction, which seems gigantic even by today's standards, was only possible thanks to engineers. The new Switzerland that began to be built in the middle of the 19th century was their work.

The demands on the engineers were high. The construction of the railways, for example, required both expert technical knowledge and practical competencies. In Switzerland, these demands took on new dimensions due to the great number of bridges and tunnels that had to be conceived, planned and built to master the topographical complexity of the country. No other European nation placed such high demands on its engineers.

The railway engineers, who began to construct the Swiss rail network in the 1850s, at first came almost exclusively from abroad. While the construction of the Gotthard Tunnel, which began in 1872, was entrusted to the firm of a Swiss citizen, Louis Favre (1826–1879), the position of chief engineer was filled by the German Robert Gerwig (1820–1885) from 1872 to 1875 and then, until 1878, by the Austrian Wilhelm Hellwag (1827–1882). The position was only assumed by a Swiss engineer, in the person of Gustav Bridel (1827–1884), in the final phase of construction. When work on the Lötschberg Tunnel began in 1913, however, the chief engineers were mostly Swiss. In the second half of the 19th century, Switzerland became a country of engineers, a fact attested to by numerous pioneering achievements.

Several factors were important in this development. There had long been outstanding building experts in Switzerland, who met demanding topographical challenges with daring bridges and also excelled at building church steeples and other large-scale structures. One of these was Hans Ulrich Grubenmann (1709–1783). As the scion of a traditional family of carpenters, he became a master in timber construction. Especially famous were his Rhine bridges in Schaffhausen and Reichenau and the interior of the Wädenswil church. As was typical of the early Swiss engineers, Grubenmann had hardly any theoretical knowledge. It was experience, passed on and added to from generation to generation, that made possible the construction of complex structures, which in Grubenmann's case bear up even to modern methods based on rigorous calculation. It is also impressive that Grubenmann used neither too little nor too much construction material. His bridges would, for the most part, meet today's exacting standards. Regrettably, his principal works were destroyed during the French invasion in 1799.

The most demanding area of construction engineering was the building of tunnels. As a relatively new field, it involved a large number of unpredictable challenges. This was clearly the case in the construction of the Gotthard Tunnel, during which the tunnel itself, but also its long access ramps, continually presented the builders with fresh problems. The rock structure and the threat of inrushing water made for the principal natural dangers. No less complex, though, were the challenges of ensuring adequate air circulation in the tunnel and channelling out the water. Then the rubble had to be removed, and dynamite and equipment transported to the building site. Finally, the many construction workers – mostly Italian – had to be lodged and fed. Violent disputes and strikes were not infrequent. The challenges increased as more and more of the tunnel was excavated. The construction of the 15-kilometre-long Gotthard Tunnel had been thought by many to be an impossible undertaking. A daring Genevan tunnel pioneer, however, took on the challenge, and the result would be his crowning achievement.

The jump from craftsman to engineer was a crucial step in the career of Louis Favre. Favre's father ran a carpentry shop in Chêne-Bourg near Geneva, and Favre served his apprenticeship there. When he was almost 20, he went to Paris to join a construction firm. He gained recognition for his technical prowess during the construction of a bridge over the Marne in Neuilly. He subsequently received various commissions for work on the Paris-to-Lyon railway line, which he undertook while attending architecture courses and studying engineering on his own. He received commissions for railway stations as well as bridges and finally, beginning in 1855, for tunnels. His tender for the construction of the Gotthard Railway Tunnel between Göschenen and Airolo was lower than that of his closest competition by a year of building time and more than 12 million francs in building costs. Given the technical possibilities of the time, his offer did not seem realistic. Favre, however, was counting on rapid technological progress being made during the course of the work.

Construction began in 1872. The first delays soon cropped up. The stone of the Gotthard massif was different than had been expected, and the labourers were suffering. Diseases broke out in their squalid barracks but were ignored by the foremen. When the workers on the north side of the tunnel went on strike, the local militia was called in and approached the strikers with weapons drawn. Deaths ensued. Delays and the extra costs they gave rise to coincided with the great railway crisis of the 1870s. Supplementary financing was arranged, but only with great difficulty. And then, in 1879, Louis Favre died during an inspection of the tunnel. In spite of all these complications, the north-south breakthrough occurred on 28 February 1880, a month earlier than had been calculated.

That the Gotthard Tunnel was only finally opened about 15 months later than had originally been planned and agreed on is of little relevance; the opening could easily have taken place earlier, in the winter of 1881/1882.[28] It was postponed only because winter seemed a less-than-ideal time of year for the inauguration of the construction project of the century. When one figures in the delays caused by legal conflicts between Favre's company and the Gotthard Railway Company after his death, and the further delays caused by strikes, as well as the fact that not only Favre but also Escher, the leading executive driving the project, dropped out before it was finished, one cannot but conclude that the Gotthard Tunnel could well have been completed by 1880, the deadline specified in the contract.

It is only natural that very few pioneers had careers that took them, like Grubenmann and Favre, from craftsmen to star engineers. These two were prodigies. The construction of a national railway network, however, required a large number of capable engineers, and therefore also an appropriate training ground for them. With the founding of the Universities of Zurich and Bern in 1833 and 1834, respectively, liberal cantons were offering wide-ranging educational opportunities at the university level. And the founding of the Polytechnic in the young Federal State also created top-level educational opportunities, particularly in technical and scientific fields. Another platform would soon follow with the establishment of the Technikum in Winterthur. This, too, helped Switzerland become a country of engineers. Previously, Swiss students looking for a technical education had had to move abroad and study at foreign universities or else come by their knowledge as autodidacts. This was the case, for example, for the engineers who first advocated for and planned a Gotthard tunnel: Gottlieb Koller (1823–1900), Karl Emanuel Müller (1804–1869) and Pasquale Lucchini (1798–1892).

Lucchini, the eldest of the three, was originally a stonemason. He taught himself both foreign languages and technical expertise. Working as an assistant chief engineer in Austria, he demonstrated his abilities and deepened his knowledge. In 1844, he returned to Ticino where, as Cantonal Engineer, he executed numerous civil engineering projects, among them the dam at Melide. In 1853, he designed the southern ramp of a standard-gauge railway over the Gotthard, for which he envisioned a number of switchbacks and a 7.5-kilometre summit tunnel.

His pioneering spirit was evident in other fields as well; he built and operated a silk-spinning factory outside Lugano and was a co-founder of the Banca della Svizzera Italiana.

Müller, on the other hand, attended the Lyzeum in Solothurn after early schooling in Altdorf and then studied civil engineering and road and bridge construction in Heidelberg and Vienna. He returned to Altdorf in the summer of 1827 and soon took up work on the construction of the new road over the Gotthard Pass. As deputy construction supervisor, he was responsible for the section from Göschenen to Andermatt, where the greatest difficulties had to be overcome. Besides building the new Devil's Bridge, he enlarged the Urnerloch Tunnel to make the entire road navigable for coaches. The road was praised on all sides and turned the Gotthard into the shortest and most popular transit route over the Alps. Müller's second major road project was the Axenstrasse, which was built from 1862 to 1864.

Figure 2.7 "Federal Palace with Helvetiaplatz," ca 1905. Postcard. Photo credit: Burgerbibliothek Bern, Sammlung Hans-Ulrich Suter 448.

In 1848, at the time of the Federal State's founding, the Parliament Building (Bundeshaus) in Bern had not yet been built. The design competition was won by Ferdinand Stadler (1813–1870), one of the many important architects active in Zurich in the 19th century. He originally made his name in church construction; in 1847, he designed the Baden train station for the "Spanish Bun Railway" (Spanisch-Brötli-Bahn). Because the Bern City Council deemed that the next stages of planning for the so-called Federal Council House were not moving forward expediently, it decided to commission the project anew on the basis of an earlier design by the Bernese Architect Jakob Friedrich Studer (1817–1879). This design was realised, and the building was festively inaugurated in 1857.

In 1853, Müller was charged with designing the northern ramp of the Gotthard Railway, at the same time as Lucchini was planning the southern one. Based on his research, Müller recommended a ramp without cable haulage or switchbacks and a long tunnel between Göschenen and Airolo. His design came remarkably close to that of the final project, which was realised 19 years later. Until his death, Müller was a leading promoter of the Gotthard Railway, involved in both technological and political aspects of the project. But he too worked on more than the construction of roads and railways. He was involved in the channelling of the Reuss in Canton Uri, founded the Postal Steamboat Company (Post-Dampschiff Gesellschaft) on Lake Lucerne, contributed to the Vitznau-Rigi Railway and bought a paper mill in Horw and a sawmill in Isleten, which was later converted to a dynamite factory.

Finally, there was Koller. He studied in Paris, as there were no opportunities for study in Switzerland. He worked as a project engineer in railway construction in France and then, at the age of 27, was appointed to a position in the newly established Swiss Railway Office (Eidgenössische Eisenbahnbureau). For the rest of his life, Koller was involved in the Swiss railway project and especially with the transalpine rail link. He travelled across Switzerland with Robert Stephenson (1803–1859) and Henry Swinburne (1821–1855), collecting information and impressions for the first expert assessment of the railway project to be delivered to the Federal Council. As deputy chief construction engineer for the Swiss Central Railway (Centralbahn), he wrote an expert opinion comparing possible sites for the transalpine rail link, himself favouring the Gotthard option. Finally, between 1862 and 1872, in his role as delegate of the Gotthard Committee and later as a construction inspector of the Gotthard Railway Company, he contributed decisively to the building of the line.

Soon after its founding, the Polytechnic – the only federal university at the time – played a key role in the training of Swiss engineers. Robert Moser (1838–1918), for example, who took over responsibility for building the northern ramp in the late phase of the construction of the Gotthard Railway, was a graduate of the "Poly." The Swiss engineers behind the great Simplon and Lötschberg Tunnels, men like Alfons Zollinger (1852–1930), Ferdinand Rothpletz (1872–1949), Carl Fridolin Bäschlin (1881–1961) and Eduard Locher (1840–1910), were also graduates. Graduates of the Polytechnic also made history abroad. Maurice Koechlin (1856–1946) stands out among the Swiss engineers of the second half of the 19th century. In 1884, as research director of the Gustave Eiffel construction company, Koechlin conceived of a 300-metre-high-tower for the 1889 Exposition Universelle in Paris. He also worked out its structure in detail, though the tower would end up bearing the name of his boss, Gustave Eiffel (1832–1923).

The success stories of Polytechnic – later ETH – engineers extend into the 20th century. Othmar Amman (1879–1965), for example, was responsible for a number of large-scale bridges in New York, among them the famous George Washington Bridge over the Hudson River. Amman's constructions, which repeatedly set new world records, had a lasting influence on the field of bridge construction.

Kaspar Wetli (1822–1889) was an exception among Swiss engineers, for he did not attend the Polytechnic. After completing vocational school, he studied mathematics at the University of Zurich. He worked as a surveyor before being hired as engineer or chief engineer for several railway projects. He undertook field surveys for the proposed transalpine rail link over the Lukmanier Pass in the 1850s and was later involved in the Gotthard project. His role at the Wädenswil-Einsiedeln Railway, for which he developed a special cog system, however, led to a tragedy. The uphill test run of Wetli's system went smoothly, but on the downhill run the brake system failed, the train ran out of control and a fatal accident occurred. Some of the carriages derailed, while the locomotive reached the Wädenswil train station and flipped over.

The prodigious amount of construction undertaken in the young Federal State called for suitable job structuring. Engineers who went it alone were not able to master the immense challenges they faced. Larger teams and efficient engineering companies were necessary. Johann Jakob Locher (1806–1861), a builder, city councillor and major, founded Locher & Cie. in Zurich in 1830. Locher had acquired his technical expertise in Paris and Karlsruhe. He was soon working with the engineers Adolf Naeff (1809–1899) of St Gallen and Peter Olivier Zschokke (1826–1898) of Aarau. Their collaboration resulted in numerous weirs, bridges and roads, and in the 1850s they began to work on railway lines. After a restructuring of the firm in 1867, Naeff and Zschokke directed their own construction company in Aarau, while Locher's sons headed the original operation in Zurich. Under the leadership of Eduard and Fritz Locher, the company's reputation and esteem grew even beyond the Swiss borders. It was a leading player in the construction of the Simplon Tunnel. The third generation of Lochers were construction engineers with ETH degrees.

Stonemasons and Reinforced Concrete: The Mechanisation of the Building Trade

The changes in the construction industry in the early years of the new, post-1848 Switzerland can be seen in the development of the Zug-based company Landis Bau AG. Leonz Landis (1813–1878) took over his family's building operation in its fourth generation and transformed it into a well-organised construction company. He received commissions to build the Zug train station (1864) and city hall (1869/1873). Leonz's son Johannes (1860–1936) expanded the company. The boom in infrastructure projects, and especially the advent of an important new building material – ferroconcrete – resulted in an uptick in the building sector. Landis Bau AG worked on the railway line accessing the Gotthard from

Zug via Arth-Goldau and built a new Zug train station (1897), the Post and Telegraph building (1899/1902), the Theatre-Casino (1907/1908) and numerous hotels. Johannes Landis converted to Protestantism and shortly thereafter was commissioned to build the Protestant church in Zug. His career unfolded in a building industry that had to harmonise two different working rhythms: the pace of the stonemason and the significantly faster one of workers in concrete. At the end of the 19th century, Landis took a step towards mechanisation by purchasing cranes and other construction machines, which accelerated the pace of construction work even more.

While the Landis construction entrepreneurs in Zug made their name building prestigious infrastructure that became symbolic of a new and modern Switzerland, there were also pioneers who excelled in the construction of single- and multi-family housing. The boom in demand for these buildings was due to the sizeable increase in the Swiss population.

The Lenzlinger family in the Zurich Oberland was among the entrepreneurs in this sector. Johann Joseph Lenzlinger (1824–1900) of Mosnang in Canton St Gallen earned his keep as a travelling carpenter in the Zurich Oberland. In 1861, he married the widowed Margaretha Zollinger-Wäckerlin (1830–1917). They purchased a plot of land in Uster on which they built a house, a stable and a workshop. Only a few years later, the Lenzlinger operations expanded significantly. A new residence was built that lodged up to 20 journeymen. The Lenzlinger company profited from a boom in residential building in the Oberland that had been triggered by the flourishing textile industry and the new Glatttal railway line (1865). Lenzlinger, who was supported by his wife in the company's administration – she took care of correspondence and managed the bookkeeping – then partnered his construction firm with a sawmill. The couple's adopted sons, Johann Jakob Lenzlinger (1856–1945) and Johann Edwin Lenzlinger (1858–1927), joined the business in 1880 and expanded the sawmill and forestry operations. Thanks to this diversification, they profited from the golden years of the building industry during the Belle Époque, when single-family houses in chalet style came into vogue in Canton Zurich. The brothers, however, did not agree about which building material was the most promising. As a consequence, Johann Edwin established his own construction business in the city of Zurich, while Johann Jakob continued to specialise in chalet-style wooden constructions.

Businesses producing iron and concrete, which emerged as building materials in the last quarter of the 19th century, also contributed to the modernisation of Switzerland. Although Switzerland was largely dependent on imports of metal and other raw building materials, it nevertheless contributed significant pioneering achievements in metal production. In 1806, Johann Conrad Fischer (1773–1854) of Schaffhausen became the first person in continental Europe to produce crucible steel, which had advantages over other kinds of steel. Fischer began to alloy cast steel with other metals, which led to a considerable number of commissions from all over Europe. He made history with his so-called Fischer metal, a steel alloy with a third part of copper. His foundry at first remained an artisanal operation. The transition to industrial production occurred in 1864, under his nephew Georg Fischer (1834–1887).

The production of pig iron required blast furnaces, which had existed in Switzerland since the end of the Middle Ages. They were markedly improved in the 19th century, and Jura and Graubünden became centres of the metal industry. The most important ironworks was founded as a public limited company under the name "Ludwig von Roll'sche Eisenwerke" in 1823. It had its origins in the blast furnaces that Ludwig von Roll (1771–1839) had built in Gänsbrunnen and in Klus in the township of Balsthal. Von Roll also owned two foundries in Matzendorf and a hammer mill in Gerlafingen. By 1862, Von Roll's had become the largest ironworks in Switzerland. Numerous takeovers and restructurings ensued. Von Roll also diversified into agriculture and forestry, founded a public limited company dedicated to silk cultivation and was involved in the expansion of the two Hauenstein roads. He was not only an entrepreneur and business pioneer but, as an enlightened patrician, he also assumed political responsibilities. He was a member of the Solothurn government from 1798 to 1833, through every change in regime, and his basic orientation was towards community well-being rather than profit.

Iron and steel found a fitting partner in concrete during the second half of the 19th century. Up until the end of the 1870s, Portland cement, which had been developed in England in 1844, had to be imported to Switzerland. Domestic production was not of high enough quality. Rudolf Zurlinden (1851–1932) of Zofingen changed that. He recognised an opening in the market and the chances it offered. In 1882, together with two partners, he founded the cement factory Zurlinden & Co. in Aarau. In its first year of operation, the factory produced 2,160 tonnes of Portland cement; by the turn of the century, annual production had climbed to 42,000 tonnes. This powerful growth was aided by tariffs that were introduced on imported cement in 1884. In 1890, a second factory opened in Wildegg, and in 1897 the two operations merged under the name Jura-Cement-Fabriken Aarau-Wildegg AG to become the largest cement producer in Switzerland.

The success of the business was based on the marriage of iron and cement. Zurlinden built the first ferroconcrete bridge in Switzerland in 1890; it spanned the Wildegg factory canal in an elegant arc. In addition to running his own operations, Zurlinden was committed to supporting the industry in general. He was the secretary of the Swiss Association of Cement, Lime and Plaster Manufacturers (Verein schweizerischer Zement-, Kalk- und Gipsfabrikanten) and its untiring advocate, and contributed to the creation of a cement cartel when revenues stagnated due to overproduction in the 1890s.

Watches: An Early Swiss Trademark

The watchmaking industry was among the early heavyweights of the Swiss economy.[29] Its point of departure was Geneva, where, starting in the mid-16th century, the know-how of refugee Huguenot watchmakers merged fruitfully with the local goldsmithing trade. Its second birthplace was in the tributary valleys of the Neuchâtel Jura, where watchmaking began to develop towards the end of the 17th century. Whether religious refugees provided the impetus here as well is a matter of dispute. In any case, the watchmaking industry certainly did not arrive in Jura as the result of the expansion of Genevan businesses in the regular course of economic development. Unlike in Geneva, where wealthy watchmakers' products sold in the highest price range, watchmaking in Jura was a secondary source of income for peasants and comprised a form of cottage industry. Thus, the Swiss watchmaking industry has its origins in two completely different political and socio-cultural milieus.

It is typical of Swiss economic history that it was religious refugees who brought the specialised professional competencies required for the craft of watchmaking to Switzerland. It is also characteristic – and this is a Swiss strength – that impulses from abroad were taken up and then further developed in innovative ways. There were numerous instances in 19th-century Switzerland in which a branch of business dominated an entire city or region so that clusters and company towns were formed. This was the case with the watchmaking industry: Municipalities such as La Chaux-de-Fonds and Le Locle – others would join them later – developed into veritable watchmaking towns.

The first watchmakers in Geneva were craftsmen who plied their trade in small workshops. They independently produced and assembled all of the components of a watch. In the next phase, specialisation and the division of labour evolved. Engraving and making casings diverged to become two different professions, and further diversification followed. The transition to proto-industrial production first occurred in the Neuchâtel Jura, in whose remote tributary valleys free trade had been the rule since the 17th century – a contrast to the guild-dominated cities with their strict economic regulations. In these valleys, farmers also worked as craftsmen, building and repairing watches, especially in the winter months.

A legend tells of how Daniel Jeanrichard (1672–1741) of La Sagne in Canton Neuchâtel came to take up watchmaking on being asked by a travelling horse trader to repair his pocket watch, which had been made in London. At this, Jeanrichard is said to have set his mind on producing such watches himself. What is certain is that Jeanrichard set up a small watchmaking workshop in La Sagne, which he soon transposed to the Le Locle region. There he also trained his employees, organising his business according to his own needs. His historical significance lies first in the fact that he compartmentalised the production process and thereby created a proto-industrial mode of manufacture. While watchmakers and their apprentices had previously put together watches from A to Z in a small workshop, Jeanrichard established an atelier with numerous workers, each of whom was tasked with a specific step in the production process. Second, Jeanrichard's products spoke to a different class of customers than did the Genevan watchmakers', which were expensive decorative items for foreign consumers. The watches produced by Jeanrichard were simple and still fairly clunky. Thanks to the structured working process and their simpler designs, however, they could be produced more cheaply than the Genevan models. The number of Jeanrichard's customers visibly increased and soon included a local clientele of artisans, clergymen and government officials who would not previously have been able to afford such products. Jeanrichard distanced himself from the export market for luxury watches, leaving that business to the Genevans.

The production of the Genevan watchmakers was initially greater than that of their Jura counterparts. But the proto-industrial watchmaking industry in Neuchâtel would soon overtake the artisanal watchmaking trade in Geneva. A process was developed in Neuchâtel that would fundamentally alter production and transform the Jura into the centre of the Swiss watchmaking industry. While Jeanrichard's production process had been essentially factory-oriented – the entire process, from the production of parts to the selling of the merchandise, took place under one roof – the next phase saw the introduction of the profession of *etablisseur*. The *etablisseur* bought parts and mechanisms and arranged for them to be assembled into finished watches by home-workers and *termineurs*. He was also in charge of marketing his products.

There are records of several hundred watchmakers working in the northern Jura valleys in the mid-18th century, some of whom had international reputations. Among the most prominent were Pierre Jaquet-Droz (1721–1790), whose large clocks attracted notice in European courts, Ferdinant Berthoud (1727–1807), who made his name with maritime chronometers, and Abraham-Louis Breguet (1747–1823), who became one of the most important watchmakers of his time by inventing the tourbillon and the overcoil spring that bears his name. His fame was crowned by producing the world's first wristwatch, which was worn by Caroline Murat (1782–1839), Napoleon's sister and the Queen of Naples. The brilliant rise of the watchmaking industry in the Neuchâtel Jura from the middle of the 18th century onwards is evident in the statistics: In the early 1750s, more than 450 watchmakers were at work, while by the end of the 1770s, the number was more than 2,000, and in 1810, it was already almost 4,500.[30]

In Geneva, too, specialisation was unstoppable. There were 30 different professions that were involved in the manufacture of watches in 1778. By the end of the 18th century, up to 100,000 chronometers were being produced annually. In 1781, for example, 40,000 gold and 45,000 silver watches were manufactured, almost all of which were exported. Remarkably, at this point more than 10 percent of the population of Geneva was active in the watchmaking industry. This percentage subsequently increased even further: 4,000 out of 30,000 Genevans were involved in the industry in 1808. In the 19th century, there were even more professions related to watchmaking in the Jura than in Geneva. In 1867, in La Chaux-de-Fonds, there were no fewer than 54. The characteristic network of home- and factory workers, deliverers and dealers that would typify the watchmaking industry was now in place. The cities along the arc of the Jura mountains became a veritable cluster. The town of La Chaux-de-Fonds was described by Karl Marx (1818–1883) as, for all intents and purposes, a watchmaking factory. The watchmaking industry provided a model of a society completely based on the division of labour.[31]

While the area around Neuchâtel had already caught up to Geneva as a watchmaking centre by the end of the 18th century, in the 19th century it surpassed it completely. In the 1840s, more than 30 percent of the population worked in professions connected to the industry. Watchmaking expanded into the surrounding regions – to St Imier in the Bernese Jura, then further to Biel and on to Grenchen in Canton Solothurn – with breathtaking speed.

The development that the Swiss watchmaking industry underwent in the 19th century is impressive: It first established itself in Europe and soon attained the leading position in the world market as well. A number of factors contributed to this. Watchmaking schools saw to systematic training, while promotional organisations provided important impulses for research. Mistakes in construction were thus rectified, and new manufacturing procedures developed. The improvement of clockwork toothing was especially decisive for the industry's success. From the 1850s onwards, increasing numbers of flat watches were produced, and these proved popular; there were also important technical innovations, for example in the manufacture of chronographs. And behind all of these developments were inventors, pioneers and entrepreneurs committed to progress.

Among the preeminent events in the history of the industry was the advent of the mechanically produced watch. A number of developments made this innovation possible. Important impulses were provided by the Audemars watch dynasty, found by Louis-Benjamin Audemars (1782–1833). Louis-Benjamin's son, Louis Audemars (1808–1854), who was also an exceptionally gifted watchmaker, invented the stem winding. The improvements introduced by the watchmaker Georges Frédéric Roskopf (1813–1889) were equally trailblazing. By simplifying watches and reducing the number of their moveable parts, he lowered material and production costs. For this he was awarded a medal at the 1867 Exposition Universelle in Paris. But Roskopf's innovations had far broader implications: They led to the beginnings of serial production.

An important contribution to the industry was made by the mechanic Pierre Frédéric Ingold (1787–1878) of Biel, who invented a machine that made possible the post-processing of wheel teethings. Ingold's life, however, was marred by misfortune. Because his work did not meet with favour in Switzerland, he emigrated to England. There he aroused the anger of watchmakers who feared for their jobs, and consequently was refused permission to found his own company by the English Parliament. He next travelled to North America, where he also had no luck – on the contrary, he had to stand by and watch as other watchmakers exploited and profited from his inventions.

The lever escapement, developed by the English watchmaker Thomas Mudge (1715–1794), was definitively optimised when the Genevan watchmaker Georges Auguste Leschot (1800–1884) developed the so-called angle of traction for anchor palettes in 1825. Leschot became a notable pioneer in the field of watch assembly, developing many inventions to a point of technical maturity. Commissioned by the company Vacheron & Constantin, he invented various machines that were capable of producing specific parts used in watchmaking; the goal was to achieve the exchangeability of individual parts. He received indispensable support from Antoine Léchaud (1812–1875), who produced machine tools that Leschot needed in order to serially produce the lever escapement with his angle of traction. In 1848, Léchaud and his brother John (1815–1882) became independent producers of lever escapements. These were of such high quality that many Genevan watch producers used them. Leschot and Ingold, avant-gardists of Swiss watchmaking, gave the Swiss watchmaking industry a decisive competitive edge, since its main competition, primarily consisting of English companies, did not modernise as quickly.

It is remarkable that Swiss watchmakers had reached a technical level that permitted the exchange of individual watch parts three decades before US producers did. Yet the voice of the prophets went unheard in Switzerland, and the shock was the more profound when Swiss watchmakers had to acknowledge, in Philadelphia in 1876, that they had rested on their laurels for too long. The competition on the far side of the Atlantic, propelled by developments in the arms industry, had made breathtaking technical progress.

The various steps taken to modernise production techniques in the Swiss watchmaking industry in the 19th century improved the quality of watches and led to a decrease in production costs. Watches thus became increasingly accessible to ever broader segments of the population. In a larger context, increased automation led to machines taking over a number of tasks in watch production – exactly what workers in the English watchmaking industry had feared. Yet rationalisation and accelerated production processes led to a product that, technically improved and externally more attractive, sold in great numbers, and this in the end created more jobs: Swiss exports tripled from 3 million items in 1885 to 9 million in 1905, while the number of industry employees quadrupled from around 10,000 to 39,000.[32]

Some Swiss watchmakers were successful pioneers even outside of the watchmaking centres – Heinrich Moser (1805–1874) of Schaffhausen, for example. He began his career as a watchmaker in his parents' business. Then came internships in the heart of the Swiss watchmaking industry, in Le Locle and La Chaux-de-Fonds. At the age of 22 he moved to Russia, where he established a company that principally dealt in watches. In order to meet the large and continuously growing demand for Swiss watches in the tsarist empire, but also to achieve greater independence, he opened his own watchmaking factory in Le Locle. From St Petersburg he supplied the Russian and Asian markets, which no one before him had done. Moser exploited this situation with zeal and determination and soon dominated these markets. He travelled repeatedly between St Petersburg, Moscow, Kiev and Le Locle – and this at a time when none of the countries he passed through had a continuous railway network. In 1848, he returned to Schaffhausen a wealthy man, built a castle-like estate and promoted the industrialisation of his native city.

MILESTONE 2.2

10 May 1876

The Centennial International Exhibition in Philadelphia: The Profound Shock of Swiss Watchmakers

The Swiss watchmaking industry has a mercurial history. Successes and crises have succeeded one another across the years and decades. It is not at all obvious that watchmaking should have been among the most successful branches of the Swiss export economy for more than two centuries. And yet, the development of the Swiss watchmaking industry is illustrative of the development of the entire Swiss export industry, which has seen itself continually confronted with booms and economic slowdowns. The evolution of the Swiss watchmaking industry shows that even a branch that produces the best products in the world is not immune from dramatic financial slumps and, in addition, will always run the risk of being overtaken by technological developments, failing to keep pace with a rapidly modernising society, and thus ending up threatened in its very existence.

This doomsday scenario confronted the Swiss watchmaking industry in the final quarter of the 19th century. The successful watchmakers became cavalier and failed to implement necessary structural adjustments in their methods of production. They assumed that they would be able to simply box their way through a crisis and failed to recognise the need for decisive action. The fact that the industry did ultimately claw its way out of its troubles is illustrative of a dynamic that would repeat itself throughout Swiss economic history up until the present day – though not in all branches of industry. The textile and engineering industries, for

(*Continued*)

example, lost their positions as global market leaders in the second half of the 20th century. The watch industry remains a keystone of the Swiss export market even today, however, and the quality of its output is valued the world over.

What happened in the final quarter of the 19th century? Swiss watches had conquered market after market. In 1870, three quarters of the watches purchased the world over were made in Switzerland. Then, in 1876, the Centennial International Exhibition took place in Philadelphia. It was a wake-up call for the Swiss watchmaking industry. The Swiss watchmakers who had been sent to the USA realised that the American watch industry had surpassed their own, and returned home in shock. The US watches were just as good as the Swiss products, but they were less expensive. The discovery that the large US workshops used modern methods of production and not the pre-industrial putting-out system that was the norm in Switzerland was downright harrowing. The Americans created watches out of machine-made, interchangeable and mass-produced parts. Certainly, these had to be assembled by hand. Yet the watchmakers profited from this kind of production, whose great advantage was that individual components were finished to a precision of a tenth of a millimetre and so fit together perfectly and interchangeably. The painstaking fitting and reworking process (the so-called repassage) required in Swiss workshops was no longer necessary in the USA, and this decreased production costs. How had the American watchmakers made this leap forward? In fact, its origin lay in the American Civil War. The US watchmaking industry had profited from advances in mechanisation that had been achieved in the field of weapons technology.

Switzerland had lost its technological edge in watch production, and its watchmakers found themselves in an existential crisis. While there had been forward thinkers in Switzerland in the first half of the 19th century who had recognised the problem, they had gone unheard. The shock induced by the experience in Philadelphia was so profound that it triggered a dramatic turnaround – a change in thinking that one would not have thought the watch industry capable of – and a wave of industrialisation set in. Watchmaking in Switzerland was transformed from a cottage industry to a factory enterprise, serial production was introduced, and the increase in productivity was enormous. While watches did continue to be made in the out-of-the-way highlands of the Jura, production increasingly moved to the Central Plateau. In Biel and Grenchen two new centres of the industry emerged, both of which were connected to the railway. The change of mindset that took place in Switzerland after the exhibition in Philadelphia was clear to see:

From 1882 until 1911, the number of watch factories increased 12-fold, from 72 to 853. The challenges the Swiss watchmaking industry faced after the First World War no longer had to do with mechanisation; they were now related to sales.

Figure 2.8 First Swatch collection with 12 models, presented on 1 March 1983. Copyright by Swatch.

The Swatch was a first-class technological product and a brilliant marketing idea. The two parts of its name – Swiss and watch – symbolised the rebirth of the Swiss watchmaking industry. To a large extent, it was Nicolas Hayek (1928–2010) who initiated this latest chapter in the success story of the Swiss watch. Obviously, other clever minds played a part, but Hayek will go down in history as the main actor: His initiative as an entrepreneur seems to have known no bounds; his flair for marketing, his feel for branding and his belief in the viability of a high-quality mechanical watch blazed a trail for the watchmaking industry.

The evolution of the watchmaking industry illustrates several characteristics typical of Swiss economic history:

- Fundamental impulses for the development of watchmaking came from abroad. While in this case they were brought by religious refugees, other branches and sectors would later profit from the contributions of political refugees and economic migrants who found new homes in Switzerland and were able to realise their ideas there.
- The entrepreneurial soil was not uniformly fertile throughout Switzerland. While the economic conditions in the city of Geneva, as in other locations with guild-oriented structures, were strictly regulated, the free-trade economic order in the Neuchâtel Jura allowed for the emergence of innovative enterprises. Here, work processes could be optimised, and this led to the development of new products.
- Watchmaking was oriented neither towards producing cheap commodities nor towards the domestic market. Both in terms of the quantity it produced and in terms of the quality of its products, the Swiss watchmaking industry soon came to dominate the global market. In 1800, every second watch in the world had been made in Switzerland.
- At first glance it appears bizarre that an industry that produced for export and had developed in the remote valleys of the Jura should have become a trademark for the entire country: Switzerland – the nation of watches.
- As was true of other products of the consumption and luxury goods industry, watch exports varied in response to economic and political events that affected global markets. Wars and revolutions influenced sales. In this, the watch industry was like other economic sectors, in particular the tourism industry. Yet not all economic sectors were affected in parallel. To the same extent that Napoleon's Continental Blockade spurred on the Swiss textile industry, it put pressure on the watchmaking industry.
- The oldest watch manufacturer in Switzerland, Vacheron Constantin, began operations in 1785. While a number of renowned watch companies were founded in the first half of the 19th century – for example, Jaeger Le Coultre and Patek Philipp (both 1839), Cartier (1847) and Omega (1848) – many important watch companies and brands that are still around today had their origins in the early days of the Federal State – Tissot (1853), Eterna (1856) and Chopard (1860) – or in the last quarter of the 19th century – Piaget (1874) and Breitling (1884).
- Even today, Swiss watches are primarily manufactured in the locations where the pioneers of the industry originally founded their firms or at least where their companies evolved during the 19th century.
- Two characteristics differentiate the watchmaking industry from other branches of the Swiss economy. First, it developed significantly earlier. Second, its interplay with other sectors of the economy

remained comparatively limited, despite the fact that there was considerable interconnectedness within the industry itself. Crucially, however, watchmaking introduced proto-industrial work, a fundamental condition for the further industrialisation of Switzerland. It was a forerunner in this respect.

- Throughout its history, the watchmaking industry has been confronted with diverse challenges and crises. In the last quarter of the 19th century, Swiss watchmakers were existentially threatened; this became apparent at the 1876 World Fair in Philadelphia. From the perspective of economic history, it is interesting how the public authorities reacted to this doomsday scenario affecting an entire branch of business. It is remarkable that, in contrast to the federal interventions during the watchmaking crises before and after the Second World War, it was the cantons and municipalities that engaged themselves for the industry in the 19th century. The federal government neither took action to support the industry nor intervened in other ways.
- With the exception of the crisis years from 1876 until the start of the 1880s, Swiss watchmaking in the 19th century was a success story. This success did not continue into the 20th century, however. Wars and other crises paralysed the market for Swiss luxury goods, and it became clear that the lessons learned in 1876 had been forgotten with the passing of time. For when the global economy began recovering in the 1950s and a financial boom set in, Swiss watchmakers once again failed to keep up with technological developments – due to hubris, an absence of foresight and an unwillingness to react to the implications of social progress. This mentality was fostered by the Watch Act (Uhrenstatut), which, with its governmental protections, misconstrued the reality of international competition. It made little difference that certain brands, like Rolex, continued to be successful. The Swiss watchmaking industry was in decline.
- Although it introduced automatic assembly machines in the 1960s, the Swiss watchmaking industry could not keep pace when production-line assembly was introduced in Japan a decade later. The Swiss watchmaking industry was displaced from the lever watch market, and the consequences were dramatic. The complete loss of standing of the Swiss watchmaking industry at the time was not connected with the rise of the electronic watch, as is still often bruited about today. That particular technological change was mastered with bravura by Swiss producers with the legendary Swatch. No, the demise was rather a consequence of the fact that Japanese manufacturers had succeeded in penetrating and then completely taking over the lever watch market. The structural foundation for the revival of the Swiss industry was provided by the landmark merger of ASUAG and SSIH to form ASUAG/SSIH AG in 1983 (SMH since 1985), from which, in 1998,

through a name change, the Swatch Group came into being. This transformation was achieved thanks to an almost 900-million-franc cash injection by the large banks and a few cantonal and regional banks, which provided a foundation for the revival. Yet it took brilliant minds, vision and products that were in touch with the pulse of the times to lead the Swiss watchmaking industry back to success.

Thanks to Cottage Industry, Switzerland Becomes the Second-Largest Textile Exporter in the World

Here too, religious refugees! In 1555, a considerable number of so-called Locarno Protestants arrived in Zurich, having been driven out of their native land for practising the wrong religion. Along with their technical know-how, they brought with them experience with the workshop system. The textile business at the time was largely an urban trade; like Genevan watchmaking, it was strictly regulated by guilds. Since spinning was not counted as a trade, however, it could be practised by anyone, both in the city and in the countryside.[33]

At the end of the 16th century, two textile pioneers, David Werdmüller (1548–1612) and Heinrich Werdmüller (1554–1627), made names for themselves in Zurich. In 1587, together with the Locarno velvet-maker Giacomo Duno (1540–1603), they founded a company that produced woollen cloth. Another religious refugee, Francesco Turrettini (1547–1628), introduced the Werdmüller brothers to silk floss manufacture. The Werdmüllers were among the first businessmen in Canton Zurich to pay out wages to workers who spun wool and raw silk into yarn and thread in their own homes. This division of labour created an efficient structure. In its deviation from the commercial practices prescribed by the urban guilds, the Werdmüllers' capitalistic business enterprise with its proto-industrial silk production constituted an economic revolution. Their success made them the wealthiest citizens of Zurich and turned their city into a centre of the silk industry. The Werdmüllers created further synergies by uniting the processing of wool, silk and cotton for the first time.

The workshop system the Werdmüllers introduced in Zurich represented an important development in economic history. The raw materials they bought were provided to homeworkers who, alongside their primary agricultural work, weaved it into cloth in return for wages. The finished goods were picked up by the businessmen and then sold. In the silk industry, this form of homework was practised even into the machine age.[34]

In time, cotton processing developed into the most important branch of the proto-industry. Peter Bion (1684–1735) of Kurpfalz furthered this development in St Gallen. The son of an official of Huguenot heritage, in 1707 he emigrated from Heidelberg to St Gallen, where he initially worked as a trader in textiles and other goods. In 1721, he became the first to produce fustian by weaving together cotton and linen. With this he introduced the processing of cotton to St Gallen, which had previously been dominated by linen weaving. Since weaving was forbidden to him as a member of the tailor's guild, he applied to join the weaver's guild, into which he was accepted. But Bion did not strictly respect the guild's regulations. By not only carrying out all of the steps in the production process but also by selling his textiles himself, he contravened the prescribed separation of production from trade. Yet since cotton production was not directly regulated by the guild, and Bion's cotton products at first did not directly compete with traditional linen, he was allowed to do as he pleased. Bion naturally endeavoured to keep the cotton business outside of the remit of the guilds. Like others before him, he organised his business according to the workshop system. In 1726, Peter Gonzenbach (1701–1799), a respected and influential merchant, joined Bion's business; he took it over in 1732 and subsequently expanded it. It was Gonzenbach who, in the 1750s, first contracted out Indian muslin to be embroidered and thereby established embroidery as an occupation in St Gallen.

One of Switzerland's economic advantages was its large supply of inexpensive unskilled labour, especially in its impoverished and rural regions. By 1790, Switzerland had become second only to England as an exporter of cotton fabrics. The Zurich Oberland, Toggenburg, Glarus and Appenzell regions were among the most intensively industrialised areas in Europe. And cotton was the raw material most processed in the textile industry.

And so it continued into the 19th century. In 1861, Gottfried Keller (1819–1890) wrote a polemic about the "cottoners" and the "disastrous white fluff."[35] In fact, it seemed at the time as if the entire country was covered in cotton, and the textile industry had all of Switzerland in its clutches. And they were all – the businessmen, the small-scale industrialists and the tens of thousands of home and factory workers – implicated in the transatlantic triangular trade that bound Africa, America and Europe.

The development of the Swiss cotton industry is baffling in many respects. How could it have happened that Switzerland, where far and wide no cotton was grown, should have become second only to England as a centre of this industry – a global processing centre in whose homes and factories thousands upon thousands of spindles turned, spinning yarn out of cotton, while other Swiss wove this yarn into cloth and still others sold the cloth to the rest of the world? Although cotton processing was one of the most important branches of Swiss industry from the Middle Ages to the beginning of the 20th century, its genesis is in many respects still nebulous today. And so it is not surprising that, 200 years ago, it was even more difficult to imagine where in the world cotton actually grew and how its raw fibres, which were usually pressed into bales, ended up in Switzerland. Indeed, many people did not even know whether cotton was plucked from plants or shorn from animals – perhaps it was even a plant/animal hybrid.

Figure 2.9 Henry Lee. *Vegetable Lamb of Tartany: A Curios Fable of the Cotton Plant*, 1887. London.

The world of textiles initially comprised linen, wool and silk. Several thousand years ago, in various places on the globe – including on the Indian subcontinent and Peru – people succeeded in making thread from cotton fibres. Many years later, in East Africa, techniques were developed for spinning and weaving cotton. Production was sufficient to meet local needs. Over time, the raw material changed: perennial bushes or small trees with sparse seed pods and underdeveloped seed hairs gave way to short, high-yielding annual plants with long fibres. At the end of the 18th century, cotton began to shape the economy and society like no other resource. King Cotton had soon established an empire and was playing the lead role in global capitalism.[36] This came about not just as a result of the plantations that existed in South and Central America, the southern USA, Southeast Asia, India and Egypt but especially because of the huge manufacturing operations that began appearing in Europe. And now these markets had to be connected to one another. This was the job of commerce.

An Abundance of Water: A Rattling Loom on a Rushing Brook

From the 1770s onwards, mechanical production of cotton fabric expanded in Great Britain. This placed Swiss producers under pressure and led to an acceleration of the mechanisation process. The widespread textile proto-industry in Switzerland provided favourable conditions for actual industrialisation, which occurred over the course of the 19th century. Without the numerous rivers and streams that provided spinning mills with the energy they needed, however, the textile industry in Switzerland would have been unthinkable.

With this we touch on an exceptional phenomenon in economic history: While the industrial revolution in Great Britain is usually equated with the introduction of the steam engine, this connection does not hold in Switzerland, where the textile industry first prospered on watercourses that were suited for the operation of waterwheels. These watercourses were not primarily great rivers like the Rhine or the Aare but rather smaller rivers and large streams such as the Linth, Lorze, Töss and Thur, and the Aa streams in the Zurich Oberland, Seetal, Obwalden, Wägital and Gasterland. While these rural areas provided favourable conditions for industrialisation, the cities, especially Basel, Zurich and St Gallen, maintained their positions as sites of textile trading.

These relationships can be clearly seen in the Glarus region. At the end of the 18th century, the textile business there, which was largely a cottage industry, experienced a crisis. Machine-produced yarn from England had set off a collapse in prices that, in turn, led to a decline in wages. Politico-military developments accentuated the crisis: In the War of the Second Coalition (1798–1802) between France and the other European great powers, many Swiss villages had been laid waste, and the billeting of foreign troops had intensified a food shortage. At this point, however, cotton printing and weaving provided a new orientation for the textile business, since the Napoleonic Continental Blockade had weakened competition to the Swiss cotton business.

Swiss entrepreneurs like Bartholome Jenny (1770–1836) seized the opportunity. In 1808, together with his brothers Kaspar (1782–1828) and Fridolin (1784–1857), Jenny founded the commercial venture Barth. Jenny & Cie. in Ennenda in Canton Glarus. The history of this firm demonstrates how business pioneers were forced to adjust their strategic orientation, their infrastructure and their palette of products in order to adapt to constantly changing markets. It also shows that proto-industrial methods were already being used in the first half of the 19th century.

Bartholome Jenny had learned hand-weaving in a muslin factory in Upper Austria and had then worked intermittently as a barber and wig-maker in Ennenda. In the company he and his brothers founded, cotton yarn was prepared for the weaving process. Boiled in stick water, dried and spooled and then wound up into "Wirpfen," it was delivered to the weavers, who worked at home all over the canton. When the material came back, it was checked and then sold as raw cloth to printing factories and cloth dealers.

Increasing demand convinced Bartholome Jenny to take on the finishing and sale of the cloth himself. He thus had the material printed at his own expense and exported it to Italy himself. To facilitate these exports, in 1818 he opened a branch of his company in Lugano, to be run by his youngest brother, Fridolin. Jenny then expanded the business further into the area of cloth printing itself. His first attempt to start his own factory was unsuccessful, as the Trümpy brothers pre-empted him in exploiting the water power of the Dorfbach, a canal diverted from the Linth River. Jenny therefore pursued a cooperative course, which led to the merging of his business with that of the Trümpys. Fridolin Jenny, who did not approve of the merger, left the company, founded his own trading firm and built a mechanical spinning mill in Ziegelbrücke in 1833, which also prospered. Fridolin recognised the strategically favourable location of Ziegelbrücke, as well as the promise of mechanical methods of production. He powered his operation with water from the various streams that flowed into the Linth in Niederurnen.

After the death of Bartholome Jenny, his son-in-law Jakob Trümpy (1808–1889) played a pioneering role in further developing the technical aspects of the company. He introduced new printing techniques and expanded the company's range of products – for example, by manufacturing so-called Turkish caps, or "yasmas," which were very popular in the Ottoman Empire. Production bottlenecks among home-weavers due to increased demand then prompted the partners at Barth. Jenny & Cie. to establish a mechanical spinning and weaving mill in Haslen, in the Glarus hinterland, in the 1840s. The choice of location was once again dictated by the water power that could be won from the Linth. The machines were commissioned from Rieter in Winterthur and Honegger in Rüti. Barth. Jenny & Cie. became the largest employer in Canton Glarus and the largest vertically integrated textile company in the Glarus textile industry. The firm was able to take imported cotton, spin it, weave it, print it and finally sell it to retail customers.

The textile industry gave a powerful boost to machine manufacture, from which it profited greatly in turn. Around the middle of the 19th century, a turn was made towards industrial production proper, leading to a previously unimaginable level of growth. The Glarus region, with its innumerable streams, once again offered favourable conditions, especially since no special governmental permission was required to exploit the streams' power. Liberal economic policies – there were no guilds – were also decisive for the "Glarus economic miracle" (Glarner Wirtschaftswunder). In 1865, when the textile industry in the Glarus region reached its zenith, it employed around 9,700 workers. This comprised no fewer than 80 percent of all employed labour in the Glarus manufacturing sector. And one out of every ten of these workers was employed in one of the several factories of Barth. Jenny & Cie.

The Legler company also profited from the upswing in the Glarus textile industry. In 1834, David Legler (1790–1865), who had up until then managed his parents' farm, set up a couple of looms in the cellar of his house in Diesbach. In 1845, together with his son Matthias Legler (1819–1866), who later gradually took over the running of the company, he erected a building large enough to house 50 looms. In 1855, Matthias Legler acquired land on which to build the mechanical weaving mill he had been planning. This was partly financed by his uncle Joachim Legler (1807–1856), who died before the company began operations in Diesbach in 1857. Ten years later the business employed around 150 people, thereby fulfilling one of the municipality's conditions for granting the concession to build the factory. Another condition had been that, whenever possible, people from the village were to be employed.

Viewed from a cultural-historical perspective, the transition to the next generation of leaders is worthy of note. Matthias Legler (1844–1932) wanted to study in order to acquire the advanced technical training that he deemed would help him run the company. His father, however, did not agree; he maintained that a secondary school degree and a commercial apprenticeship would provide all the education his son needed – he himself, after all, had completed no more than five years at the village school. Matthias Jr accepted this and took up work in the company office. Soon, in addition to the operation in Diesbach, he was also running an affiliate in Ponte, Italy. It began operations in 1876 with 7,000 spindles and 200 looms and by 1890 employed around 700 people.[37]

Heinrich Kunz and the Issue of Social Welfare

In 1787, around 34,000 men, women and children in Canton Zurich – no less than a fifth of the population – were employed in the manual spinning of cotton. In certain regions, for example in the Zurich Oberland, spinning occupied as much as half of the population. After 1790, however, there was a massive decline in cotton spinning, which was only partly compensated for by the up and coming silk industry. The reason for the decline lay in the nascent mechanisation of cotton spinning in England. Cheap imports from England now reached the Continent, forcing Swiss manufacturers at the start of the 19th century to mechanise their own spinning operations. At first this development mostly affected smaller businesses, many of which shut down as time went on. The final demise of hand-spinning followed the repeal of the Continental Blockade, after which continental Europe was once again flooded with inexpensive English machine-spun yarn. The famine of 1817 compounded the economic crisis and turned the decline of hand-spinning into a true catastrophe.

Machines were the hallmark of the emerging industrial revolution. The enormous growth that they enabled is evident in statistics: In 1827, there were 106 textile factories in Canton Zurich, most of which had fewer than a dozen spinning frames. In 1830, there were already 5,000 factory jobs. Home-weaving took off at the same time as did spinning in factories. In 1840, the textile industry was already providing 16,000 jobs, two thirds of them in the Oberland. Yet the factories and the machines, and the rapidly growing numbers of factory workers, brought about a fundamental change in working conditions. The transition from cottage industry to factory work led to unemployment. Many of those affected emigrated. The employment situation remained precarious in the 1830s, and when mechanisation won out in the weaving industry as well in the 1840s, the situation became critical. Resistance to mechanisation by incensed homeworkers who had lost their jobs arose early on.

In this time of fundamental transformation, a controversial figure in 19th-century Swiss industrial history stepped into the spotlight: Heinrich Kunz (1793–1859).[38] Kunz has gone down in history as the king of the spinning industry, and both the size of his manufacturing empire and his immense wealth justify this title. Generous donations and charitable works financed from his legacy contribute to his aura; his heirs made donations of no less than 750,000 francs. More than half of this went to the canton to finance the construction of the Burghölzli lunatic asylum, while a bequest of 100,000 francs contributed to easing the critical financial situation of Kunz's hometown, Oetwil am See.

These generous charitable acts contrast, however, with the severity with which Kunz treated his employees. He displayed little understanding for the often miserable lives of his factory workers – men and women, children and teenagers – who suffered due to overlong work days and night and Sunday shifts. Like so many early factory owners, Kunz was blind to the dark sides of industrialisation and in no way open to altering working conditions and labour laws to improve the welfare of his employees. This attitude was certainly not unique to Heinrich Kunz; the path to socio-political reform was a long one. Mentalities had to change, and resistance of various kinds be overcome, before the first factory laws would be enacted.

Heinrich Kunz came from a respectable and wealthy family in Oetwil am See. His father, Hans Heinrich Kunz (1766–1825), served as treasurer of his municipality, a member of the Cantonal Parliament and a captain in the infantry. After attending the village school and then a private school in neighbouring Männedorf, 16-year-old Heinrich received training as a merchant in a trading company in Guebwiller in Alsace, where he developed practical know-how in the field of cotton processing. In correspondence with his family from Alsace, Kunz was already reckoning up the possibilities of earning money through cotton spinning and suggesting that the family invest in the industry. When he returned home at 18, he set up a hand-driven spinning workshop in the family home. In the same year, 1811, he began to build up a spinning mill in Schaffhausen with a local industrialist. Just two years later, in 1813, he was installing machines in the Zurich Oberland, and in 1816 he used his earnings to build his first large-scale spinning mill in Oberuster. He established a second operation in Niederuster in 1825.

Kunz was the first to recognise the potential of the water power of the Aa River, and the Aa valley would subsequently become a centre of the Swiss textile industry. Kunz's father, who worked as a cotton merchant with a workshop system and ran a number of small-scale spinning mills, died in 1825, and Kunz inherited his mills. In 1828, he built a cotton factory in Windisch in Aargau. Relentlessly driven to make his operations more efficient and productive, Kunz ignored rules and regulations – he expanded his operations without the required concessions, for example – and repeatedly came into conflict with the authorities. His drive to expand was not dampened when his factory in Oberuster burned to the ground in 1831; he rebuilt the factory and, in 1835, purchased a spinning mill in Adliswil. In 1839, he acquired another, in Linthal, and two years later he took over a spinning mill each in Rorbas and Oberkemptthal, the owners of which had gone bankrupt. This phase of expansion lasted until the beginning of the 1850s and included a new operation in Fehraltorf, the expansion of the factory in Adliswil and the opening of a large-scale spinning mill in Unter-Aathal. At the height of his empire, Kunz employed around 2,000 employees and dominated the Swiss cotton industry. His operations included 150,000 spindles (9 percent of all the spindles in Switzerland) and accounted for around 15 percent of Swiss production. Even on the larger European stage, no manufacturer operated more spindles than Kunz or took in more annual revenue than his 3.5 million francs. Heinrich Zollinger, Kunz's nephew, and Johannes Wunderly (1816–1873), Zollinger's brother-in-law, took over the company after Kunz's death, retaining the well-known company name. They expanded the empire to 245,000 spindles; in 1880, with 2,700 workers, they were among the largest employers in Switzerland. From 1891 onwards, they operated under the name Wunderly, Zollinger & Cie.

Kunz had a good reputation among clients and suppliers. He was dependable, met his financial obligations and offered a wide range of high-quality yarns. He knew his field inside out. He invested his profits not in personal luxuries but in his factories; he lived ascetically and parsimoniously. The strict standards that he lived by, however, translated into ruthless severity in his treatment of his factory workers. Kunz was feared in his own home and despised outside of it. The sometimes catastrophic social injustice and the appalling conditions in his factories and workers' quarters led to multiple complaints and grievances and involved him in a number of court cases.

Kunz remained unmarried. As he aged he increasingly lost control over his many-branched company. His competition exploited this, as was evident in a sensational case tried in 1857 before the Zurich Court of Assizes. The proceedings concerned alleged theft, mainly of yarn, which was disappearing "by the cartload," especially from the Adliswil factory. A treacherous conspiracy within the factory involved everyone from packers "up to top-ranked clerks."[39] The stolen goods were disposed of on the black market and hawked ever more blatantly until the cover of the conspirators was blown. The court sentenced the chief defendants to prison and penal servitude; Major Kunz, as the lieutenant colonel was referred to, did not demand compensation. Already in this trial, which undermined his previously unshakable aplomb, it was obvious that Kunz's physical and psychic powers were in decline. His deteriorating health subsequently became increasingly evident. Heinrich Kunz died in 1859. The cause of death was recorded as typhus.

Escher Wyss: From the Textile to the Engineering Industry

Hans Caspar Escher (1775–1859) remains present in the cityscape of Zurich, as the main guard house on the Rathausbrücke (1824/1825) was built to his design. But Escher was not destined for a career in architecture. In fact, he does not seem to have been very fond of school. His spirit was too lively, and his imagination too rich. He followed his father's wish and trained to be a businessman in Livorno, but his heart was not in it. He took no pleasure in office life. His experience in Livorno was portentous, however – not because he decided to give up business and jump into architecture but rather because his experiences in Italy would shortly lead to his engagement with a much more extensive professional field. Fascinated by sea travel, he followed the traffic of the ocean-going ships down the Tuscan coast and listened to tales of faraway countries. Shipbuilding increasingly interested him, and he began to dabble in it as a draughtsman.

In 1797, Escher returned to Zurich and began work as an architect. Despite a number of successes, he was unhappy in the profession. And soon the political and economic circumstances that climaxed with the occupation of Switzerland by French troops and the establishment of the Helvetic Republic drained him of all hope of better times. He pulled himself out of this negative spiral, however, and took a decisive step: Escher became a cotton spinner. By the turn of the century he was already running a small cotton-spinning mill, which allowed him to indulge his passions for tinkering and technology.

The idea of designing spinning machines especially fascinated Escher. He had heard that secret attempts were being made in England to spin cotton with machines, and he travelled there to attempt to get in on the secret. This turned out not to be so simple. Escher is said to have often snuck up to the mysterious machines under adventuresome conditions; once he crouched down for hours, spying through a cellar window. He was engaged in nothing more or less than industrial espionage! Escher sketched out what he had seen and then, from memory, made more detailed drawings. He would soon succeed in building his own machines.

In 1805, Escher endeavoured to "expand [his assets] to include bigger things, as the British do"; he purchased the "New Mill" (Neumühle) from the Zurich government.[40] Together with the banker Salomon von Wyss (1769–1827) and other Zurich investors, he founded Escher, Wyss & Cie., a large-scale cotton-spinning company. A pioneering aspect of the operation was that the spinning mill was joined to a mechanical workshop from the beginning. At first, this workshop merely served to carry out repairs on the company's own textile machines.

In 1800, the Swiss cotton industry was in full bloom, drawing its inspiration from technical achievements in England. The demand for suitable machines was everywhere apparent. Escher Wyss's next step was to stop acquiring manufacturing machines and main engines from England and instead to produce them itself. Once the company's own need for machines was satisfied, however, the question arose of what to do with the 12 mechanics who had made them. Escher saw great potential in the field of machine-building. He therefore proposed that the company not simply employ its mechanics to make repairs to its own machines but rather that the entire team embark on making machines for other customers.

The new strategic orientation was settled on in 1810. And this was the decisive turning point, both for Escher's company and for the development of the entire Swiss engineering industry. Since revenues in the yarn trade subsequently fell, while machines sold at a torrential pace, the machine-manufacturing and the cotton-spinning operations were separated from one another in 1831. By the early 1830s, Escher Wyss had become the largest machine manufacturer in Switzerland. In the process, it diversified into other fields: Besides textile machines, the company began to manufacture water wheels, water turbines and transmission systems; beginning in the late 1830s, it manufactured steamboats, including their boilers and steam engines. In the 1850s, with the railway triumphing in Switzerland, Escher Wyss also began building locomotives.

Figure 2.10 Escher Wyss & Cie. machine factory, Zurich. View into the assembly workshop, 1875. Lithograph. Zurich, Zentralbibliothek Zürich.

Hans Caspar Escher was the heart and soul of the company. His vision determined business policy; he regularly kept up with developments in Germany, France and England; and he lent a hand himself when it came to improving machines and devices. He received support from his son, Albert Escher (1807–1845), who became the director of the technical division of the company and later a partner. It was expected – and taken for granted – that the young Escher, like other successful Swiss machine builders, would go to England to acquire experience. His stay there would go down in business history. Albert Escher died when he was only 38 years old.

Interplay between different economic sectors is a typical feature of Swiss industrial history and was important in the development of Escher Wyss. That the company did not limit itself to the manufacture of textile machinery, but rather developed new fields of business as the transport industry became mechanised, was characteristic of pioneering enterprises of the time. It started with steamboat construction. The first steamboat engines, like the first textile machines, were imported from England. French suppliers only entered the game later on. Escher Wyss first became involved in steamboat production in 1835, when the firm was entrusted with the assembly of the first steam-driven boat on Lake Zurich, the *Minerva*. This provided a decisive impulse. It is significant that Escher Wyss not only assembled the boat but also had the confidence to make alterations in the design. The first steamer to be completely built in the Neumühle workshops was the *Linth-Escher*, which was commissioned in 1836 and made its maiden voyage on Lake Walen on 4 September 1837. The *Stadt Luzern* was also launched in 1837 – and so it went, one boat after the next. Thus began the astonishing rise of a new Swiss industry, one that would make global history. Soon Escher Wyss steamers operated not only on all the larger Swiss lakes and rivers but also on other European and even transatlantic inland waters. And with the *Languedoc*, Escher Wyss became one of the first manufacturers of larger steamers.

What is most astonishing here is not that Switzerland made a name for itself in an area of manufacturing for which most raw materials had to be imported. This was no different in the textile industry and would be repeated in the chemical industry as well. The surprising thing is that in taking up shipbuilding, the Swiss engineering industry presumed to enter a field that would seem to have greatly favoured companies from other countries. As a landlocked country, Switzerland lacked the experience that seafaring nations had in abundance. And this same geographical aspect, viewed through another lens, also distinguishes the historical achievement of Swiss shipbuilding: for Escher Wyss, like Sulzer later on, was not able to deliver its ships to purchasers via watercourses but had to transport them in pieces and re-assemble them on site.

Escher Wyss's decision to get into the business of manufacturing textile machines was doubtless influenced by the Continental Blockade. After the collapse of Napoleonic rule, however, English competition was once again overwhelmingly present in global markets. Escher Wyss in Zurich would have seemed, in comparison to the English companies, a completely insignificant machine manufacturer, one that had only just begun to produce and sell textile machinery. In the middle of the 19th century, however, the power relations began to change. In 1835, Escher Wyss built its first stationary steam engine; in 1841, its first paper machine; and in 1844, its first turbine. Thanks to the great demand for steamers on Swiss lakes, Swiss shipbuilders, with Escher Wyss at the fore, were able to continually increase their market share in European steamboat manufacture. After the Sulzer brothers launched their first steamer in 1867, all steamers on Swiss lakes were built by these two firms, with a single exception – the *Stadt Luzern*, built in 1928 by the Sachsenberg brothers in Rosslau on the Elbe. Starting in the mid-19th century, Switzerland had gradually developed into one of the leading shipbuilders worldwide – and Escher Wyss was the unchallenged leader among Swiss shipbuilders, well ahead of Sulzer. An indication of its strength was the fact that in 1874/1875 Escher Wyss delivered two dozen steam engines for passenger travel on the Thames. And to the triumph of the steamboat was added that of the steam locomotive. As early as the 1850s, Escher Wyss delivered its first locomotives to the Northeast Railway (Nordostbahn) and the United Swiss Railways (Vereinigte Schweizerbahnen).

During the first phase of the mechanisation of the textile industry, waterwheels were the principle source of energy. Just as they had previously been used to power mills and sawmills, so they were now used to drive mechanical looms. Mechanical weaving operations not only profited from existing knowledge regarding the construction of canals and dams but also from the proven designs of the waterwheels, whose gear mechanisms were still almost exclusively made of wood. Soon, however, these wooden waterwheels were no longer able to meet the demands placed on them for increased performance. Thanks to Walter Zuppinger (1814–1889), an employee and one-time mechanical apprentice who specialised in the improvement of waterwheels, Escher Wyss was able to manufacture cast-iron rims and optimised sheet-metal vanes for its wheels. This innovation, which was patented in 1849, made history as the "Zuppinger wheel": an extremely high-performing water wheel, with an efficiency 80 percent that of a turbine. It is still used today for situations with small vertical drops and lesser water flows.

Escher Wyss took another innovative step in 1844, when it became the first Swiss company to manufacture turbines. These were based on the design of the French engineer Nicolas-Joseph Jonval (1804–1844) and were capable of converting up to 80 percent of the kinetic energy of water into motive power. Six years later, Escher Wyss built double-rimmed Jonval turbines that performed at more than 100 metric horsepower. And on it went: in 1870 with Girard turbines and then with ever-improving designs and higher performance. The many rivers with steep gradients and the growing demand for water turbines promised good business. Other firms followed suit, including Rieter in Winterthur, Bell in Kriens, Piccard-Picter (later Charmilles) in Geneva and the Ateliers de Constructions mécaniques in Vevey. All of them exported the majority of the machines they manufactured.

The imposing rise of Escher Wyss was not slowed down by the death of Hans Caspar Escher. A cleverly managed succession gave the company security and stability. In the great halls and workshops of the firm – in the foundry as in the hammer, copper and boiler forges, in the factory hall as in the power plant – the manufacture of tried and tested products was complemented by that of machines responding to the exigencies of the times, which sometimes broke new ground. Having recognised the potential of water power for the production of electrical energy, the firm built pumping stations in Zurich, Geneva and Bucharest in the 1890s. By the end of the 19th century, Escher Wyss had delivered a total of around 7,000 products, among them 500 ships and ship engines, 2,600 turbines, more than 1,000 steam pumps and compressors, and 1,700 steam boilers – and also 200 paper machines and 140 naphtha launches.

Meanwhile the number of the firm's employees rose continually. Already in its early years, the company had been characterised by its rapid development; in 1829, it employed around 100 mechanics; by 1835, 400. The continual and sometimes striking growth made it necessary to adjust the company's legal status, and in 1889 the limited partnership Escher Wyss & Cie. became a public limited company. But this did not solve all of its problems; the increases in production and the growing number of workers led to an acute lack of space in the Neumühle. Other logistical challenges also arose: Transport of the finished products to the train station was cumbersome, time-consuming and costly. There was only a small footbridge between the factory grounds and the station, so a detour had to be taken via the Limmatquai, the Münster bridge and the Bahnhofstrasse. The firm thus decided to build a new large-scale plant in Hard, for which a private power station in Bremgarten in Canton Aargau would provide the necessary electricity. By 1895, the move was complete. At this time the novel steam turbine developed by the engineer Heinrich Zoelly (1862–1937) had proven so successful that the global demand for it already necessitated further expansion and construction – the more so as the Zoelly turbine was soon being used by navies on all the world's oceans.

A significant portion of Escher Wyss's shipbuilding served military purposes, and Austria was the firm's best client. In 1849, the first commission rolled in as Construction Number 36: the reconnaissance vessel *Franz Joseph*, which was to be used on Lake Garda. In the early 1850s, Austria placed three further orders for steamers destined for Lake Langen: the *Radetzky*, the *Benedek* and the *Ticino*. These warships were unusual in that, in times of peace, they were used to carry passenger and freight traffic.

They still belonged to the state, however, and their crew always consisted of military personnel. Vienna envisioned similar solutions for Lake Garda and the Po, and Escher Wyss received the commissions. Escher Wyss also supplied ships for the Danube: first, in 1854, the engine for the imperial yacht *Adler*, and later the hull and engines for several gunships. At the same time, however, Escher Wyss was producing engines and steamers that could carry arms in the event of war for the Kingdom of Piedmont-Sardinia. Thus it came about that during military actions in the 1859 Austro-Sardinian War, warships produced in Zurich were used by both sides in operations on Lakes Garda and Langen.

The fate of the Austrian ships on Lake Langen makes for a noteworthy case study in the history of mentalities. As the Austrian army retreated from Milan, its warships were left behind, with more than 600 men on board. At this point the Austrians gave up their base at Laveno and had themselves – together with their war material – interned in Switzerland. Suddenly presented with three warships, Federal Councillor Jakob Stämpfli (1820–1879) thought the moment had arrived for Switzerland to arm itself for the expansionist foreign policy that he favoured: While two of the ships could serve civilian purposes – so Stämpfli – the *Radetzky*, renamed the *Elvezia*, should become a Swiss warship. Such plans for playing at war found no political backing, however. Yet situations in which military equipment made in Switzerland was used by opposing sides in a war would be repeated – for example, in the Third Italian War of Independence between Austria and Italy in 1866 – and would continue to be the subject of political debate.[41]

Escher Wyss supplied the recipe for a Swiss firm's success in the global market of the 19th century: It had to be at the forefront of technological development, ensure the dependability of its deliveries and inspire confidence in its repair work. In order to live up to these demands, Escher Wyss took pains to conduct its own research and to invest where it saw a potential for innovation. The competitiveness of its prices was important but, compared to these other factors, not decisive. Then, in addition to the factors that the company could itself influence, there came the imponderables: the situational advantages from which it profited, and in particular the role of Switzerland as a small neutral country, which allowed deliveries in all directions. But Escher Wyss also showed itself equal to worldwide economic crises and natural disasters and thus provides a prime example of the development and success of a firm in the Swiss export economy.

The Engineering Industry: Honegger's Looms

The number of Swiss textile companies increased markedly between 1806 and the end of the Continental Blockade in 1813. In 1814, there were already around 70 mechanised spinning mills in Canton Zurich and more than two dozen in St Gallen and Appenzell.

Salomon Honegger (1774–1830) ran a small farm in Rüti in Canton Zurich. Like many others, he worked as a handweaver on the side. Demand was high. Honegger therefore expanded his handweaving operation, step by step, into a spinning mill. At first, with only around 2,000 spindles, it was modestly outfitted. Salomon's son Caspar Honegger (1804–1883), however, made history as an industrial pioneer. As a 15-year-old he was already required to work in his father's business. In 1821, now all of 17, he took over the technical leadership of the company. Soon afterwards he took over responsibility for the entire business, in which he and his brother Heinrich (died 1866) became partners. Their pioneering spirit became evident in 1834, when the brothers expanded operations to Siebnen, on the Schwyz side of Lake Zurich. The opportunity was enticing. Since the Honegger brothers were willing to make an investment, and in particular to build a factory that would stimulate the economy of the impoverished region, they received the land and the water rights for free.

Without having tried them out beforehand, Caspar and Heinrich Honegger purchased 50 mechanical looms. In their desire to exploit the favourable circumstances of the day, they were willing to run great risks. Even the positioning of a factory outside of their home canton revealed progressive thinking for the time. The Honegger business flourished, but the brothers were not satisfied with the quality of the English looms imported to Switzerland in the 1830s. Caspar Honegger, who had only attended the village school – and even that only irregularly on account of the work he had to do at home – felt he had no choice but to tackle the problem himself. He expanded his technical knowledge of machine construction by carefully examining the English machines on his own.

Critics have described industrialists such as Honegger as "robber barons," but such simplistic descriptions fail to do justice to Honegger's achievement.[42] In fact, Honegger permanently improved the English product. In 1841, the first mechanical loom constructed in Switzerland appeared; under the name Honegger, it would spread through the entire world and become legendary. His success motived Honegger to construct his loom serially and put it on the market. He therefore built a mechanical workshop abutting his spinning mill.

In 1847, during the run-up to the Sonderbund Civil War, Honegger's loom manufacturing operation moved and expanded. Caspar Honegger feared that the workers in Siebnen, as citizens of Canton Schwyz, might be recruited to fight on the side of the Conservative Sonderbund; this would have aligned neither with his political convictions nor with his business interests. He therefore covertly transferred the personnel and equipment of his mechanical workshop to Rüti in Canton Zurich. He left the spinning mill as it was, as its predominantly female workforce was in no danger of being summoned to military service. Honegger's fears were not realised; the area around Lake Zurich was not involved in the military conflict, and production continued without interruptions or limitations. Now, however, his mechanical workshop had found a new home in the Zurich Oberland, and there it would develop into a machine factory known around the world. By 1870, an impressive 30,000 Honegger looms had been sold.

When Caspar Honegger died in 1883, the Maschinenfabrik Rüti (Rüti Machine Works) and its operations in Siebnen and Bavaria were hived off and restructured. In 1850, Honegger had also built a cotton weaving plant in Rüti, which was transformed into a silk weaving plant in 1881. The machine factory had started producing mechanical silk looms in the 1860s. With the transition from cotton to silk, Caspar Honegger's goal had been to have a pilot plant for the most modern models of silk looms on hand in the immediate vicinity of the textile factory.

Honegger's story is illustrative of several phenomena in Swiss economic history, harbingers of which could already be observed in the watchmaking industry. Swiss pioneers were capable of taking ideas and innovations developed abroad and adjusting them to meet their own needs. They understood how to develop existing products further and in doing so to qualitatively surpass their foreign competition. Even in quantitative terms, Swiss entrepreneurs were soon able to assume leading roles worldwide. Thus the Maschinenfabrik Rüti developed into an international leader in the production of weaving machines. The opening of agencies abroad, which was also typical for the Swiss engineering industry, was a logical consequence. By the end of the 19th century, the company had representatives in all of Switzerland's neighbours, and from 1914 onwards also in Moscow, Manchester, Damascus and Constantinople. After 1930, steps were taken to expand into South America, India, South Africa and Australia.

Rieter and Sulzer: The Heavyweights from Winterthur

The Swiss engineering industry stepped out from under the shadow of its English counterpart in the mid-19th century and, in certain branches, even became a global leader. While Switzerland is struggling as a manufacturing location today, in the 19th century it was attractive because of the availability of cheap labour. The Swiss engineering industry was unusual for its time in that it was not centred around a single product or location. In contrast to the industry in other countries, it was not concentrated in urban agglomerations. Instead, 19th-century Swiss companies found their places in the world market from widely dispersed manufacturing locations and with very diverse products. Among these companies were Sulzer and Rieter, both from Winterthur.

Like both Escher Wyss and the Maschinenfabrik Rüti, Rieter emerged from the textile sector. Johann Jakob Rieter (1762–1826) founded a cotton-trading company in 1795. The company soon took up textile production. Here, too, Napoleon's Continental Blockade was the crucial factor in the shift. The mechanical workshop abutting Rieter's textile operation developed into a machine factory, and soon engines and locomotives were being produced alongside textile machines. Such diversification was typical in the 19th century. The pioneers of industry were continuously seeking new sales possibilities and finding them in new branches of industry, which led to an expansion of their product ranges. In the 20th century, instead, a phase of concentration and specialisation would take place, for Rieter as for other machine builders.

The second-largest machine factory in Winterthur was founded by the brothers Johann Jakob Sulzer (1806–1883) and Salomon Sulzer (1809–1869). They were among the machine manufacturers who did not grow out of the textile business but rather emerged from artisanal operations. The Sulzers' soon-to-be-famous iron foundry developed directly from the turning plant that Sulzers had already been running for two generations. The development of their business was similar to that of Rieter and Escher Wyss. While at first they produced heaters and boilers, they were soon manufacturing steam engines and finally entire steamships and steam locomotives. Sulzer set up agencies in Italy and Germany in the second half of the 19th century and opened a branch in Ludwigshafen. The company grew at a breathtaking pace. The number

Figure 2.11 The Sulzer Brothers, Winterthur. Forging a crankshaft under the 1,000-tonne forging press, 1910. Postcard. Private collection.

of employees rose from just 12 journeymen in 1836 to 500 employees in 1860; by 1906, the employees numbered 4,500, and the company was still growing. Employee numbers reached their peak in 1970, when, together with Escher Wyss, which had been incorporated into the company, more than 30,000 people worked for Sulzer worldwide. At that time, at least one out of every five ships on the world's oceans was propelled by a Sulzer diesel engine.

SIG Neuhausen: Carriages, Weapons and Milk Cartons

In 1853, in the promising atmosphere of the young Federal State, a train carriage factory was founded in Neuhausen am Rheinfall. With 150 employees on board from the start, it was a considerable enterprise. Like other Swiss industrial operations, the carriage factory continually expanded its range of products. In 1860, the company began to produce weapons; the so-called Vetterli-rifle was its first big seller. A repeating rifle developed by Friedrich Vetterli (1822–1882), it attracted international attention, combining as it did various elements of existing weapons into a novel whole. The Vetterli rifle was the first service weapon of the Swiss army; the Sturmgewehr 57 (in 1959/1960) and the Sturmgewehr 90 (in 1983), both of which were produced in Neuhausen, also became standard military issue. Vetterli was able to construct a successful new Swiss weapon based on existing foreign designs with impunity because there was no patent protection in Switzerland at the time.[43] A proposal to introduce a national law for the protection of intellectual property was defeated in a referendum in 1866. It was only in 1888 that such a law was passed, and it initially only applied to inventions that were representable by models. The protection of processes was only integrated into Swiss patent law in 1907.

In 1863, in the course of diversification, the original name of the Neuhausen carriage company (Schweizerische Waggon-Fabrik) was changed to Schweizerische Industrie-Gesellschaft (Swiss Industrial Company, SIG). In 1906, the company began to manufacture packaging machines for the food industry. Between 1918 and 1955, it also built road vehicles. After the Second World War, its range of products was rescaled, and the company only concentrated on certain areas. Weapons manufacture was hived off from SIG and sold, and the automobile branch was given up. The rolling stock business now only produced individual parts for carriages, and this branch, too, was later divested; the surviving SIG Combibloc Group today only produces packaging machines.

The founders of the Neuhausen carriage company were Friedrich Peyer im Hof (1817–1900), Heinrich Moser (1805–1874) and Johann Conrad Neher (1818–1877) – each a pioneer in his own right. Neher came from a family of Swabian Catholic entrepreneurs who had become citizens of Canton Schaffhausen. His father Johann Georg Neher (1788–1858) was a specialist in iron smelting who had directed an ironworks in Messkirch. Later he settled in Schaffhausen and purchased the copper hammermill in Laufen, which he transformed into an iron forge and fitted out with a blast furnace.

Like many other Swiss industrialists, Neher took an educational journey to England. During his absence from home, his eldest brother, Anton Neher, succeeded in thoroughly squandering the family fortune through ill-considered speculation. Johann Georg paid off the family debts through his hard work over the course of many years. In 1813, he married Esther Seiler (1790–1864) and was granted Schaffhausen citizenship. This occurred on the explicit condition that all of their children would be raised Protestant. Despite his marriage into a patrician family, however, Neher was not treated as an equal by Schaffhausen Conservatives, for whom it was incomprehensible that a man would devote himself to commercial or industrial work. Earning one's bread or slogging away as a manufacturer did not befit the rank of a patrician. This attitude persisted until the end of the 1840s. The fresh wind that blew in with the young Federal State also touched Schaffhausen, sweeping away this and other conventions of the old order.

Neher remained undeterred and continued on his entrepreneurial journey. The industrial momentum that enveloped Schaffhausen in the early 19th century thanks to the work of Johann Conrad Fischer led to a boom in ore mining. Neher significantly expanded his operations in Laufen. When he learned of a completely ruined ironworks in Plons and an abandoned iron quarry in Gonzen, he bought them up. In 1831, after some initial difficulties, he discovered manganese – a mineral essential for the smelting of iron – in the old ore mines. Neher's new enterprise flourished.

Finally, he purchased a hammer mill in Thorberg, near Lucerne. Family stories tell of events there during the Sonderbund War. Vagrant Bernese troops broke furniture and household possessions to bits and perforated a "valuable and large fire hose with their bayonets."[44] Neher, who had remained Catholic but openly sympathised with the troops of the Confederation – in whose army two of his sons were serving – immediately submitted a demand for reparations to Chief of General Staff Frey-Herosé (1801–1873). It will hardly come as a surprise that the response he received was to Neher's complete satisfaction.

In 1851, Neher transitioned to steel production in Thorberg. He worked indefatigably right up until his death and died as one of the wealthiest citizens of Schaffhausen. That in Protestant Schaffhausen he remained faithful to his Catholic confession, energetically helping to build up Catholic institutions, shows him to have been an undeterred individualist.

Neher's son Johann Conrad, the co-founder of the carriage factory, studied at the Karlsruhe Polytechnic and then joined his father's company, for which he first directed the ore-smelting operation and the manufacture of cast-iron products. Thanks to deft marriage politics and, doubtless, the help of Providence, the Neher family became more strongly anchored in the company with each passing generation.

In the case of the carriage factory, this embedding of the family in the company is especially apparent. Johann Conrad Neher had two brothers and a sister. His sister, Sophie (1821–1893), married Neher's business partner Peyer im Hof; one brother, Bernhard (1814–1865), married Peyer im Hof's sister Pauline; the other, Johann Georg (1826–1885), married Emma (1835–1916), the daughter of the third partner in the firm, Heinrich Moser. And Johann Conrad himself? He married Caroline Stokar von Neunforn (1820–1894), who came from a patrician Schaffhausen family.

Peyer im Hof and Moser had no direct connection to machine construction. Their goal was simply to further the economic development of their home city, Schaffhausen. After his apprentice and journeyman years, Peyer im Hof took over his family's cloth business in 1838. In 1848, with the founding of the Federal State, he became a politician at both the national and cantonal levels. He was a National Councillor and a member of the Cantonal Parliament for many years, in which capacities he devoted himself particularly to infrastructure projects. In 1850, he co-founded the Lake Constance and Rhine Steamboat Company (Dampfbootgesellschaft Bodensee und Rhein), which was later taken over by the Nordostbahn. At the same time as the founding of the carriage factory, he launched the Rheinfall Railway (Rheinfallbahn), which was to connect Schaffhausen with Winterthur and Zurich. Even before the Rheinfall Railway began operations, however, Peyer im Hof supported its merger with the Swiss Northern Railway (Schweizerische Nordbahn) to form the Northeastern Railway Company. Schaffhausen was still not linked to Zurich, but it was at least integrated in the network of one of the largest Swiss railway companies. Peyer im Hof held an executive position in the Northeastern Railway for around two decades.

Advances in the banking industry were closely linked to the building of railways and to commercial activities. Here, too, Peyer im Hof played a pioneering role; he founded the Bank in Schaffhausen and the Schaffhausen Commercial Bank (Handelsbank Schaffhausen). He was one of the major players of the pioneering age who fell from grace in the end, however. Speculation in various companies in Hungary lost him his entire fortune. He was also affected by the crisis in the Swiss railway industry in the 1870s and in 1877 had to step down from his executive positions.

After an absence of 20 years and a successful career as a watch manufacturer, Heinrich Moser returned to his native Schaffhausen. He was not cut out to merely live off his private fortune, however. In building the first run-of-river power station in Schaffhausen, he pulled off a

Figure 2.12 "An early lorry model by Saurer, Arbon," 1907. Photograph. Source: Saurer Museum Arbon, photo archive.

Many twists and turns mark the history of the Saurer machine company. In 1852, Franz Saurer (1806–1882) of Veringendorf (Württemberg) established a foundry in St Georgen. In 1863, he moved to Arbon, where his second wife, Pauline Stoffel, had inherited a factory. Saurer built this operation into the Mechanische Werkstätte und Eisengiesserei F. Saurer-Stoffel (F. Saurer-Stoffel Mechanical Workshop and Iron Forge). His son, Adolph Saurer (1841–1920), established himself as a pioneer. Together with his brother, Anton Saurer (1835–1872), he developed an embroidery machine, which was first sold in 1869. In 1896, Adolph Saurer assumed the leadership of the company. He now pioneered the construction of trucks, to which he dedicated himself from 1903 onwards. This diversification allowed the company, which in 1910 already counted around 1,500 employees, to free itself from its dependence on the crisis-prone embroidery industry. Adolph Sauer's son, Hippolyt Saurer (1873–1936), increasingly took over responsibility for automobile production. He developed numerous innovations, including the engine brake in 1904.

pioneering accomplishment – especially because, at the time he built the dam in 1850/1851, electricity had not yet been recognised as a means of transmitting energy. Moser's system instead transmitted mechanical energy – via large gear mechanisms, belts and cables – over distances of several hundred metres to a number of workshops and factories. Between 1863 and 1866, Moser built a larger dam spanning the entire Rhine; it has gone down in history as the "Moser Dam."[45] Initially, this dam produced 600 horsepower and served around 20 customers. In order to transport material and workers to and from the power plant, Moser had the Rieter company build a small aerial cableway over the

Rhine – the first aerial cableway in Europe. In 1887, the transmission belts were replaced by electrical power lines. The dam itself survived until 1961, when it was replaced during the construction of the current Schaffhausen power plant.

Alongside his involvement in the power plant and the SIG, Heinrich Moser held an interest in a steamboat business that operated on the Rhine and Lake Constance. Then there was the Society for a Rheinfall Railway (Gesellschaft für eine Rheinfallbahn), of which he was the principal shareholder. Finally, he also traded in grain. Moser ruled over an industrial empire. He is said to have led in a strictly hierarchical manner but to have understood how to foster the loyalty of his workers through generous remuneration. In return, he expected outstanding contributions to his company. Differences of opinion between Moser, Neher and Peyer im Hof led to Moser bowing out of the SIG after a few years.

Educational Journeys to England

Johann Georg Bodmer (1786–1864), one of the founding fathers of Swiss industry, was born to be a pioneer. In 1807, after completing an apprenticeship as a mechanic, he set up a mechanical workshop in Küsnacht on Lake Zurich; two years later he was in St Blasien in Württemberg, where he directed a textile factory and later established a spinning mill, a weapons factory and an ironworks. Then the time came for him, too, to embark on lengthy stays in England. There, in the heyday of industrialisation, he ran a textile-machine factory and an experimental workshop in Bolton, and later on a foundry in Manchester. He next headed off for Lanzendorf, near Vienna, where he manufactured metal goods.

Bodmer's biography speaks volumes about the history of industry and about Switzerland as a business location in the first half of the 19th century. His choice of apprenticeship already pointed towards a promising career, as there was a shortage of mechanics at the beginning of the 19th century. The maintenance of textile machines and their drive systems required specific expertise, which at the time of the Continental Blockade could not be learned in England. Bodmer's mechanical workshop satisfied an important need, and his reputation spread across the border to southern Germany. That he was active as an industrialist and manufacturer in Württemberg demonstrates that Swiss industry had already reached a level equal to that of its southern German competition.

The most important element in Bodmer's early years, however, was his stay in England. Once again, the remarkable attraction exerted by England on textile and machine manufacturers from other countries becomes evident: England was the cradle of industrial development and the pacesetter for industrial progress. Everyone wanted to follow developments on location and become acquainted with new skills and manufacturing processes early on in the game. English industry was the measure of all things. Bodmer was among the first Swiss industrialists to escape the narrowness of cantonal perspectives and set out to gather experience abroad in the early 19th century. He helped establish what would become a common practice, first for textile industrialists and later for leaders in the engineering industry: heading off to learn and gain experience in the place where the latest developments and the most impressive competencies were to be found – in England.[46]

At around the same time as Bodmer, two other heavyweights of Swiss industry were on their own educational journeys: Hans Caspar Escher of Zurich, founder of Escher Wyss, and Johann Conrad Fischer (1773–1854) of Schaffhausen. The latter was not only the founder of today's Georg Fischer AG but also left a legacy of vibrant contemporary accounts of industrial development in Continental Europe and England.

"*Nulla dies sine linea*" was his motto – no day without a written record of what he had observed and experienced. Fischer accordingly has bequeathed us many diaries and notes. His account of a six-week trip in 1814 via Paris to London and some of the manufacturing towns in England – Birmingham, Leeds, Manchester – is among the most splendid of his writings. It is of particular interest to cultural and social historians, as it provides technically competent analyses and comparative evaluations of the industries he encountered.

Fischer was enthusiastic about the beauty of England and of the cities and villages he visited, from Dover to London – "such an appearance of wellbeing and prosperity you will find nowhere else, and it is no wonder that the French were jealous of it, for the difference between the two countries is all too striking."[47] In light of his observations and notes about other regions that he travelled through in the 1790s, such as Germany and Scandinavia, Fischer's testimony can be taken seriously. Thanks to his professional expertise as a coppersmith and an entrepreneur in the casting industry, he was in a unique position to assess the proprietary development of crucible steel in the context of the industrial metamorphosis of England. Fischer was received by the industrial magnates of England. They exchanged ideas, and he was afforded a backstage view of English manufacturing – even at Boulton & Watt, the pacemaker of the industry. Fischer realised that England's post-1780s boom in manufacturing had been kicked off by the newly developed steam engines. He compared English iron production with his own; he saw that vehicles could be propelled by steam engines in place of horses; he investigated how gas lighting functioned and compared English watchmaking with that in Le Locle and Fleurier. He marvelled at what he saw and was "full of reflections about how far diligence, understanding and tenacity can bring people." Yet he also showed understanding for the weavers in Nottingham and elsewhere, for the bitterness of those who had lost their jobs to machines. And Fischer noted down all that he saw and heard.

Figure 2.13 Adolph Menzel (1815–1905), *Eisenwalzwerk (Moderne Cyclopen) (Iron Rolling Mill (Modern Cyclopes))*, 1872–1875. Oil on canvas, 254 cm × 158 cm. Berlin, Staatliche Museen zu Berlin, Nationalgalerie. Photograph by Andres Kilger.

In the mid-19th century, trips like Fischer's to England were compulsory for Swiss industrialists. And while previously they had been the province of textile producers, now they were increasingly undertaken by machine manufacturers. But the purpose of the stay abroad remained the same: to learn from the English competition. In 1849, Johann Jakob Sulzer (1806–1883) spent several weeks in England. Sulzer's earlier research trips through Germany, France and Austria left a less profound mark on him than did his visit to England. He was profoundly impressed with the high level of technology employed in English industry. He saw that, in many areas, British companies really were among the most modern in the world.

What especially struck Sulzer, however, was the importance of steam engines, which were essential to English factories and drove the most varied manufacturing machines. While in England, he came up with a plan to manufacture steam engines at his company in Winterthur. For this he needed a specialist, however, and a specialist could only be found in England.

The stars seemed to have aligned, for Sulzer's brother-in-law Gottlieb Hirzel (1828–1904) was working as an engineer at Maudslay, Sons & Field in London – a company that produced, among other things, steam engines. The company was well known as a leader in the field of steamboat and machine tool construction, and its renown was nurtured by commissions from the Royal Navy.[48] Hirzel was contacted by Sulzer but did not wish to return to Switzerland himself. Instead, he recommended a young man whom he credited with all the necessary skills: Charles Brown (1827–1905).

The Brown Dynasty: British Know-how Gains Currency

Sulzer did not hesitate, and Brown arrived in Winterthur in 1851. The young Englishman from Uxbridge (today part of Greater London) had been trained in the royal armoury after attending a religious school. Formal training in industry was not available in the England of his day. He set up a small machine workshop in his home and began tinkering. As a 19-year-old he found employment at Maudslay, Sons & Field.

The circumstances that moved Brown to transfer to Sulzer in Winterthur are not precisely known. What is certain is that this still unmarried Englishman with no university training found very promising prospects in Switzerland. Sulzer, for his part, depended on Brown because the manufacturing workshops and technical facilities of his company were primitive in comparison with English ones.

Brown set to work designing machine tools, and his modernisation of Sulzer's facilities catapulted the company to the forefront of technological development on the Continent. He built the first steam engines in Winterthur and brought Sulzer onto the world market in this area as well. The Swiss firm rapidly gained recognition as the manufacturer of one of the most powerful steam engines – at the 1867 Exposition Universelle in Paris, for example. Brown was a genius at technology and construction, a tinkerer and a researcher. He was also impatient, and a poor businessman, but Sulzer covered him here. What especially distinguished Sulzer was that he let Brown do as he pleased, giving him as much freedom as possible. This was the key to their success.[49]

English know-how was in demand in Switzerland. That two English engineers – Stevenson and Swinburne – were chosen to assess the possibilities for the Swiss railway network in 1850 attests to England's leading role in early industrialisation and railway construction. British engineers and specialists left their mark in many areas of Swiss industrial history: Matthew Murray Jackson (1821–1892), a senior engineer at Escher Wyss, raised the manufacture of steamboats to a new level as the firm became a leading producer of steamers for European inland waters. Jackson soon earned an almost legendary reputation, reminiscent of that of his grandfather, the famous engineer Matthew Murray (1765–1826), the designer of the *Salamanca* steam locomotive. Other British specialists also served in leadership roles at Escher Wyss: A Birmingham native surnamed King, for example, was in charge of the foundry. His son, Edward King (1861–1920), followed in the footsteps of both his father and his godfather, Matthew Murray Jackson, serving as foreman of steam engine and steamboat construction at Escher Wyss before founding his own machine factory in Wollishofen in 1861.[50]

The need for this kind of knowledge transfer sheds light on the shortage of technical experts in Switzerland. This deficit became increasingly accentuated as the railway project took off. Until the Federal Polytechnic and the Winterthur Technikum began producing trained Swiss engineers, the growing demand had to be met by foreign specialists. And nowhere in Europe was there such a reservoir of tried and tested experts as in Great Britain. That said, the fact that these British specialists were willing to move shows that Switzerland was an attractive location for them. And this again says neither more nor less than that the Swiss engineering industry in the middle of the 19th century had attained a level that was viewed as competitive with the English one.

While Switzerland had too few homegrown specialists, it had sufficient unskilled labour on hand for factory work. John Stuart Mill (1806–1873), the political theorist and founder of modern liberalism, provided a notably positive assessment of working conditions in Zurich. That a Swiss farmer could supplement his income through homework (textiles) or a factory job, without giving up his work in the stable and the farmyard, was a revelation to Mill. The labourer in Zurich was today a craftsman, tomorrow a farmer again. He changed his occupation in harmony with the seasons of the year. In the union of these two occupations Mill saw the explanation for why the unskilled Swiss labourer had a better foundation from which to achieve financial stability than employees in large companies. In another passage, Mill cited the "engineer and cotton manufacturer" Albert Escher (1807–1845), the son of the founder of Escher Wyss, who employed almost 2,000 workers from many different countries. In discussing the character of English labourers and the difference between them and continental workers, Escher came to the conclusion that an employer looking for broadly capable workers would do best to hire Swiss and Saxons. If he had to choose between them, he should choose Saxons, for they received an outstanding general education. After only a short settling-in period, they were capable of performing many different jobs – in contrast to the English worker, who might do his job well when building a steam engine, for example, but was capable of no more than this.[51]

After working at Sulzer for 20 years, Brown left the firm in 1871. He had trained the junior director himself and had even worked with him on the development of the valve-fitted steam engine, but had then fallen out with him. It also hurt his feelings that the younger Sulzer had not offered him partnership in the firm. And this all the more when, in 1872, Johann Rudolf Ernst (1836–1890), a friend of Sulzer since their youth, became a partner. Now that he would be able to realise his own entrepreneurial plans, Brown was also better able to accept his failure to convince Sulzer to get into the locomotive business, which the Sulzer family had regarded as too risky. At the age of 44, Brown established a locomotive company in Winterthur: the Schweizer Lokomotive- und Maschinenfabrik (Swiss Locomotive and Machinery Works, SLM).

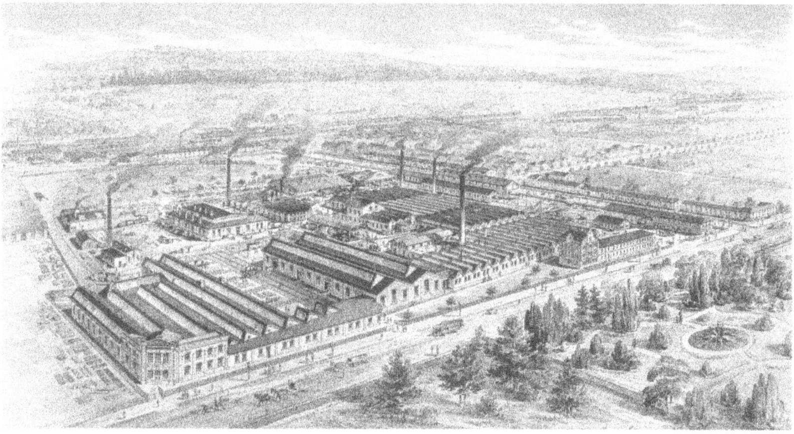

Figure 2.14 "Swiss Locomotive and Machine Works, Winterthur: View of the factory," 1896. Windisch, SBB Historic.

Yet now Brown's weaknesses became apparent: a lack of business experience and a poor ability to assess markets. By the time he got into locomotive construction with SLM, important railway networks in the Swiss Central Plateau had already been built, and the previously unbridled demand for locomotives was largely covered. His exceptional talents as an engineer, which had turned Sulzer, a small Swiss company, into a world-class business whose steamships were inseparable from his name, did not help him manage his own company. He left SLM.

Brown's relationship with Sulzer had broken down, and he had failed as an entrepreneur at SLM, but another path now opened up before him. His work with Peter Emil Huber (1836–1915) would bring Brown back to the top of the world of industry and technology. Huber, a Zurich engineer from a wealthy and established family, was in the first class that graduated from the Polytechnic in machine construction. Brown got to know the young Huber in 1859, when, just after his graduation, he earned his stripes at Sulzer. It was also at Sulzer that Huber came into contact with Murray Jackson, the legendary head of steamboat construction. When Huber returned to Zurich in 1862 after a lengthy stay in England, he and Jackson developed the idea of building a foundry for processing scrap iron. Despite its promise, the plan came to naught, as most Swiss machine manufacturers continued to import their forgings from England. The English industry had developed a new process that drastically reduced costs, so the market was difficult for new producers to enter.

In 1867, Huber gave it up. He had effectively run the company by himself, since Jackson had remained at Escher Wyss. It was this failure, however, that became the starting point for his success story. In choosing the location for his foundry, Huber had wanted to ensure that it was on the Zurich–Winterthur axis, that it was connected to the railway and that it was near a train station. He had thus decided for an insignificant hamlet by the name of Oerlikon. The consequences of this decision were soon unmistakable; the engineering works that he built there would make the name of this little town known around the world. The previously tiny village grew rapidly, from 176 inhabitants in 1850 to 3,982 in 1900.

After the collapse of the scrap iron project, Huber became involved in social and political activities for several years. Then, in 1873, he was contacted by Brown. Brown suggested that he offer his unused land in Oerlikon, together with the empty factory, to a company in Rorschach that was seeking a new and more accessible location. So it happened that Daverio, Siewerdt & Giesiker moved to Oerlikon, and Huber became a partner in the firm. In 1878, Huber and a partner became the majority shareholders. The manufacture of machine tools, which had at first dominated the business, was superseded by the production of other kinds of machines, and the Machinenfabrik Oerlikon (Oerlikon Machine Works, MFO) was born.

Despite its diversification, the company did not develop satisfactorily. This changed when Brown became involved again and recommended that Huber "devote special attention to the electrical sector."[52] Moreover, he offered to build up the electrical engineering division himself. In 1884, Brown began work at MFO, accompanied by his two sons Charles and Sidney, the one 21 years old and the other 19. Only a few months later, however, for reasons that are not completely clear, Brown left the company, recommending that Huber make his son Charles the head of the electrical engineering division. Huber followed Brown's advice, and it would prove a happy choice.

Charles Eugene Lancelot Brown (1863–1924) had studied machine technology at the Technikum in Winterthur, as did his brother, Sidney Brown (1865–1941). The Technikum had been founded in 1874 and was the first institution of its kind in Switzerland. In 1882, the young Brown began an apprenticeship at Bürgin & Alioth, a producer of generators and electric motors in Basel. Networking had played a role in this choice as well: Bürgin, a graduate of the Polytechnic, had worked for Charles Brown Sr at SLM. The younger Brown remained at Bürgin & Alioth for a year, improving his electrical engineering skills. This branch of industry was arousing increasing interest in Switzerland in the early1880s, leading to the founding of companies that produced electrical devices of many different kinds. The younger Charles Brown at first had little success building up the electrical division at MFO. He had to persist through a dogged dry spell, during which the termination of the division was threatened several times.

Still, Huber seemed to have unshakeable faith in the young Brown. Huber's business partner Friederich Wegmann (1832–1905) saw things differently; when he had had enough, he sold his share of the company to Huber. Then, in 1885, Brown succeeded in transmitting electrical power along the eight-kilometre-long transport route from Kriegstetten to Solothurn. This positioned the MFO handsomely in the area of electrical engineering. In 1891, it received a landmark commission: to set up electrical transmission from Lauffen am Necker to Frankfurt am Main, a distance of 175 kilometres. Brown accomplished this, which caused a sensation, and the MFO took off.

The year 1891 was a critical one, during which Brown set the course for his further professional career and for a new core area of Swiss industry. He moved to Baden in Canton Aargau as one of the most renowned engineers and electrical pioneers in the world, and the man at the forefront of the second generation of the electrical-engineering revolution. Yet though he was by now an international star, he did not dare to found an electrical company on his own. Instead, he relied on the support of a man who had come to Switzerland in 1885, had worked as a trainee at MFO, and had distinguished himself there as a specialist in plant construction and as a project leader: Walter Boveri (1865–1924), the son of a physician from Bamberg, who was two years younger than Brown. Brown was not only the older of the two but also had unquestionably been Boveri's boss at the MFO. Despite this, even in the early years of their new firm it was clear that Boveri's strengths as a leader were just as essential as Brown's abilities as an innovative technician. Technical expertise, innovation, risk management and business skills complemented one another ideally at Brown and Boveri.

When Brown and Boveri were setting up their company in Baden, the electrical engineering industry in Europe was already established. It thus seems all the more astonishing that they were successful in gaining a footing among the foreign competition and were soon keeping pace with the largest electrical companies in the world. This may be partly due to the fact that, as they entered the market, Brown and Boveri were able to profit from the findings and experiences of the older pioneering companies and thus were not plagued by the same teething difficulties that some of their competitors had faced earlier. They possessed the most up-to-date technologies from day one. Just as decisive for their success, however, were the characters of the two founders.

Brown and Boveri were allowed to set up an industrial operation in Baden because the city was practically bankrupt. Like many other cities and towns, it had invested exuberantly in the Swiss National Railway (Schweizerische Nationalbahn), whose failure in 1878 left behind a gigantic mountain of debt that the investing towns suffered under for years or even decades. It is thus understandable that Brown and Boveri were offered the opportunity to establish their firm in Baden: The city was counting on jobs and tax revenues. Besides these considerations, the product created by Brown and Boveri was a decisive factor; the construction of an

Figure 2.15 "First BBC steam turbine, 1901." Photograph. Historisches Archiv ABB Schweiz, N.1.1.3383.

The future ABB was restructured many times. Pictured (from left to right): the brothers Eric, Charles and Sidney Brown; Walter Boveri; designer Albert Aichele; Director of Finances Fritz Funk; and three fitters.

electric power station was in the interests of the city, and electric lighting would meet a key need of its innkeepers. For the electric age had been rung in, and in various locations hotels already had electric power.

Baden quickly became a company town. The electrical engineering firm Brown Boveri & Cie (BBC) was founded in 1891 as a medium-sized enterprise. Over the course of only a few years, it developed into the most innovative company in the Swiss engineering industry and one of the largest electrical concerns in the world. This was reflected in the number of its employees, which rose from 74 in 1892 to 1,600 within eight years, and more than doubled again by 1910, when it reached 3,500.

The Transformation: From Water to Electricity

At the end of the 18th century, the exploitation of water power by the textile industry contributed significantly to the first wave of industrialisation in Switzerland. Around 100 years later, beginning in the 1870s, electrification led to the emergence of new branches of commerce, and these branches produced numerous pioneers. The first low-voltage devices, many of which were used in telecommunications, were followed in the 1880s by increasing quantities of high-voltage equipment such as electric motors, generators and illumination systems. Finally, a new sector of industry was formed. It was called electrical engineering.

In the early days of the electrification of Europe, it could hardly have been foreseen that Switzerland would play an important role in it. Conditions may have been favourable, given the country's abundant sources of water power, but it took more than water to develop and manufacture electrical products. For that, technical and entrepreneurial talent was required – and at the beginning of the age of electricity, such talent was lacking in Switzerland.

In the 1870s, however, Emil Bürgin (1848–1933) engineered the first direct current machines in Switzerland. In 1881, he founded a firm that manufactured generators and electric motors. Bürgin found a business partner in Ludwig Rudolf Alioth (1848–1916), also an engineer. The company moved to Münchenstein; in 1883, Bürgin left the firm, which then operated under the name Elektrizitätsgesellschaft Alioth (Alioth Electrical Company, EAG) and merged with BBC.

In order to produce electricity, generators had to be powered. In a hydroelectric plant they were driven by turbines, which are nothing more than continuous-flow machines that produce mechanical power, a refinement of the waterwheel. In Switzerland water was abundantly available as a source of energy, both in the form of rivers and in the form of steep mountain slopes where pressure mains could be laid. In 1897, Conradin Zschokke (1842–1918) built Europe's first modern run-of-the-river power plant in Rheinfelden – three decades after Heinrich Moser (1805–1874) had built the first dam across the Rhine in Schaffhausen.

Progress in electrical engineering, in hydraulic engineering and in power plant construction allowed for an increasingly efficient supply and transmission of energy. At the same time, hydroelectric plants were continually becoming larger. The linkage of these phenomena demonstrates that electrical engineering and power plant construction, although different branches of industry, support one another in their development. The electricity business had become a key industry in Switzerland by the end of the 19th century. In its turn it benefitted other industries, such as the engineering and construction industries. Soon both small and large hydroelectric plants were to be found all over Switzerland. Alongside Zschokke and Moser, men such as Eduard Will (1854–1927) and Gottfried Bangerter (1847–1923) made pioneering contributions. With the Hagneck power plant, the plants on the Kander and the Wynau plant, they played a key role in the relatively late industrialisation of Canton Bern.

Eduard Will came from a poor family. After the early death of his father, he had to provide for his mother and siblings. In 1878, after completing an apprenticeship as an engraver, he began to work as an ironmonger, first in Nidau and later in Biel. His prospects began to

Figure 2.16 "In the foreground, the spa town of Baden; in the background on the right, the BBC industrial area," ca 1907. Coloured postcard. Private collection.

Baden's transformation, or, the industrialisation of a health resort. For centuries, Baden was a leading Swiss health spa. Hoteliers and innkeepers made up its elite society. Industry was practically non-existent. And precisely during the Belle Époque, when tourism was flourishing and the whole elegant world found its way to luxury hotels, when baths, whey and climatic cures transformed Switzerland into a wellness-landscape, Charles Brown and Walter Boveri brought industry to Baden. This point of departure is striking; it was the beginning of a remarkable company history, which brought about the transformation of the city from an illustrious health resort to a place of industry. Thanks to the arrival of Brown and Boveri, spa operations rapidly began to lose their economic, cultural and social significance relative to industry. The transformation was irreversible. The industrialisation of a spa city was a rare occurrence in the 19th century – Baden was an exceptional case. The population grew comparatively rapidly, from 4,215 in 1888 to 8,732 in 1919; in neighbouring Wettingen, in the same period, there was an increase of more than 300 percent, from 1,991 to 5,986. With this growth, social structures changed: out of the small-town, Catholic health resort, which had promoted healing and enjoyment, there developed a future-oriented industrial city with a Protestant ethos. Brown and Boveri were foreigners: While Boveri, a German, became a citizen of Baden in 1893, the Englishman Brown was awarded honorary citizenship in 1916. Additionally, almost the entire leadership of BBC was made up of foreigners or men from other cantons. Many of these new residents became part of elite Baden society.

improve in the military. He completed officers' training, became Chief Corps Commander (Oberstkorpskommandant) of the Third Army Corps, and during the First World War was responsible for the defence of the southern border from 1914 to 1916. As a municipal councillor in Nidau, he was instrumental in initiating the building of the Hagneck power plant and was its first director. This was his first step into the electricity business. After the merging of the Hagneck power plant with the power plants on the Kander, Will became the director of the new company, which was dubbed the Bernische Kraftwerke AG (today's BKW) in 1909. During Will's tenure, which lasted until 1926, the Kandergrund power plant, which supplied energy to the Lötschberg railway, and the power plants in Kallnach and Mühleberg became part of the company, in 1911, 1913 and 1920, respectively. All of these plants were built by BBC.

Will was also active as a politician. Alongside and following his work as Municipal Councillor in Nidau (1889–1893), he represented the Radicals in the Cantonal Parliament (1887–1909), was President of the Cantonal Parliament in 1909 and was a National Councillor from 1896 to 1919. Deeply engaged with military policy, he contributed significantly to the 1907 structuring of the armed forces (Militärorganisation 1907) and the 1911 order of battle (Truppenordnung 1911).

Gottfried Bangerter launched numerous business initiatives and held several political offices. Although he lived a generation after the great founding figures of the mid-19th century, he proved himself to be cast from the same mould. After completing a commercial apprenticeship, he became co-proprietor of the Stettler & Bangerter cloth firm in Langenthal. In 1893, he founded the carbonation company Kohlensäurewerk AG in Bern (the predecessor of the Carba public limited company); two years later he became the first president of the Wynau power plant. He supervised the merger of the Hagneck and Kander power plants into the Bernische Kraftwerke AG (BKW) and was the first president of its governing board. Later he was involved in the founding of the children's food producer Galactina, the Utzenstorf paper mill, the Hallwag publishing house and the Schweizerische Speisewagen-Gesellschaft (Swiss Restaurant Car Company). For years he presided over the governing boards of these companies. He was also a member of the board of the Swiss National Bank. Bangerter was also politically active: In 1874, at the age of 27, he was elected to the Langenthal Municipal Council; between 1877 and 1882, he served as a Radical in the Bernese Cantonal Parliament; and in 1877 he was elected a National Councillor, in which position he served for 12 years.

Electricity thanks to water power: This formula also played a decisive role in the history of Swiss railways. The synergy between transportation and electrical engineering demonstrates, yet again, how two very different branches of industry can help each other advance. Rail routes with steep gradients over large altitude differences were energy-intensive propositions for the railways. This can be seen, for example, in the sections of the Gotthard Railway between Erstfeld (475 metres) and Göschenen (1106 metres), and between Biasca (293 metres) and Airolo (1142 metres). Here electrification was plainly called for. Since coal had to be imported to Switzerland, while water was present in great quantities, the idea of electrifying the Swiss railway network had in fact arisen at an early stage.

The first generation of electric locomotives operated in the 1840s – predominantly in Scotland – but was powered by batteries and confined to short routes. The first use of electricity to power trains over longer distances only occurred in the 1870s, when a continual supply of electricity became available. The first electric trains in Switzerland travelled between Vevey and Territet (1888), Sissach and Gelterkinden (1891) and Burgdorf and Thun (1899). The MFO and BBC were the companies most deeply involved in this process of modernisation. The electrical units of most Swiss locomotives came from these two companies, with the chassis usually supplied by SIG. Added to the challenges of actual construction was that of choosing the appropriate system: Questions regarding voltage, frequency and direct or alternating current had to be answered. Expert opinion was often divided on these questions, and what was right and what was wrong could often only be discovered after the engines became operational.

The discussion about the right kind of current was a tempestuous one. The MFO, for example, operated a test stretch between Seebach and Affoltern with alternating current between 1905 and 1910. For the Simplon Tunnel, however, it was finally decided that rotating current was the only type that would be practicable over the long distance involved.

The actual electrification of the Simplon Tunnel was a bold and highly risky undertaking. This almost 20-kilometre-long transalpine rail link was the longest tunnel in the world. Originally planned for steam engines, it was only electrified because BBC insisted on it shortly before the tunnel's completion, declaring that it would undertake the installation at its own cost and risk. Electrifying a tunnel of this length at first appeared utterly unrealistic. Besides, there was no time for experimentation or evaluation. BBC assumed the costs of the electrification in order to be able to gain experience and was prepared to remove the system at its own cost if it did not work.

But it did work. And so, the Simplon Tunnel, opened in 1906, made history as the first electrified transalpine rail link.

Flushing Away Basel's Chemical Waste

Like the engineering industry, the chemical industry developed in the wake of the textile industry. Because textile companies needed large quantities of acids and other fundamental chemicals for their bleaching and dyeing, and these materials could only be delivered in fragile glass bottles, transport was a challenge. Practice and experience had shown that the waterways were far safer than roads for transporting breakable items. This led chemical companies to situate themselves near textile companies, which themselves depended on flowing water for their energy needs.

The first chemical factory in Switzerland was built in 1778 in Winterthur, at the foot of the Töss Valley textile region. Johann Sebastian Clais (1742–1809) and Johann Heinrich Ziegler (1738–1818) produced so-called commodity chemicals in their laboratory: sulphuric acid, and later also hydrochloric acid, sodium carbonate, chlorinated lime, nitric acid and copper sulphate. The nascent textile industry in Glarus and in the Zurich Oberland led to the emergence of numerous chemical factories around Lake Zurich, which, taken together with the Linth and Limmat Rivers, formed a continually navigable waterway from Glarus to the Rhine. In Horgen, the Käpfnach chemical factory was built near the coal mine of the same name, which supplied its energy needs. In Wädenswil, which had become a regional centre of the textile industry, several chemical companies were founded. And on the opposite shore, in Uetikon, there were chemical companies as well, for example those of Johann Rudolf Rusterholz (1773–1836) and the previously mentioned Schnorf brothers. The latter company was founded in 1818 and became the largest producer of sulphuric acid in Switzerland. Almost all of the other producers of commodity chemicals ceased operations after the middle of the 19th century, when the tempo of the railways not only made goods transport on the waterways unprofitable but also allowed exports to undercut the domestic production of acids. The Schnorf brothers' chemical factory, however, maintained and even expanded its position on the market, not least because it continually optimised its production processes. As a family business that did not have to distribute profits, it was able to survive economically lean years. The Uetikon chemical factory later proved to be of national strategic importance, especially during the world wars, as it provided Switzerland with acids.

In the second half of the 19th century, the chemical industry in Basel followed a different path, concentrating on high-value specialty chemicals – first bitumen colours and later pharmaceuticals. There are a variety of reasons that the jump from commodity to specialty chemistry in Switzerland succeeded only in Basel. The local silk industry and the Alsatian calico industry (colour textile printing) provided good markets. Since the patent protection laws introduced in 1888 did not affect the chemical industry, many French chemists moved to Basel, which was close to France and other export markets. In contrast to the situation in the 20th century, when the chemical industry was largely consolidated and its companies were strongly interested in the protection of intellectual property, the dye industry at the close of the 19th century was characterised by very short-term innovations that rapidly succeeded one another. In this environment, the lack of patent protection had generally advantageous effects.

Basel was connected to the Alsatian railway network as early as 1844 – years before the railway project was successfully launched in Switzerland. Raw materials could therefore be transported to Basel more cheaply and easily than to other Swiss cities. But the Rhine, too, played an important role. Thanks to its large volume of flowing water, the highly poisonous wastes produced by the industry could be disposed of – and even better, disposed of directly into foreign countries.

No other Swiss city offered such favourable conditions. Robert Bindschedler's (1844–1901) application for permission to build a chemical plant in Winterthur was rejected in 1871, for example, because the City Council was concerned about the pollution and health problems it might cause – both of which were widely feared. Bindschedler therefore moved to Basel, where, together with a fellow student from Winterthur, Albert Busch (1836–1884), he founded Bindschedler & Busch – the future Schweizerische Gesellschaft für Chemische Industrie in Basel (Swiss Society for Chemical Industry in Basel, Ciba). The move to Basel brought Bindschedler even more advantages: The Rhine was not only a convenient place to dispose of chemical waste but also served as an important transport route for raw materials and product delivery – despite competition from the railway.

These underlying conditions and situational advantages were important. Yet the ultimate reason for the enormous growth of Basel's chemical and pharmaceutical firms was the optimal way that different businesses became interlinked. The phenomenon of several pioneers influencing a given area in such a way that their achievements worked together synergistically had already been a factor in the success of the watchmaking industry; now it became manifest in the Basel chemical industry as well.

The aniline dye industry in Basel was launched – as was so often the case for new Swiss industries – by a foreigner, the silk dyer Alexander Clavel (1805–1873) of Lyon. Clavel became a citizen of Basel and began production in 1859. In the same year, Johann Rudolf Geigy (1830–1917) also began to produce aniline. In 1865, Robert Bindschedler became the technical director at Geigy. After a short stay abroad, he found a job with Clavel, whose firm he acquired in 1873. One of the chemists at Bindschedler & Busch was Alfred Kern (1850–1893); in 1886, together with Edouard Sandoz (1853–1928), he founded the chemical company Kern & Sandoz. Sandoz had previously worked for Louis Durand (1837–1902), who, in turn, had been a Clavel employee from 1866 to 1870. It may be more than a coincidence that Geigy, Bindschedler, Busch, Kern, Sandoz and Durand, whose companies would merge to become Novartis 100 years later, were so closely connected with one another as pioneers.

The pharmaceutical company founded by Fritz Hoffmann-La Roche (1868–1920) had no close connections to other chemical manufacturers.

Hoffmann completed a banking apprenticeship in Yverdon, transferred to the pharmaceutical sector in 1889 and then completed an additional commercial apprenticeship. In 1894, with the support of his wealthy father, the silk-ribbon manufacturer Friedrich Hoffmann (1838–1897), Fritz Hoffmann and Max Carl Traub (1855–1919) founded Hoffmann, Traub & Co. Just two years later, after the departure of Traub, the company was renamed F. Hoffmann-La Roche & Co.[53] It experimented with a number of medicines and remedies for wounds but without much success, and the debts piled up. In this critical phase, Hoffmann showed himself to be a true pioneer, continuing to believe in his idea as he found ways to defray his mounting debts. This was possible not least due to his wealthy background. In 1898, he and his chemists achieved a breakthrough by producing Sirolin cough syrup. That Fritz Hoffmann became an influential and successful businessman in the matter of only a few years was not just due to Sirolin, however. Three other factors played a role: First, he manufactured his products industrially, while other pharmaceutical firms were still relying on manual work; second, he effectively advertised his products; and third, he massively expanded his foreign operations.

Another phenomenon that characterised the Basel chemical and pharmaceutical concerns was their loyalty to their location. Even if over the course of time they transferred parts of their business abroad, their legal headquarters remained on the crook of the Rhine. Significant portions of their research and development activities still take place in Switzerland today – for F. Hoffmann-La Roche, about a quarter. The companies' loyalty is also evidenced by the number of their employees who still work in Switzerland. Of the approximately 94,400 people employed by Roche in 2018, 13,600 worked in Switzerland; of Novartis's approximately 129,000 employees in the same year, around 13,000 worked in Switzerland.

Alongside the development of the large chemical and pharmaceutical companies in Basel in the 19th century, other small, locally embedded institutions formed. Some of these became known for the production and especially the sale of medicines, chemicals and exotic products. The Finsler company in Zurich provides an example.

The physician Johann Jakob Finsler (1796–1858) opened his first chemist's shop on the Münsterplatz in Zurich in 1833. From there he built up his trade in medicines, drugs and chemicals. Finsler supplied the pharmaceutical and chemical departments of the university, an important factor in the further development of his business. His son Georg Jakob (born 1826) inherited his father's pioneering spirit. He was one of the first businessmen in Zurich to recognise the importance of advertising for the success of a company. In the mid-1850s, as railway lines were opening one after another at a breakneck pace, Finsler printed train schedules featuring advertisements for his products. He thereby informed travellers not only about the departure and arrival times of trains but also about which ointments and perfumes were in vogue: fly glue, tinctures, Persian insect powders, floor polish. But Georg Finsler had still more expansive plans. He became involved in chemical production and built a factory in Oerlikon. He was also an innovator in sales and distribution and built up a field sales force. His effervescent spirit, which knew no bounds, ended up putting enormous strain on the management of his warehouses, as he attempted to offer his customers some 3,000 different products. This high-flown enterprise eventually landed on the hard ground of operational reality. The business was taken over by Adolf Finsler (1852–1907), who ran it until 1903.

Steamboats and Chocolates

The abundance of water in Switzerland was not only a decisive factor in the success of the textile industry. At various times it was a fundamental condition for other areas of commerce – for example, steamer traffic and tourism. Waterways were the birthplace of motorised transport in Switzerland, and they remained a key part of the transport system even when the first railway lines were built. For these lines did not run along the shores of lakes but rather ended at them. From there, the onward journey required a change of conveyance.

It all began on Lake Geneva, and once again it was a foreigner who provided the decisive impulse: Edward Church (1769–1847). An American diplomat in France, Church was surprised to see that there were no steamers coursing across Lake Geneva. It was incomprehensible to him that a free and enlightened nation in the heart of Europe should be without this gift of technological progress, which was highly prized in America, and he decided to do something about it. Church, who had already established a steamer business on the Seine, met with the Genevan authorities, who approved his project – and in 1823, the *Guillaume Tell*, the first steamboat in Switzerland, left the shipyard.

In pursuing this initiative, Church revealed certain remarkable aspects of his character, for he was himself neither a shipbuilder nor a businessman. In fact, he had no professional interest in steamer traffic on Lake Geneva. But as a believer in progress, as a man fascinated by new technical possibilities, he had felt the need to get something going. A certain spirit of adventure must have motivated him as well, as was reflected in the name of the boat: The republican-minded American wanted to celebrate the heroic freedom fighter of the Old Swiss Confederacy, and thereby show his reverence for a sister republic.

The steamboat was built around 700 kilometres from Lake Geneva, in Bordeaux, by Mauriac Père & Fils, as there were not yet any comparable shipyards in Switzerland. The novel conveyance caused a great sensation well beyond the Swiss borders, and it was not long before steamer projects were developed for other Swiss waterways. Church himself was later involved in launching steamboat traffic on Lake Constance – not, however, from the republican Swiss side but on behalf of the Württemberg and Bavarian monarchies.

Three years after the first voyage of the *Guillaume Tell* on Lake Geneva, the first steamer plied the waters of Lakes Neuchâtel and Biel. The initiative in this case was taken by Jean-Beat Albert du Thon (1791–1838) of Canton Vaud, who joined forces with the Nidau businessman Ferdinand Piccard. The two men came up with the idea of establishing a steamboat connection between Yverdon and Biel. In contrast to Church, who deployed the *Guillaume Tell* for passenger traffic, du Thon and Piccard planned to haul freight from the start. The initial rejoicing at the launch of the ship in the summer of 1826, however, soon yielded to disillusionment. Repeated breakdowns due to the inattention of the crew led to a loss of confidence in the new form of transport. The amount of goods transported and the number of passengers decreased after only half a year. The company was dissolved less than two years after its formation.

It appeared that the time was not yet ripe for navigation on the Jura lakes. But now the next pioneer, Philippe Suchard (1797–1884), appeared on the scene and met with success. For 14 years, beginning in 1834, he himself captained the *Industrielle* on the waters of Lakes Neuchâtel and Biel. As was the case for Edward Church, it was not exclusively business interests that moved Suchard to take up with steamboats. Enthusiasm for the new, a will to modernise and a belief in progress also played their parts. And Suchard was also an adventurer. His steamer, which was built in Paris and constructed solely of iron, was the first of its kind on Swiss waters. The iron hull allowed for a leaner and more efficient design than was possible for the wooden ships that were the norm for the time.

To the public it seemed inconceivable that such an iron colossus would actually float. Even the authorities had serious concerns. It is thus not surprising that Suchard, like many pioneers, met with obstacles and public disdain. There were a number of reasons for this. One very substantial one was that the *Industrielle* represented overpowering competition for local boatmen, who up until then had transported goods and passengers on sailboats and rowboats. Suchard and his steamer were torpedoed – the man with accusations of personal intrigues and the boat with wild rumours about the dangers of the new means of transport. The situation was further complicated by the cantonal borders that had to be respected on the Jura lakes. The bureaucratic and financial hurdles were sometimes ridiculous. While the Neuchâtel government maintained friendly relations with Suchard as one of its own, and created favourable conditions for his project, the sympathies of the Fribourg and Bernese customs officials were with their own local ships. They harassed the *Industrielle* with endless inspections and other chicaneries. Added to these difficulties was the fact that, since Suchard had no luck in hiring competent Swiss technicians, he was compelled to recruit expert personnel abroad. These, however, quickly realised their indispensability, repeatedly made new demands and even went on wildcat strikes.

Suchard was a picture-book pioneer. Receptive to all that was new, he was active in many areas of business. He became world-famous for his chocolate, which he began producing in 1825. He had designed a mixing machine with which he could blend sugar and cacao in precisely prescribed ratios; the fundamental procedure is still used in the chocolate industry today. He moved his production workshop to an old mill and used its water power to run both his mixing machine and his cacao grinder. His first successes were with wealthy foreigners, who became enamoured of his sweet product. He principally made a name for himself at the Prussian court, which he could easily supply because Neuchâtel was a Prussian dominion at the time. The demand for chocolate increased markedly in the second half of the century.

Suchard continued to run his shipping business in parallel with his chocolate company, but he also undertook other new and adventurous enterprises. In 1837, he began raising silkworms – an undertaking for which he received state support, since dependence on foreign suppliers was viewed as an encumbrance to the silk trade. The climate on the banks of Lake Neuchâtel seemed favourable for both mulberry trees and the silkworms that fed on their leaves. Suchard planted around 3,000 mulberry trees. In 1844, the great moment arrived: He was able to present the Neuchâtel city government with the first product of his workshop in Serrières, a foulard woven from threads produced by silkworms he had raised himself, that had been nourished by the leaves of his own mulberry trees. This happily initiated project foundered, however, when a disease annihilated the silkworm population.

In 1841, Suchard became the managing director of an asphalt sales company in Val de Travers. For publicity purposes, he had the roof of his chocolate factory asphalted, while during sales trips in Germany undertaken for the asphalt company, he vigorously advertised his chocolate. When the demand for asphalt declined, he summarily liquidated the young company.

Suchard was fascinated by faraway foreign lands. In 1846, after buying some inexpensive land in Utica, New York, he founded a public limited company to assist the settlement of Swiss emigrants in America. The goal was to construct a kind of reception and training camp, where the emigrants, alongside their farming, would mine the rich treasures he suspected lay hidden beneath the soil. He aimed to provide an alternative to the many fraudulent arrangements whereby emigrants "bought" American land while still in Europe – land they would never see on their arrival on the other side of the Atlantic. For this purpose, Suchard himself travelled to the USA and assessed a number of locations. The project, however, was ultimately unsuccessful. The mining treasures he had expected to find did not exist, settlers showed little interest and Suchard ended up swallowing an enormous financial loss.

Suchard subsequently concentrated on chocolate production, but his enthusiasm for the wider world remained intact and became visible for all to see in Neuchâtel. Full of impressions from his travels in the Near and Far East, and still in the thrall of a five-and-a-half-month trip around the world that he took at the age of 76, Suchard decorated his house with half-moons and built a minaret – surely the first in Switzerland.

The chocolate that bore Suchard's name made him famous around the world. But that was only one side of the coin – the sweet one. On the other side, bankruptcies piled up. It is only when these two sides are considered together that Suchard is revealed as a typical pioneer of the Sturm und Drang period, marked by fortune and failure, trial and error. Pioneers both succeeded and failed, and often had to begin over again from scratch more than once.

Alongside commerce and the thirst for adventure, tourism was a driving force behind the development of steamboat navigation in Switzerland. Such was the case on Lake Thun. The brothers Johann Jakob (1790–1867), Johannes (1793–1865) and Johann Friedrich (1796–1871) Knechtenhofer ran the *Hotel Bellevue* in Thun, which was among the most distinguished hotels in all of Europe. In order to enliven their own tourism business, and at the same time ensure that their hotel remained easily accessible – a new road was planned, but for the opposite side of the lake – they founded a steamboat company. Based on advice they received from Suchard, the Knechtenhofers commissioned their first steamer in 1835 – notably from the same Paris shipbuilders as had built Suchard's *Industrielle*. They gave the steamboat the name *Bellevue*, thereby linking it both to their hotel and to the tourist industry in general. Johannes, the second-oldest brother, became its captain. A steam-driven mechanical trumpet, mounted on the bow and capable of belting out no fewer than 16 different tunes, proved to be a huge attraction. The reception given British visitors became legendary: The Knechtenhofers had adroitly installed the melody of "God Save the Queen."

In the course of just a few years, most of the large bodies of water in Switzerland began to be traversed by steamships. In 1835, Franz Carl Caspar (1794–1838) and Johann Jakob Lämmlin (1805–1854) launched the first steamer on Lake Zurich. The boat had been built in Manchester. It arrived in Kaiseraugst after an adventurous crossing of the North Sea and a journey up the Rhine via Mannheim and Basel. It was disassembled in Kaiseraugst, loaded onto ox- and horse-drawn carts, and driven to Zurich. After its reconstruction in Zurich, its name was changed from *Vulkan* to *Minerva*.

Casimir Friedrich Knörr (1808–1882) and David Gottlieb Matti (1804–1851) became steamboat pioneers on Lake Lucerne and Lake

Brienz in 1837 and 1839, respectively. Somewhat later, in 1852, a steamer belonging to Johann Friedrich Peyer im Hof's (1817–1900) Rhine and Untersee Steamboat Company (Dampfschifffahrtsgesellschaft Rhein und Untersee) was launched on Lake Constance. A steamer had been running on the German side of the lake since 1824.

Tickets to the Mountaintops

Niklaus Riggenbach (1817–1899) was the director of the engineering workshop of the Swiss Central Railway (Schweizerischen Centralbahn, SCB) in Olten. He was looking for a system that would allow locomotives to function on steep gradients, and found it in cog railway technology. Riggenbach refined this technology and commercially exploited his design. In 1873, the Rigi became the first mountain in Switzerland to be climbed by a train. The two-year construction period was due to legal reasons. The technology created a sensation, and business boomed. In its first year of operation, the train carried 60,000 people up the Rigi, despite the fact that it moved little faster than the hikers walking beside it. Once again, the pioneer did not remain alone in his enterprise; lively competition ensued, and Switzerland soon led the world in cog railway construction.

Only a few years after the opening of the Rigi railway, Carl Roman Abt (1850–1933), an employee and student of Riggenbach, developed an optimised cog system that was both quieter and less expensive. Meanwhile, the inspector of the Berner Oberland Railway and the Lauterbrunnen-Mürren mountain railway, Emil Strub (1858–1909), was planning a railway up the Eiger and developed his own cog system to propel it. His project was never realised; the ambitious and above all very wealthy railway pioneer Adolf Guyer-Zeller (1839–1899) beat him to the punch with his project for a Jungfrau Railway. After some initial hesitation, Strub gave up his resistance and threw his lot in with the Jungfrau Railway. He became its technical director, which allowed him to implement his own cog system on the tracks leading to the highest train station in Europe.

For the steepest cog railway in the world, which opened on Pilatus in 1889, Eduard Locher designed his own novel system, in which two horizontally oriented cogs meshed with the rack. Although it was ideal for such extreme gradients, the Pilatus railway remained the only one to use this system. Today, almost all cog railways in the world use Riggenbach's, Abt's or Strub's systems.

By providing access to the mountains, railway construction became even more important for tourism. While steamship operations had served touristic purposes from the start, freight transport had been the first priority for the railways on the Swiss Central Plateau. This was not the case, however, for the Alpine regions oriented towards tourism, where passenger transport became increasingly important. Yet the railroad was not only decisive for the success of the Alpine hotspots of the last quarter of the 19th century. The accessibility of a given region by rail generally determined its touristic development. The same principle applies to mountaintop destinations: Säntis, for example, was less of a tourist attraction than Pilatus because it was not accessible by a mountain railway. Tourism and the railways provided one another with stimuli for their mutual development. This was especially true during the Belle Époque.

The Schindler company provides a good example of how tourism fostered economic development. Robert Schindler (1850–1920), the son of a physician from Schwyz, spent time abroad as a journeyman after serving an apprenticeship as a mechanic. In 1874, he partnered with Eduard Peter Villiger (1848–1913) to found Schindler & Villiger in Lucerne, a mechanical workshop dedicated to the production of lifting devices and machines of all kinds. The company built a first freight lift in 1890 and an electric lift with a belt drive two years later. The demands of the growing hotel industry soon moved Schindler to exclusively manufacture lifts. In 1902, the company built the first electric passenger lift with push-button controls. Since then, Schindler has become the global market leader in lift production; in 2017, the company boasted over 60,000 employees.

Dairy Products: From Mountain to Factory

In the 19th century, Switzerland was known as the Alpine country *par excellence*. And even if today three quarters of the Swiss population lives in cities, the Alpine landscape is still, in historic terms, of immense significance in many respects. As a buffer between north and south, east and west – and as the keeper of the major Alpine passes – Switzerland was allowed to retain its sovereignty by the great European powers. The great mountains and the isolation of the Alpine valleys materially shaped the federalism that became one of the Swiss recipes for success. And the wealth of waterways in the Alps played an essential role in the history of Swiss industry.

Since the Middle Ages, the Alps have also played an important role in the Swiss economy. The first significant Swiss export product – cheese – emerged from the practice of keeping livestock on the alps in summer, and the domestic food industry is also closely tied to the mountains. There is evidence of cheese being used to pay duties to overlords as early as the Middle Ages. In the 16th century, the transition was made from soft and whey cheeses to hard cheese, which has a much longer shelf life and is therefore a fitting product for export.

Growing demand in Swiss cities and neighbouring countries led to a rapid increase in cheese production. Sbrinz, Emmental and Gruyère became the best-known kinds of Swiss cheese. As an easily stored and calorie-rich foodstuff, cheese became important during wartime, both for the nourishment of civilian populations and as rations for soldiers. Accordingly, cheese exports increased steeply during the Thirty Years' War (1618–1648) and developed into a flourishing business. That trade in Swiss cheese became increasingly lucrative during the 17th century is evidenced by the monopolies established by patrician families. In order to safeguard the local butter markets, some Swiss towns even regulated cheese exports. The success and expansion of grass-based dairy farming led to a decrease in the production of grain.

Until the early 19th century, cheese production remained concentrated in the Alpine and pre-Alpine regions. A dramatic transformation took place after 1830, when cheese dairies began to appear in the valleys and cheese production moved from mountain huts down to the villages. Thanks to improved production techniques, valley-produced cheese was able to hold its own against cheese made on the alps. In contrast to the latter, it could also be produced all year round. Increasingly rapid transport connections in the following decades, and especially in the 1860s, led to a further increase in demand and to a downright boom in cheese. After 1870, however, a rapid decline in cheese production occurred in the hinterlands of newly formed powdered milk and chocolate factories, such as the areas around Vevey (Nestlé) and Cham (Anglo-Swiss Condensed Milk Company). These industrial concerns became the main customers for the milk produced in their regions.

Tilsit cheese occupies a memorable place in Swiss history. How can it be that one of the best-known Swiss cheeses bears the name of an eastern European city? Tilsit, today's Sowetsk, belonged to East Prussia up until the Second World War. At the beginning of the 18th century, after the plague had killed about a third of the Prussian population, King Frederick I (1657–1713) introduced policies designed to entice immigrants to settle in his realm. Swiss immigrants soon arrived, and continued to flow in until the early 19th century. In their new home, they made their living as farmers and dairymen.

Around 1890, two cheesemakers from Thurgau, Otto Wartmann and Hans Wegmüller, arrived in Tilsit independently of one another. Inspired by the cheesemaking they saw there, they made their way back to Switzerland, where they began to make cheese according to the East Prussian recipe in 1893. They made a few changes to the original, forming a wheel instead of a loaf of cheese, and the new product was favourably received in Switzerland. At the Swiss Agricultural Exhibition of 1903 in Frauenfeld, no fewer than 17 different Tilsit cheeses were on display.

Milk was the fundamental raw material for the first product made by Nestlé, today the largest food company in the world. Heinrich Nestle (1814–1890) was born in Frankfurt am Main, where he served an apprenticeship in a pharmacy. In 1839, fearing reprisals for his contacts with the Liberal opposition to the government, he fled to Switzerland

and settled in Vevey. Here he gave his name a French twist and was henceforth known as Henri Nestlé. After passing an examination to qualify as an assistant pharmacist, he began to produce, with modest success, oils, liqueurs and vinegar, and later also fertiliser and mineral water. He developed a liquefied gas that he sold to the city of Vevey for its streetlights and invented a procedure for producing Portland cement and prefabricated building blocks. Nestlé's breakthrough, however, came in 1867, with the production of a baby cereal containing milk. A story about his cereal saving the lives of two sick and emaciated infants made Nestlé and his product well known. He began to produce the baby cereal industrially. Enormous population growth, the poor health of many segments of society and the economic crisis of the 1870s all led to great demand for the product. In 1875, atypically for a pioneer of the time, Nestlé retired to private life at the age of 60, selling his company to three other industrialists. He had by then earned a fortune that would safely see him through his twilight years.

In 1905, Nestlé merged with the Anglo-Swiss Condensed Milk Company in Cham. This company, founded in 1866 by a group led by the American Vice Consul in Zurich, Charles Page (1838–1873), was the first producer of condensed milk in Europe. It grew rapidly, established

Figure 2.17 "Women at work in the packaging facility for bouillon cubes of the Maggi company in Kemptthal," 1913. Photograph. Archives Historiques Nestlé, Vevey. © NESTLE S.A./Société des Produits Nestlé S.A.

several branches in Switzerland and abroad, and at the time of the merger with its competitor, Nestlé, was by far the larger of the two companies. That Nestlé today bears the name it does is due to the fact that Nestlé & Anglo-Swiss Condensed Milk Company, the original name of the merged firm, was felt to be too awkward and was therefore shortened.

Milk from the mountains also played an important role in the chocolate industry, but only after Daniel Peter (1836–1919), the son-in-law of François-Louis Cailler (1797–1852), mixed it with chocolate at scale and thereby created a new product. For this he has gone down in history, despite the fact that other individual confectioners had previously used milk in their own creations. Peter, who was a friend of Nestlé, first used powdered milk in his recipe but, in 1875, decided in favour of condensed milk. By this point, however, Switzerland had already become a nation of chocolate. Not only had Philippe Suchard revolutionised the procedure for making chocolate in 1825, thereby turning it into an affordable product, but he had also succeeded in building Suchard up into a global brand with his considerable advertising skills. The image of Switzerland as an idyllic country, a place of health and natural life, again and again played a key role in Suchard's publicity. Switzerland is still associated with chocolate today, although nary a cacao bean has been grown on its soil. But then, Switzerland also grows no cotton and has hardly any iron ore, and despite this was long associated with the processing of these two raw materials and became a global leader in the textile and machine industries.

The Mechanisation of Agriculture

Developments in Swiss agriculture affected more than just farmers and the milk-processing industry. They also impacted other areas of the economy – for example, the manufacture of agricultural machinery.

Specialisation within the agricultural sector led, on the one hand, to the outsourcing of the production and repair of machines and tools. On the other hand, it led to mechanisation, which in turn led to a demand for professional mechanics. In the first half of the 19th century, agricultural machinery was used only in a few large operations, mostly in western Switzerland. Machines served to accelerate simple but time-consuming activities such as the grinding of livestock fodder, the harrowing of fields, the sharpening of knives and the honing of scythes. Starting in the 1850s, the use of British and American haymaking machines became increasingly widespread in Switzerland, and in the 1860s, threshing and feed-chopping machines, which were still operated by hand or by horse capstans, made their appearance; they were followed in the 1880s by steam-powered threshers. By contrast, work in the fields was still largely performed using muscle power – mostly that of horses. In the last quarter of the 19th century, mouldboard ploughs came into use. These needed no special steering, which spared a worker. The mechanisation of mowing arrived in 1895, with the domestic serial production of horse-drawn mowing machines.

These developments are reflected in the history of agricultural machine manufacture. At the start of the 19th century, the village blacksmith manufactured and repaired agricultural machines – when farmers did not carry out this work themselves. Over time, specialised mechanical workshops were established. These fostered the development of machines and other equipment, in synergy with the activities of pioneers in other fields.

An example of this can be seen in the Bucher company, which still produces agricultural machinery and all-terrain vehicles at its original location in Niederweningen in Canton Zurich today, while also employing around 13,000 workers on five continents as a globally active technology concern. The firm had its origins in one Heinrich Bucher (1784–1850), who started his own smithy in 1807. This Heinrich Bucher, however, remained a conventional blacksmith. In the 1850s his son, also named Heinrich Bucher (1815–1876), transformed the smithy into a mechanical workshop. He used a nearby stream to power his machine tools. Among his first products were slurry pumps, hand-operated threshing and feed-shredding machines, and hand mills. The third generation of the Bucher enterprise, in the person of Johann Bucher-Manz (1843–1919), further pursued the path of mechanisation and expanded the firm's product line with fruit and grape presses. At the same time, Bucher began to trade in foreign machinery, in particular McCormick mowing machines from the USA. He thus became an important contributor to the mechanisation of agriculture at the turn of the century.

The increasing demand for agricultural machines in Switzerland can be seen in the development of Bucher: While up until the end of the 1880s the company had only a handful of employees, in the 1890s the number grew to 29. This expansion called for the construction of new facilities and the extension of old ones, in the course of which, in 1896, the company name "Maschinenfabrik" (Machine Factory) gained currency. In 1904, Jean Bucher-Guyer (1875–1961) took over the business. In its fourth generation, Bucher became a technological leader in hydraulic fruit and grape presses, which now, along with hand and slurry pumps, made up a part of the firm's core business. The trade in agricultural machinery continued, and when foreign models proved deficient, Bucher took pains to develop alternatives of its own construction and to bring these to the market.

While Bucher's core business was in the trade and sales of agricultural machinery, two other pioneers dedicated themselves to the production of this machinery: Johannes Rauschenbach (1815–1881) and Johann Ulrich Aebi (1846–1919). After his journeyman years, Rauschenbach worked as an independent mechanic in his home city of Schaffhausen. When Heinrich Moser built the first water-power plant on the Rhine,

Rauschenbach took advantage of the opportunity and, with Moser's support, moved his workshop to the river. In 1846, Rauschenbach, who produced machine tools of all kinds, became one of the first manufacturers in Switzerland to produce threshing machines. The market was dominated by British and American competition, however, and Rauschenbach's sales were sluggish. At first, he was unable to sell more than a single machine per year. By 1866, however, he was selling 212. And then, in the 1870s, sales downright exploded. The second agricultural revolution and the mechanisation it involved had a resounding effect. In 1872, an in-house foundry was built onto the mechanical workshop, and in 1876, sales of threshing machines reached 11,210.

Rauschenbach was active as an industrialist in other companies as well. In 1847, he and his brother Conrad founded a brad and cotton-wool factory. He was known as one of the richest men in Schaffhausen. Alongside his commercial activities, Johannes Rauschenbach was a member of the Schaffhausen City Parliament (Grosser Stadtrat) (1856–1881), the Cantonal Parliament (1867–1876/1878–1880), the Municipal Building Commission (1866–1872) and the Constitutional Council (1873–1876). In 1879, he took over the bankrupt watch manufacturer IWC (International Watch Company) and led it back to profitability. IWC was inherited by the industrialist Erst Jakob Homberger (1869–1955) and then by his son Hans Homberger (1908–1986), before being taken over by the German company VDO Adolf Schindling AG in 1978. Since 2000, it has been part of the Richemont Group.

Johann Ulrich Aebi built a mechanical workshop on his parents' farm between Wynigen and Burgdorf in 1868. Like Rauschenbach and the Buchers, he avidly visited technical expositions, especially world fairs, where he picked up inspiration for his own constructions. Aebi at first concentrated on the replication of and technical improvements to selected machines: fire hoses, mowers and steam- and water-power-driven engines. Good business results led him to build a factory, first under collective proprietorship as Aebi & Mühlethaler (1883) and from 1888 onwards as an individual enterprise. In 1876, he built the first mowing machine of his own design. He achieved a breakthrough with the "Helvetia" mower, serial production of which began in 1887.

Adolf Bühler (1833–1896), a pioneer in mill construction, was another agricultural supplier. In 1860, he opened a small iron foundry in Uzwil, to which he appended a mechanical workshop in 1871. He first manufactured embroidery machines but soon afterwards expanded and made products for the milling industry. The development of Bühler Uzwil is illustrative of the agricultural industrialisation process. In 1872, Bühler produced the first chilled-casting roller, in 1876 the first roller mill, and from 1890 onwards he was making entire grain mills and silos. The number of his employees increased from 3 in 1860 to over 500 in 1895. Bühler simultaneously expanded his business internationally, with a branch in Paris (1891) and agencies in Milan and Barcelona (1896). Under the leadership of his son, Adolf Bühler (1869–1939), the firm developed into an international concern, with more than 2,800 employees in the late 1930s.

The Bühlers, father and son, are exemplars of the first and second generations of industrial pioneers. While the elder Adolf Bühler completed an apprenticeship as a caster and only became a master after several years of professional practice, his son studied engineering sciences at the Polytechnic (Zurich) and in Karlsruhe. He took over the leadership of the firm in 1896 and was a promoter of the kind of well-connected and organised industry that characterised Switzerland until well into the 20th century. The younger Bühler, for example, sat on the boards of numerous companies and was active in the leading associations in the engineering and metal construction industries. He was also a Municipal Councillor for the Freisinnig-Demokratische Partei (FDP) from 1897 to1912) and a member of the Cantonal Parliament (1898–1906). He developed and implemented a number of company-internal social services, such as the housing cooperative "Uze" in 1926.

The progress of agriculture depended not only on practical experience but also on scientific findings, as is illustrated by the career of Hermann Müller-Thurgau (1850–1927). Like grain cultivation, viticulture was in a difficult situation in the second half of the 19th century. There were several reasons for this. Large quantities of wine were being imported into Switzerland, and it was not only generally less expensive than Swiss wine but also often of a superior quality. And with this wine, novel pests also entered the country. Swiss winegrowers, who were often poorly trained, were not up to meeting these challenges.

In 1891, 14 German-speaking Swiss cantons bonded together to found an experimental agricultural institute, the Versuchsstation und Schule für Obst-, Wein- und Gartenbau Wädenswil (Experimental Station and School for Fruit, Wine and Garden Cultivation in Wädenswil). Müller-Thurgau was its first director (1881–1924). One of the early pioneering achievements of this institute was its research into diseases and pests afflicting cultivated plants. Its best-known accomplishment was Müller-Thurgau's breeding of the new Riesling-Sylvaner grape variety, which was characterised by its fertility, early maturity, high sugar content and moderate acid content. Riesling-Sylvaner grapes, known abroad as Müller-Thurgau grapes, were soon among the most widely cultivated in the German-speaking world. Müller-Thurgau's research on the preservability of fruit and grape juices and on the importance of pasteurisation were also pioneering achievements. From this research sprang the "Erste schweizerische Aktiengesellschaft zu Herstellung unvergorener und alkoholfreier Trauben- und Obstweine" (First Swiss Corporation for the Production of Unfermented and Alcohol-Free Grape and Fruit Wines), which was later subsumed by the Migros supermarket chain.

Commerce: From Generation to Generation

In 1851, Salomon Volkart (1816–1893) and Johann Georg Volkart (1825–1861) launched a commercial venture in Winterthur and Bombay. Salomon, the elder of the two brothers, had completed a commercial apprenticeship at Caspar Schulthess & Cie., a renowned Zurich bank and trading company that today goes by the name of Rahn + Bodmer Co. He subsequently moved to Genoa, where he assumed a position in an olive oil firm. This job involved travelling intensively throughout Italy. He next worked for a German company in Naples. Finally, a long journey in 1844/1845 brought him to India. There he met his brother, Johann Georg, who had begun travelling after his own commercial training at the Hüni & Fierz textile trading company in Horgen. In Bombay, Johann Georg worked as a cotton purchaser, taking advantage of Great Britain's repeal of the so-called Navigation Acts, which cleared the way for free trade with the British crown colony.

The two brothers blazed new trails as Swiss entrepreneurs with their business activities: In 1853/1854, they maintained their own mercantile fleet of three sailboats. These boats, which operated under the flags of Hamburg and Bremen, established a direct link between the firm's two headquarters in Switzerland and India. To operate the fleet, the Volkarts formed a consortium with the Ziegler sulphonated castor oil dye-works. The connection to Switzerland and in particular to their home city of Winterthur was expressed in the names of the ships: *Winterthur*, *Ida Ziegler* and *President Furrer*. Johann Georg directed the Bombay branch of the company, while Salomon organised the business from Switzerland. Post always travelled with the shipped goods, for at that time neither telephones nor telegraphs were yet in use. The trip around Africa by ship took around two months; the Suez Canal would only open in 1869.

That the Volkarts were able to successfully build up and develop their business under these circumstances was a considerable accomplishment. Business competency, knowledge of their field and mutual trust, all of which the Volkarts possessed, had to be supplemented by a readiness to take on risks. But the Volkarts were successful. Their business flourished, first in raw cotton and then also in seeds, tea, oils, coffee and spices, which came from India to Switzerland, and in sugar, soap, paper, clocks and textiles, which were shipped in the other direction. Already in the first year of the business they opened branches in Colombo, Kochi and Karachi, and in 1868 an office was opened in London.

Salomon Volkart provides yet another example of the entrepreneurial breadth and diversity that characterised the pioneering era of the young Federal State. He was involved in the founding of numerous companies in Winterthur, such as the Bank in Winterthur, the Schweizerische Lokomotiv- und Maschinenfabrik (Swiss Locomotive and Machine Works) and the Schweizerische Unfallversicherungs-Gesellschaft (Swiss

Accident Insurance Company). He also served in the Zurich Cantonal Parliament for several years as an Economic Liberal.[54]

Doctor Alfred Escher of Zurich: *A La Bonne Heure*, This Is a Man *Comme Il En Faut Pour La Suisse*

Most politicians, business leaders and entrepreneurs fade into obscurity when they die.[55] The 19th century gave rise to certain personalities, however, who would hardly be possible today, and who therefore have remained in our collective memory. Such a figure was Alfred Escher (1819–1882) of Zurich. His achievements and influence would surely seem to justify a place of honour in the Swiss pantheon.

Yet political heroes are taboo in Switzerland. When someone becomes too powerful for too long, the Swiss people instinctively revert to a defensive republican attitude, one nourished by resentment and petty jealousy. At this point, the hour is ripe for the opposition. Escher was among those who experienced this tipping point and its consequences. It is understandable that, in their contemporary context, the epochal changes that he wrought went unrecognised, that his unbridled potency was seen as excessive, his dominance as provocative. Truly, Switzerland is not used to dealing with individuals of such a calibre. For Escher was a titan. And today, in our equitable society, even more than in his lifetime, such a figure, with so strong a mind of his own, will necessarily appear suspect and maladjusted.

Escher achieved the extraordinary on the most diverse levels; he demolished contemporary expectations of what was possible. It would be exhausting to list all of his offices and functions. Yet a brief overview will make evident the contours of his work, which was unique even for the second half of the 19th century, both for the scale and for the rapid succession of the projects it consisted of. It is downright astonishing how much he was capable of doing and being simultaneously: He was a member of both the executive (Government Council) and the legislative (Cantonal Parliament) branches of the Zurich cantonal government, was a Federal Parliamentarian (National Councillor), a chief executive (railways), a president of boards of governors (railway and finance), a member of the executive committees of various companies and institutions (business and academic), and an initiator and promoter of Swiss infrastructural projects in general.[56] The three temples that Alfred Escher erected in his lifetime keep his memory alive more effectively than the rather static monument to him on the Bahnhofplatz in Zurich: the temples of transport (the Zurich Main Train Station), of science (ETH Zurich) and of finance (Schweizerische Kreditanstalt). A fourth temple, that of the arts, he never built, but this gap was closed, at least conceptually, in the dreams and plans of his daughter Lydia.[57]

Figure 2.18 Richard Kissling (1848–1919). *Alfred Escher.* Dedicated in 1889. Photograph. Private collection.

Alfred Escher, represented with the bearing of a titular monarch, turns his back to the crowds rushing out of the Zurich main station. His gaze is towards the south, down the Bahnhofstrasse.

Alfred Escher's family, which became domiciled in Zurich at the end of the 14th century, was a branch of the Escher vom Glas family, originally from Kaiserstuhl. Alfred Escher was born in 1819 in the "Neuberg" house on the Hirschengraben, three years after his sister Clementine (1816–1886), the future Frau Stockar-Escher. In 1831, the family moved into the Belvoir estate in Enge. Firmly settled, and submerged in a sea of tasks and obligations undertaken on behalf of Switzerland and Zurich, Alfred Escher married a German woman, the 19-year-old Augusta Uebel (1858–1891), in 1857. The marriage produced two girls: Lydia (1858–1891), the later Frau Welti-Escher, who had no children, and Hedwig (1861–1862), who died in infancy. Alfred Escher's family is thus no longer with us. Escher was buried in the old Enge cemetery; on its deconsecration in 1925, his remains were moved to the Mannegg cemetery.

The great diversity of his areas of expertise allowed Alfred Escher to assume the role of the omnipresent player and networker – as a well-versed politician (finance, science and scholarship, education, transport, business, social issues, culture, foreign policy) and as a business leader and citizen (from the landmark Gotthard project to the rebuilding of a local schoolhouse). And although it might be objected that other politicians, too, were successful businessmen, and that the interaction between political and business forces was a general characteristic of the young Federal State, still no one else exploited this institutional interweaving to the same extent or with the same intensity as Alfred Escher. That his fine-meshed network has become known as a "system" in the jargon of political philosophy illustrates his influence.[58]

Escher exuded the Spirit of '48 and stood for what would become the foundation for the success of the new, post-1848 Switzerland: capital and science. He furthered development in Switzerland after 1848 like no other business leader or politician. He was the creator of modern Switzerland – a man who, at the time of the young Federal State, delighted not in Medieval heroes but in train stations and industrial plants, in the magnificent buildings of the finance industry and the academy. Escher dedicated his life to creating this Switzerland. And he did so, at least in part, out of love for his native country.[59]

It was once fashionable for emperors and kings to promote themselves by appending to their names the epithet "the Great." Yet when is a person great? When can someone be said to have achieved greatness? Jakob Burkhardt (1818–1897), the (great) Swiss cultural historian, measured greatness in terms of time.[60] He differentiated between true greatness, possessed only by a few, and great power, which often accrues in the hands of leaders. When Burckhardt places Alexander the Great (356–323 BCE) at the top of the list of Greats, followed by Karl the Great (Charlemagne, ca 747–814), Peter the Great (1672–1725) and Frederick the Great (1712–1786), his criteria are evident: Historical greatness is attributed those individuals who lead the people of a given culture from an old into a new condition. At first it might seem presumptuous to compare Escher with the Greats of the world, with emperors, kings and sultans who conquered half-continents and established world powers. Yet let us look at the matter more closely.

Alfred Escher was a politician in a nation that, up until the middle of the 19th century, would have to be called a developing country. Yet he was more; he was a founding pioneer and a visionary. He led Switzerland from one condition into another, formulated the fundamental principles of Swiss politics, established the strategic and conceptual pillars of a small nation and staked out the possibilities and limits of its power politics. He was the founder of important business enterprises and the operational leader of several of them. He recognised that developing Switzerland via the railways was the key issue of his time and understood what it would take to realise this development; he created essential public and private infrastructure and determined which tasks belonged to federal and which to cantonal administrations; he helped the idea of a transalpine rail link to its breakthrough and, as President of the Board of Directors of the Gotthard Railway Company, oversaw the construction project of the century, one compared by contemporary media to the building of the Egyptian pyramids. In all of this, Escher followed his vision of a new, modern, future-oriented nation. When he stepped down from the socio-political stage, the one-time developing country had become a nation of a completely different character: a leading industrial nation, its railway network – and in particular, the Gotthard Railway – a brilliant symbol of technical progress that radiated far and wide.

And his contemporaries? Where can we find a comparable personality, one responsible for so many epochal achievements in so many areas? Not in Switzerland. Here there is only Alfred Escher. In Europe? Where, even in the whole world? Let us have a look. We will not be stopped by the fact that the effectiveness of individual leaders cannot be stringently and empirically measured. That is not what this is about. And while the circumstances of the cases we consider might appear too diverse to enable a sensible comparison of the individual actors, temporal and cultural differences ultimately do not alter the fundamental profiles of historical figures. Seen from a distance, structural parallels and constants reveal themselves even among the multiplicity of their manifestations.

What got in Escher's way were the national and political structures that differentiated Switzerland from dynastic, monarchic systems. Or – was it perhaps precisely the characteristics of this unique environment that created the conditions for his success? There is much to be said for the idea that only small, republican Switzerland, with its federalist makeup and its representative democracy, could have provided a setting that would have allowed Escher to become the exceptional phenomenon that he was; the idea that a figure like Escher was only possible in the context of the political institutions, parliamentary procedures and power relations characteristic of the Federal State at its beginnings – while in the third quarter of the 19th century, as direct democracy gathered strength, he could not have retained his dominating influence; the idea that only in Switzerland with its political militia system would a figure like Escher have been able to assume so many political, business and academic roles at the same time.

To whom can Escher be compared? In the Germany of Escher's time, Imperial Chancellor Bismarck (1815–1898), who led his country into a new order, comes to mind. But Bismarck was wanting in entrepreneurial talent. Frederick I of Baden (1826–1907) lastingly reformed his Grand Duchy, promoted the expansion of railways and waterways and developed southwest German industry. He also helped develop important educational institutions, such as the Technical University of Karlsruhe (today's Karlsruhe Institute of Technology), still also known as the "Fridericiana." Yet he was not a business leader. King Ludwig II of Bavaria (1845–1886) also had little business savvy. He was a passionate builder of castles and spent more money than he possessed. And Emperor Franz Joseph I (1830–1916) in Vienna? He was too occupied with holding together his multi-ethnic state and navigating his way through the dangerous shoals of foreign policy.

And what about the greats of German industry? Alfred Krupp (1812–1887), say, or August Borsig (1804–1854)? They furthered machine construction and the metals industry and controlled entire branches of the economy. But they were not politicians. Is Escher comparable to Friedrich List (1789–1846), Germany's great railway pioneer, who was simultaneously an economic theorist, a businessman, a diplomat and a politician? Or the brothers Friedrich (1793–1880) and Gustav Harkort (1795–1865), who taken together might have made up an Escher? The one was an entrepreneur in the engineering industry and the other in the textile industry, and both were also politicians and railway pioneers. Gustav, in addition, was the founder of the Allgemeine Deutsche Credit-Anstalt (German National Credit Institution) in Leipzig, a sponsor of Escher's own Kreditanstalt. List and the Harkort brothers: why not?

And what about the USA? Abraham Lincoln and the other US presidents of Escher's time were politicians who promoted transport networks and educational institutions but were not themselves entrepreneurial pioneers and business leaders. And no leading politicians are to be found among the greats of American business: not John Pierpont Morgan (1837–1913), the bank founder with the railway conglomerate; not John Davidson Rockefeller (1839–1937), the petroleum magnate and patron of the arts. Cornelius Vanderbilt (1794–1897)? He was one of the country's most successful businessmen, first as a shipowner, then as a railway mogul. No, not he, either. Perhaps Leland Stanford (1824–1893) comes closest to Escher – a railway entrepreneur who laid tracks that crossed the continent, he was also a governor and senator, an inventor and a founder of Stanford University.

In all of these men, we find qualities and attributes that also distinguished Escher. Yet not in their fullest expression. Escher was a symbol of the capital analysed by his near-contemporary Karl Marx. Yet he was not a proponent of the organised capitalism whose development led to the founding of associations, parties and unions in the last quarter of the 19th century in Switzerland, and which exerted a strong influence on direct democracy. This all happened towards the end of Escher's life, during a time that was no longer his. Escher, who was a millionaire but not among the richest men in Zurich, was a big businessman who was committed to and sacrificed himself for the welfare of his society. His unceasing activity was criticised as a sign of political ambition, but this explanation falls short. Escher was in fact seized by a sense of purpose, by a commitment to Switzerland.

We do not know what Marx thought of Escher. His comrade-in-arms and co-author Friedrich Engels (1820–1895), however, expressed his own view clearly. Engels attended a session of the National Council in Bern at the end of 1848. He had barely taken his seat when his gaze immediately fell on Escher, then the Vice President of the Council. His impression and his assessment are captured in a memorable description: "Herr Doktor Alfred Escher von Zürich. A la bonne heure, das ist ein Mann, comme il en faut pour la Suisse." (Doctor Alfred Escher of Zurich. Just at the right time, just the right man for Switzerland.)[61]

Alfred Escher was an exceptional Swiss politician of statesmanlike calibre, and his legacy and influence have endured. What he brought about in the fields of business, academics and politics has survived him and still recalls him today: railway lines and train stations, banks and insurance companies, research and educational institutions. Theodor Mommsen (1817–1903), who taught at the University of Zurich thanks to Escher, said it in a nutshell: Escher had the presence of a true sovereign – all the more so, because he did not bear that title.[62]

Life Insurance: Johann Conrad Widmer

Johann Conrad Widmer (1818–1903) felt out of place as a theology student in Zurich, so in 1837 he enrolled as a law student at the University of Basel. He began practising law in 1839. As a young lawyer, he once won a bet by pleading a case before the district court of Frauenfeld entirely in doggerel; he was fined for breach of protocol. He was part of the most illustrious social circle in Thurgau, which included personalities like Karl Kappeler (1816–1888), later President of the ETH board; Philipp Gottlieb Labhardt (1811–1874), future member of the Government Council and National Councillor; and Abraham Roth (1823–1880), future editor of the *Bund* and *Grenzpost* newspapers. The circle also included Johann Konrad Kern (1808–1888), future national politician, railway pioneer and Swiss ambassador in Paris, and Christian Beyel (1808–1858), publisher of the *Thurgauer Zeitung* and cofounder of the Zürcher Industrieverein (Zurich Industry Association). Widmer was known for his delightful humour and sharp wit, which enlivened the friendships he later developed with greats of business and society such as Jacob Burckhardt (1818–1897), Gottfried Keller (1819–1890) and Alfred Escher (1819–1882), and with painters, composers and artists from the most varied milieus, among them Wilhelm Baumgartner (1820–1867) and Richard Wagner (1813–1883).

In 1847, Widmer's wife Margaretha Bohny (1818–1847) died, leaving him with three children. Two years later he married Virginia Rogg, with whom he had four more children. Virginia and Johann went to Basel on their honeymoon in the summer of 1849, while in the neighbouring Grand Duchy of Baden, rebellious liberals and republicans were fighting against the ruling dynasty, which was supported by Prussian and Hessian troops. Johann was eager to see the fighting from up close. After extracting a promise from him to be back in Basel by the evening, his new wife allowed him to go.

In Freiburg im Breisgau, Widmer sought out the camp commandant to gain access to the theatre of operations, but in vain. Undeterred, he rode on his own to Baden-Baden and then continued on foot, always following the thundering of the cannon. He climbed a small hill and gazed down on the burning village of Gernsbach, at which point he noticed some soldiers approaching him. He retreated to a nearby inn, where he was arrested and accused of espionage. In the end, he talked his way out of the jam, but only with great difficulty. He returned to his wife, who had surely feared for his life, on the following day.

When the position of director of the Zurich cantonal prison in Oetenbach was advertised, Widmer applied and was selected for the job. In 1852, he moved to Zurich with his family, to a gloomy building with overfilled rooms and desolate sanitary facilities that was home to around 400 prisoners. The inmates were divided into several categories: chained convicts, convicts, prisoners, pre-trial detainees, arrestees, teenagers under 16 years of age, serial criminals and criminals awaiting the death penalty. It was a sad, pitiful scene and stood in sharp contrast to the economically and culturally developing city. Widmer took his job seriously and demanded that the authorities take action to mitigate the situation. He established a protective association (Schutzverein) for released prisoners and made his reforms publicly known. Once the prison had been reorganised, he considered his mission fulfilled, although his principal desire, for a new building, would only be realised in 1901 in Regensdorf.

In his work at the Oetenbach prison – formerly a nunnery – Widmer showed himself to be a man who felt ethically bound to combat social wrongs and help people in distress. In Widmer, the young Federal State had a founding figure on its socio-political stage who began to construct a social safety net on the basis of private industry. Widmer laid the foundations for the emergence of Switzerland as a welfare state – a later trademark of the country – with the same social welfare institutions that define it up until today: the Schweizerische Unfallversicherungsgesellschaft (Swiss National Accident Insurance Fund, Suva) and the Alters- und Hinterbliebenenversicherung (Old-Age Insurance System, AHV). His social engagement was apparent in a number of his undertakings. After the Great Fire of Glarus in 1861, for example, a school was established for children from Glarus who were being put up in Zurich, and Widmer taught there for a year and a half – despite the fact that, as Executive Director of the Rentenanstalt (today's Swiss Life), he already had more than enough to do.

Widmer was born in the farming village of Altnau in Canton Thurgau. His childhood and adolescence were marked by frequent moves. His father, a physician, did not do well financially and was never able to settle down in one place. Widmer's mother died when he was 12, and as a child he switched schools as often as his father moved. This changed when, outfitted with a scholarship and a no-interest loan, he was admitted to the second class of the upper secondary school (Obergymnasium) in Zurich. The effect this opportunity had on Widmer was greater than the few kilometres between Thurgau and the city of Zurich might suggest, for a whole a new world now opened up before him. He established acquaintanceships with peers from Old-Zurich society and became friends and networked with ambitious young men who would soon be playing leading roles in government, business and society. Among them was Alfred Escher, now Widmer's schoolmate.

Switzerland was in the grips of change on many levels around the middle of the 19th century. Its transformation, spurred on especially by the railway project, led to the founding of a great number of private businesses. Key new industries sprang up; the emergence of industrial banks, which had not previously set roots in Switzerland, also provided an indication that, alongside this major economic transformation, the social structures and ways of life of large segments of the population were changing.

In the emerging industrial society, the demand for insurance products grew rapidly. And the labour movement, which was gaining both social and political clout, now began to demand that Switzerland become a more comprehensive welfare state.

The need for some kind of insurance against the financial consequences of ageing and death were not new at the time. The first modern life insurance company to cover these needs by working with mathematical models had been founded in London as early as 1762. Similar establishments were founded in France in 1787 and towards the end of the 1820s in Germany. In Switzerland, the mathematician and economist Christoph Bernoulli (1782–1863) dared an attempt in Basel in 1830, while in Zurich, in 1839, Professors Johann Caspar Bluntschli (1808–1881) and Joseph Ludwig Raabe (1801–1859) were commissioned by the Charitable Society to take action. These and other assays, however, were unsuccessful. In 1840 in St Gallen, the Survivors', Widows' and Old-Age Fund was founded by the Commercial Directorate as an institution oriented towards all of Switzerland; a lack of trust on the part of the population, however, led to its early demise. The underlying cause of the failure lay in the insufficiency of its insurance-mathematical basis. Mathematical models were employed, to be sure, but the number of insured people was too small to allow for a dependable reliance on mortality statistics.

A basic requirement for the success of an insurance business was, then as now, the assured ability to provide benefits. Revenue from premiums was not enough to guarantee this, particularly in the beginning stages of a business, so additional capital was needed. In light of these multifarious difficulties, it is easy to understand why foreign insurers dominated the Swiss market in the 1850s.

Widmer recognised these connections. Furthermore, it disturbed him that the premiums flowing into foreign companies represented money exiting the Swiss economy. Yet his principal desire was to confront the negative consequences of contemporary socio-political developments in such a way as to ward off both acute and latent societal misery. With all this in mind, he began to develop a pension system. As an essential foundation for his calculations, he needed statistical data; this, however, was not easy to obtain. Even the first national census, carried out in 1850, did not meet his needs, for though it contained statistical data, they were not ordered demographically. Widmer needed mortality tables, and no such tables encompassing the entire Swiss population existed. He thus contacted the healthcare authorities of the cantons, collected the results of local and regional compilations and consulted foreign data for comparison. A mortality table with data from seven cantons published by the Bernese engineer Alexander Kocher (1814–1893) in 1845 provided him with a valuable resource. Widmer finally succeeded in producing a reliable basis on which to calculate premiums – and thus became the first real Swiss insurance specialist.

He next worked on the legal and organisational elaboration of his project, which turned out to be unexpectedly difficult. Since the number of clients targeted during the founding phase of his enterprise was necessarily small, Widmer was in danger of losing his financial solvency if an unusually large cluster of fatalities were to arise. Buyers of insurance knew this and therefore demanded additional guarantees for the money they were laying down. Widmer developed a proposal that addressed this problem and presented it to the Leu Bank. The bank, he suggested, should assume liability with all of its equity capital, which at the time was 10 million francs – an idea he had taken from the one-stop finance model of France's Crédit-Mobilier Institute. Widmer's proposal was rejected by the tradition-bound Leu Bank. Widmer then considered setting up a public limited company, but in the end rejected the idea.

At this point, the Schweizerische Kreditanstalt jumped in. Its Vice President, Johann Jakob Rüttimann (1813–1876), who appreciated Widmer's previous work on the Zurich Government Council, examined the plan; Widmer's high-school friendship with Alfred Escher, the President of the bank, didn't hurt either. Escher recognised the promise of Widmer's model of cooperation between banking and insurance. He was guided by the idea that the bank's backing would make possible an institution that would serve the social welfare of broad segments of the population, would be economically advantageous for Switzerland and in the end would even bring in profits for the Kreditananstalt. And thus came about a sensational structure: The Kreditanstalt assumed liability with its entire equity capital of 15 million francs and even invested additional money. In exchange, it was due a 40 percent share of the profits of the insurance business, determined the management of the company, maintained a strong presence on the supervisory board and was generally authorised to intervene in strategic and important operational processes.

Thus was the Rentenanstalt (today's Swiss Life) founded. Hostile voices spoke of it as "nothing but a simple office of the Schweizerische Kreditanstalt," but the Government Council of Canton Zurich granted its license in November 1857.[63] The integration of structures and personnel between the bank and the insurance agency became increasingly disentangled towards the end of the 19th century, and from the mid-1880s onwards, the bank was loosed from its obligations as guarantor.

In 1892, Johann Conrad Widmer gave up the operative leadership of the Rentenanstalt. His place in history was already assured by that institution and by his promotion of life annuities and life insurance. He was also occupied with other questions and challenges facing the insurance business, such as the founding of the Schweizerische Rückversicherungsgesellschaft (Swiss Reinsurance Company, today's Swiss Re) and – on commission from the Federal Council – with the Union Winkelried, which was ultimately never established. He took on many societal obligations and worked under Alfred Escher as the general secretary of the Gotthard Committee. His multifaceted and wide-ranging commitments have earned him a place among the pioneers of the young Federal State. He was indefatigable, inventive and creative, "a whole person," an early riser from his youth. "By the time most other people begin their day's work, (he had) already done half of his. Only so was it possible for him to fit in so great an amount of both work and pleasure."[64]

Transport Insurance, Fire Insurance and Reinsurance: Moritz Grossmann

It was largely due to the founding of the Schweizerische Kreditanstalt in 1856, and to the accelerated commercial activity spurred on by the bank's president, Alfred Escher, that Zurich became the financial hub of Switzerland in the second half of the 19th century. The founding of the Rentenanstalt in 1857 added another pillar to the city's finance industry. Escher and Widmer were two pioneers who understood how to take ideas and concepts that had been realised elsewhere, adjust them to fit Swiss conditions and realise them in Switzerland. Their achievements led to the establishment of further insurance companies in Zurich.

But first the tale moves to St Gallen, where, at the end of 1858, a group of textile industrialists were engaged in founding Helvetia, the first Swiss transport insurer. The project was at an advanced stage, but they were still looking for a director. The initiators of the project made an effort to fill the position with a Swiss citizen, but in vain. In point of fact, at the time it was hardly possible to find a specialist in transport insurance who was Swiss. The Swiss insurance market at mid-century was dominated by foreign companies. The only Swiss establishments of any significance were the cantonal fire insurance institutions, but they only insured buildings and were unwilling to offer contents insurance. This they left to private companies, of which only the Schweizerische Mobiliar-Versicherungs-Gesellschaft had any stature. There were thus no insurance institutions in Switzerland that were able to even partially fulfil the needs of a modern industrial society. The contradiction was apparent: The private insurance industry was mismatched with the industrial strength of the nation.

The lack of specialists in Switzerland forced the St Gallen businessmen to extend their search to foreign countries. Their gaze particularly fell on Trieste, an important location for European transport insurers. There they happened upon Moritz Grossmann (1830–1910), an Austrian with Galician roots. Though he was only 28 years old, Grossmann had proven business experience in Vienna. The complication was that he had only just assumed his position in Trieste. Since the St Gallen businessmen saw no alternative, they had to entice Grossmann away. And he turned out to be a stroke of good fortune, not just for St Gallen but for the entire Swiss insurance industry. Grossmann became assimilated in Switzerland, was naturalised and distinguished himself as a patron of the arts – he was a member of the theatre committee and the concert association and was active on behalf of the concert hall. For "charitable endeavours of every kind," he "always lent a helping hand."[65]

In St Gallen, Grossmann built up his insurance company, and Helvetia grew quickly and vigorously in the thriving transport market. It was the first public limited company in the Swiss insurance sector that was able to hold its own on the market. Then, on the night of 10–11 May 1861, a conflagration reduced the cantonal capital of Glarus to dust and ashes. The damages came to around 10 million francs – around half the annual revenues of the federal government. Glarus building insurers were incapable of meeting the compensation claims, and the state had to step in. The Great Fire of Glarus provided the catalyst for the founding of several private contents insurance companies, which operated across cantonal borders and focused on fire damage. Since the risks in this field were difficult to calculate, these institutions were mostly structured as public limited companies.

In St Gallen, meanwhile, Grossmann had long been engaged with the problems posed by fire insurance. And while providing such insurance would have been possible according to the statutes governing Helvetia, another structure seemed more suitable. Thus, in 1861, the Helvetia

Schweizerische Feuerversicherungs-Gesellschaft (Helvetia Swiss Fire Insurance Company) was founded as a sister company – it, too, with Grossmann at its head.[66]

Yet Grossmann's plans went even further. In the summer of 1863, he presented the governing board of Helvetia with an "expert opinion concerning the founding of a reinsurance company in Zurich by the Schweizerische Kreditanstalt." In the field of reinsurance, too, foreign companies had taken the lead, especially in the German states. The same unsatisfactory situation that had arisen in Switzerland in the context of primary insurance was also present with reinsurance – namely, that a portion of the "money held in Switzerland is flowing back to foreign institutions via the reinsurance channel."

In the German states of the 1850s, a development had taken place that – so Grossmann reasoned – might occur in Switzerland as well. As they had done in Switzerland, in the first half of the 19th century English and French reinsurers had moved into the German market, which had become ever more lucrative as industrialisation and urbanisation had progressed. And while the risks were effectively spread around in this way, the consequence was still that premiums and profits were flowing out of the country. The German primary insurers also recognised this, and some of them founded reinsurance businesses as subsidiaries. This model, however, did not prove successful, as conflicts between the primary insurers and their subsidiaries were preordained. Merchants and bankers therefore met in Cologne in 1842 to found an independent reinsurance company. It would be ten years before this company began operations, however.

It was with all these connections in mind that Grossmann produced the concept accepted by the governing board of Helvetia in the summer of 1863. Now, however, more money and additional expertise were needed. In order to help the idea conceived in St Gallen take form, and to ensure the success of its realisation over the long term, it had to be cast on a grander scale. Thus did Alfred Escher's Schweizerische Kreditanstalt and Johann Conrad Widmer's Rentenanstalt come into play. The bank drew up the foundation agreement and the articles of association, which were approved by Canton Zurich in the same year – as is confirmed in a document dated 19 December and signed by the writer Gottfried Keller, then the First Official Secretary of the canton. The constitutive meeting of the governing board, led by Grossmann, took place a week later and included representatives of the major shareholders Helvetia, the Kreditanstalt, the Basler Handelsbank and Lloyd-Transport, as well as Widmer of the Rentenanstalt, who was elected president, and the Zurich silk industrialist Johann Gustav Siber-Gysi (1827–1872), who assumed the vice-presidency.

The Schweizerische Rückversicherungs-Gesellschaft (today's Swiss Re) had barely been founded, however, before a conflict broke out that brought the institution to the edge of the abyss. The problem arose at the first meeting of the governing board and escalated at the second. The dispute concerned the choice of a director. Two camps faced off: On the one side was the group around Widmer, which proposed Heinrich Fick (1822–1895), a German lawyer about to assume a professorship of Roman law, trade law and exchange law at the University of Zurich, and who represented the interests of the Kreditanstalt and the Rentenanstalt; on the other was the group around Grossmann, which included Siber-Gysi and the representatives of Helvetia and the Basel bank, and which proposed Georg Schmidt (died 1864), former director of the Austrian insurance company Phönix. Schmidt, who unlike Fick had practical experience in the insurance industry, was elected by secret ballot at the first meeting of the governing board. Widmer, however, was not prepared to accept this decision and placed the issue on the agenda of the second meeting. The result of the second vote, however, was the same. At this, Widmer resigned as president of the governing board; Hüni-Stettler, the representative of the Kreditanstalt, resigned as well. Yet all was still not well. Ten months after taking on the leadership of the company, Schmidt died. The circumstances of his death were not completely cleared up at the time. Rumours of suicide quickly made the rounds, mentioning large business losses by the reinsurance company for which Schmidt was allegedly responsible. In its commemorative publication on the occasion of its centenary, the reinsurance company itself backed the suicide hypothesis. Another explanation that made the rounds attributed Schmidt's death to a stroke.

In the midst of the personnel crisis that now fell to the governing board, and in acute political difficulties within the firm, Grossmann found a new director: Giuseppe Besso (1839–1901). The two worked well together. Besso had been employed by the same insurance company as Grossmann in Trieste, his native city. But more than nostalgia was involved: The young Besso brought specialist knowledge with him, and in Zurich developed into a true expert in his field. Like his mentor before him, he proved to be a stroke of good fortune for the firm.

The first years in business posed significant challenges, and the losses accumulated. Grossmann had imagined things differently; he had assumed that primary insurers would reinsure their risks with his company to a greater extent than they actually did. In fact, business essentially remained in the hands of the English and French primary insurers. The situation was difficult, for in addition to these structural challenges, the domestic market for a Swiss reinsurer was very small compared to that for the competition.[67] Grossmann's company was thus quickly forced to look abroad, and this brought with it other risks. The situation was so tense that, up until the end of the 1860s, the company often seemed close to failing. Things only began to improve when Grossmann and Besso began to terminate contracts. They studied various options for which branches they might give up. At this point, business picked up again, and in 1869, for the first time in five years, the company paid out dividends. Still, other steps were necessary before the consolidation process was successfully concluded at the end of the 1870s.

Since the reinsurance business was in an existential crisis for many years, it is understandable that Grossmann, who according to the statutes should have left the governing board in 1866, kept his seat until 1870. Even after leaving, though, he remained in touch with the director. Besso had by now taken on the same overwhelming stature that Grossmann had assumed during the founding phase of the company. It may be due to Besso's dominant leadership and extensive expertise that the governing board, which was theoretically his supervisor, neglected to fill the positions of president and vice president for several years. Besso had carte blanche and did as he pleased – an unsustainable leadership situation.

Like Grossmann, Besso considered Switzerland his new homeland and became a Swiss citizen. His son Michele (1873–1955) was also consumed with enthusiasm for Switzerland. He moved from Trieste to Zurich and studied at the Polytechnic, where he became friends with Albert Einstein (1879–1955), to whose Special Theory of Relativity his ideas contributed.[68]

Disaster in Winterthur: Swiss Lloyd and the Financial Bust

The socio-political awakening of the mid-19th century led to the establishment of new branches of the Swiss economy and to a veritable flood of new companies. In many cases, however, entrepreneurs' experiences of practical business leadership and strategy were inadequate, and their readiness to take risks was excessive. Impressive numbers on a business's balance sheet were often deceptive. Insufficient insurance backing, a poor assessment of reserves at the founding, problematic dividend payments, risky deals and rushed phases of expansion abroad all combined to create the disaster that unfolded in Winterthur. Yet there is more to be said. The rumours that arose in the wake of the death of Georg Schmidt, the Director of the Rückverischerungs-Gesellschaft, point to a phenomenon prevalent in the Sturm-und-Drang era: the assumption of personal responsibility for the failure of a business. In extreme cases, this could lead to suicide, especially when fraudulent or even criminal activities were involved. Another way out involved flight from one's responsibilities, or in order to escape criminal charges; in such cases, the USA was often the preferred destination.

In Winterthur, such events followed hard on one another when Lloyd-Transport went bankrupt and pulled half of the city into the abyss with it.[69] The Schweizerische Lloyd Transportversicherungs-Gesellschaft

(Swiss Lloyd Transport Insurance Company) had been founded in 1863. Twenty-three-year-old Ewald Moritz Lengstorf (1840–1883) became its director; his deputy was the 27-year-old Albert Busch (1836–1884). Both had previously worked in Antwerp. Lloyd-Transport was successful at first; it grew at a breathtaking pace and became the largest transport insurer on the Continent. Revenues from premiums seemed inexhaustible, and, up until 1874, dividends averaged 22.8 percent; in some years they were higher than 30 percent. But this apparent success was, as would later be seen, no more than a bubble.

In 1874, another company, the Schweizerische Lloyd Rückversicherungs-Gesellschaft (Swiss Lloyd Reinsurance Company, known as Lloyd-Rück) began operations in Winterthur – though up until 1877, the only business it reinsured was Lloyd-Transport. Lloyd-Rück then branched out into other areas, including fire insurance. After two years with small deficits, in 1882 the losses in the Lloyd transport and reinsurance businesses shot up to around 3 million francs each. In 1884, insolvency was declared. It later came out that, in addition to an irresponsible and speculative business strategy – which the governing board ultimately bore responsibility for – both Lengstorf and Busch had caused losses to the Lloyd companies with corrupt and fraudulent practices. They had brokered business transactions with two French insurance companies and kept the commissions of more than 1.5 million francs for themselves. In return, they had taken on great risks on behalf of their Parisian confederates, granting them long-term ship collision insurance that other insurers had declined to provide. They had also committed other offenses.

In 1875, the Schweizerische Unfallversicherungs-Aktiengesellschaft in Winterthur (Swiss Accident Insurance company in Winterthur, known as "Winterthur") was founded.[70] As was the case for the Versicherungs-Verein in Zürich (today's Zurich Insurance Group) and other companies of the time, here too Gottfried Keller, as the First Official Secretary of the canton, signed the Government Council's document of approval. The young Winterthur, whose business at first yielded profits, ran up a large deficit in 1881. In May 1882, the president of the governing board, Heinrich Rieter (1814–1889), a textile machine industrialist and Liberal member of the Council of States, resigned his post. Vice President Lengstorf, who was at the time heading towards bankruptcy with Lloyd, declared his willingness to step in and run the company. Half a year later, however, the presidency was again vacant. Lengstorf had thrown himself into the Limmat River in a fit of depression, according to internal communications in the insurance world. Then the affair became public. "Lengsdorf, Director of Lloyd in Winterthur, gave away his watch and his money yesterday in the Zurich train station and has since disappeared. Suicide is suspected." So read the report in the *Schaffhauser Intelligenzblatt* of 5 January 1883. And Lengsdorf had indeed committed suicide, after his machinations at Lloyd had become known.

Still, the turbulence at Winterthur continued. Director Carl Widmer-Kappeler, who wished to get to the bottom of the crisis affecting his company, held the governing board partially to blame for it in his report of spring 1883. The governing board, he claimed, had downplayed the severity of the crisis. But Widmer-Kappeler must have then gotten cold feet himself. In April 1883, the day after the dramatic shareholders' meetings of the two defunct Lloyds, and only a few days before that of Winterthur, he headed overseas via Basel – not, however, before helping himself to securities valued at around 100,000 francs.

The collapse of the two Lloyds, the fraud on the part of its top-ranking executives, the suicide of the president of Winterthur's governing board, and the dip into the safe and flight of its director left the city in a state of shock. Memories of the collapse of the Swiss National Railway in 1878 were still fresh, and now, only five years later, such a disaster! It was a disgrace for Winterthur society, prominent members of which had sat on the supervisory boards of the companies and apparently noticed nothing. That they would now have to pay back fees and bonuses could be endured. But the disgrace sat deep.

And that was not yet all. The city of Winterthur was shaken yet again when, still in the 1880s, the Bank in Winterthur had to be restructured – and not for the first time in its short history. President Salomon Volkart (1816–1893) and Vice President Johann Ulrich Zellweger-Waeffler, who had both also sat on the governing board of Lloyd, stepped down. Further resignations followed. Then came numerous private bankruptcies, due to the fact that many citizens of Winterthur – dazzled by increasing share prices and dividends, which reached dizzying values year after year – had invested in these local companies. And there were not only private bankruptcies; small- and mid-sized firms that had invested in Lloyd were also shaken by financial turbulence in a chain reaction.

The career of Johann Ulrich Zellweger-Waeffler had a spectacular end. A cotton trader who had sat on the governing board of Lloyd since 1868, Zellweger-Waeffler went into a financial tailspin when he was required to fully pay up his shares. Since he was also highly in debt to the Bank in Winterthur, he was not in fact able to pay and so went bankrupt. The auction of his property was announced in the *Landboten.* Zellweger-Waeffler was discredited in society and had to accept that his "assuming of any official function was forever excluded."[71]

Others who had underestimated the dangers of partially paid-up shares of stock also experienced Zellweger-Waeffler's fate. They were the victims of a deceptive enchantment that seemed especially appealing in the founding era of Swiss industry. It is easy to sum up: Partially paying up shares made possible the ownership of more shares than fully paying for them would have. The danger was that a company could demand that the shares be paid in full at any time. This could do the shareholders in if they were unable to source the necessary funds.

A Breakneck Pace: Hotel Pioneers and Their Empires

The international tourism routes of the 18th century, which were primarily frequented by noblemen, businessmen and artists, generally passed Switzerland by. The country did not have much to offer aristocratic, wealthy and well-educated travellers and was considered backward and unsafe. With the exception of certain inns in cities, on the trade routes and at spas, the hospitality industry in Switzerland in the early 19th century was of little economic importance; it had no promotional value abroad, nor did it contribute to a sense of national identity at home. To this rather bleak assessment should be added, however, that there were certain inns in Switzerland that enjoyed excellent reputations, and had for decades and even centuries. But these few were hardly representative of the general state of the industry.

Given this not exactly inspiring past, it is natural to wonder how Switzerland could have developed a leading international hotel industry over the course of the 19th century. The modernisation process commenced in the 1830s. It did not encompass the entire country but was at first concentrated in cities and a few early tourist destinations. Yet it is astonishing how quickly the business was transformed. In less than a single generation, the hotel scene had changed beyond recognition. Already in the mid-1840s, Switzerland was deemed the country with the best hotels in the world. And while this ranking may seem exaggerated, there can be no doubt about the brilliant ascent of the Swiss hotel business in the 1850s and 1860s, and especially in the Belle Époque. Switzerland now not only put up British alpinists in its tributary valleys but also attracted an international clientele – a clientele that stayed in magnificent and luxurious buildings and celebrated its glamorous lifestyle in high-altitude Swiss locations and other dramatic settings.

The impressive development of the Swiss hotel industry in the 19th century was conjoined with the country's political and economic modernisation. Ultimately, transport was the decisive factor. It was initially the expansion of the road network, and even more so of the waterways, that opened up new possibilities. But no other transport infrastructure was more closely and fatefully bound to the boom in tourism than the railways in their various forms. Without their explosive development in the young Federal State, Switzerland as a tourist country would have been unthinkable.

Still, the development of transport networks throughout the country only provided a necessary condition. For the hotel industry to be able to take off and then maintain a high level of quality, much more was required. More than most other economic branches, the hotel business is a "People's Business." It stands to reason, then, that individual pioneers and daring entrepreneurial personalities should have proved as indispensable in the hospitality business as they had in other successful areas of industry. Such pioneers combined organisational talent with a keen sense of style and had a sure eye for identifying the advantages of their location – one of which was their country's policy of neutrality. In Switzerland, VIPs from far and wide could spend their vacations without worrying about political tensions. The distinction between friend and foe blurred in the glamour of high society. In addition, the hotel pioneers knew how to exploit their country's distinctive topography. Especially in the second half of the 19th century, iconic scenes from the Swiss landscape became effective advertising vehicles all around the world.

It is only natural that the hotel pioneers who ran flourishing inns in the first half of the century were to be found in cities and at a few other tourist destinations – such as Thun and Interlaken, or the Rigi. As tourism spread to other parts of the young Federal State, hotels were built in these areas as well. Hotel pioneers who built their inns in tributary valleys not yet linked to a transportation network especially stand out. These hoteliers could not have foreseen that their hotels would one day be connected with the Swiss Central Plateau via a road or rail corridor. Among these visionaries was, for example, Alexander Seiler (1819–1891) of Zermatt. Yet Seiler's investment in the Gletsch transit junction shows that he, too, recognised the potential contribution of transport networks to the growth of tourism in a given location.[72]

A further factor differentiates the new hoteliers of the 19th century from the innkeepers of earlier times. Their accommodations no longer merely served as places to spend the night on a through-journey. These hoteliers did not primarily want guests in transit but rather tourists who would spend their entire holidays at the hotel.[73] As a consequence, the demands on hotel infrastructure in the new age were of a different order from those in the 18th century. Hotel guests wanted more. Even in a hotel in the Swiss mountains, they wanted to participate in sporting activities and live out their own culture.

In the new age, the social profile of the hosts changed as well. In earlier times, when through-travellers were forced, for want of alternatives, to spend the night in parish houses or with village doctors, the question of the provenance of their hosts was irrelevant. They would soon be on their way again, and then everything would be as it was before: The pastor would be a pastor again, the doctor a doctor. But the hoteliers of the new generation no longer fit this mould. They were highly visible professionals. This led to many dissonances and disagreements, since the local population could now see that the foreign visitors, who were coming in increasing numbers to their village, were also bringing foreign ideas and peculiar mentalities with them; that the village hotel was continually being extended and expanded; that additional hotels and tourism infrastructure of all kinds was being built; and that the hotelier was becoming wealthy and basking in the glow emanating from his aristocratic guests. This often did not sit well with the locals, not least because the hoteliers who stepped into the spotlight during the last half of the 19th century were often themselves immigrants: They came from other regions in Switzerland, sometimes even from abroad, and even if they were citizens of the same canton, they were considered foreigners and treated accordingly. It was not normally the local folk who constructed Grand Hotels in the tributary valleys. This socio-cultural and mental distance from the local population could be quickly overcome only if the newcomer married a villager.

In the course of the 19th century, some Swiss hoteliers expanded their businesses to such an extent that they became powerful forces in politics and society. In the young Federal State of the 1850s and 1860s, the danger of a concentration of power in the hands of a small number of industrialists was evoked, and talk of textile, financial and other "barons" made the rounds. From the 1870s to the outbreak of the First World War, one might similarly have spoken of Swiss hotel "kings," who exerted their influence on business and political institutions far beyond the realm of tourism. And while the social profiles of these pioneers, who were active in every corner of the country, were necessarily diverse, still certain characteristics and attributes can be made out that mesh together to form the image of a typical hotelier.

The inns that were built in the 1830s and 1840s were mostly run by hoteliers born around the turn of the century. The new cultural era can be said to have begun in Zurich with Johannes Baur (1795–1865) and in Interlaken with Peter Ober (1813–1869). The former was an Austrian who had earlier worked as an innkeeper, while the latter was a physician and private tutor from Alsace. Travelling with an English family, Ober fell in love with the Bernese Oberland and also with a woman from Interlaken named Elisabeth Beugger (1812–1861). Thanks to his marriage to a local woman, Ober was accepted in the ruling circles in Interlaken and became a hotelier. He also had a knack for writing and published several travel guides. Three decades after Franz Niklaus König (1765–1832) launched the first Unspunnenfest, Ober became the great promoter of tourism in Interlaken. He wrote the first French-language travel guide to the Bernese Oberland.

Friedrich Seiler (1808–1883) of Bönigen in Canton Bern had a somewhat different profile than Ober. Although he took over the *Pension Jungfrau* in Interlaken from his father at just 21 years of age, he was at first less a hotelier than a politician. Already a member of the Cantonal Parliament in his youth (1837–1858, with interruptions), he was elected to the National Council in 1848. With the exception of the decade between 1852 and 1862, he remained a National Councillor until his death. His political stance was Radical. He belonged to the left-central wing of Parliament and associated with the Internationalists of the world.

Seiler was a controversial figure, and not only among Bernese Conservatives. That he had participated as an irregular soldier in the Freischaren campaigns (attempts to topple the Conservative-clerical government in Lucerne), and that his brother died in the second Freischaren campaign in 1845, made the Catholic-Conservative faction in the young Federal State seethe. Seiler was one of those committed citizens of the new Switzerland who became a businessman after serving in political office. He founded a brickworks and a match factory and was active in the founding of a flooring factory. But mainly he was a manufacturer of Oberland chalets – a business he ran from Paris, where he lived for several years.

Seiler's business ventures, however, seem not to have been terribly successful. The fact that he was a guest of Napoleon III on several occasions did little to change this. He eventually returned to Interlaken, where he slipped into the role of a hotelier. His *Jungfrau* hotel flourished. In 1864, he inaugurated a new hotel building on the Höheweg, a choice of location that has left its mark on tourism in Interlaken up to the present day.

Seiler was a prominent personality who was interested in questions of social welfare and other contemporary issues. It is not surprising, therefore, that he became involved in the field of transport. He had a particular interest in establishing a link between Lakes Thun and Brienz, for which he developed several ideas. He was an important promoter of the Bödeli and Brünig Railways, as well as other train lines in the area.

Eduard Ruchti (1834–1902) should be mentioned in the same breath as Seiler. Ruchti came from Homberg in Canton Bern and was a generation younger than Seiler. He was a new kind of hotelier, as his career reflects. After receiving a comprehensive education in hotel management in France and England, Ruchti returned to Switzerland in 1855. There he started off modestly, with the purchase of the 15-bed *Pension Victoria* on the Höhenweg in Interlaken. This purchase was possible thanks to the support of Friedrich Seiler, who was a friend of Ruchti's father. Ruchti's hotel projects at first developed in Seiler's wake. As his mentor took on the new *Hotel Jungfrau*, Ruchti followed with his *Pension Victoria*, which he rapidly transformed into the new *Hotel Victoria* in 1864/1865. Ruchti rode the wave of progress and showcased it in the Bernese Oberland: in 1875, with one of the first lifts, and in 1882, with the installation of electric lighting in the dining hall.[74]

When Ruchti took over the *Hotel Jungfrau* after Seiler's death and the tragic accident that claimed the life of Seiler's son, he founded a public limited company into which he brought both his and Seiler's operations, thereby creating the configuration of today's *Victoria & Jungfrau*. Ruchti also became a politician – he sat in the Cantonal Parliament (1865–1902) and on the National Council (1896–1902) – but in contrast to Seiler, only after he had become a successful hotelier. Through his political activities, he promoted tourism in Interlaken and the Bernese Oberland. There was not a transport project, on rails or cables, that he did not examine with a sharp eye for its possible utility for the tourist industry overall and for his own operations in particular. What distinguished him from Seiler was his participation in the new form of business leadership that emerged in the last quarter of the 19th century. Ruchti sat on the boards of innumerable railway companies. His hotel career was further distinguished by the fact that he acquired other hotels besides the one he inherited – first in the local neighbourhood, with the *Jungfrau* and the *Eiger*, and then abroad, with a hotel in Cannes.

The dovetailing of politics and the hotel business was typical for the time. Though there were some precursors to it in the 1840s, the phenomenon became more prevalent in the young Federal State. It found its strongest expression in the 1870s, when business, political and social interests formed associations as a reaction to the introduction of direct democracy at the federal level. The political sway of the hoteliers on the municipal, cantonal and national levels in the second half of the 19th century can be seen in any number of examples: Jean Anzévui (1835–1926) built hotels in Arolla, Evolène and Sion and was also the Mayor of Evolène and a member of the Valais Cantonal Parliament; his son Jean (1865–1945) served in various political offices, including as President of the Valais Cantonal Parliament; the Genevan city councillor Adolf-Rudolf Armleder (1847–1930), patriarch of a hotelier family, built the *Richemond* in Geneva in 1875 and co-founded the Swiss Hotel Association in 1882; the Nidwalden Government Council member Kaspar Blättler (1791–1872) opened the *Hotel Klimsenhorn Pilatus* and the *Kurhotel Rotzloch* in 1856; the Schwyz Government Council member and National Councillor Ambros Eberle (1820–1883) was linked not only by family ties but also as a member of the Cantonal Parliament to Fridolin Fassbind (1821–1893), the founder of the *Waldstätterhof* in Brunnen, and to other hoteliers in the Swiss Parliament.

An especially powerful network formed on Lake Geneva around Ami Chessex (1840–1917) and had a decisive influence on tourism around Montreux. At the centre of the group was Chessex, who, from his magnificently situated hotel facilities in Territet, built up a hotel empire on Lake Geneva like no other in Switzerland – owing in part to connections established through his marriage to Rosine Emery. Chessex was a Municipal Councillor in Les Planches and a member of the Vaud Cantonal Parliament. He became a member of various institutions in Territet and Montreux that played an important role in the development of tourism: the Société d'Embellissement, the Société d'Utilité Publique, the Société des Divertissments et Sports, the Hotel Association and the Kursaal society. Many of these institutions hailed from his own initiatives, and he was the founding president of some of them. Chessex initiated and oversaw; he ruled not only over his own hotel empire but also over the development of the rapidly growing town of Montreux. That Chessex was among the founders of the Société Romande d'Electricité in 1903 and was President of the Swiss Hotel Association from 1886 to 1889 brings his profile into even sharper relief.

Chessex was able to play this outstanding role not least due to his marriage into the Emery hotel family of Yverdon in Canton Vaud. His brother-in-law Alexandre Emery (1850–1931), who first worked for Chessex as Chef de Réception, took over the *Du Cygne* in Châtelard (Montreux) in 1882, from where he built up his own hotel empire which included the *Montreux Palace*. Like Chessex, he was a founder of railway companies and other operations and establishments. No important development in Montreux passed him by. Emery was also politically active on all three levels of government: he was the Syndic (mayor) of Châtelard (1902–1912), a member of the Vaud Cantonal Parliament (1889–1893) and eventually a National Councillor (1906–1917). Like Chessex, he was a member of the central committee of the Swiss Hotel Association. Together with Alexander Seiler II (1864–1920), he introduced the 1911 motion that eventually led to the establishment of the Schweizerische Verkehrszentrale (today's Switzerland Tourism).

All Montreux lay at the feet of these two hotel kings, Chessex and Emery, who had divided up their dominions geographically. Around these two central figures a circle of local politicians and businessmen formed, including the syndics of Veytaux, Alfred Chatelanat (1857–1921) and of Planches, Philippe Faucherre-Vautier (1844–1932) – the latter also a hotelier. This coalition had so much political power that no important decisions could be taken in the region around Montreux without their consent. They initiated and executed projects in line with their interests – roads, quays, pavements, canals, bridges – and they knew how to obstruct whatever projects might get in their way.[75]

The Swiss hotel industry did not only exist in Switzerland. In the last quarter of the 19th century and beyond, hotels in select locations in cities around the world began to be associated with the Swiss label, either because they had been built and run by Swiss or because Swiss hoteliers lent new lustre to already-existing operations. Some Swiss hoteliers left their home country and concentrated on their operations abroad. Several became international stars in the metropolises of the world, either by running their businesses themselves and acting as hosts or by having others run their luxury hotels for them. Cäsar Ritz (1850–1918) became the best-known Swiss hotelier on the international stage, but he was not alone. Charles (Karl) Albert Bähler (1868–1937) of Thun, for example, changed careers after an apprenticeship as an accountant and took up the hotel business, first in Italy, then in Germany. As a 20-year-old, he sailed to Egypt. In Cairo, he restructured the bookkeeping system at the world-famous *Shepheards* hotel, whose renovation he oversaw in 1891. Together with other financiers, he purchased several hotels and founded Egyptian Hotels Ltd., which ran hotels in and around Cairo and in Alexandria. When the tomb of Tutankhamen was discovered in 1922 and tourists streamed to upper Egypt in ever-increasing numbers, Bähler followed them, building hotels along the way. Soon the new Upper Egypt

Hotel Co. owned several hotels in Luxor and Aswan. The activities of this hotelier and investor from the Bernese Oberland knew no bounds. His empire soon comprised several thousand beds. He built a hotel in Jerusalem as well, and it soon became one of the most renowned in the Near and Middle East: the *King David*.

Two hoteliers from Obwalden, Franz Josef Bucher (1834–1906) and Josef Durrer (1841–1919), were also active beyond Switzerland's borders. Like Bähler, they were not classical hoteliers who saw their calling as involving daily contact with their guests. They were mavericks, and their role was primarily that of entrepreneurs building modern facilities. Yet these two colourful figures had a lot to do with hotels. On the one hand, Bucher and Durrer illustrate how the Swiss hotel industry was oriented in the Belle Époque; on the other, they represent exceptions, for their empire stands alone in the Swiss hotel business of the 19th century in terms of size, rate of expansion and creation of new infrastructure. And while many hotel owners who achieved fame and honour over the course of their careers came from humble beginnings far removed from their later field of work, the contrast is especially astonishing in the case of these two men from Obwalden. Bucher grew up on his parents' farm in Kerns and was actively involved in its operation. Durrer came from Sarnen, where he owned a small carpentry workshop. The two came together when Bucher married Durrer's sister; they subsequently founded the Bucher & Durrer company. Many rags-to-riches stories are recounted in America, but what happened at Bucher & Durrer verges on a fairy tale.

At first Bucher and Durrer built sheds and wooden houses in Obwalden and attempted to sell them off as quickly as possible. The two thus gained skills in the real estate business. Durrer was a gifted craftsman with technological savvy; he is usually depicted as the quiet creator, a cool and sober calculator. Bucher, by contrast, was unmistakably cut from a different cloth: a visionary, full of effervescent ideas, but with an instinctive feeling for business opportunities. Bucher and Durrer built a flooring factory in Kägiswill, which was followed by similar factories in other locations in Obwalden. This kind of wood processing was in vogue at the time, and the boom in housing and other building construction in Switzerland that began in the 1850s as the railways were being developed promised profits without great risks. And in fact, Bucher and Durrer's business was on a successful path. In 1870/1871, they built their first hotel, the *Sonnenberg*, in Engelberg. They sold it to Alfred Landry for a good price after a single summer season and now had capital at their disposal as never before. They bought the alp then known as Tritt, built a Grand Hotel on it and renamed it Bürgenstock. The street running from Stansstad to Bürgenstock was also their work.

Figure 2.19 "Hotel Ritz, Paris," ca 1900. Photograph. Wikimedia Commons.

Cäsar Ritz (1850–1918) belongs in a category of his own among hotel pioneers. In the middle of the 19th century, when Alexander Seiler and Johannes Badrutt were gradually building up their empires in Zermatt and St Moritz, respectively, Ritz had only just been born. In contrast to other leading figures, Ritz was not among the hoteliers who made names for themselves politically, or who distinguished themselves through their contribution to tourism infrastructure in the final quarter of the 19th century – men like Alexandre Emery or Ami Chessex, at whose feet all of Montreux bowed. There were of course other Swiss citizens who established and operated luxury hotels around the world, but none made such a name for themselves as a hotelier or proprietor as did Cäsar Ritz. The "gastrophilosophy" and gastronomy that he and his master chef Auguste Escoffier (1846–1935) purveyed became legendary.

That the farm boy Cäsar Ritz from Niederwald in Valais would one day make hotelier history as an ambassador of Switzerland, and even transform the luxury hotel world with his high standards, could not have been predicted from his family history. Similarly improbable is that both Alexander Seiler of Blitzingen and Cäsar Ritz of Niederwald were from the remote Goms region of Valais. At 12 years old, Cäsar Ritz left Niederwald and entered the Kollegium (secondary school) in Sion. Three years later he began an apprenticeship as a waiter in Brig, which he soon broke off. Between 1867 and 1873, he started his career as a waiter. In 1874, he became the restaurant manager of the *Grand Hôtel Nizza*. After joint leadership roles at the *Grand-Hotel* in Locarno (1875) and the *Hôtel de Nice* in San Remo, Ritz became the director of the *Hôtel Viktoria* in San Remo (1877), the *Grand-Hotel National* in Lucerne (1877) and other hotels. From 1880 to 1887, he was the director of the *Grand Hôtel* in Monte Carlo and the *Grand-Hotel National* in Lucerne. In 1888, he married Marie-Louise Beck (1867–1961). In 1888/1889, Ritz purchased the *Restaurant de la Conversation* and the hotel *Minerva* in Baden-Baden, as well as the *Hôtel de Provence* in Cannes. In 1889, he took over the leadership of the *Savoy* in London, and in 1891 he began building the *Grand Hôtel* in Rome. Further highlights of his career were the inauguration of the *Hôtel Ritz* in Paris (1898) and the *Carlton* (1898) in London. After the turn of the century, Cäsar Ritz became physically and psychically ill. He had to bid adieu to glamour, and for 16 years, until his death, he led a secluded life.

This step into large-scale entrepreneurship, which for others might have represented the culmination of a career, was for Bucher and Durrer only the beginning of a future that would have been impossible to predict. After a first, temporary separation (1877–1879), Bucher and Durrer reunited and became involved in the funicular business. Their first project was the connection between the train station and the city of Lugano (1886). Then came funiculars up the Bürgenstock (1888), Monte San Salvator (1890) and the Stanserhorn (1893). They then built the *Park-Hotel* on the Bürgenstock and the *Summit Hotel* on the Stanserhorn. From the funicular business, they expanded to power plant construction, building plants, for example, on the Engelberger Aa (1888) and in Maroggia (1891).

Around the same time, they built the electric tram line in Genoa (1890/1891). This project marked the end of their partnership, however. They had by now drifted apart; their divergent personalities and conflicting interests, which had already led to disputes, now left no other alternative. Their emotional breakup was triggered by a dispute about the million-franc proceeds from the sale of the Genoan tram line. Bucher, euphoric at their success, had himself photographed at his home together with these million francs. For Durrer, such excess was too much. Disputes about the distribution of the money and about further investments may also have contributed to the break-up.[76]

In 1895, Bucher & Durrer was dissolved. Durrer took over the wood-processing operations and continued to do well. He ran and extended his company in Obwalden and expanded his operations significantly into eastern Europe. He built a funicular and a hotel in Braunwald in 1906/1907, adding to his string of successes.

Bucher took over the hotels and the funiculars. He too continued his triumphal march, acquiring and building more hotels. His international business dealings are the more surprising since he knew no foreign languages and, in fact, spoke only the Obwalden dialect. Truth and invention commingle in the many stories told about Bucher and his language skills.

In 1897, Bucher leased the *Hotel Continental* in Cairo, and in 1900 he purchased the *Hotel Euler* in Basel. In the same year, he founded the Schweizerische Hotelgesellschaft (Swiss Hotel Company), which built the *Palace* in Milan. In 1901, he acquired the *Hôtel du Parc* in Lugano, which he transformed into a Grand Hotel. In 1904, he built a new *Palace Hotel* on the Bürgenstock, thereby strengthening his presence there. Still on the Bürgenstock, he built the daring Hammetschwand lift, which led to a walking path of his design, hewed out of a cliff. In Lucerne, where he had leased the *Hotel Europe* since 1883, he built the *Palace* in 1906. To top off his career, he planned to build a luxury hotel in Cairo. For this purpose, he founded the Schweizerische-Egyptische

Hotelgesellschaft (Swiss-Egyptian Hotel Company). Franz Josef Bucher died at the inaugural ceremony of the *Semiramis*, his first-class hotel in Cairo.

A further characteristic of Swiss hotel history is that certain pioneers founded hotel dynasties. This was a pervasive phenomenon: In smaller destinations as in tourist hotspots, hotel families often operated their businesses over two, three or even more generations. Dynasties were responsible for some of the flagships of the Swiss tourism industry. These outstanding families not only influenced the culture of their own hotels but also advanced the image of their whole village or region, and even of the whole country. Among these families were the Gredigs in Graubünden and the Bürgis, Cattanis, Buchers and Pfyffers in Central Switzerland. Three great family dynasties in particular reflect the history of the development of the Swiss hotel industry and Swiss tourism in the 19th century: the Badrutts, the Seilers and the Bons.[77]

Johannes Badrutt (1819–1889) and Alexander Seiler (1819–1891), two hotel pioneers of almost the same age, appeared on the scene around the middle of the 1850s. The age in which they were born was such that they were able to launch technical, cultural and athletic initiatives that later generations arrived too late for. Promoting St Moritz as an outstanding winter tourist destination and thereby providing an incomparably strong boost to winter tourism in Switzerland from the late 1860s onwards, or operating the first electric power plant in the Engadin and switching on the first light bulb in a Swiss hotel (1878) – these things could only happen once. Johannes Badrutt thus holds a unique place as a pioneer and promoter; no one after him would be eligible for these laurels.[78]

It is notable that Badrutt and Seiler began their hotel careers not at well-known locations but in two peripheral regions that were not yet developed for tourism. At the time when Badrutt acquired the modest *Pension Faller* and made of it the imposing *Kulm-Hotel*, St Moritz, despite its ancient baths, possessed nothing in the way of modern infrastructure. Its population of less than 300 was poor and oriented towards emigration. The situation that Seiler met with in Zermatt was similar. These two great men and their hotel businesses turned St Moritz and Zermatt into internationally leading tourist destinations and into symbols of Switzerland as a nation of tourism. Their business achievements were so imposing that their hotels dominated local tourism.[79] In Zermatt it was even the case that, for a time, the Seiler empire controlled every single hotel room in the village.

Although both Badrutt and Seiler also built or acquired inns beyond their home base, they remained in their respective regions and did not expand to other parts of Switzerland or abroad. This concentration differentiated them from the Bon hotelier family, which became prominent a generation after Badrutt and Seiler, and represented yet another type of hotelier – not because its first inn was on a transit route but because its rise began on the Rigi and Lake Lucerne, that is, in a region of Switzerland that was already highly developed in terms of tourism.

The founders of the Bon hotel dynasty were Anton Bon (1854–1915) and Maria Nigg (1854–1944).[80] Anton Bon came from Bad Ragaz. He was the son of Sebastian Bon (1816–1900), the mayor and owner of a sawmill, who was friends with Bernhard Simon (1816–1900). Simon and the elder Bon convinced Anton to go into the hotel business rather than study at the Polytechnic in Zurich and become a machine engineer. During his school vacations, Anton sometimes worked at the *Quellenhof*, and after completing his Matura school-leaving examination he found, with Simon's help, internships in leading French, English and Italian hotels.

Maria Nigg, meanwhile, worked as a housekeeper at the *Hotel Hof Ragaz*. The young married couple planned to run a hotel themselves, and the opportunity presented itself earlier than they had expected. In 1879, when they were both 25 years old, they took over the lease of the *Bodenhaus* hotel in Splügen, Canton Graubünden. The location seemed well chosen, for an important north-south transit route ran over the Splügen Pass. Three years later, however, things looked different, as the newly opened Gotthard Railway stripped the Splügen of most of its goods traffic. The Bons left Graubünden and moved to Central Switzerland, where they leased a first-class hotel on the Rigi, the *Rigi First*. This location was easily accessible and was a magnet for tourists. When "Regina Montium," the owner of the hotel, went bankrupt, Bon exploited his right of first refusal and purchased the hotel. Thus, at the age of 33, he was the proprietor of his own establishment. And now the acquisitions began to snowball. He purchased land and property down in Vitznau on Lake Lucerne, which was connected to the *First* by the Rigi railway. Bon bought the *Vitznauerhof* and the *Bellevue* and built the *Park Hotel*, which resembled a fairy-tale castle. Prospects seemed brilliant in the Belle Époque, and Central Switzerland was a hotspot of tourism. Yet Bon saw that not all was well, for his hotels were not in a position to profit from a development that would influence the Swiss hotel business increasingly towards the end of the 19th century: winter tourism. He took action: In 1911, he founded a public limited company in Zurich, the Suvretta. In 1912, he built a new luxury hotel in Chasellas, outside of St Moritz, with a "vue imprenable" (breathtaking view) of the lakes of the upper Engadin. This hotel was called *Suvretta House* and was placed "in God's custody."

In 1915, three years after the opening of *Suvretta House*, its founder and builder died. His eldest son, Anton Bon (1881–1959), took over the direction of the hotel until 1916, after which he worked at the *Hotel Dorchester* in London. But times had changed; the dream of golden years had been dreamed out, the First World War swept Swiss hotels empty and the Bon family's hotels ran into financial difficulties.

After the war, however, the prospects of the tourist industry slowly began to improve, even in the Engadin. During the critical wartime years, changes took place in the leadership of *Suvretta House*. Anton Bon became president of the governing board, while his brother Hans Bon (1882–1950) presided over the directorate, a function that he carried out until 1950. His younger brother Primus Bon (1884–1974) took over the station buffet in the Zurich main train station; under his leadership, it developed an international reputation. The hotel empire of the Bon family, which had already been expanded by investments beyond the Swiss borders in the days of the first Anton Bon, grew through the participation of the six children of the second generation and expanded to include the Bally and Candrian families. For many years, beginning in 1890, Anton Bon was on the central executive committee of the Swiss Hotel Association, as were his sons Anton and Hans Rudolf later on. This points to a characteristic of the times: Hotel companies were strongly influenced by Swiss personalities who remained in their home country and engaged in politics and public life after building up their businesses, realising that this was not only good for Switzerland but also paid off for their hotels.

And now, finally, to the crowning conclusion: Alexander Seiler (1819–1891) of Blitzingen in Goms in Canton Valais, the future hotel pioneer and entrepreneur of Zermatt. Seiler's early biography reflects essential socio-political factors that characterised peripheral Swiss regions in the first half of the 19th century, and he and his hotel dynasty provide an example of developments that were typical in Swiss tourism history.

Seiler was a business pioneer who broke out of the narrowness of the limited and melancholy 1840s, recognised the dynamic unleashed by the young Federal State as an opportunity and was prepared to take risks and commit himself to the modernisation of his country. He was fearless in his exploitation of new technical possibilities and became a flag-bearer of progress. For Seiler, the new beginning meant an open spirit, infrastructure and yet more infrastructure. Alexander Seiler incorporated the values of the new Switzerland in an exemplary fashion. His story shows that economic success after 1848 had nothing to do with religious denomination and that the dynamics of modernisation took hold in peripheral regions as well as in the cities of the Swiss Central Plateau.

Alexander Seiler and the hotel pioneers who emerged from the 1850s onwards embodied the new Switzerland as no other professional group did. As hoteliers, they were also politicians, businessmen and promoters of tourism; they invested daringly in new technologies and initiated the building of roads, railways and power plants. They recognised the importance of education and training as an investment in the future, despite the fact that many of their own careers had no such foundation. With their multifaceted entrepreneurial activity they created local and regional infrastructure that was decisive for the success of their country. These hoteliers became makers of a new Switzerland and calling cards for the nation.

Alexander Seiler was born into a family of mountain farmers.[81] His parents, Christian and Maria Seiler-Bürcher, led lives of self-sufficiency; his father's carpentry work brought in only a small extra income. Alexander generally went to school only in winter, since work on his parents' farm came first in the other months. His eldest brother, Joseph, studied theology in Milan and later worked as a vicar and pastor. This corresponded to the usual practice in the Catholic milieu of the time. In the first half of the 19th century, even a large farming family could find ways and means to make it possible for a son – generally the eldest – to become a priest, while single daughters normally either remained on the farm or entered nunneries.

When Alexander Seiler was 22 and his work on the family farm was no longer required, he followed the example of many men in Valais who found their village too confining and for whom there were no professional prospects at home: He emigrated. At the recommendation of the pastor of Goms, who came from Württemberg, Seiler left Blitzingen in 1841 and travelled to southern Germany, where he learned to make soap and candles. He returned to Switzerland a year later and traversed the country as a travelling salesman, exchanging and selling goods – from matches to calfskins. He also furthered his soapmaking skills at a chemical factory in Wädenswil.

At this point, and not for the first time, his brother Joseph assumed a game-changing role as a spiritual father in Alexander's life. Joseph brokered business contacts and organised seed money for the establishment of a business, and in 1843, Alexander Seiler settled in Sion. Together with his brothers Christian and Franz, he set up a so-called soap and light factory – which was nothing more than a workshop for the manufacture of soap and candles. The partnership agreement envisioned the possibility of pursuing other businesses as well. The company did not do well, however, and Seiler was compelled to travel around the country again, selling his goods. Times were hard. The political unrest and civil-war-like conflicts that dominated Valais in the 1840s were not good for business. Soon these conflicts would spread to other regions of Switzerland and lead to a veritable civil war.

In the meantime, Joseph Seiler had completed his studies and been consecrated as a priest. His bishop assigned him work as a chaplain in Zermatt. As early as 1848, he wrote home describing a daring idea: Together with the Zermatt pastor Joseph Ruden (1817–1882), he planned to build an inn on the Riffelberg, at the foot of Monte Rosa, at an altitude of 2600 metres. After the mountain hotel on the Faulhorn (2681 metres), it would be the highest inn in Europe, and certainly the one with the best view. Chaplain Seiler encouraged his brother to come to Zermatt and join the project. Shortly afterwards, however, Joseph was reassigned to the college in Brig, and the construction of the inn went forward without him; other clergymen supported Pastor Ruden in the endeavour.

The inn on the Riffelberg was typical of the Valais hospitality industry in the first half of the 19th century, in that clergymen acted as the pioneers and promoters of tourism. Alexander Seiler's subsequent career would be decisively influenced by this brief engagement on the part of his brother. It was only a fleeting episode, but its areas of concern would soon thoroughly saturate his biography. For although Seiler remained a soap boiler and a salesman for now, his brother's brush with the hotel business had planted a seed in his mind.

In 1851, Alexander Seiler went to Zermatt for the first time in his life, and what had to happen, happened. His brief stay there was a revelation: The view of the Matterhorn bewitched him. Two years later he would move to Zermatt and lease the six-room, twelve-bed pension owned by the physician Josef Lauber – which, for a short time now, had borne the high-flown name of *Hôtel du Monte Rosa*.[82]

In 1854, Seiler bought the building; he subsequently expanded it to a 35-bed hotel. The lease and sale contract with Lauber was signed by both Alexander and Franz Seiler. The 4,000 francs they were short was covered by a mortgage and by sureties. With this, the cornerstone of Alexander Seiler's hotel empire had been laid, and the Seiler hotel dynasty began its rapid development. The impending onslaught of British alpinists would help the *Monte Rosa* attain legendary status.

In the same year, 1854, Seiler leased the inn on the Riffelberg, and in 1867 he acquired the *Mont Cervin*, which had been built opposite Lauber's pension by Joseph Anton Clemenz (1810–1872) in 1852. During his first years in Zermatt, Seiler already sought to buy up strategic plots of land for future buildings. Piece by piece, he built up his reserves. By 1871, Seiler was running all of Zermatt's hotels; including those on the Riffelberg, he had more than 150 beds at his disposal. Over time, purchases and leases brought yet more hotels and plots of land into his possession. In the 1860s, he expanded a small hostel he had purchased with his brother in Gletsch, at the foot of the Rhône glacier, into a modest inn he called the *Glacier du Rhône*, which he then expanded further into a mountain hotel. In 1879, he leased the 150-bed *Zermatterhof*, which had been built by the Zermatt Citizens' Community opposite the *Monte Rosa*. In 1881 came the *Hôtel des Alpes*. In 1884 – a highlight – the *Hotel Riffelalp* opened after several years of construction. The building of this hotel constituted a great challenge for both men and animals, as its construction materials had to be carried by mules and horses from Visp – a difficult, ten-hour expedition up to an elevation of 2222 metres. The hotel was run by Katharina Seiler's sister, Marie Clausen-Cathrein, the wife of a future federal judge. The hotel was designed with a largely British clientele in mind, and Seiler built an Anglican chapel beside it. The guests arrived in hordes. In 1887, a Catholic chapel was consecrated, giving the unique location at over 2200 metres altitude an additional place for spiritual practice.[83]

In 1890, the 71-year-old Seiler leased the *Schwarzsee* hotel. In 1891 – the year of his death – he and his wife ran seven hotels in Zermatt with a total of around 1,000 beds – four of these they owned, while three were leased. He also owned the *Glacier du Rhône* and the *Belvédère* in Gletsch and held shares in the Cathrein *Jungfrau* hotels on the Eggishorn, at Riederalp and on the Riederfurka.[84]

Alexander Seiler moved with the times. He had no anxiety about dealing with British nobles or other famous personages. He enthusiastically maintained relationships with members of London's Alpine Club, who were among his regular guests, and with the many other alpinists who appeared in the world of Zermatt's 4000-metre peaks in the late 1850s and afterwards. He foresaw that Zermatt would boom as a tourist destination, as it indeed did after the Matterhorn tragedy of 1865. His later investments in the construction of hotels and tourism infrastructure were therefore not particularly risky.

Seiler's impressive personality was evident in his first trip to England. The hotelier, who carried only a light satchel with him and knew no more English than what he had learned through his everyday interactions with international guests, left Brig on 1 March 1863 and travelled via Geneva and Paris to London, where he stayed until the end of the month. His travel notes are of interest for the light they shed on cultural and social history.[85] On reading them, one feels immediately how the hotelier from Zermatt was impressed by the great city; by English parks, cultural landmarks and monuments; by steamers on the Thames, railway bridges and underground trains; by the Houses of Parliament, Westminster Abbey and Oxford Street – where his eye lit on commerce, warehouses and luxury goods –, by the unceasing jostling of the crowds and the turmoil of carriages, fiacres, wagons and omnibusses, and by the cries of the merchants. Finally, it all made him dizzy; it seemed to Seiler as if the entire world had flowed into this place and was confusedly rolling about him – he dreamed of being in a world that had no end. He became aware of how much human beings are capable of, thanks to their wealth of insights, their science and their art. One is astonished at the ingenuousness with which he – all on his own – left this gigantic city to explore its surroundings. He regretted that his English was not good enough to allow him to make more extensive excursions. Nor can the reader help being impressed by how this Alexander Seiler was received in the homes of high-ranking personalities and introduced to elegant society – even into the salon of a famous chemistry professor, where he regretted, but without undue stress, that his English was not good enough for him to be able to follow the discussions. And finally, Seiler paid a visit to the exclusive Alpine Club. There he dined in the company of noblewomen and the renowned British alpinists who had been his guests in Zermatt summer after summer, and with whom he interacted as a friend.

Valais owes much to Alexander Seiler's forward-looking initiatives. He busied himself with everything. He paid a visit to Sion and obtained a subsidy from the state treasury to improve the main street in Zermatt; he financed hiking trails to scenic spots; to the delight of tourists, he began to collect and exhibit cultural objects, laying the foundation for the future Alpine Museum. He looked after the Zermatt postal depot and, from 1873 on, also held the office of postmaster. Seiler also sat in the Valais Cantonal Parliament (1868–1891), in which capacity he was especially involved in the correction of the Rhône, which regularly flooded the valley floor with the annual snowmelt, creating a swampy landscape rife with disease. His second-most-pressing concern was for the creation of jobs for the mountain population. With his own businesses, he set a shining example on this front.

Seiler was a man who solved problems creatively, as the following example shows. Despite the fact that there was a line of sight between the inn on the Riffelberg and the *Hotel Monte Rosa*, there was no technical means to communicate between the two establishments to ascertain, for example, how many rooms each had available. No problem: The hotels communicated by code, via coloured sheets hung out of their windows. A more reliable method arrived with the advent of the telegraph, which allowed for communication with the entire world. In 1871, Seiler provided one of his hotel rooms to house the telegraph machine.

The improvement of the way between Zermatt and the Rhône valley was high up on Seiler's agenda, for in the early days only a mule path led up the Matter Valley. Seiler submitted an application to the canton for the construction of a carriage road, and at the same time applied to be the construction supervisor himself. He got the job, but the financial support offered by the state amounted to no more than a few thousand francs – far too little for such a road. But Alexander Seiler set to work, and the road was built. He was a key promoter of the railway line that linked Zermatt with Visp, thereby establishing a connection to the larger railway network. It is an irony of history that the first regularly scheduled train on the line, which left Zermatt for Brig in 1891, carried Seiler's coffin.

In the 19th century, hotels in Zermatt were only open for the summer season. In late autumn, Alexander Seiler would leave the Matter Valley and would only return to Zermatt in early summer. At first, he maintained his business in Sion and continued to work as a trader in the winter. From 1855 onwards, however, he committed himself full-time to his calling as a hotelier. This did not change the fact that he was only present in Zermatt for half the year, but now in the winter he only went as far as Brig.

This distance between Brig and Zermatt is symbolic of the fundamental unease felt by the mountain inhabitants of Zermatt with the hotelier, who was still seen as a foreigner. And the more successful Alexander Seiler and his family became, the wider the cleft between them and the local families grew. The cultural discrepancies were apparent and led to the many forms of resistance that Seiler was to encounter throughout the years. The tensions between the Seilers and the village escalated when Seiler submitted an application to become a citizen of Zermatt. This citizenship, refused to him for 18 years, was only finally granted 2 years before his death, and after he had pursued all conceivable legal means to attain it – a process that ultimately involved the Federal Supreme Court and the Federal Council, which took his side.

Alexander Seiler only married when he was 38. He refrained from entering into a politically motivated marriage that might have improved his relations with the local population. Instead, in 1857, he married the 23-year-old Katharina Cathrein (1834–1895) of Brig. And if Alexander Seiler appeared to be a picture-book hotelier, and if his praises as a host were sung in the highest terms by the most illustrious guests, this was only possible because his wife played an equally decisive role in the business. She was responsible for the office, the bookkeeping and the correspondence, and her social skills were evident even in her dealings with French- and English-speaking guests. She also had a considerable influence on the expansion of the hotel business.

Katharina Seiler-Cathrein bore 16 children, of whom 5 died in childhood. The surviving second generation consisted of five sons and six daughters. From an early age, the children were entrusted with regular tasks in the hotel and assigned additional chores as needed. The large flock of children gave the family dynasty many chances to branch out. The traditionally close ties between the Seiler family and the Jesuits offered the family opportunities for reflection. Alexander Seiler's second-oldest son Julius Seiler (1859–1936) was himself a member of the Society of Jesus, and even in the following generation, the relationship remained a close one, especially between the Seilers and the Stella Matutina seminary in Feldkirch. The family's international outlook was maintained by its manifold friendships with guests from all over the world.

Alexander Seiler II (1864–1920), Hermann Seiler (1876–1961) and Joseph Seiler (1858–1929) stand out among the second generation of Seilers for their contributions to the hotel business and to tourism. Of the Seiler daughters, one remained unmarried, while the five others married prominent personalities from Valais and other cantons and thereby strengthened the family's social network. Alexander and Katharina Seiler's sons-in-law included the important topographer and cartographer Xaver Imfeld (1853–1909); the editor of the *Neue Zürcher Zeitung*, Albert Fleiner (1859–1902); Joseph von Stockalper (1868–1955) of the long-established Brig family; and Elias Perrig (1856–1942) – the latter two both lawyers and notaries. They all contributed to the success of the Seiler family. Yet there were also plans mooted in Zermatt that could not be realised, even with all the family's connections – for example, a railway line from Sierre to Zermatt via Zinal.

After the death of Alexander Seiler, the leadership of the business passed into the hands of his widow, Katharina Seiler-Cathrein. From her, the business passed in 1895 to her second-oldest son, Alexander II, who had earned a doctorate in law. Before taking over the Seiler empire in Zermatt, he worked as an independent lawyer, notary and district judge. He was elected to the Cantonal Parliament in 1891 and to the National Council in 1905 and served in both these bodies until his death. As a politician he was especially active in matters of transport, finance and foreign policy. As a hotelier, he worked hard to continually improve the Seiler hotels and expand tourism in Zermatt. In this he followed in his father's progressive footsteps. He was active in pursuing the connection of Zermatt to the Swiss telephone network and in developing a water supply and sewage system for the village. He was a co-founder of the tourist office, and as its first president applied himself to upgrading and expanding roads, building walking and hiking paths, and setting up benches. In 1917, he became the first president of the Schweizerische Verkehrszentrale (today's Switzerland Tourism), which was brought into existence thanks to a motion that he introduced in the Swiss Parliament in 1911.

Alexander Seiler II was considered a first-rate hotelier in the mould of his father.[86] He also followed in his father's footsteps in continually expanding the empire, through leases like that of the *Hotel Belvédère* on the Gornergrat, and through takeovers like those of the inn on the Schwarzsee or the *Hotel Victoria*, which he extended with an imposing annex. The solution to the problem of access to the *Hotel Riffelalp* gave brilliant expression to his creative power but also provides an example of the poor relationship between the Seiler family and long-established Zermatt locals. Alexander Seiler II planned an access road from the Gornergrat railway station, which was then being built, to the *Hotel Riffelalp*. Because his application for a right of way through the Burgerwald (Burger Forest) was rejected, rendering the planned access road unrealisable and leaving the hotel inaccessible, he turned to a ruse. Instead of continuing to insist on the access road, he went directly to the Swiss Parliament and applied for a concession to build a connecting tram line. The concession was granted, and in 1899 Alexander Seiler II inaugurated what was both the most elevated and the shortest tram line in all of Europe.

The legal status of the business left behind by Alexander Seiler on his death was at first established through the founding of a company belonging to the three brothers Alexander, Joseph and Hermann Seiler. In 1908, this became the Société des Hôtels Seiler S.A. (Seiler Hotels Company, Inc.), to which, among other assets, ownership of the hotels and the greater part of the land owned by the Seiler empire in Zermatt was transferred. This public limited company was controlled by Alexander and Hermann Seiler. Other land and buildings outside of Zermatt were privately held by the two brothers. Thus, in 1909, another record was set in Seiler hotel history: As owners or lessees, the Seilers now had over 1,285 beds – around two thirds of the total capacity of the Zermatt region. No fewer than 750 employees worked for the Seiler Company.

Although he was tightly bound to the hotel business in Zermatt, and himself ran the *Zermatterhof* and the *Riffelalp* during several summer seasons, Hermann Seiler, Alexander's younger brother by 12 years, chose to pursue a career in law. After earning his doctorate, he worked as a lawyer and notary. At 28 he became the Mayor of Brig, in which capacity he faced many challenges during the construction of the Simplon and Lötschberg Tunnels. He was elected to the Valais Cantonal Parliament in 1910 and to the National Council in 1920. He had to give up his promising political career, which paralleled his rise to regiment commander in the army, when his brother Alexander died in 1920.

Like the Swiss hotel industry overall, the Seiler business found itself in a financially critical situation at the end of the First World War. Hermann Seiler gave up all his political offices and took over the leadership of the Seiler Hotels Company. Like his father and brother before him, he made tourism history in Zermatt. Seiler recognised that Zermatt would have no future without winter tourism. As early as the turn of the century, he had himself attracted attention as one of the first practitioners of winter sports in Switzerland. In 1902, in Zermatt, he had organised the first ski course for mountain guides ever to be offered in Switzerland and had later organised ski races as well. Now, in 1927, a quarter of a century later, he inaugurated the first Zermatt winter season – still absent a rail connection between Visp and Zermatt, for the train did not yet run in winter – by driving in 180 invited British guests on 50 horse-drawn sledges. This successful venture broke the ice; the train line was subsequently protected by avalanche barriers, as were the tracks up to the Gornergrat, and a year later the first regular winter season was launched. Zermatt could now position itself as a tourist destination in winter as well.

Joseph Seiler, the oldest son of the elder Alexander Seiler, was also active in the hotel business. Among his father's hotels had been, as mentioned earlier, a mountain hotel in Gletsch. This location had become significantly more important with the completion of the road over the

Furka Pass in 1866. The *Hotel Belvédère*, newly constructed at the upper hairpin curve of the road in the 1880s, took advantage of the popularity of the pass. Up until 1892, the Seiler hotels in Gletsch proper were run by a leaseholder. When this leaseholder ran into trouble, Joseph Seiler took over the running of the hotels; he also took on responsibility for the postal stagecoach and private coach operations. It was the heyday of stagecoaches and pleasure journeys over the passes; in the summers, around 150 horses were put up in Seiler's stables.

Joseph Seiler broke off his connection to his father's original empire completely when, in 1907, he left the Zermatt hotel company. The brilliant atmosphere that had enveloped the tourism regions of Gletsch/Furka at the turn of the century vanished with the outbreak of the war, however, and after 1918, Seiler was unsuccessful in relaunching his business. Technological revolutions, like the supplanting of stagecoaches by post buses, may have contributed to this failure. In contrast to Zermatt and other villages, the region was not well suited to winter sports. Out of feelings of solidarity with his brother, Hermann Seiler took over the operation of the troubled hotels in Gletsch in the mid-1920s.[87]

Swiss Industry in the 19th century: Dynamics and Structure

The Swiss economy was fundamentally transformed over the course of the 19th century. Agriculture, the sector that had employed most Swiss workers and strongly shaped Switzerland's image, became less important. Between 1850 and 1910, the fraction of the labour force engaged in agricultural work sank from over 50 percent to under 30 percent. Meanwhile, the industrial and service sectors grew. Workers in the service sector accounted for 13 percent of the labour force in 1850 and 27 percent in 1910, placing service on a level comparable to that of agriculture. The industrial sector, meanwhile, clearly became the strongest of the three; employment in industry rose from 30 to 46 percent of the total workforce. From the turn of the century onwards, more people were employed in industry than in agriculture.

The Swiss economy, then, was dominated by industry. Alongside England and Germany, Switzerland became a beacon of industry in Europe in the second half of the 19th century, with numbers surpassing even those in the USA. With the possible exception of Belgium, there was no other country in which industry attained as much importance as it did in Switzerland. Meanwhile, by 1870 the service sector in Switzerland had matched the agricultural sector in terms of the number of workers employed. The development in these sectors – decrease in agriculture, increase in service and a high level of industry – continued to play out over the course of the 20th century.

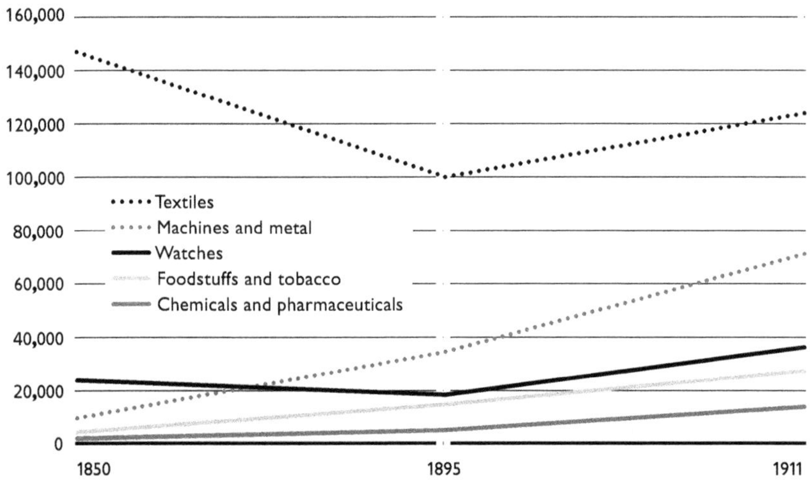

Figure 2.20 Number of persons employed in selected branches of Swiss industry in Switzerland, 1850–1911.

After a boom in the 1850s, the direction in which agriculture was heading became increasingly evident. It retreated from grain production – its dominant form before the age of the railways – and shifted to dairy and livestock. In 1846, Stefano Franscini (1796–1857) estimated that grain production in Switzerland would be capable of providing bread for the Swiss population for 290 days each year. Less than 20 years later, it would only have sufficed for 220 days. While Bavaria and Swabia were the principal suppliers of grain to Switzerland up until the mid-19th century, in the 1860s Austria-Hungary, France and even Russia – thanks to the railways – took on significant roles. Imports of cattle also surpassed exports in the second half of the century – in 1866, for example, by some 20,000 head. Domestic meat production, then, also failed to cover the needs of the population. The balance then deteriorated even further. In 1870, domestic production would have sufficed for only 200 days. At the end of the Franco-Prussian War in 1871 there were hopes of an economic upswing, but already in the mid-1870s a severe agricultural crisis developed. It lasted until the early 1880s. The state took no effective measures, and thousands of farmers went bankrupt. Many moved into industry and commerce, while others emigrated.

The early-capitalist business form of the workshop system proved successful for the textile industry: The industry became established in rural areas, where there were numerous workers at hand, while production centres were erected in the cities – in Zurich, for example, at the Seidenhof and the Wollenhof. In the 17th century, the production of raw silk became more important. Silk doubling was in demand, and Zurich developed into the main supplier of the silk-cloth factories in southern

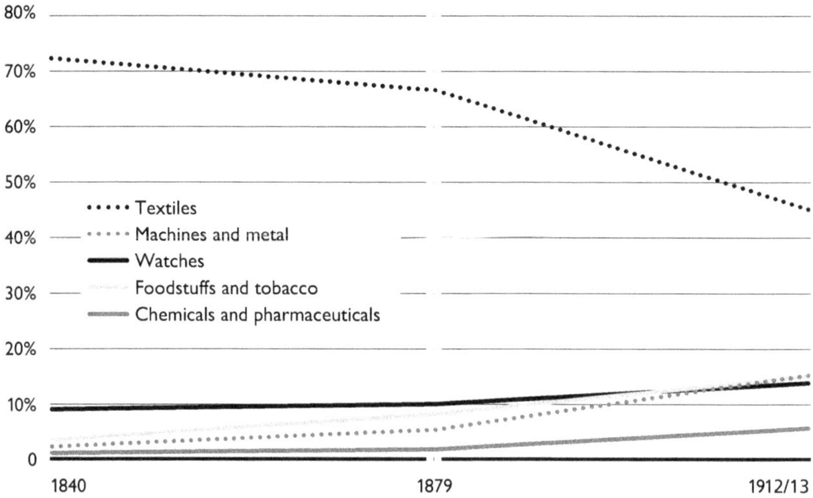

Figure 2.21 The Swiss export economy from 1840 until 1912/1913 (in percent of total exports).

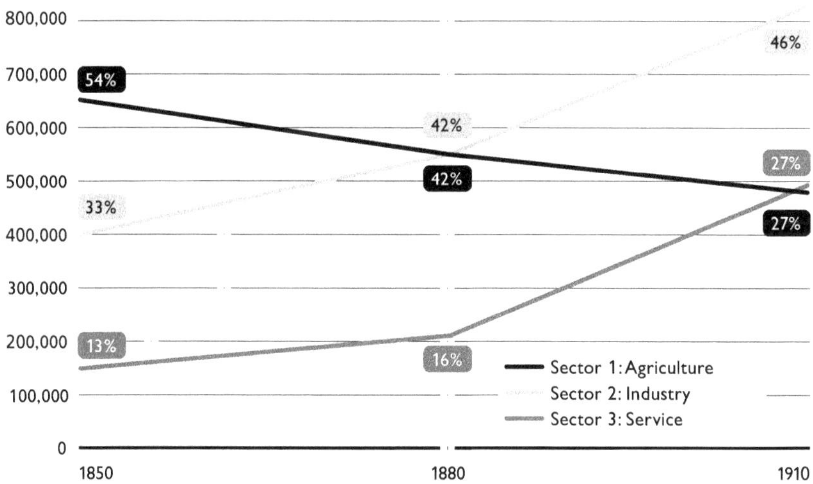

Figure 2.22 Number of persons employed by sector, 1850–1910.

France. The rise of the cotton industry followed hard on the heyday of the silk industry. In the turmoil and then the aftermath of the French Revolution, the early-capitalist business form collapsed along with the Old Swiss Confederacy in 1798. In the early 19th century, new industrial centres formed in Winterthur and the Zurich Oberland. Mechanisation fundamentally transformed the textile industry.

Industrialisation in Switzerland began in rural areas. By the end of the 18th century, with the boom in the textile industry, the Zurich Oberland,

Glarus, Appenzell and the Toggenburg became the most densely industrialised regions in Europe. Water power was the dominant source of energy. Industrialisation in England had earlier developed quite differently: There it was steam engines that delivered the energy, and industry was concentrated in the cities. While spinning mills in Switzerland were first set up along streams in order to use water as their motive power, the cotton mills that were established along larger streams and rivers led to the building of much larger power plants. Most of the textile operations in the early 19th century were run by smaller companies.

Self-financing by manufacturers was standard practice for textile operations. Only occasionally were silent partners involved. Many of the private banks that were founded in the 18th and early 19th centuries were originally parts of trading firms. This explains why industrial banking only came into being rather late across the whole of Switzerland – predominantly in connection with the railway project. Up until the 19th century, spinning frames were hand-operated, but the Vorwerk needed stronger motive forces. When the embargo against England was lifted in 1814, inexpensive machine-produced yarn flooded the Continent. A response was called for: Improvement in yarn quality and higher production volumes were needed. Spinning operations were moved to riversides, and mechanical spinning mills were retooled so that water power could be used to drive the spinning frames.

The engineering industry emerged from the textile industry and artisan enterprises and was concentrated in urban areas. It developed in three phases. First, repairs were carried out on English textile machines; next, these machines were emulated and optimised; and finally, machines for other branches of industry were produced: turbines, steam engines, ships and locomotives, and later electrical machines. In England and Germany, coal deposits formed the raw-material foundation of early industrialisation. The locational disadvantage of Switzerland in this respect became less pronounced with the possibility of large-scale freight transport via the railways. In addition, water power stood in for coal-powered steam engines as an energy supplier for fixed installations. These two factors allowed Switzerland to push to the fore of technical development in the second half of the 19th century, despite its scarcity of raw materials.

An orientation towards exports has been a defining feature of the Swiss economy throughout history. The reasons for this range from the topographical peculiarities of the country to the social structure of its population, and on to its political architecture. As early as the 18th century, the textile and watchmaking industries manufactured their wares primarily for foreign markets. In the 19th century and up until 1914, the dynamics of industrialisation led to the Swiss economy becoming dependent on exports to a greater extent than any other economy in Europe.

Notes

1 See Switzerland Global Enterprise, accessed 20 September 2019, https://www.s-ge-com/de/aktuell/20181-ranking-patents; Sylviane Chassot, "China überholt die Schweiz bei den Patenten," *Neue Zürcher Zeitung*, 7 March 2018, accessed 20 September 2019, https://www.nzz.ch/wirtschaft/china-ueberholt-die-schweiz-bei-den-patentanmeldungen-ld.1363654; Andreas Flütsch, "Wie unterschiedlich die Schweiz und China sind," *Tages-Anzeiger*, 17 January 2017, accessed 20 September 2019, https://www.tagesanzeiger.ch/schweiz/standard/wie-unterschiedlich-die-schweiz-und-china-sind/story/23074667.

2 "Pioneering entrepreneurs dominate the Swiss Market Index." Jung Joseph, ed., *Schweizer Erfolgsgeschichten: Pioniere, Unternehmen, Innovationen*, vol. 100 of *Schweizer Pioniere der Wirtschaft und Technik* (Jubiläumsausgabe), ed. Verein für wirtschaftshistorische Studien (Zurich, 2013), 84f.

3 I first used and contextualised the term "Spirit of '48" in my celebratory speech marking the occasion of the 150th anniversary of the Turicia Academic Association in 2010. Joseph Jung, "Projekt Schweiz oder der 'Spirit of 48': Abdruck der Festrede am Festakt zum 150-Jahr-Jubiläum der Akademischen Verbindung Turicia vom 22. Mai 2010 im Kongresshaus Zürich." In *Stolzes Banner am Limmatstrand: Die Geschichte der Akademischen Verbindung Turicia 1860–2013*, ed. Alt-Turicia Zurich (Zurich, 2014), 15ff.

4 Eveline Hasler has written about Dunant's tragic life story. Eveline Hasler, *Der Zeitreisende: Die Visionen des Henry Dunant* (Nördlingen: dtv Verlagsgesellschaft, 2018).

5

> As a small country in the heart of Europe that has no significant domestic sources of raw materials, never had its own colonies and never pursued an imperialistic foreign policy, [Switzerland] was already engaged in significant intermediary trade in raw materials in the 19th century, and at the turn of the 21st century was the largest global hub for commodity trading.

Lea Haller, *Transithandel: Geld- und Warenströme im globalen Kapitalismus* (Berlin: Suhrkamp, 2019), 19.

6 "According to estimates, Swiss companies were directly or indirectly involved in the deportation of 172,000 slaves." Lea Haller, *Transithandel: Geld- und Warenströme im globalen Kapitalismus* (Berlin: Suhrkamp, 2019), 49.

7

> The Industrial Revolution fundamentally changed work, human society and individual lives. A couple of examples: The small family would be unthinkable without it, since it drastically reduced child mortality; our social welfare system and our nation states are both consequences of it, as only with the emergence of the railway could larger territories be governed and administrated, and we would not have been able to afford universal education without it. One can go through practically every area of our society and establish that the Industrial Revolution represented a caesura.

Thomas Gull, "Die Wucht der Veränderung," furrerhugi, accessed 20 September 2019, https://www.furrerhugi.ch/en-us/influence/2019/%C2%ABdie-wucht-der-veranderung%C2%BB.

8 The cantons that adopted liberal constitutions in 1830/1831: Zurich, Bern, Lucerne, Fribourg, Solothurn, Schaffhausen, St Gallen, Aargau, Thurgau,

Vaud and Ticino. Basel-Landschaft followed in 1833 after its secession from Basel-Stadt.

9 "It is therefore not surprising that contemporary observers spoke of factory workers as 'modern slaves'...According to a report by the Attorney General's Office there were 21 fatal accidents in Zurich factories between 1834 and 1857." Robert Fritzsche, Fritz Heberlein and Heinrich Schmid, *Hermann Müller-Thurgau: Gründer der Schweizerischen Versuchsanstalt für Obst-, Wein- und Gartenbau, Wädenswil*, vol. 29 of *Schweizer Pioniere der Wirtschaft und Technik*, ed. Verein für wirtschaftshistorische Studien (Zurich, 1974), 53.

10 *Die Käserei in der Vehfreude* was made into a film by Franz Schnyder in 1958.

11

> In an essay about British entrepreneurship during the Industrial Revolution, Joel Mokyr has pointed out how often this [division of responsibilities between a brilliant technician and a commercially oriented entrepreneur] was the case, and discussed several examples. He speaks here of "couplings": "The couplings of individuals with technical skill and those with commercial acumen personalize the great advantage that Britain enjoyed in this dimension, namely the complementarity of human capital and favourable institutions."

Markus Somm, *Elektropolis an der Limmat: Baden und die BBC, 1870 bis 1925; Die Beschreibung einer Transformation* (Bern: Stämpfli Verlag, 2019), 146f.

12 I have published several studies on the history of Swiss banking. A comprehensive one appeared in the context of my work on the Schweizerische Kreditanstalt in 2000. See Joseph Jung, *From Schweizerische Kreditanstalt to Credit Suisse Group: The History of a Bank* (Zurich: NZZ Verlag, 2000). The present discussion is based on this earlier work. Some of the content has been expanded on or reworded.

> The business model of Crédit Mobilier consisted on the one hand of pooling large amounts of capital to realise important infrastructural projects. On the other hand, railway construction and industry were promoted by the bank itself acquiring the relevant companies' securities in the issues it arranged, and maintaining them in its portfolio until they could be sold at a profit.

Joseph Jung, *Alfred Escher 1819–1882: Der Aufbruch zur modernen Schweiz*, vol. 3 (Zurich: NZZ Libro, 2006), 738.

13 "Very soon after its inception, SKA had become a strong driving force in the economy, a role that was only to intensify in subsequent years." Joseph Jung, *From Schweizerische Kreditanstalt to Credit Suisse Group: The History of a Bank* (Zurich: NZZ Verlag, 2000), 46.

14 "In 1914, the total assets of SBV, the largest Swiss bank, did not amount to even a quarter of the assets held on the balance sheets of the big banks in Britain, Germany and France." Joseph Jung, *From Schweizerische Kreditanstalt to Credit Suisse Group: The History of a Bank* (Zurich: NZZ Verlag, 2000), 33.

15 I have written extensively about the history of the Swiss insurance industry in my work about the history of Winterthur Insurance: Joseph Jung, *Die Winterthur: Eine Versicherungsgeschichte* (Zurich: NZZ Verlag, 2000). The present discussion draws on this earlier publication; some of the content has been expanded on and reworked.

16 "The Swiss insurance business grew to such an extent that its foreign revenues were comparable to the export revenues of the most important industry groups." Joseph Jung, *Die Winterthur: Eine Versicherungsgeschichte* (Zurich: NZZ Verlag, 2000), 33.

17 "The maintaining of convertibility, and, to protect this, the guarantee of a generous gold backing, also became the central goal of the monetary policy of the National Bank." Ernst Baltensperger, *Der Schweizer Franken: Eine Erfolgsgeschichte; Die Währung der Schweiz im 19. und 20. Jahrhundert* (Zurich: NZZ Libro, 2012), 137f.

18 I have written extensively on the history of the cultural policies of the young Federal State in my work on the Gottfried Keller Foundation. See Joseph Jung, *Das imaginäre Museum: Privates Kunstengagement und Staatliche Kulturpolitik in der Schweiz; Die Gottfried Keller-Stiftung 1890–1922* (Zurich: NZZ Verlag, 1998). The present discussion draws on this earlier work. Some of the content has been reworked and expanded on.

19 *Neue Zürcher Zeitung*, 24 February 1888.

20 The following discussion refines, concretises and conceptualises the 17 theses about the social characteristics of Swiss pioneers that I published in simplified form in 2013. See Joseph Jung, ed., *Schweizer Erfolgsgeschichten: Pioniere, Unternehmen, Innovationen*, vol. 100 of *Schweizer Pioniere der Wirtschaft und Technik* (Jubiläumsausgabe), ed. Verein für wirtschaftshistorische Studien (Zurich, 2013).

21 I am grateful to Dr Andrea Grossi of the Federal Department of Home Affairs for his kind assistance on 18 September 2019.

22 "There is nothing new under the sun…" Remarks made by Johann Salomon Hegi about Lydia Welti-Escher's autobiographical sketches ("The Thoughts of a Woman"): Joseph Jung, *Lydia Welti-Escher 1858–1891*, with a foreword by Hildegard Elisabeth Keller, 5th ed. (Zurich: NZZ Libro, 2016), 528 and 206ff. See also: 93f., 206 and 218.

23

> The search for lodgings was even more difficult for the first tourists. Besides on the post-horse road from St Gingolph to Domodossola, with its hostels in Leuk, Turtmann, Visp, Brig and on the Simplon Pass, there were hotels only in Leukerbad, and a small inn each in Saas, Zermatt and at the [foot of the] Rhône Glacier. Even in these villages, foreigners preferred to lodge with the pastors, who up until 1839 were unrestrictedly allowed to operate taverns. Travellers after 1830 generally spoke positively of lodging with the village pastor.

Marianne-Franziska Imhasly, *Katholische Pfarrer in der Alpenregion um 1850*, vol. 9 of *Religion – Politik – Gesellschaft in der Schweiz*, ed. Urs Altermatt (Freiburg: Universitätsverlag Freiburg, 1992), 291f.

24 The Appenzell almanac of 1852 reported that Simon built 12 palaces in a single year and employed some 3,000 workers. It described Simon as follows:

> The extent of the architectural genius he developed there [in St Petersburg] is evidenced by the known fact that the emperor himself once patted him on the shoulder and said, "You are the little Napoleon of architects." Mr Simon is truly a very small man of somewhat neglected appearance, but for that all the better equipped with spirit and talent.

25 The Swiss economy increasingly had need of factory and construction workers in the second half of the 19th century. These often came from abroad:

> A further large wave of immigration occurred in connection with the so-called Second Industrial Revolution as well as with the expansion of the

> railway network between 1888 and the First World War. The immigrants replaced the labour force represented by the approximately 12 percent of the Swiss population that left the country in the second half of the 19th century. They were allowed to settle in Switzerland without restriction and to change jobs at will.

Marcel Heiniger, "Einwanderung (Immigration)," Historisches Lexicon der Schweiz, 7 December 2016, accessed 2 October 2019, https://hls-dhs.dss.ch/de/articles/007991/2006-12-07/.

26

> In 1855, the Dufour map won a gold medal at the World Fair in Paris, and numerous other distinctions at other international expositions followed. Thanks to its fitting degree of generalisation, the harmony of the linear elements and the writing, the velvety softness of the copper printing and especially the representation of the terrain, which was the apex of what was possible in black and white, it was described as the "most exquisite map in the world" (August Petermann, 1864). Its shortcomings lay in the variable quality of the trigonometric and topographical data it was based on. Buchwalder and the Alpine researcher Gottlieb Studer justifiably criticised the appellations chosen for certain localities.

Hans-Peter Höhener and Thomas Klöti, "Geschichte der schweizerischen Kartographie," in *Kartographische Sammlungen in der Schweiz* (Bern, 2010), 26.

27

> Seen from this perspective, it is clear that with the leadership and the multifaceted competencies that Favre and Escher had demonstrated up until the end of the 1870s, the project could have been completed on time and according to contract on 1 October 1880.

Joseph Jung, *Alfred Escher 1819–1882: Aufstieg, Macht, Tragik*, 6th ed. (Zurich: NZZ Libro, 2017), 402.

28 I would like to thank Dr Bruno Bohlhalter for his many suggestions and his critical engagement with the text.

29 "The oldest surviving watch manufacturer in Switzerland, Vacheron Constantin, opened its doors for business in 1785. In 1788, around 3,000 people were employed in the Genevan watchmaking industry – a considerable number for a city of around 26,000 inhabitants." Bruno Bohlhalter, *Unruh: Die schweizerische Uhrenindustrie und ihre Krisen im 20. Jahrhundert* (Zurich: NZZ Libro, 2016), 18.

30 Marx distinguishes between heterogeneous manufacturing (watches) and organic manufacturing (locomotives). For him, the typical form is the heterogeneous one. In the transformation from artisanal to industrial operations, this form stays closer to its origins, as the division of labour occurs under a single roof. Organic manufacturing, on the other hand, became transformed into large-scale industry. In his *Critique of Political Economy* (*Capital*), Marx extensively discusses manufacturing. In this context, he takes the watch as an example of the "division of labour in manufacturing" and describes "an immense number" of "suboperations." Karl Marx, *Das Kapital, Kritik der politischen Ökonomie,* vol.1 of *Karl Marx – Friedrich Engels – Werke 23* (Berlin, 1968), 362f.

31

> This change in thinking [the Philadelphia shock] also resulted in an explosion in factory construction in the last two decades of the 19th century. From 1882 to 1901, the number of watch factories in Switzerland

> increased from 72 to 647; by 1911 the number was already 853. Despite this huge increase, the overall structure remained more artisanal than truly industrial.

Bruno Bohlhalter, *Unruh: Die schweizerische Uhrenindustrie und ihre Krisen im 20. Jahrhundert* (Zurich: NZZ Libro, 2016), 27.

32 I would like to thank Professor Alexis Schwarzenbach and Dr Roman Wild of the Lucerne University of Applied Sciences and Arts for their suggestions and their critical reading of my discussion of the Swiss textile industry.

33 The term "Locarneser" also referred to Italian religious refugees who came to Switzerland via Locarno. My thanks to Professor Alexis Schwarzenbach for pointing this out.

34 *Zürcher Intelligenzblatt*, 27 March 1861.

35 When the US Civil War caused existential problems for the cotton industry in Switzerland, the *Winterthurer Landbote* (21 June 1862) commented that Europe should not get involved in the war. "King Cotton" was not "almighty" enough to justify European intervention. In its estimation of almightiness, however, the *Landbote* was off the mark. *King Cotton: Eine Geschichte des globalen Kapitalismus* (*King Cotton: A History of Global Capitalism*) is the German title of a book by Sven Beckert of Harvard University, the second edition of which appeared in 2015. The original title is *Empire of Cotton: A Global History* (2014).

36 Matthias Legler "finally chose the small village of Ponte San Pietro on the Brembo river, west of Bergamo and right on a railway line." Andréa Kaufmann, *Spinnen – Weben – Drucken: Pioniere des Glarnerlandes*, vol. 99 of *Schweizer Pioniere der Wirtschaft und Technik*, ed. Verein für wirtschaftshistorische Studien (Zurich, 2014), 28.

37 Werner Bosshard is currently working on a comprehensive history of Oetwil am See. In it, using previously unexploited sources, he devotes a long chapter to Heinrich Kunz, who grew up there. I am grateful to him for allowing me to read the manuscript.

38 *Neue Zürcher Zeitung*, 6 February 1857.

39 Eugen Hermann, *Ein Jahrhundert Zürich und die Entwicklung seiner Firmen*, vol. 1/2 (Zurich: J.H. Müller, 1946/1947), 72.

40

> One could fill an entire book with a list of the warships and trading ships that fell victim to one or another military conflict and were equipped with engines built by Escher Wyss. In the 19th century, Switzerland was one of the leading shipbuilding countries.

Barbara Stolba, *Neue Zürcher Zeitung* archive, 10 January 2018, accompanying commentary to the article "In Zürich gebaut – im Ausland versenkt: Schicksale Schweizer Schiffe" (Built in Zurich – Sunk Abroad: The Fate of Swiss Ships), originally published on 8/9 April 1978.

41

> Denounced as "practices of robber barons" and "a system of parasitism" by foreign competitors, this institutional anomaly is believed to have facilitated the emergence of powerful food processing, chemical, and engineering industries in the late nineteenth century, as Swiss entrepreneurs could adopt new technologies without having to bear any of the high development costs.

Roman Studer, "When did the Swiss Get so Rich? Comparing Living Standards in Switzerland and Europe 1800–1813," in *Journal of European Economic History*, 37, no. 2 (2008): 405–452.

42

> The Vetterli rifle appears as a perfected emulation of the Winchester or Henry rifle, with individual ideas imported from the Lindner and Zündnadel rifles. It has therefore justifiably been commented that it provides new evidence of the great advantages of the absolute freedom of commerce from the privileges granted by patents for inventions. Without this freedom, this rifle would never have appeared.

Schweizerische Militarzeitschrift (Swiss Military Journal), 23 December 1867.

43 Karl Schib, "Johann Georg Neher (1788–1858)," in *Schaffhauser Biographien des 18. und 19. Jahrhunderts,* part 1: *Schaffhauser Beiträge zur vaterländischen Geschichte,* no. 33 (1956): 236.

44

> This so-called "Moser Canal" helps...prevent floods in the industrial neighbourhood, without leading to a loss of rise, meaning that the force of the water can be fully exploited. Moser's solution to this construction problem was considered ingenious by contemporary experts.

Roger Nicholas Balsiger, *Heinrich Moser 1805–1874: Internationaler Uhrenfabrikant – visionärer Industriepionier*, vol. 85 of *Schweizer Pioniere der Wirtschaft und Technik*, ed. Verein für wirtschaftshistorische Studien (Zurich, 2007), 45.

45

> Bodmer kept a meticulous diary on this trip [to England and Scotland in 1816/17]...it sparks fascination in the reader. Bodmer's notes communicate to us a very vivid picture of England as a land of technical miracles before the emergence of the railways...At one point Bodmer spitefully comments on how well he has succeeded in appearing naïve, so that his host is unaware that he has an expert before him.

Norbert Lang, *Johann Georg Bodmer (1786–1864): Maschinenbauer und Erfinder*, vol. 45 of *Schweizer Pioniere der Wirtschaft und Technik*, ed. Verein für wirtschaftshistorische Studien (Zurich, 1987), 35.

46 Johann Conrad Fischer, *Tagebuch einer im Jahr 1814 gemachten Reise über Paris nach London und einigen Fabrikstädten Englands vorzüglich in technologischer Hinsicht* (Diary of a journey made during the year 1814 via Paris to London and a number of industrial cities in England, seen from a technological perspective) (Aarau, 1819), accessed 26 October 2019, http://dx.doi.org/10.3931/e-rara-18795.

> During his many journeys through Europe, Johann Conrad Fischer kept... diaries, in which he described his visits to production facilities and his general observations...Fischer considered himself...a writer as well, and lived according to the maxim "Nulla dies sine linea" (No day without a line).

See Johann Conrad Fischer, *Tagebücher 1773–1854*, ed. Karl Schib (Schaffhausen: Georg Fischer AG, 1951), accessed 2 October 2019, https://www.eisenbibliothek.ch/content/gf/ironlibrary/de/libraryuser/lieblingsbuch/fischer/tagebuecher.html.

47

> That Brown was offered an opportunity here may have to do with the fact that he came from the Royal Arsenal...Brown may have been an autodidact, and never went to university, and yet this may give the wrong

> impression; in fact he received his training at one of the best schools of the epoch, namely, the Arsenal.

Markus Somm, *Elektropolis an der Limmat: Baden und die BBC, 1870 bis 1925; Die Beschreibung einer Transformation* (Bern: Stämpfli Verlag, 2019), 157.

48

> If we here recall the phenomenon of Coupling...The relationship between Johann Jakob Sulzer and Charles Brown senior was characterised by a productive cooperation of this nature, in which the two complemented each other so well that the weaknesses of the one were made up for by the strengths of the other, and vice versa.

Markus Somm, *Elektropolis an der Limmat: Baden und die BBC, 1870 bis 1925; Die Beschreibung einer Transformation* (Bern: Stämpfli Verlag, 2019), 159.

49

> From the perspective of the [Swiss] industrialists, it is clear, why they recruited these English experts – but what made these experts want to come to Switzerland? To answer briefly: Switzerland was no longer a developing country; its companies had something to offer to ambitious and talented people.

Markus Somm, *Elektropolis an der Limmat: Baden und die BBC, 1870 bis 1925; Die Beschreibung einer Transformation* (Bern: Stämpfli Verlag, 2019), 155.

50 See John Stuart Mill, *Principles of Political Economy with Some of Their Applications to Social Philosophy*, abridged, ed. and with an Introduction by Stephen Nathanson (Indianapolis: Hackett Publishing Company Inc., 2004), 42f.

51 Peter Emil Huber, personal records 1863–1917, quoted in Markus Somm, *Elektropolis an der Limmat: Baden und die BBC, 1870 bis 1925; Die Beschreibung einer Transformation* (Bern: Stämpfli Verlag, 2019), 165.

52 "In the same year [1894], Hoffmann married Adèle La Roche-Passavant, who came from an established family of traders in raw silk. After Traub's departure in 1896, the firm took on – in 1897 – the famous double name Fritz Hoffmann-La Roche." Mario König, *Besichtigung einer Weltindustrie, 1859–2016*, vol. 1 of *Chemie und Pharma in Basel,* ed. Georg Kreis and Beat von Wartburg (Pliezhausen: Christoph Merian Verlag, 2016), 42.

53 "Volkart had not only built up a multi-branched purchasing organisation in India in the second half of the 19th century, but also a continually growing network of sales agents in Europe." Christof Dejung, *Die Fäden des globalen Marktes: Eine Sozial- und Kulturgeschichte des Welthandels am Beispiel der Handelsfirma Gebrüder Volkart 1851–1999*, vol. 85 of *Industrielle Welt: Schriftenreihe des Arbeitskreises für moderne Sozialgeschichte*, ed. Andreas Eckert and Joachim Rückert (Vienna: Böhlau Verlag, 2013), 113.

54 I first wrote about forgotten political heroes in 1994, in connection with the Alfred Escher exhibition that was held in the Le Point Gallery on the occasion of the 175th anniversary of Alfred Escher's birth. See Joseph Jung, "Vom Wehen des Zeitgeists: Alfred Escher und die Maximen der schweizerischen Aussenpolitik" in the exhibition catalogue of the Galerie "le point" (Zurich, 1994), 62ff. I subsequently pursued the idea and have written on it on several occasions. Although the present discussion draws largely on these works, some of the content has been newly conceived and restructured.

55 I have extensively documented Escher's business and political work and his innumerable offices and functions in my biographies of him. The most up-to-date presentation of Escher's official positions from 1839 to 1882 and his work on commissions from 1845 to 1881 can be found in my condensed 2019 publication in the "Swiss Pioneers of Business and Technology" series. See Joseph Jung, *Alfred Escher: Visionär, Grossbürger, Wirtschaftsführer*, vol. 114 of *Schwiezer Pioniere der Wirtschaft und Technik*, ed. Verein für wirtschaftshistorische Studien (Zurich, 2019), 120f. For more extensive depictions see Joseph Jung, *Alfred Escher 1819–1882: Der Aufbruch zur modernen Schweiz*, 4 volumes (Zurich: NZZ Libro, 2006); Joseph Jung, *Alfred Escher 1819–1882: Aufstieg, Macht, Tragik*, 6th ed. (Zurich: NZZ Libro, 2017).

56 I first introduced the image of Escher's four temples in connection with my remarks on Richard Wagner. See Joseph Jung, "Zürichs Herrscher und der Asylant: Alfred Escher und Richard Wagner," special edition printed in honour of the Zurich "Festspielen" 2013, reprinted in *Mitteilungen der Gottfried Keller-Gesellschaft* (Zurich: NZZ Libro, 2014).

> Escher was the darting flame that consumed itself after it had set off the initial spark of modern Switzerland...Alfred Escher and the 1848ers were surely proud of the young Federal State, but they celebrated it not in heroic images but in tracks and train stations, in the temples of science, in industry and in finance.

Joseph Jung, "Der Aufstieg der Schweiz hat einen Namen," *Neue Zürcher Zeitung*, online, no. 45, 23 February 2019, 4–5.

57

> Escher's love for his home country centred around two focal points: the area around Lake Zurich and Switzerland itself. The great goal that Escher pursued in all his founding activities was to promote Zurich to national prominence – and, above all, to secure the independence of Switzerland.

Joseph Jung, "Der Aufstieg der Schweiz hat einen Namen," *Neue Zürcher Zeitung*, online, no. 45, 23 February 2019.

58 Jacob Burckhardt, *Werke: Ästhetik der bildenden Kunst; Über der bildenden Kunst; Über das Studium der Geschichte*, critical complete edition, vol. 10 (Munich: C.H. Beck Verlag, 2000).

> Historical greatness is thus dependent on the standards of each epoch and is at the same time the result of an ever new discursive understanding about whether the acts of a ruler demonstrate true greatness or merely great power. In this connection Burckhardt uses the image of history loving to condense itself into a human being, whom from this point onwards the world will obey.

See Berthold Seewald, "Eine Frage der Grösse," *Welt*, 3 July 2011, accessed 2 October 2019, https://www.welt.de/print/wams/vermischtes/article13464578/Eine-Frage-der-Groesse.html.

59 *Neue Rheinische Zeitung*, 10 December 1848. Quoted in Karl Marx, *Das Kapital, Kritik der politischen Ökonomie*, vol.1 of *Karl Marx – Friedrich Engels – Werke 23* (Berlin, 1968), 90f.

60

> I have not yet seen Escher; he is in Bern. I am curious about him and would like to believe that he is better than the party, and that he is utterly in the right, but he stands there just like a sovereign, all the more in that he does not bear the title.

Mommsen to Jahn, Zurich, 4 May 1852. Lothar Wickert, ed., *Theodor Mommsen – Otto Jahn. Briefwechsel 1842–1868* (Frankfurt am Main: Klostermann, 1962), 106.

61 Joseph Jung, *Alfred Escher 1819–1882: Der Aufbruch zur modernen Schweiz*, 4 volumes (Zurich: NZZ Libro, 2006), 825ff.

62 *Neue Zürcher Zeitung*, 12 April 1903.

63 *St. Galler Tagblatt*, no. 56, 8 March 1910.

64 It was also recognised in Basel that private fire insurance could be a profitable business: In 1863, the Basel Insurance Company for Fire Damage (Basler Versicherungs-Gesellschaft gegen Feuerscaden) was founded. In 1864 came the Basel Life Insurance Company (Basler Lebensversicherung Gesellschaft) and the Basel Transport Insurance Company (Basler Transport-Versicherungs-Gesellschaft), and in 1869, the Basel Reinsurance Company (Basler Rückversicherungsgesellschaft). In Zurich, meanwhile, the fire-insurance business was not taken up; neither was it in Winterthur. See Joseph Jung, *Die Winterthur: Eine Versicherungsgeschichte* (Zurich: NZZ Verlag, 2000), 23.

65

> In contrast to what the founders of Swiss Re had expected, the special reinsurers had a long and very difficult time establishing themselves... Specialised reinsurers, who were crucially dependent on a high volume of premiums to be able to cover large damages, were only used sporadically.

Tobias Straumann, "Die unsichtbare Reise: Die Geschichte von Swiss Re 1863–2013," in *Swiss Re und die Welt der Risikomärkte: Eine Geschichte*, ed. Harold James (Munich: C.H. Beck, 2014), 346.

66 I am grateful to Tobias Straumann for directing my attention to the friendship between Einstein and Besso. See Tobias Straumann, "Die unsichtbare Reise: Die Geschichte von Swiss Re 1863–2013," in *Swiss Re und die Welt der Risikomärkte: Eine Geschichte*, ed. Harold James (Munich: C.H. Beck, 2014), 346.

67 I first published on the collapse of the Lloyd companies in Winterthur in 2000. The discussion that follows draws on this earlier work; the content has been modified in some places, and the wording has been changed. Joseph Jung, *Die Winterthur: Eine Versicherungsgeschichte* (Zurich: NZZ Verlag, 2000), 25f., 63.

68 I published extensively on the history of the Winterthur Insurance Company in 2000. The present discussion draws on this earlier work; some of the content has been modified and reworded. Joseph Jung, *Die Winterthur: Eine Versicherungsgeschichte* (Zurich: NZZ Verlag, 2000).

69 Adrian Knoepfli, "Als die Lloyd-Versicherung pleiteging," in *Der Landbote*, 17 August 2013.

70 Thanks to Dr Mark Andreas Seiler for his helpful suggestion.

71 For example, the relay function of the *Glacier du Rhône* hotel:

> The "well-invented" town of Gletsch was a "transit station for Alpine traffic", a "wonderful reloading point for hikers", and an Alpine "caravanserai for travellers" as well as a horse-changing station for public and private stagecoach traffic, and the hotel was perhaps at times the "largest...inn in Switzerland before or after the coach ride (or hike) over the passes that connected Canton Valais with Cantons Bern and Uri".

Mark Andreas Seiler, *Ein Gletscher – ein Hotel – eine Familie. Horizonte einer Walliser Hotelierdynastie* (Visp: Rotten-Verlag, 2012), 175.

72 "The decisive impulse for the dissemination of electric lighting in Swiss hotels was provided by the first international electricity exhibition in Paris in 1881,

which was accompanied by a great deal of propaganda." Roland Flückiger-Seiler, *Hotelträume: Zwischen Gletschern und Palmen; Schweizer Tourismus und Hotelbau 1830–1920*, 2nd ed. (Zurich: Hier und Jetzt, 2005), 33.

73 "En réunissant ces éléments, nous constatons...une importante multipositionnalité des principaux acteurs, actifs tant au sein des entités politiques que dans les conseils d'adminstration (CA) des sociéteés touristiques et économique (en patriculier les banques)." Géraldine Sauthier, *Pouvoir local et Tourisme: Jeux politiques à Finhaut, Montreux et Zermatt de 1850 à nos jours* (Neuchâtel: Edition Alphil, 2016), 59.

74 With the legendary Genoa million, Bucher became the first millionaire in Canton Obwalden. "Franz Joseph Bucher used the 'Genoa million' as seed capital for his own company, whose name he altered only slightly: He replaced Bucher & Durrer with his own surname, Bucher-Durrer." Romano Cuonz, *Der Hotelberg: Geschichte und Geschichten vom Bürgenstock-Resort 1871 bis heute* (Basel: NZZ Libro, 2018), 98.

75 "Pioneers show up across the entire hotel industry. Their concentration in specific areas depends on the vagaries of fashion." Louis Gaulis and René Creux, *Schweizer Pioniere der Hotellerie*, foreword by Werner Kämpfen, trans. Herbert Meier (Paudex: Fontainemore, 1976), 37.

76 Romana Costa, "Der Hotelpionier, der Licht nach St. Moritz brachte," in Schweizer Radio Fernsehen 4. Zeitblende, 29 June 2019, online, accessed 16 October 2019, https://www.srf.ch/sendungen/zeitblende/der-hotelpionier-der-licht-nach-st-moritz-brachte.

77 My thanks to Diane Conrad-Daubrah for her helpful suggestion.

> The investors from St Moritz-Bad...soon noticed that they were being outstripped by the village [St Moritz Dorf]. There the Badrutts had set up a hotel empire, and had discovered a lucrative field of business in winter tourism. With the construction of the *Schweizerhof* hotel in 1898...a first breach was made in the Badrutt empire.

Susanna Ruf, *Fünf Generationen Badrutt: Hotelpioniere und Begründer der Wintersaison*, vol. 91 of *Schweizer Pioniere der Wirtschaft und Technik*, ed. Verein für wirtschaftshistorische Studien (Zurich, 2010), 57.

78 My thanks to Dr Reto Bon for his helpful suggestions.

79 Thanks to Stephan Seiler for his helpful suggestions and for generously allowing me a look at unpublished materials related to the Seiler family's history.

80

> Contrary to popular opinion, the change in name of the old inn to *Hôtel Monte Rosa* was made in the summer season of 1852 by the surgeon Joseph Lauber, and not in 1855, when the hotel was owned by the Seiler brothers.

Roland Flückiger-Seiler, "Streiflichter zur Hotel- und Tourismusgeschichte von Zermatt," in vol. 47 of *Blätter aus der Walliser Geschichte*, ed. Geschichtsforschenden Verein vom Oberwallis (Brig, 2015), 139–248.

81 My thanks to Dr Mark Andreas Seiler for his helpful suggestion.

82

> Eggishorn, a mountain terrace with an extensive panoramic view, had already entered Seiler's imagination as a possible site for a hotel in 1854. With the clear eye of a land speculator who saw the travel-hungry and close-to-nature spirit of the second half of the century approaching, he selected the

locations at which in a few, perhaps five, perhaps ten years, this yearning for natural scenery and mountain air would stop in and feel at home.

Mark Andreas Seiler, *Ein Gletscher – ein Hotel – eine Familie: Horizonte einer Walliser Hotelierdynastie* (Visp: Rotten-Verlag, 2012), 215.

83 My thanks to Stephan Seiler for allowing me to read his unpublished manuscript.

84 Leslie Stephen, a regular guest at the *Monte Rosa* for decades, described Alexander Seiler in his obituary as "the best of all proprietors of Alpine Hotels." Elsewhere he wrote, "Everybody chatted with him, and everybody found him cordial as well as courteous." Mark Andreas Seiler, *Ein Gletscher – ein Hotel – eine Familie: Horizonte einer Walliser Hotelierdynastie* (Visp: Rotten-Verlag, 2012), 12, 196.

85 My thanks to Dr Mark Andreas Seiler for his helpful suggestion.

3 Headlines

From Developing Country to Laboratory of Progress

Almost Passed By

In the first half of the 19th century, Switzerland fell behind modern states in decisive areas of development. Despite its already world-famous watch and textile industries, it was a largely agricultural country with a severely deficient infrastructure. But the main problem lay in the political structure of the Confederation, as the following example makes clear.

The Swiss engineering industry excelled in the construction of boats and turbines in the 1830s, but a transition to the manufacture of locomotives did not ensue – just as the railway project itself was unable to get on track before 1848. Why was this? It is evident that there was no lack of technical ability in Switzerland. But the decentralised political structure of the country made the execution of large-scale, nationwide projects impossible. The backwardness of pre-1848 Switzerland was not the fault of its businesses but rather of its political architecture.

In 1829, an envoy from the Grand Duchy of Baden suggested that nothing would ever come of Switzerland. Baden's foreign minister expressed the same sentiment in 1836: Switzerland, he explained, was a canker gnawing away at Germany's tranquillity. In 1843, an Austrian spy referred to Switzerland as "Europe's cloaca magna." In 1847, the King of Württemberg chimed in, adding that Switzerland protected criminals and served as a home for all the scum of Germany.[1]

The smoke had barely cleared after the Revolutions of 1848, however, before Switzerland came to be regarded rather differently. Now many German observers quietly compared Switzerland to their own nation and wondered at the simplicity, calm and punctuality of the Swiss administration; the altruism and frugality of the administrators; the many great undertakings accomplished with relatively low budgets; the perfection of the transport companies; and, generally, the transparency and accessibility of everything and everyone involved with government finances – at least according to the report of a Bavarian diplomat in 1856. In 1864, another diplomat stated that "one can safely say that the small country of Switzerland is one of the world's largest industrial states."[2] What a

DOI: 10.4324/9781003243144-3

stark turnaround in the foreign perception of Switzerland – and this, in an incredibly short period of time! Questions leap off the tongue. What led to this reversal? What fuelled the country's brilliant rise? How can it be explained that, within a few years, Switzerland had quite clearly changed from a "rogue state" to a flagship state, a model country in terms of business and transport and a perfect example of many qualities that are today often dismissed as cliches? A first and fundamental answer to this question is that the Swiss turnaround was due to the founding of the Federal State in 1848.[3]

Peace and Threats to Peace

In comparison to other countries, Switzerland boasts an above-average level of historical continuity and stability. This is most obvious in its keeping of the peace. Since 1848, Switzerland has had no military conflicts with neighbouring countries, nor has it known internal wars. This phenomenon is both unique worldwide and of great significance for its economic development; while its neighbours have had to rebuild war-ravaged economies more than once, Switzerland has been able to operate continuously with an intact infrastructure and according to well-established procedures.

When considering war and peace, it is worth taking a brief look back into the era that preceded 1848. An exact analysis reveals that the epoch of peaceful development in Switzerland dawned in large measure in 1799/1801, at the end of the Coalition Wars. In contrast to surrounding countries, Switzerland remained largely unscathed by the Napoleonic wars that followed – with the exception of certain violent suppressions of uprisings and pillaging. Throughout the entire 19th century, then, Switzerland experienced no large-scale destruction as a result of military violence.

Nevertheless, there was a very decisive difference between the two halves of the century: The uncertainty, unrest and riots that characterised the era before 1848 were followed by tranquillity and order. Up until 1848, there were repeated conflicts between Swiss in the form of armed raids, acts of violence and looting; there were vagabond bands that roamed and pillaged, burning down houses and farms; there were conflicts that led to the burning down of a factory in Uster in 1832, to the division of Basel into two Cantons in 1833 and to the civil war in Valais in 1840, in which Liberals and Conservatives from Upper and Lower Valais opened fire on one another. One might play down the significance of these events by pointing out that they were locally or regionally rooted and that they had no tangible effect on the Swiss economy as a whole. But this would be to underestimate their seriousness in a number of respects.

The Freischarenzüge of 1844/1845, meanwhile, comprised a more serious breach of the peace. By crossing cantonal borders, these campaigns provoked a nationwide civil war. Here, too, one could point out that the

Freischarenzüge – and even the Sonderbund Civil War of 1847 – were not of overwhelming importance in terms of destruction and casualties. And it is true that, from a military perspective, the civil war was largely parenthetical: With a duration of around three weeks, around 100 dead and 500 wounded (some through self-inflicted accidents), no large-scale destruction in any single region and only a handful of roads and bridges destroyed, it did not seriously impair the economy. The Sonderbund War hardly left a mark on the histories of most businesses and is often considered an insignificant event and even left unmentioned. This contrasts starkly with the First World War, which, despite leaving Switzerland territorially intact, was far more detrimental to its economy: For some sectors, including the tourist industry, these war years had the worst consequences imaginable.

The military inconsequentiality of the Sonderbund War, however, stands in clear contrast to its pivotal importance in Switzerland's transition from a traditionally static and unpromising Confederation to a dynamic and modern Federal State. The personal fates of individual citizens, such as the Catholic-Conservative women of Lucerne raped by marauding Confederation troops, are to be measured with an entirely different metric than the military death toll. And even the Sonderbund War could have consequences for individual businesses, as when the threat of military conflicts affected a company's decision about where to set up operations. But the Sonderbund War's impact on the economy went well beyond the level of individual business decisions; it created different conditions for the winning and losing cantons in the new Federal State. While a euphoric mood broke out in most of the victorious Liberal-Radical cantons, leading to widespread investment that boosted the economy, the defeated Conservative cantons did not at first profit to the same extent. Overcome by a defeatist attitude, resentful of what they felt to be a foreign Federal State and afflicted with an unpatriotic image, the wealthy elites of the losing side were initially significantly less motivated to invest in the new Switzerland. The situation was made worse by the fact that the losing cantons were forced to pay the debt incurred in the war. These monies were then not available for building up new public infrastructure. The criminal proceedings brought against the political and military leaders of the Sonderbund, the confiscation of cultural goods, the looting of monuments and, in particular, the secularisation of the monasteries did not exactly create a climate in hard-hit Central Switzerland that motivated investment in the new state. The power the victors wielded over the losers cast a long shadow.

While the losing Conservative side did not disappear from the economic scene altogether, for a long time there were only a few businessmen among its number who had much influence at a national level in the young Federal State. Instead, the federal political sphere was dominated by Liberal and Radical politicians. That said, on the local, regional and cantonal levels, it did not take long after 1847/1848 before Conservative pioneers and entrepreneurs emerged in Central Switzerland and Valais, men who recognised new economic opportunities and knew how to take advantage of them. This was especially the case in the tourism sector, whose upswing also makes clear that economic development is the right recipe for healing political wounds.

War on the Doorstep

Anyone who thinks the violent and warlike conflicts that took place in Switzerland before 1848 were relatively insignificant overlooks the effect that internal discord and strife in Switzerland had on neighbouring countries and the great powers of the time. In the first half of the 19th century, Switzerland was considered an unsafe, even dangerous country, where law and order were trampled underfoot. Political assassinations like the killing of the charismatic leader of the Lucerne Conservatives, the farmer and politician Josef Leu (1800–1845), added up to more than merely a collection of individual events. The surrounding monarchies and dynasties considered them a clear sign that this unstable and backward republic was careening towards its end. The politically decreed abolition of monasteries, which had its beginnings in Aarau in 1841, was a breach of the Federal Treaty on which the Confederation was founded. There is ultimately no other conclusion to be drawn: The goings-on in Switzerland in the 1830s and 1840s painted a picture of a country on the brink of the abyss on numerous fronts, one in which the rule of law was being undermined by capriciousness. The political structures were in no way appropriate and were incapable of peaceably solving internal political problems and meeting the other challenges of the time. Switzerland's political image suffered in the 1830s and 1840s as it never had before.

The conflicts between conservatives and progressives were even more explosive in view of contemporary European monarchic and dynastic power dynamics. The fact that many political refugees settled in Switzerland and used it as a base from which to agitate against their home countries transformed Switzerland into a powder keg. On multiple occasions, the emotionally charged situation threatened to devolve into a war with foreign powers. The internal political situation also came close to spiralling out of control. The danger of more bloodshed, which had seemed unthinkable in the aftermath of the Sonderbund War in 1847, could no longer be ruled out in 1848. This is evident when one considers events that took place in Canton Ticino in the summer of 1848. Two representatives of the Federal Diet were sent to the south with a military contingent, effectively placing Canton Ticino under the control of the Confederation.[4] This caused an uproar in certain parts of Switzerland. The task of maintaining peace and order in Ticino, and of preventing Lombard refugees from using Swiss soil as a base from which to attack the Austrian forces occupying their country, was a difficult and delicate operation. The ideologically based self-aggrandising of certain

Radical-Liberal politicians pushed the humanitarian reasons for taking in refugees into the background and brought neutral Switzerland into a difficult position vis-à-vis Austria.

Given these circumstances, the severely critical descriptions of Switzerland by observers from Baden, Bavaria and Württemberg cited above are hardly surprising. The situation in Switzerland in the first half of the century was certainly unpromising. The country seemed like a weather-beaten shed that would sooner or later collapse – one that patchwork and repairs would no longer be sufficient to save.

And yet it was precisely this backward Switzerland, lacking the economic and socio-political infrastructure of a modern state, that became the only country in Europe to successfully bring about a liberal revolution, and that enacted the most progressive constitution on the entire continent: a work of genius that marked the birth of the new Federal State.

Before it improved, however, the country's image would first become even more tarnished. After the failed Revolutions of 1848, thousands of political refugees flowed into Switzerland, where they found safety and protection. This happened on a scale that surpassed even the political immigrations of the 1830s. As a result, European royal families came to regard the Alpine republic of Switzerland as a stronghold of revolutionaries and a danger to aristocratic rule. In Geneva, French refugees campaigned against France. In Thurgau, exiles operated revolutionary printing presses, and from Zurich and Schaffhausen, commandos slipped over the border to the Grand Duchy of Baden and the Kingdom of Württemberg, where they perpetrated attacks before crossing back over the Rhine to safety.

And, as mentioned above, things were heating up in the south of the country as well. Not only did the Ticino government allow Italian ringleaders to organise anti-Austrian resistance in Lombardy from the safety of Swiss soil but they even actively supported attacks themselves. Such actions also occurred in other locations, including, unabashedly, in Geneva: In their Radical fervour, Swiss figures of authority identified with the political aims of the refugees and with the people's fight for freedom.[5] In doing so, they interfered in the domestic affairs of other countries. Switzerland was therefore said to be more dangerous than the worst nests of pirates on distant oceans. This was the sentiment expressed in the military camps of Austrian Field Marshal Joseph Radetzky (1766–1858), who was stationed in Northern Italy with his troops in 1848/1849, ready to invade Ticino and put an end to the activities of the revolutionaries and their Swiss sympathisers.

The crossfire from the European wars and revolutions, as well as the expansionist fantasies of Switzerland's own Radicals, brought the country into existential difficulties in the middle of the 19th century. This critical situation forced the young Federal State to formulate the guiding principles of its foreign policy, and in particular to clarify its neutral status. It was lucky for Switzerland that political realists were able to carry the day with regard to these dicey and emotionally loaded questions. These realists rejected an expansionist foreign policy and conceived of military interventions in foreign countries only as a last resort for protecting the sovereignty of their own nation. In these fundamental matters of national policy, which led to difficult balancing acts, the Federal Council was generally supported by the Economic-Liberal politicians. These politicians rebuffed the reckless and adventuresome politics of the Radicals.

Among the trailblazing figures in the Swiss Parliament who took this stance was, once again, Alfred Escher (1819–1882) of Zurich. Escher formulated the precepts of Swiss foreign policy and championed the importance of neutrality. This fact makes clear that political power in the young Federal State lay with the cantons and in Parliament – and in particular, with the National Council. The President of the National Council, who conducted himself in a statesmanlike manner on multiple occasions when Parliament was in session, as well as the President of the Foreign Policy Commission, could effect more change than could a member of the Federal Council. It was indicative of the power dynamics of the time that a Swiss Parliamentarian like Alfred Escher preferred to give important speeches about the state of the nation not just in his capacity as President of the National Council but also in front of a cantonal audience, in his further role as President of the Zurich Cantonal Parliament.

Mass Emigration and Italian Migrant Workers

In some parts of the country, for example in Valais and in the valleys of Ticino and Graubünden, a bitter poverty reigned in the first half of the 19th century. The year 1817 was the most climactically disastrous one of the entire century. It was called "the year with no summer": Seeds germinated too late, vegetables rotted, potatoes grew to the size of cherries, fruit remained puny and hay harvests were meagre. Hunger became so rampant that in some places fields were guarded, and entering them at night was forbidden. Fruit and vegetable thieves were executed to deter others from following their example. As death by starvation became widespread and the end of days seemed near, the suffering and confusion of the impoverished rural population appeared in the cities in the form of flocks of beggars seeking sustenance. In the face of emaciated fathers, despairing mothers and hollow-eyed children, the distress could not be overlooked. Eastern Switzerland in particular was afflicted by scarcity and want, but the federal government was too weak to effectively address the situation. As a result, emperors and kings rushed to the aid of the desperate: Tsar Alexander I (1777–1825) donated 100,000 rubles to Eastern Switzerland in the spring of 1817, and the Kings of Bavaria and Württemberg followed suit. The Swiss, however, were unable to agree on how to distribute the financial aid. As a result, the town of Flawil, for example, was forced to wait more than 20 years to receive the emergency relief. The situation in the country appeared so hopeless that, for many citizens, leaving appeared to be the only option.

Thus, Switzerland became a country of emigration. Even after the fear of famine had long passed, the waves of emigrants persisted. While the economically liberal measures that had been introduced in the early years of the Federal State had led to a rush of investment activity, an appetite for risk and a plethora of visionary ideas and innovations, it was only towards the end of the 1880s that the effects this economic awakening began to be felt by the population at large. At this point, thanks to the founding of companies, the emergence of new sectors of industry and the expansion of infrastructure, tens of thousands of jobs were created across the country. Swiss citizens were rare among the workers on dangerous large-scale construction sites like that of the Gotthard Tunnel, however. Here migrant workers were needed, and they mostly came from Italy. Immigration and emigration were not mutually exclusive.

Synchronisation and Punctuality

Switzerland's transformation during the second half of the 19th century is illustrated by developments in a wide range of areas. Its most important drivers were the transport and communication systems. While in 1850 the only Swiss railway company employed barely a handful of employees, railway enterprises soon began to shoot up like mushrooms. By 1860, they employed a combined total of around 5,400 workers; 20 years later, no fewer than 25,000.

MILESTONE 3.1

12 September 1848

The Enactment of the Federal Constitution

The enactment of the new Federal Constitution by the Federal Diet on 12 September 1848 was an austere affair, but for that all the more important in terms of constitutional law. But let us take a step back. The political conflicts that had played out over many years, and had paralysed Switzerland both economically and socially, were settled by the outcome of the Sonderbund Civil War. The levers of power were now in the hands of the Radical-Liberal victors. Inspired by the spirit of progress, a new constitution was drawn up within a very short time. A draft was presented to the male electorate in the cantons and was approved over the course of the summer of 1848. The Constitution was officially ratified by the Federal Diet on 12 September 1848.

The first elections for the National Council and Council of States were watched with concern, as they appeared to offer a potential for conflict. But they went off successfully; the discriminatory measures of the Radical-Liberal authorities did not trigger a nationwide revolt. The leaders of the Conservative camp were demoralised and politically silenced by their military loss in 1847. They had retreated to their cantonal refuges. There were others, however, for example the writer and priest Jeremias Gotthelf (1797–1854), who had no scruples in loudly proclaiming their disgust. They spewed bile and gall against the impious new state and its Constitution. On 6 November 1848, the newly elected Swiss Parliament convened for the first time in Bern. Some members were exhilarated by the historical event; others arrived in a defeatist mood, filled with resentment and anger. Ten days later, the Federal Council was appointed, and the old Federal Treaty of 1815 definitively rescinded.

On 12 September 1848, a new era of Swiss history was rung in. The Constitution was enacted, making Switzerland – at least on paper – the most progressive country in Europe. It satisfied important Liberal demands while at the same time addressing Conservative concerns. Seen in these terms, the Federal Constitution was a compromise. Yet this in itself must be considered a great accomplishment. By leaving sensitive socio-political issues like education, religion and culture under cantonal authority, the Constitution respected regional differences and diverse mentalities. Thanks to this approach, cultural diversity remained one of Switzerland's fundamental pillars, and this led in just a short time to the social and economic integration of the overwhelming majority of the population into the new Federal State. A further indication of the success of the Constitution was that, in 1848, hardly anyone honestly wished to return to the way things had been before.

The Constitution of 1848 reveals numerous signs of external influence. The political equality of citizens was a democratic demand of the Enlightenment and the French Revolution. Women, non-Christians, the clergy and foreigners, however, were at first, and for varying lengths of time, excluded from this franchise. The two-chamber system was based on the model set out in the US Constitution. In fact, the US system enjoyed widespread sympathy, which came to be shared by its "sister republic." The economic innovations introduced by the Federal Constitution were decisive for Switzerland's success. These included the standardisation of weights and measures, the introduction of a uniform currency, freedom of trade and commerce, and the lifting of domestic tariffs. These were all elements of economic liberalism and were the foundation of modern industrial states. They created a communal economic area, which made possible the development of a Swiss domestic market and at the same time took into account the goals of the export economy.

(*Continued*)

With the Constitution of 1848, Switzerland remained an outlier on the European continent; the Federal State was an island republic, surrounded by monarchies. Making foreign and international trade policy therefore required negotiating considerable risks. The major powers initially were taken aback by the small country and regarded it suspiciously. Official Switzerland was forced to navigate a path between its liberal foundational principles, the safeguarding of its sovereignty and the challenges of national defence. There was no lack of border disputes or conflicts about sovereignty, but confrontations and even looming military conflicts were ultimately resolved peacefully. This was the case, for example, with the negotiations over Büsingen (1849), Neuchâtel (1856/1857), Savoy (1860) and the Dappen Valley (1861/1862). The cantons, which had only recently been engaged in hostilities with one another, came together on 12 September 1848 – in some cases involuntarily – and placed themselves under federal authority. Sovereign power thus passed from the cantons to the federal government.

The Federal Constitution provided the foundation for the development of modern Switzerland. Despite the momentous dynamism it triggered, it enabled levels of stability that had not previously been thought possible. The Federal Constitution of 1848 was a work of genius.

Figure 3.1 The Constitution of the Swiss Confederation (excerpt), Caspar Studer, Winterthur (1848). Zurich, Zentralbibliothek Zürich.

By stagecoach, a dispatch sent from Lake Constance to Lake Geneva and back took between four and five days. Priority mail that needed to travel a lesser distance was carried by messengers, using a relay system when necessary. This all changed with the introduction of the telegraph in 1852. Now, a message could be transmitted from Geneva to St Gallen, and a response received, within an hour. In the first year of the telegraph, around 2,900 telegrams were sent in Switzerland; in 1875, more than 3 million. Communication was made even easier by the introduction of the telephone. Spectators attending the Swiss Singing Festival (Sängerfest) in 1880 were able to try this new form of communication out for themselves; in August of the same year, the first telephone network in Switzerland began operating on a private basis.

While the railway redefined distance, telecommunication rendered it altogether insignificant. Both required a standardised method of timekeeping – the more so as the natural rhythm of day and night had become blurred due to the introduction of street lights in 1840. In 1848, however, when the constitutional outlines of the new Switzerland were being drawn up; the communal, toll-free economic market was being created; and the introduction of the Swiss franc was on the agenda, timekeeping was not addressed. Despite the general process of standardisation and unification, the clocks in Eastern Switzerland still did not show the same time as those in the west of the country. The difference between Müstair on the eastern Swiss border and Geneva in the west amounted to 18 minutes.

When the first telegraph lines began operations, the Federal Council decreed that the postal services and telegraph offices were to run according to the local mean time in Bern. The railway companies agreed to follow suit. Beginning in 1860, the exact time was determined by the observatory in Neuchâtel. The time signal was passed on to the telegraph and railway stations via Bern. Because local times continued to be used outside of these institutions, the relationships between the various times remained confusing. This was particularly difficult for people who had to travel through numerous local time zones. This was not a uniquely Swiss problem, however; it affected all countries until 1884, when time was standardised at the International Meridian Conference in Washington, DC. The reference point would henceforth be the prime meridian in Greenwich in Great Britain. By the 1890s, most European countries had set their clocks accordingly. Switzerland, however, initially remained an island. The Federal Council was in favour of the change but met with too much resistance. The proponents of synchronised time argued that standardisation was an economic necessity, however, and eventually the Federal Council did take action: Beginning on 1 June 1894, Swiss time was no longer Bernese but rather Central European Time (CET).

The Changing Faces of Cities

The transformation of Swiss society over the course of the 19th century also affected the appearance of cities. From the 1830s onwards, bulwarks, redoubts and towers, whose construction dated back to the 16th and 17th centuries, began to be razed. This made room for new structures. Light and air swept into cities in the second half of the 19th century. Periods of intensive construction changed their look and feel within a short time. In addition to the train stations, the palaces of the finance industry, the enlargement of existing industrial facilities and new public and private buildings with cultural, social, and health- and justice-related purposes, there were many smaller signs of change. These might on their own have seemed inconsequential amidst the great storm of transformation, and yet they were symbolically important. One was the felling of the 250-year-old "Tiefenhof" lime tree on the Paradeplatz in Zurich. This queen among trees was not brought down by a storm, but rather fell victim to the money-obsessed spirit of the times. "The felling of this beautiful ornament of the city brings to mind the glaring difference between the old romanticism and our current sober prose," a bitterly angry commentary proclaimed.[6]

The population of Switzerland increased from around 1.7 to 2.4 million in the 50 years between 1800 and 1850. In the 50 years that followed, it grew by almost a million and reached 3.3 million. It had thus doubled within a century. This growth changed the relationship between the cities and the countryside. In 1850, 41.6 percent of the population lived in towns with fewer than 1,000 inhabitants; by 1900, this figure was 27.3 percent. Seen in other terms: In 1850, 6.4 percent of the Swiss population lived in cities with more than 10,000 inhabitants; by 1900, 22 percent did. There was also considerable growth in the number of foreign residents. In 1850, there were 72,000 foreign residents in Switzerland, representing 3 percent of the total population; in 1910, there were around 550,000 foreign residents, accounting for more than 14 percent of the Swiss population. The number of foreigners in rural areas was low, but in industrial cities it was strikingly high. In Zurich, the foreign population increased from 8.9 percent of the population in 1850 to 29 percent in 1900.

In Search of the Secret to Quality

In 1835, an Englishman travelled through Switzerland on a special, economically important mission. The background was as follows: In the early 19th century, Napoleon's Continental Blockade had not only strengthened the position of the Swiss textile industry – to England's detriment – but had also facilitated the birth of the Swiss engineering industry. Industry in Switzerland now attracted English attention for a number of reasons. Visits paid by Swiss entrepreneurs to Britain, which had become a standard part of their training, had not gone unnoticed. And Swiss manufacturers and inventors, who had made advances in core areas that had once been considered sovereign English territory, were also admired in Britain. It thus seemed advisable to take a closer look at the industrial country that Switzerland had become.

It was for this reason that John Bowring (1792–1872) travelled to Switzerland in 1835 as a British envoy. He was tasked with carefully inspecting factories and industry and trade practices and writing a report on his findings. And what were these findings? According to his report, Bowring was convinced that nowhere was industry more robust, healthy and flexible than in Switzerland.[7]

On the face of it, this professional assessment is astonishing. Bowring's report, which was limited to the state of Swiss industry, could easily lead one to draw false conclusions about the general state of Switzerland and Swiss society. In point of fact, there was a disheartened and hopeless mood in most of the country.

By the 1830s, the English had considered the Swiss textile industry to be their main competitor for decades, so this was hardly news. Naturally, because there was considerable contact between Swiss and English industrialists, the English had also noticed that the Swiss were in the process of building up a tool and engineering industry. Bowring concluded that Swiss industry was flexible, and his conclusion was certainly justified. How else could the rapid expansion of skills in the engineering industry be explained? It is also true that Swiss companies were healthier and more robust than those in many other countries.

That said, Bowring's brief was not to comprehensively and critically discuss the sizes of Swiss companies compared to English ones, nor the strength and structure of their respective branches. That the Swiss watch industry had already established itself as a world leader at the time of Bowring's visit, and that Switzerland and England were competing neck and neck in the textile business, were facts already known to the English Parliament and would hardly have called for investigation. Rather, Bowring's critical attention was to be directed at the Swiss tool and engineering industry.

Soberly considered, it is evident that in this area there were still worlds between the two countries. Saying this, however, was not Bowring's job. He had a competitor to inspect, and to speak ill of it would have made little sense. Yet the English knew full well that, besides Escher Wyss, there was no machine manufacturer in 1830s Switzerland worth taking seriously. Most Swiss workshops that made tools and repaired machines were not factories on the English scale but rather small, artisanal operations. This was certainly true of Reiter in Töss, and even Escher Wyss in Zurich did not come close to rivalling the dimensions of the large English operations. The same could be said of Sulzer in Winterthur: At the time of Bowring's visit, Johann Jakob Sulzer (1782–1853) and his sons were busy setting up an iron foundry. They were supported in their efforts by two journeymen and two day-workers. So much for large-scale operations!

Decisive areas of manufacturing in which Swiss companies would soon dominate the global market, including the construction of steamers, locomotives and other machines, could not be examined by Bowring – neither in Zurich nor in Winterthur – for the simple reason that they did not yet exist. And nothing could yet be said of the foodstuff, chemical and pharmaceutical industries that would develop either, nor of the tourist destination and financial hub that Switzerland would soon become. And where, in 1835, were the railroads? They were on paper or were the stuff of fantasy.

But back to Bowring's assessment. The imposing rise of the Swiss engineering and tool industry to world-leading positions only occurred after the middle of the 19th century and was only possible thanks to conditions that had not existed earlier. Furthermore, the size and structure of the Swiss domestic market were hardly comparable to those of the British market. To make a comparison of this kind between the two countries as they stood prior to 1848 would have been to distort reality to an almost grotesque extent. In fact, it is difficult even to speak of a Swiss domestic market before the second half of the 19th century. Prior to 1848, the political structures of the Swiss Confederation seriously impeded inter-cantonal economic development.

This all raises the question of why the Switzerland of 1835 drew the attention of the English in the first place. The answer is that the British interest was not in analysing a competitor in terms of its output and volume but rather in examining its innovative strength and the quality of its manufacturing and production. And the inspection by Bowring concluded that, according to these criteria, individual Swiss industrial firms had in fact achieved a technical standard that was in no way inferior to that of British companies.

It was only after the middle of the 19th century that the Swiss engineering industry began to develop vigorously. It is true that it had been competitive before then and had made Switzerland independent of its foreign neighbours. But because of Swiss domestic tariffs, its development had remained restricted up until 1848. The truly decisive factor for its flourishing, though, was the rapid construction of railway lines in the 1850s. The vast scale of railroad construction generated new demand for locomotives, rolling stock and cranes. The railway also made it possible for the Swiss engineering industry to import large quantities of the necessary raw materials and to more easily transport finished machines and deliver them to customers. It was only in this context that the Swiss engineering industry was able to establish itself in the global market.

The industry received an additional boost because other sectors of the economy, propelled by innovations in science and technology, were also in need of high-performing machinery. Thus, in the 1850s, alongside Escher Wyss, Reiter and Sulzer, other machine companies began cropping up that would soon make their mark as large-scale enterprises. Among them were Saurer in St Gallen, which would soon relocate to Arbon; the rolling stock factory in Neuhausen by the Rhine Waterfall, the later SIG; Bell in Kriens; and Bühler in Uzwil. For all these enterprises – as well as for Brown Boveri in Baden, the Maschinenfabrik Oerlikon and the other companies that would later emerge in the machine and electrical sector – railway connections had become indispensable.

Turning Obstacles into Advantages

Given Switzerland's vast, largely uncultivable mountainous terrain, its topography was considered a natural disadvantage in the first half of the 19th century. The largely meagre and only partially usable soil rendered farmers' harvests insufficient to feed the population. The generally small-scale nature of farming operations made efficient exploitation of what land there was impossible, which further aggravated the situation.

The fundamental nature of its territory affected the Swiss economy and the foreign image of Switzerland for centuries. In comparison to other European countries, it was generally regarded as a deficit – all the more so when 19th-century industry began to centre around iron, mineral ores and coal, which other countries readily found in their own ground. Switzerland was largely lacking in these resources.

This initial disadvantage would, however – paradoxical as it may sound – become one of the country's greatest strengths. Because Swiss industry could not rely on natural resources buried in the country's own soil, it was forced to import them. And importing the required quantities was only possible via the railway. This circumstance would initially appear to be a further economic disadvantage. But on closer examination, it is evident that this drawback was at least neutralised. Because 19th-century Switzerland was not able to rely on its own natural resources, it was less dependent on fundamental technological changes than were other countries.

In an era in which iron and coal were decisive for development, the Swiss economy had to decide what course to set. It chose to depend on the import of raw materials and goods and their refinement by clever minds and skilled hands. In improved and enhanced form, these goods were then re-exported.

But this process of upgrading, and the orientation of the economy towards export, would only be successful in the competitive environment of the second half of the 19th century if the country created the requisite economic framework. Beginning in 1848, the young Federal State did precisely this, and on two counts. First, it endeavoured to keep import tariffs low, so as not to increase the expense of the raw materials required by its industrial economy; and second, it endeavoured to strike trade agreements with as many countries as possible.[8]

The Federal Council's decision to initially leave these negotiations in the remit of the private sector was a clever one. In point of fact, it had no other option, since the young Federal State had very few diplomats. And so, driven by private enterprise, imports and exports increased in the second half of the 19th century, and the country quickly developed structured trade relationships. The wide range of international contacts that Swiss trading companies had established prior to 1848 was thus upgraded to official status in the Federal State. Business relationships with foreign countries were brought into alignment with a Swiss economic policy that was, for the first time, worthy of the name.

It thus came about that the Swiss economy made a quantum leap after 1848. This was due partly to an increased emphasis on exports.[9] This traditional pillar of the Swiss economy, which had until then been grounded in the watch and textile industries and in specific Swiss regions, was expanded in the second half of the 19th century to become a comprehensive economic structure comprising new sectors such as the tool, engineering and electrical industries; chemical, pharmaceutical and foodstuff manufacturing; and, not least, tourism. The second defining pillar of the new economy was the development of the Swiss domestic market. Having been weighed down by a variety of restraints and restrictions prior to 1848, this market now harboured serious potential for growth. It thus came about that, little by little, an economic structure was established that began to rely equally on exports and internal trade.

MILESTONE 3.2

17 February 1863

The Founding of the ICRC

Advances in weapons technology had made wars more gruesome and battlefields bloodier, yet an awareness of the fates of the victims of wartime violence only began to awaken in the middle of the 19th century. This awareness marked the start of a development that would lead, at least to some extent, towards the realisation of a more humane world.

The horrific carnage of the Battle of Solferino, a clash between Austrian and French-Italian forces on 24 June 1859, traumatised the Genevan businessman Henry Dunant (1828–1910). Dunant had travelled to Lombardy to ask Napoleon III for his support in a dispute with the French colonial government in Algeria that had escalated to such a point that Dunant's trading and finance company was on the brink of ruin. The terrible suffering of Solferino's battle-wounded, and the impotence of the medical services in its face, cried out for a new way of dealing with wounded soldiers. Dunant wrote *A Memory of Solferino*, which he published in 1862. In it, he proposed the creation of voluntary national aid organisations that would support and protect wounded and ill soldiers. Dunant's ideas were rapidly disseminated in the Swiss media and were discussed in philanthropic circles. The decisive impulse for the institutional realisation of his vision was provided by the Liberal-Protestant elite of Geneva, and, in particular, by members of the Geneva Public Welfare Society (Société d'utilité publique genevoise). There a commission formed that, at its first meeting, on 17 February 1863, established itself as a permanent international committee for the establishment of national aid societies for care of the wounded. Since 1876, it has been called the International Committee of the Red Cross (ICRC).

In record time, numerous preparatory meetings led to a diplomatic conference that was held from 8 to 22 August 1864 in Geneva on the invitation of the Federal Council. The fact that the Federal Council succeeded in constructing an international platform of this kind and was able to get 18 high-powered representatives of 12 European countries to come to Geneva is surprising, as Swiss diplomatic presence was underwhelming in the early years of the Federal State. In fact, in the early 1860s Switzerland only maintained three embassies – in Paris, Vienna and Turin. The aim of the conference in Geneva was to anchor Dunant's idea in international law. In the end, a declaration was signed that unleashed a worldwide movement and transformed international law: It has gone down in history as the First Geneva Convention. In Article 7, the symbol that would identify individuals and facilities that were thenceforth not to be targeted in warfare was defined: A red cross on a white background. This red cross became the symbol of the entire movement and gave it its name.

The Geneva Convention of 1864 was significant for Switzerland in a number of ways. First of all, it was a positive development that, only a few years after 1848, representatives of monarchies met for a conference on republican Swiss soil. Now Switzerland was no longer synonymous with subversion, revolution and piracy but rather with a benevolent code that would develop into one of the great humanitarian institutions. The Convention of 1864 made Geneva the seat of the globally active ICRC and thereby strengthened the city's international profile. The founding and activities of the ICRC reflected values and principles that belonged to the DNA of the young Swiss nation: voluntarism and private initiative. These are what inspired Henry Dunant. And in fact, it is striking that the members of the original committee for the establishment of aid societies also acted as private individuals: the head of the

(*Continued*)

Geneva Public Welfare Society Gustave Moynier (1826–1910); the engineer, military officer and politician Guillaume-Henri Dufour (1787–1875); and the two doctors Louis Paul Amédée Apia (1818–1898) and Théodore Maunoir (1806–1869).

The ICRC is independent of Switzerland and communicates with its manifold interlocutors on equal footing. This is especially true of its president, who is required to be Swiss. ICRC presidents converse with heads of state as well as with the leaders of opposition groups and guerrilla fighters. They can also take the floor in the UN General Assembly, the UN Security Council, the European Parliament, the OSCE and NATO. The fact that the ICRC remains so closely associated with Henry Dunant is surprising for two reasons: First, Dunant was never its president, and, second, he was disavowed and publicly discredited by some of the members of the committee.

Figure 3.2 ICRC emblem, International Committee of the Red Cross, Geneva. Courtesy of the ICRC Library.

The ICRC stands for an open Switzerland, for a Switzerland of good offices and humanitarian international law. This humanitarian tradition, which continues to distinguish Switzerland today, was founded in the second half of the 19th century. It has contributed significantly to the international reputation of Switzerland up until the present day. The link between Switzerland and the ICRC can be seen in their emblems: The white background and red cross of the ICRC mirror the red background and white cross of the Swiss flag.

An important factor should not be overlooked here. That ideas from abroad often fell on fertile soil in Switzerland, where they were further developed and gave rise to important innovations, was not only due to low import tariffs. Swiss businesses also profited from other country-specific advantages that made their products competitive, among them the fact that workers' rights, environmental protection and especially the safeguarding of intellectual property were, for a long time, effectively non-existent.

And even in its topographical character, the country in fact harboured unique advantages. The Swiss economy drew on one particular resource that was available on an almost boundless scale: water. Waterways had formed the most important transport infrastructure since the Middle Ages and, in the early 19th century, were the point of departure for motorised transport. The textile industry was the first to profit from the country's numerous rivers and streams. Because there were no other sources of energy, it relied on water power. The presence of readily available water was also a necessary precondition for the growth of other sectors of the economy and left its stamp on Switzerland's overall industrialisation. Without water there would also have been no steamboats and no tourism. Without the Alpine landscape, there would have been no "Swiss reservoir." The mountains, a natural resource in themselves, were also transformed. Rock became the material out of which vast numbers of tunnels were constructed. And while mountainous areas may have been at a disadvantage compared to the Swiss Central Plateau during the onset of the era of industrialisation and modernisation, the situation changed after the middle of the 19th century, when the British elite discovered the Alps and Switzerland became "the playground of Europe." The High Alps were then transformed from an obstacle and a disadvantage into a profitable resource. As a result, even high Alpine valleys that initially appeared entirely unsuited to tourism developed an industry of their own, and on an unprecedented scale. Here, too, it held true that economic prospects only showed promise to the extent that natural locational advantages and synergies could be exploited by new technologies.

The 1848 Constitution: A Stroke of Genius

The multifaceted developments that set in in Switzerland in the middle of the 19th century, and that soon dynamised the entire country, all had in common that they were only possible thanks to the country's new political framework and, especially, the Constitution of 1848. It is evident that Switzerland's shortcomings prior to 1848 resulted from its political structures. But it would be overly simplistic to explain the tremendous economic and societal modernisation that took place after 1848 and that transformed Switzerland within a very short time solely as a result of changes in its political architecture. The fact that the Constitution provided the foundation for this change is incontestable – and that already represents a great accomplishment. But once the Constitution had been ratified, it took minds and hands to accomplish the wide-ranging rebuilding of Switzerland; it took pioneers and entrepreneurs with clever ideas and a willingness to take risks. The generation of 1848 was inspired by its faith in progress. It exploited the chances it was offered, initiated projects and saw them through. To be sure, there were hundreds of pioneers in the first half of the 19th century too, as well as in earlier times. But what happened after 1848 surpassed everything that had come before. The need to make up for Switzerland's infrastructural deficit was already immense, and the waking of additional needs created an enormous number of new economic, academic and social areas of activity that had to be taken up. The number of new projects – large and small, on the local, regional and national levels – became legion. They make clear how essential the "Spirit of '48" was for the evolution of modern Switzerland.[10]

This insight is key: The Swiss institutions of the first half of the 19th century were incapable of keeping pace with the demands of the times and the needs of a modern society. Switzerland seemed bound in a corset that restricted its development and creativity. The Constitution of 1848 liberated it from these constraints, and the country embarked on an intensive phase of modernisation. The Federal Constitution of 1848 marked a caesura in Swiss history precisely to the extent that it made the new Federal State possible. It provided the foundation for a forward-facing Switzerland, defined its framework and clarified the structures and processes of its institutions. Though not everything was newly made over by the Constitution, very much was.

A constitution is an abstract thing, and it is not especially clear just which provisions in this one were the drivers of the success that distinguished the Federal State from the pre-1848 Confederation. Yet while each of the 114 constitutional articles may have been appropriate and meaningful in its time, there are a few that stand out. Among these are the articles dealing with the economy and with higher education. The fact that, for whatever reason, important areas were omitted from the Constitution might be considered an oversight from a bookkeeper's perspective. From an overarching strategic perspective, however – one that assesses the results that might have been achieved and those that were in fact achieved thanks to the Constitution – a completely different conclusion emerges: The Federal Constitution of 1848 was a great success, both in terms of what it included and in terms of what it did not.

Now, one might ask whether it is not somewhat excessive to praise in such high terms a constitution that survived for less than three decades. By no means. The Constitution of 1848 gave wings to an age of development that could not have been more impactful, and from which – though in a different spirit – later generations would profit, from the last quarter of the 19th century until the present. That a work like the Constitution of 1848 was written in just a few weeks, and yet performed its demanding balancing act with such aplomb, navigating between the abysses of Radical one-sidedness, a ruthless civil-war mentality and a lack of consideration for cultural differences, is hardly conceivable today. The Constitution was the foundation on which it became possible to break out of the blood-spattered 1840s and begin a new course towards a successful future. And the recipe for success was representative democracy. It alone was capable of holding steady in the face of the furious waves of modernisation in the 1850s and 1860s. Direct democracy would have been the wrong prescription; it would have stood in the way of the young Federal State's success. In the middle of the 19th century, the time had not yet come for a Switzerland that balanced out the demands of political parties and interest groups.

Transport Is the Key to Almost Everything

Transport is generally the single most decisive issue for a country's development. The modernisation of Switzerland in the second half of the 19th century was closely tied to the resolution of the transport question. The construction of the railway was epochal. The modernisation it brought about surpassed everything that had come before. In contrast to the steamboat traffic that preceded it, it rendered accessible not just individual regions and areas but the entire country. Just as the textile industry became the point of departure for the development of new areas of the economy in 1800, so did the railway 50 years later – and how! It appears that ultimately all areas of business, and even of society, were transformed by the railway, which connected them over mountains, down valleys and across lakes as technology overcame all natural barriers. Switzerland's structural deficit as a location of industry in a period of reliance on iron, ore and coal was no longer relevant when, beginning in the 1850s, the railway enabled the transport of goods on a massive scale. The trains, initially conceived of primarily for the transport of goods, increasingly also served passengers and became an indispensable part of the nation's infrastructure.

But even an idea like the railway, which changed the whole world and overrode the laws of nature, was still no guarantee of transformation and progress. Railroad lines had to be planned correctly and exploited properly. There was only *one* promising solution for Switzerland, and it was effected through the landmark decision of 1852: The railways had to be built and operated by private enterprise. This insight was essential, and this point cannot be too strongly emphasised, nor written too largely or with bright enough colours on the proverbial wall. That the bulk of commercial traffic in Switzerland occurred on the rails was decisive for the country's success. The railway became the most efficient mode of transport.

The construction of a close-knit railway network and other infrastructure – the Polytechnic in Zurich (today's ETH Zurich) and modern banks, insurance companies and hotels – quickly added to the stability and stature of the young Switzerland and transformed it into a modern state. This dynamic process helped create a new image of Switzerland both at home and abroad. Just how fundamentally and rapidly this transformation occurred is evidenced by the landmark north-south rail link through the Alps – a showpiece for Switzerland's transport system. In building the Gotthard Railway between 1872 and 1882, a private Swiss railway company took on the largest and most demanding construction project in the world. It took pioneering spirit, know-how and a willingness to take risks to realise this masterful accomplishment. The financial engagement of the consortium that sourced the lion's share of the project's funding on the international capital market and the subsidies provided by the German and Italian governments both provide evidence of a new-found trust in Switzerland. The country was now perceived in a dramatically different manner than it had been just a generation earlier. But it was equally characteristic of the circumstances and profile of the country that the Federal State did not initially contribute a single centime to this historic undertaking.

Soon after mid-century, privately owned railways were already operating across the entire country. They restructured the landscape and determined the routes of main and branch lines not on the basis of political considerations but with an eye only on the bottom line. It may appear paradoxical that the new Switzerland became increasingly unified at the same time as the railway companies were divvying the country up among themselves. But in fact, these railroads connected both regions and cultures. Train stations, bridges, viaducts, ramps and tunnels were the pillars on which the new country was built. Switzerland's railway architecture inspired international awe and acclaim. Within a short time, the country came to be regarded in a new light. It was a bastion of technology and skill and a symbol of safety and stability. The railway brought with it a new kind of time, and trains in the young country came to embody punctuality, commitment, precision and reliability – values which continue to be held in high esteem today in the land of the Swiss watch and which were a precursor for the standardisation of timekeeping.

With the trains came the tunnels. There had previously been individual tunnels, such as the Urnerloch, excavated in 1708 as an alternative to the Devil's Bridge and certainly one of the oldest Swiss tunnels, but it was only with the introduction of the railway in the second half of the 19th century that tunnels became a quintessential part of Switzerland. With the Gotthard Railway, tunnels and ramps became the primary showcases of infrastructural expansion: Today these vast works are monuments. Tunnels have been a part of the Swiss image for more than a century and a half. In the 19th century, they were arguably its most sophisticated constructions. The Gotthard Tunnel went above and beyond; it was a world wonder. In 1907, Robert Walser (1878–1956) put it in a nutshell: "Soon there won't be any colossal mountains remaining that are not being bored through for the sake of traffic and civilisation and pleasure."[11]

Politics and Business, Hand in Hand

A further secret to the success of Switzerland in the second half of the 19th century was the close interlinking of politics, business, and science and technology. This combination became a magic formula in the young Federal State of the 1850s and 1860s. Many national, cantonal and local politicians – some of whom were all three at once – simultaneously held high-ranking positions in private companies. The generation that came to power in 1848 generally entered politics first and later became involved in business. The exceptions to this rule were the politicians from families with businesses in the textile and trade sectors, who could already look back on generations of commercial activity when they became politically active in the young Federal State. In the 1850s and 1860s, however, businessmen cut from a different cloth also began to emerge on the political stage. And here, too, the railway played a role! The Railway Act of 1852 led to the founding of private railway companies by top-level politicians, who often also took on operational or administrative leading roles in them. This interweaving of politics and the railway took on yet other dimensions when some of these "railway barons" – as these businessmen-politicians came to be somewhat disparagingly called, often without a full understanding of their enormous contributions – founded banks and insurance companies, and here, too, assumed executive positions.

Who Pulls the Strings Behind the Scenes?

Riflemen, gymnasts and singers are often said to have played an important role in laying the groundwork for a Swiss national consciousness from the 1830s onwards. Such observations about the importance of inter-cantonal and nationally oriented clubs and associations are certainly justified. But with the birth of the Federal State, other groups also began to assume importance. First there were the student associations, which were defined by their political leanings. The representation in the Swiss Parliament of the three most important student associations – the politically Liberal Zofingia, the Radical Helvetia and the Catholic-Conservative Swiss Student Association – increased sharply between

1848 and 1881, from 25 to 42 percent.[12] Initially, the Zofingia dominated. In 1875, for the first time, there were more Helvetians than Zofingers in Parliament – 31 of the former to 29 of the latter. The Swiss Student Association only began to catch up in the 1870s.

The numerical strength of the student associations in Parliament was correlated with power dynamics in the Federal Council. In the first Federal Council, Jonas Furrer (1805–1861) and Ulrich Ochsenbein (1811–1890) were Zofinger. In 1857, there were two Zofingers and two Helvetians on the seven-man Federal Council. In 1866, the number of student association members increased again, and the Federal Council included two Zofingers and three Helvetians. Clearly, the young Federal State sourced its political minds from the reservoir of the student associations.

The networks of Freemasons generally receive less attention than do the student associations, even though they were in fact more influential in the young Federal State. Not only was the first Federal Council President, Jonas Furrer, a Freemason; so, too, were three other members of the seven-man Federal Council – Friedrich Frey-Herosé (1801–1873), Stefano Franscini (1796–1857) and Henri Druey (1799–1855). The fact that Druey contributed importantly to the writing of the 1848 Constitution testifies to the political influence of the Freemasons. That said, policies and even interpersonal relationships were not necessarily defined by membership in particular associations in the early years of the Federal State. How else can one explain, for example, that tensions over Alfred Escher between the two fellow Masons Jonas Furrer and Heinrich Gysi escalated to such an extent that they almost led to a schism in the Zurich Lodge Modestia cum Libertät and even in the Grossloge Alpina (Grand Alpine Lodge)? Or Furrer's practice of providing confidential information about the workings of the Federal Council to his non-Masonic friend Escher, and his comparing notes with Escher as he did with none of his politically active fellow Freemasons? The inevitable conclusion is that neither student associations nor Masonic lodges were truly unified communities. And in fact, a new kind of network became increasingly effective and efficient in the young Federal State: the management structures that developed during the rapid rise of public limited companies in the 1850s and which were then anchored in the newly established merchant banks. Against this backdrop, and helped along by the opportunities created by representative democracy, a few exceptional personalities and entrepreneurial heavyweights emerged, whose companies powerfully propelled the development of the new Switzerland. And this brings us to "capital" as a further key concept. Who, after all, could deny that capitalists set the course Switzerland took after 1848? Hotel kings, entrepreneurs, manufacturers, tradesmen and big businessmen called the shots and pulled the strings, unabashedly and in plain sight.

MILESTONE 3.3

20 November 1815

Switzerland's Neutrality Is Recognised under International Law

No other country has asserted its neutrality for as long as Switzerland: 500 years. One could qualify this statement by pointing out that the nature of the neutrality of the Old Swiss Confederacy, as it gradually developed starting at the end of the 15th century, cannot be compared with what was officially established in the 19th century. And yet there is no disputing the fact that neutrality, whether in its older or newer form, has long been essential for Switzerland's existence, for reasons related to both domestic and foreign policy.

The years of Napoleonic rule definitively ended with the Battle of Waterloo, and establishing a new European order was the primary concern of the Congress of Vienna. It was in this context that Austria, Prussia, France, Great Britain and Russia recognised Switzerland's so-called perpetual neutrality in the Treaty of Paris on 20 November 1815. The interests these five major powers had in a neutral Switzerland were the driving force behind this momentous act. Charles Pictet de Rochement (1755–1824) of Geneva formulated the essential aspects of Switzerland's internationally recognised legal status in a judicious and long-sighted manner so that the guarantee of Swiss neutrality could not be interpreted by the great powers as carte blanche for intervention in Swiss affairs.

Neutrality remains a central element of both Swiss independence and the Swiss identity. How else could the small country of Switzerland, a republican thorn in Europe's side, have maintained its role as a bystander in the conflicts of the major powers for more than half a millennium? And how could this state, which to this day is stitched together from the corners of the larger language regions that surround it, have been able to prevent its own implosion? Though a critical analysis may come to the conclusion that, in light of its economic connections with warring states and its refugee policies, Switzerland's neutral positioning has sometimes been a sham, this perspective can be countered by the argument that even a small state has the right to survive and will have to position itself accordingly both in the market and in the diplomatic arena. Swiss neutrality blossomed into a success story in the 19th century; because of it, Switzerland was able to stay out of wars and armed conflicts, which was not always easy for it.

Considering all this, describing neutrality as a gift from on high might seem justified. But without earthly personnel, neutrality would not have achieved its Swiss polish. Neutrality not only had to be

(*Continued*)

cleverly earned in 1815; it also had to be subsequently protected. Alfred Escher gave the principle clear contours: Switzerland was not capable of becoming a major power, and even if it had been, there would have been no reason to desire this. Switzerland – so Escher – had to take a back seat and not get mixed up in external affairs unless there was a desperate need for it. But no country was too small to defend its independence. The Swiss policy of neutrality, according to Escher, was precisely one of independence, in that it involved not relying on others. Instead, the country had to be prepared to defend itself against every attack. As a result, Switzerland needed a good army.

In contrast to the situation in the era of the Old Confederation, during which every town was in principle allowed to develop its

Figure 3.3 Johannes Meiner, Helvetia in her floral crown with her lance and Swiss escutcheon, 1896. Photograph. Zurich, Swiss National Museum.

own foreign policy, at the time of the young Federal State Switzerland had to establish a consensual foreign policy. One might have expected neutrality to be enshrined in the articles of purpose of the Federal Constitution. But the Confederate Diet avoided doing so, instead describing neutrality as a means to end. The Federal Constitution did, however, ban cantons from entering into alliances with foreign countries, and it introduced compulsory military service. Asylum law represented another problematic area, since the taking in of political refugees and the tolerance – or even active fostering – of agitation and provocation, as practised by some cantons, put a severe strain on Switzerland's policy of neutrality. Finally, level-headed forces were also able to damp down cravings for an expansionist military policy. These, along with the ban on mercenary service that was enacted in stages up until 1859, were the essential elements of the young Federal State's foreign policy. It is inconceivable that Switzerland could have found its way through the foreign policy minefields of the second half of the 19th century and maintained its territorial integrity without its policy of armed neutrality. And only on this basis was it able to master the challenges it faced in terms of domestic policy.

The Ties of Federalism

That a new era of Swiss history was rung in in 1848 was first and foremost the result of political developments. The debilitating disputes and self-destructive conflicts that had given rise to the Sonderbund War of 1847 were brushed aside in one fell swoop by the creation of the new Federal State. Now the spirit of progress gave wings to business-friendly circles, who made up absolute majorities in the young Federal State and in most cantons. Switzerland was thus also able to liberalise its economic policy. Cantonal borders, which had previously presented barriers to trade and restricted where companies could be established, were now set aside. All parts of Switzerland were tied together in a single economic market, and the brilliant ascent of the country to a nation of industry, research and services began.

Despite attempts at centralisation that some politicians, in their Radical exuberance, tried to push through in 1848, a pronounced federalism reigned in Switzerland. Restricting the authority of the federal government in favour of that of the cantons was exactly the appropriate method for providing private business with the freedoms necessary for its development. As paradoxical as this might appear, it was the pronounced federalism of the young nation that provided fertile ground for its successful economic development. In contrast to the pre-1848 Confederation, however, in which central civic institutions and national structures were almost entirely absent in practice, certain responsibilities were centralised in the Federal State of 1848. As a result, cantonal sovereignty was cut back to a certain extent; this loss, however, could be borne, since political power in the new Federal State still generally lay with the cantons.

The centralised institutions and national policies that began to be introduced in stages in 1848 were decisive for further economic development. Under these new conditions, the state did not ultimately infringe on the autonomy of the private sector, and no transfer of authority took place from the private to the public sector. Instead, this limited centralisation created frameworks that came to be of existential significance. The establishment of a nationwide domestic market was indispensable for the coming economic upswing. This involved, among other things, the standardisation of systems of weight and measurement, the elimination of domestic tariffs and the introduction of the Swiss franc. In hindsight, it is clear that the model employed in the young Federal State for the division of powers between the federal and cantonal governments, as well as between the state and private business, likely achieved the optimal balance, both for the Swiss economy and for the socio-political development of the country. There is no telling what consequences would have ensued if, already at the time of the founding of the Federal State, regulations and standardisations had been imposed that were in fact only put into place at a later point, when the nation had achieved a certain stability and confidence. Only in the final quarter of the 19th century, and only based on political experience, hard-won authority and economic stability, could adjustments to the model set out by the Constitution of 1848 be successfully made. One example of such an adjustment is the Swiss Civil Code (Zivilgesetzbuch, ZGB), which was unanimously approved by the Swiss Parliament in 1907 and enacted in 1912. This work would not have been possible in 1848. At that time, neither the necessary technical competencies nor the vision existed to produce a forward-facing and systematic civil code – an entirely different construct than the Constitution. That the cantonal law codes of the time were not detrimental to the evolution of business in the young Federal State – and thus, that their replacement was not immediately necessary – is clearly shown by the economic development that took place after 1848.

No, in the middle of the 19th century the time was not yet ripe for Eugen Huber's masterpiece, the ZGB. It could neither have been conceptualised nor implemented in the circumstances that existed in 1848. The situation was completely different when the need for a nationwide corpus of civil and obligation law was unmistakable, and the necessary conditions existed for the creation and implementation of the ZGB. The fact that, at the time of its enactment, this legal code was considered the most modern in Europe affirms that the politicians of 1848 did well not to throw everything overboard when constructing their new country, and instead to continue working with what was tried and tested.

The Hour of Big Gambles

In the early years of the Federal State, politicians found themselves in a wide-open landscape that presented unique opportunities – a state of affairs which only arises once in a hundred years in the history of nation-states. In rebuilding their country, they faced fundamental questions: What infrastructure did the country need? Which part of this infrastructure was the responsibility of the state? Which of the private sector? What matters should remain in the remit of the federal government, and which should be devolved to the cantonal level? Ultimately, all the big questions of the time were on the table: questions of currency, of a federal university, of foreign policy. And furthermore: How should the financial system be structured? How should the education system be organised to meet the needs of industry and politics? What role ought Switzerland to play internationally? How should it position itself in international conflicts? How would it shape its relationships to neighbouring countries? In the middle of the 19th century, the dominant conception was that ultimately only those areas that were necessary for the building of a functioning economy and the safety of the country should fall to the authority of the federal government and that these included, in particular, the standardisation of measurements, weights and currency; tariffs; and national defence and foreign policy. Everything else, it was thought, should remain the responsibility of the cantonal authorities. Moreover, all areas that did not need to be in the hands of the state in order to ensure the smooth functioning of society were to be left to the private sector. This essentially included the three primary economic sectors – agriculture, industry and services – but also, for example, institutional measures to promote foreign trade, and cultural matters.

The wave of modernisation that gripped Switzerland in the 1850s and 1860s gave rise to processes and projects that have remained decisive for the country's success up until the present day. These changes came about at lightning speed and by way of decision-making channels that were no longer viable under the system of direct democracy that was in place in the last quarter of the 19th century. But the 1850s and 1860s were the heyday of representative democracy, and the power structures in which the businessmen-politicians moved had the approval of a clear majority.

The political transfiguration that took place in the mid-19th century created the foundation for manifold economic and societal transformations. Within a few decades, Switzerland became a new country. Someone who had died in 1750, if brought back to life, would have easily recognised the Switzerland of a century later, for essential societal and infrastructural realities remained unchanged. Then, however, in the dynamic unleashed by the founding of the Federal State, these realities – beginning on the Central Plateau – changed more fundamentally in two decades than they had over the course of the entire preceding century. This brief period of rapid change fell in the 1850s and 1860s. And when the Belle Époque brought modernity to the mountains, Switzerland was no longer recognisable. Someone who had died in 1850 would have regarded the Switzerland of 1900 as a foreign country.

Neutrality and Good Offices

Within a relatively short time, the Federal Council and the Swiss Parliament succeeded not only in restructuring domestic affairs but also in outwardly presenting Switzerland as a reliable and consistent partner. The young Federal State's policy of neutrality contributed to this image. Its model for success also included the good offices that the Swiss state was already rendering directly to other countries and in the resolution of international conflicts, as well as services performed by the private sector. The fact that Switzerland became an increasingly sought-after platform for international organisations is evidence of the self-confidence that the young Swiss Federal State had already developed, which was reflected in Swiss foreign policy as well as in the image Switzerland projected abroad.

In this context, the creations of Henry Dunant (1828–1910) should be mentioned: The Red Cross and the ICRC are still a part of Switzerland's DNA today. That a systematic Swiss diplomatic service was almost entirely absent at the time of the founding of the Federal State is a reflection of the aversion that the politicians of 1848 felt towards the notoriously conservative and reactionary ceremonial conduct expected of ambassadors, envoys and ministers on the international stage. A debate that took place in the National Council in 1860 is telling: The opinion was expressed that, bearing in mind its republican constitution and political attitudes, Switzerland should stray as little as possible into the world of diplomacy. Later, however, Switzerland prudently recognised the importance of diplomacy and began to use it as a tool both for its own purposes and in support of other countries. It became a forum for good offices, peace negotiations and courts of arbitration. As early as 1872, the conflict between the United Kingdom and the USA over the Alabama Claims was resolved in Geneva – further evidence of how quickly Switzerland had gained international respect during the second half of the 19th century. The numerous non-governmental organisations that were established in Geneva after the founding of the ICRC solidified this good reputation.

On the Way to Direct Democracy

The direction taken by Switzerland in the middle of the 19th century is striking because, considering the socio-political context, things might have gone rather differently. The year 1848 is remembered in European history as the year of revolution, and yet in Switzerland it marks the beginning of a phase characterised by the rapid creation of new institutions.

In Switzerland, the transition from the revolutionary epoch to the age of capitalism and science took place in paradigmatic fashion. The

Constitution of 1848 created the framework for a rapid socio-political upswing. Its Liberal-Radical creators were seen as equals by revolutionaries all across Europe, and this made Switzerland even more attractive as a place of refuge and a country of exile. But the creators of the young Federal State were not ideological revolutionaries who saw the violent destruction of old institutions as an end in itself. Quite the opposite, in fact: They created new institutions. Road and railway networks were built, production and trade companies founded, hotels and inns constructed, and productive land created through the realignment of watercourses. In the young Federal State, an economically liberal outlook reigned.

Constitutional amendments in individual cantons at the end of the 1860s augured an imminent change; this change was realised when the Federal Constitution of 1874 launched the Switzerland of direct democracy. This Switzerland has remained intact until the present day. But simply speaking of the transition from one constitution to another does not adequately characterise this process of transformation. The change involved much more than a new formulation of certain constitutional articles; it was of a more foundational nature. The Switzerland of the Constitution of 1874 was no longer the Switzerland that had been rung in by the Constitution of 1848. In 1848, the influence of private business on politics was enormous: With the enactment of the Federal Constitution of 1848, Switzerland became an experimental field for business and science – a laboratory of progress. With the 1874 introduction of federal referendums – popular initiatives would follow in 1891 – this phase of economic liberalism reached its definitive end at the national level.

The process initiated by the new Constitution of 1874 led to a fundamental shift in power dynamics: Powers which had been devolved to the authorities of the cantons in the young Federal State were now given over to the federal government; matters previously in the remit of private business were now made the responsibility of the public purse. Hand in hand with this reduction in the importance of the private sector went the diminishment of cantonal authority. This process culminated when, in a state of national emergency, wartime monopolies were established during the First World War. The contrast between this centralised economy under full state oversight and the conditions in the young Federal State could not have been more pronounced. Subsequently, the wartime constraints were loosened, and the monopolies done away with. But the developments affecting the allocation of authority that have occurred in Switzerland since the war have continued to contrast sharply with the conditions of the young Federal State. The Constitution of 1874 set off a process that has persisted until today, increasingly reallocating cantonal authority to the federal government and increasingly shrinking the remit of the private sector in favour of the state. And this development is precisely *not* what the politicians, businessmen and pioneers in the young Federal State had in mind when they made the "Spirit of '48" the guiding light of the first act of the Swiss success story.

Figure 3.4 Auguste Baud-Bovy (1848–1899), *Lioba! Ruf des Berner Oberländer Hirten* (*Lioba! The cry of the Bernese Oberland shepherd*), 1886. Oil on canvas, 130 cm × 98 cm. Acquisition, 1900. Inv. 1058. © Musée cantonal des Beaux-Arts de Lausanne.

Just as the word *Heimweh* (roughly, nostalgia or homesickness) had no adequate translation in any other language, so was the feeling it described long considered a peculiarly Swiss experience. *Heimweh* became a notorious "Swiss illness" that paralysed Swiss mercenary troops. At the end of the 17th century, a medical dissertation coined the neo-Latin word *Nostalgia* to describe this Swiss *Heimweh*, after which the word was also adopted in other languages. The motif of the "Ranz des Vache" or "Kuhreihen," a melody traditionally played on horns as cattle were driven to or from the pasture, was strongly linked to the *Heimweh* of Swiss mercenaries. Hearing it sung was said to induce so strong a *Heimweh* that they would desert. Swiss soldiers serving in the French army were therefore forbidden to sing the "Ranz des Vaches," under penalty of death. This extreme measure has not been verified by legal historians, but this did not stop it from achieving notoriety throughout Europe – not least thanks to Rousseau's intervention in the *Heimweh* discussion. The tragic motive of the good soldier driven by homesickness to desert and then executed for it fell on fertile ground in the contemporary Romantic milieu. Later, the melody of the "Ranz des Vaches" found its way into the European-American opera tradition, and can be found in works by Haydn, Beethoven and Wagner.

The Swiss Miracle

Seen from a geopolitical perspective, the Swiss miracle is that in the second half of the 19th century, 40,000 square kilometres of largely unnavigable terrain and 3 million inhabitants became a global brand denoting machinery, electrical engineering, cheese, chocolate, financial savvy, tourism and humanitarian aid. Swiss turbines equipped the Niagara Falls power plant, and after Swiss watches and textiles came to dominate world markets, the Swiss engineering, electrical engineering, chemical and pharmaceutical industries followed suit. Such a concentration of successful enterprises is unique in all the world.

It is difficult to reflect on the history of Switzerland in the 19th century in its entirety. It is too evidently separated into two parts by the caesura of 1848. At the dawn of the century, Swiss people still found it difficult to open up their towns, regions and cantons to one another. But then, almost overnight, a page was turned. And just as the Swiss railway network sought connections to international lines, so too the desire to open up, inspired by the belief in progress, extended past the Swiss borders. The circles of clients and suppliers expanded rapidly. Family-run hotels were succeeded by the luxury hotel palaces of the Belle Époque, which could only have been built and run by public limited companies. Everything became more anonymous and distant, and yet, simultaneously, the traits attributed to Switzerland became the object of a kind of nostalgia. Even visitors from faraway countries found their way to Switzerland, where the world was still in order.

Yet behind the Swiss miracle were not in fact chalets and cows but rather factories, machinery and train stations, which at times seemed the temples of a new religion. In the second half of the 19th century, the present age was born between Lake Constance, Lake Maggiore and Lake Geneva. Thenceforth, Switzerland would make world history.

Notes

1 Quotes from Alexander von Dusch (envoy from Baden), Friedrich Landolin Karl Freiherr von Blittersdorff (foreign minister of Baden), a spy from Ludwigsburg and Wilhelm I (King of Württemberg) taken from Josef Inauen, *Vom "Schurkenstaat" zur vertrauenswürdigen Republik: Die Beziehungen zwischen Baden, Württemberg und Bayern und der Schweiz im Vormärz 1840–1848 und der Wandel in der Wahrnehmung der Eidgenossenschaft durch die süddeutschen Staaten bis 1871* (PhD diss., University of Freiburg, 2013), 25.

2 Quote from the Bavarian envoy Wilhelm von Doenniges taken from Josef Inauen, *Vom "Schurkenstaat" zur vertrauenswürdigen Republik: Die Beziehungen zwischen Baden, Württemberg und Bayern und der Schweiz im Vormärz 1840–1848 und der Wandel in der Wahrnehmung der Eidgenossenschaft durch die süddeutschen Staaten bis 1871* (PhD diss., University of Freiburg, 2013), 28.

3 "Die Schweiz als Schurkenstaat" (Switzerland as Rogue State) was the title of a seminar that I held during the winter semester of 2006/2007 at the University of Fribourg.

4

> The troops of the Confederation had to guard the armouries and make sure that the Lombard refugees did not carry weapons on Swiss soil. Once when guards attempted to bring escaped internees back into custody in Bellinzona, the masses screamed and ran riot, and they had to let the refugees go free again, in order not to be forced to open fire on the inhabitants of Ticino.

From the notes of Alfred Escher, quoted in Joseph Jung, *Alfred Escher 1819–1882: Der Aufbruch zur modernen Schweiz*, 4 volumes (Zurich: NZZ Libro, 2006), 965.

5 For example, Alfred Escher, who

> at the beginning of his political career still [marched in step] with the Radical movement...He retreated from this ideological position as soon as he had to reconcile diverse interests in his role as Zurich Government Councillor and President of the National Council. Now he pragmatically oriented himself according to circumstances rather than manifestoes, and thus developed from a Radical to an Economic Liberal.

Joseph Jung, *Alfred Escher 1819–1882: Aufstieg, Macht, Tragik*, 6th ed. (Zurich: NZZ Libro, 2017).

6 "Von Dorf-, Grenz- und Tanzlinden," 1 November 2007, *Neue Zürcher Zeitung*, https://www.nzz.ch/von_dorf-_grenz-_und_tanzlinden-1.577629.

7 "It could not, indeed, but excite the attention of any reflecting person, that the manufacturers of Switzerland – almost unobserved, and altogether unprotected, had been gradually, but triumphantly, forcing their way into all the markets of the world, however remote." John Bowring, *Report on the Commerce and Manufacturers of Switzerland: presented to both Houses of Parliament by Command of His Majesty* (London, 1836), 3.

8 The young Federal State signed trade agreements with Piedmont-Sardinia (1851), the USA (1850/1855), Great Britain and Ireland (1855), Belgium (1862), France (1864), Hawaii (1864), Japan (1864), Italy (1868) and Austria-Hungary (1868).

9 The changes in patterns of employment and especially the labour market, which had grown significantly since the first half of the century, led to Switzerland's transformation from a country of emigration to one of immigration. The growing importance of the export economy in the second half of the 19th century has been shown in various contexts throughout this book.

10 "The Spirit of '48: A small group of economically liberal pioneers – I call them the '48ers – made Switzerland what it is today: a major economic power." Joseph Jung, "Projekt Schweiz oder der 'Spirit of '48,'" in *Stolzes Banner am Limmatstrand: Die Geschichte der Akadmischen Verbindung Turicia 1860–2013*, ed. Alt-Turicia Zurich (Zurich, 2014), 27.

11 Quoted from Robert Walser – "in one...[of his]...cryptic feuilletons" after Steffen Richter, "Tunnelblicke: Durchbohrte und ausgehöhlte Berge sind dankbare literarische Motive für kritische wie parodistische Bilder der Schweiz," *Neue Zürcher Zeitung*, 7 April 2012.

12 I have discussed the presence of members of student associations in the Swiss Parliament and the Federal Council in my four-volume biography of Alfred Escher: Joseph Jung, *Alfred Escher 1819–1882: Der Aufbruch zur modernen Schweiz*, 4 volumes (Zurich: NZZ Libro, 2006), 101ff. The discussion that follows is based on these earlier works. Some of the content has been abridged and reworded.

Appendix
Brief Glossary

Act of Mediation (1803) – Act issued by Napoleon putting an end to the Helvetic Republic and returning much of its centralised power to the cantons while keeping Switzerland a vassal state to France.

Cantonal Parliament – The term used in this book for the legislative body of a cantonal government. The individual cantons use a variety of names for this body.

Council of States (1848 to the present) – The chamber of the Swiss Parliament representing the cantons. It is made up of two representatives elected by each canton.

Federal Council (1848 to the present) – The chief executive of the post-1848 Swiss government, comprising seven members elected by the Swiss Parliament (q.v.), with a rotating and purely ceremonial presidency.

Federal Diet (15th century–1848) – The legislative and executive council of the Old Swiss Confederacy. It existed in various forms from the beginnings of Swiss independence until the formation of the Swiss Federal State in 1848.

Government Council – The term used in this book for the chief executive body of a cantonal government. The individual cantons use a variety of names for this body.

Helvetic Republic (1798–1803) – Republic incorporating most of the territory of modern Switzerland, established as a "sister republic" to France after invasion by the French Revolutionary Army in 1798. The Helvetic Republic centralised many powers that had previously been held by the cantons and was deeply resented by much of the population. Swiss resistance led to the dissolution of the Helvetic Republic through the Act of Mediation (q.v.) in 1803.

National Council (1848 to the present) – The chamber of the Swiss Parliament representing the people. It is made up of 200 members elected by the cantons in numbers proportional to their populations.

Old Swiss Confederacy (ca 1300–1848, except for 1798–1803) – The precursor of the modern state of Switzerland, the Old Swiss Confederacy was a loose confederation of independent small states known as cantons. It was initially part of the Holy Roman Empire. It was briefly interrupted when the Helvetic Republic was founded in 1798 after the

French invasion but established again in 1803. It ended in 1848 with the passing of the Federal Constitution.

Sonderbund War (1847) – Civil war pitting Liberal/Radical, generally Protestant Cantons, which favoured economic liberalism (the Confederation), against Conservative and generally Catholic Cantons favouring patrician rule and semi-feudalism (the Sonderbund). The war lasted only three weeks and caused only about 200 deaths, but the decisive victory of the Confederation set the stage for the political and economic restructuring of 1848.

Swiss Federal State (1848 to the present) – The form of government first established by the Constitution of 1848. Authority is divided between the cantons and the federal government, with a clear separation of powers on the US model. From 1848 to 1874, the Swiss Federal State was a *representative democracy*; after 1874 (with the introduction of optional referendums on federal legislation) and further after 1891 (with the introduction of popular initiatives to introduce constitutional changes), Switzerland became a hybrid between a *direct democracy* and a *representative democracy.*

Swiss Parliament (1848 to the present) – The legislative branch of the Swiss government, consisting of the National Council (q.v.) and the Council of States (q.v.).

Bibliography

The bibliography lists a selection of the literature referenced in this work and consulted during its writing. It concentrates on more recent literature. A comprehensive list of more than 800 titles, grouped according to the four main chapters and the concluding chapter of the book, can be found in the German version (Joseph Jung, *Das Laboratorium des Fortschritts: Die Schweiz im 19. Jahrhundert*, 615–645. Basel: NZZ Libro, 2020.)

Series and Lexica

Altermatt, Urs, ed. *Das Bundesratslexikon.* Basel: NZZ Libro, 2019.

Historisches Lexikon der Schweiz, online, accessed 29 October 2019, https://hls-dhs-dss.ch/.

Rucki, Isabelle, and Dorothee Huber, eds. *Architektenlexikon der Schweiz 19./20. Jahrhundert.* Basel: Birkhäuser, 1998.

Schweizer Pioniere der Wirtschaft und Technik. Edited by the Verein für wirtschaftshistorische Studien (Zurich). As of 2020, there are 117 volumes in German, 15 in French and 5 in English. See https://www.pioniere.ch.

Selected Publications in English

Arengo-Jones, Peter. *Queen Victoria in Switzerland.* London: Robert Hale Ltd., 1995.

Breiding, R. James. *Swiss Made: The Untold Story behind Switzerland's Success.* London: Profile Books, 2013.

Conrad-Daubrah, Diane. *Nineteenth-Century British Visitors and Their Church in Pontresina. Personalities, Tradition and Architecture 1860–1900.* Catalogue for the expedition of the same name in Pontresina, December 2016 to October 2017.

Curtis, Ashley. *"O Switzerland!" Travelers' Accounts, 57 BCE to the Present.* Basel: Bergli Books, 2018.

James, Harold, Peter Borscheid, David Gugerli, and Tobias Straumann. *The Value of Risk: Swiss Re and the History of Reinsurance.* Oxford: Oxford University Press, 2013.

Jung, Joseph. *From Schweizerische Kreditanstalt to Credit Suisse Group: The History of a Bank.* Zurich: NZZ Verlag, 2000.

Jung, Joseph. *Winterthur: The History of an Insurance Company.* Zurich: NZZ Verlag, 2000.

Jung, Joseph. *Switzerland's Success Story: The Life and Work of Alfred Escher (1819–1882)*. Zurich: NZZ Libro, 2015.

Seger, Cordula, and Bettina Plattner-Gerber. *Engadin St Moritz: Ein Tal schreibt Geschichten; A Valley with Stories to Tell*. Zurich: AS Verlag, 2016.

Studer, Roman. "When Did the Swiss Get So Rich? Comparing Living Standards in Switzerland and Europe, 1800–1913." *Journal of European Economic History*, vol. 37, no. 2 (2008): 405–452.

Wraight, John. *The Swiss and the British*. Bodmin-Cornwall: M. Russell, 1987.

Selected Publications in German

Altermatt, Urs. *Vom Unruheherd zur stabilen Republik: Der schweizerische Bundesrat 1848–1875*. Basel: NZZ Libro, 2020.

Anker, Daniel, ed., Helvetia Club: 150 Jahre Schweizer Alpen-Club SAC (Bern: SAC, 2013), 74. Published for the exhibition "Helvetia Club: Die Schweiz, die Berge und der Schweizer Alpen-Club," at the Alpines Museum in Bern, 20 April–30 March 2014.

Baltensperger, Ernst. *Der Schweizer Franken: Eine Erfolgsgeschichte; Die Währung der Schweiz im 19. und 20. Jahrhundert*. Zurich: NZZ Libro, 2012.

Bärtschi, Hans-Peter. "Industrialisierung, Eisenbahnschlachten und Städtebau: Die Entwicklung des Zürcher Industrie- und Arbeiterstadtteils Aussersihl; Ein vergleichender Beitrag zur Architektur- und Technikgeschichte." Doctoral thesis, ETH Zurich, 1980.

Bätzing, Werner. *Die Alpen: Geschichte und Zukunft einer europäischen Kulturlandschaft*. 2nd rev. ed. Munich: C.H. Beck, 2003.

Bergier, Jean-François. *Wirtschaftsgeschichte der Schweiz: Von den Anfängen bis zur Gegenwart*. Zurich: Benziger: 1990.

Betschon, Franz, Stefan Betschon, Jürg Dominik Lindecker, and Willy Schlachter, eds. *Ingenieure bauen die Schweiz: Technikgeschichte aus erster Hand*. Vol. 1. 2nd ed. Zurich: NZZ Libro, 2014.

Betschon, Franz, Stefan Betschon, and Willy Schlachter, eds. *Ingenieure bauen die Schweiz: Technikgeschichte aus erster Hand*. Vol. 2. Zurich: NZZ Libro, 2014.

Bodmer, Walter. *Schweizerische Industrie- Geschichte*. Zurich: Verlag Berichthaus, 1960.

Bohlhalter, Bruno. *Unruh: Die schweizerische Uhrenindustrie und ihre Krisen im 20. Jahrhundert*. Zurich: NZZ Libro, 2016.

Breiding, R. James, and Gerhard Schwarz. *Wirtschaftswunder Schweiz: Ursprung und Zukunft eines Erfolgsmodells*. 2nd ed. Zurich: NZZ Libro, 2011.

Caminada, Paul. *Pioniere der Alpentopografie: Die Geschichte der Schweizer Kartenkunst*. Zurich: AS Verlag, 2003.

Conrad-Daubrah, Diane. *Johannes Badrutt (1819–1889): Ich habe den schlauen Moment benutzt – Ich wagte und es gelang*. St. Moritz: Self-published, 2009.

Creux, René, and Louis Gaulis. *Schweizer Pioniere der Hotellerie*. Foreword by Werner Kämpfen. Translated by Herbert Meier. Paudex: Ed. de Fontainemore/Schweizerische Verkehrszentrale, 1976.

Dejung, Christof. *Die Fäden des globalen Marktes: Eine Sozial- und Kulturgeschichte des Welthandels am Beispiel der Handelsfirma Gebrüder Volkart 1851–1999*. Vol. 85 of *Industrielle Welt*: *Schriftenreihe des Arbeitskreises für moderne Sozialgeschichte*, edited by Andreas Eckert and Joachim Rückert. Vienna: Böhlau Verlag, 2013.

Erhart, Alfred. *Zur Entwicklung der schweizerischen Seeschiffahrt 1848–1941.* Siegen: Vorländer, 1950.

Flückiger-Seiler, Roland. *Hotelpaläste: Zwischen Traum und Wirklichkeit; Schweizer Tourismus und Hotelbau 1830–1920.* 2nd ed. Zurich: Hier und Jetzt, 2005.

Flückiger-Seiler, Roland. *Hotelträume: Zwischen Gletschern und Palmen; Schweizer Tourismus und Hotelbau 1830–1920.* 2nd ed. Zurich: Hier und Jetzt, 2005.

Halbeisen, Patrick, Margrit Müller, and Béatrice Veyrassat, eds. *Wirtschaftsgeschichte der Schweiz im 20. Jahrhundert.* Basel: Schwabe, 2012.

Haller, Lea. *Transithandel: Geld- und Warenströme im globalen Kapitalismus.* Berlin: Suhrkamp, 2019.

Holenstein, Rolf. *Ochsenbein: Erfinder der modernen Schweiz.* Basel: Echtzeit, 2009.

James, Harold, ed. *Swiss Re und die Welt der Risikomärkte: Eine Geschichte.* With contributions by Peter Borscheid, David Gugerli, and Tobias Straumann. Munich: C.H. Beck, 2014.

Jung, Joseph. See next section.

Kley, Andreas. *Verfassungsgeschichte der Neuzeit: Grossbritannien, die USA, Frankreich, Deutschland und die Schweiz.* Bern: Stämpfli Verlag, 2008.

Kopf, Martina. *Alpinismus – Andinismus: Gebirgslandschaften in europäischer und lateinamerikanischer Literatur.* Stuttgart: Springer, 2016.

Kunsthaus Zürich, ed. *Von Anker bis Zünd: Die Kunst im jungen Bundesstaat 1848–1900.* Zurich: Scheidegger & Spiess AG Verlag, 1998.

Lütscher, Michael. *Schnee, Sonne und Stars.* Zurich: NZZ Libro, 2014.

Mathieu, Jon. *Die Alpen: Raum – Kultur – Geschichte.* Stuttgart: Reclam, 2015.

Mathieu, Jon, Eva Bachmann, and Ursula Butz. *Majestätische Berge: Die Monarchie auf dem Weg in die Alpen 1760–1910.* Baden: Hier und Jetzt, 2018.

Piatti, Barbara. *Von Casanova bis Churchill: Berühmte Reisende auf ihrem Weg durch die Schweiz.* Baden: Hier und Jetzt, 2016.

Rucki, Isabelle. *Das Hotel in den Alpen: Die Geschichte der Oberengadiner Hotelarchi- tektur von 1860 bis 1914.* Zurich: Institut für Geschichte und Theorie der Architektur, ETH Zurich, 1989.

Sauthier, Géraldine. *Pouvoir local et Tourisme: Jeux politiques à Finhaut, Montreux et Zer- matt de 1850 à nos jours.* Neuchâtel: Edition Alphil, 2016.

Schiedt, Hans-Ulrich, Laurent Tissot, Christoph Maria Merki, and Rainer C. Schwinges, eds. *Verkehrsgeschichte: Schweizerische Gesellschaft für Wirtschafts- und Sozialgeschichte*, vol. 25. Zurich: Chronos Verlag, 2010.

Schild, Heinz. *Visionäre Bahnprojekte: Die Schweiz im Aufbruch 1870–1939.* Zurich: AS Verlag, 2013.

Siegenthaler, Hansjörg. "Warum ist die Schweiz reich geworden?" *NZZ Geschichte*, vol. 22 (May 2019): 25–38.

Somm, Markus. *Elektropolis an der Limmat: Baden und die BBC, 1870 bis 1925; Die Beschreibung einer Transformation.* Bern: Stämpfli Verlag, 2019.

Stalder, Helmut. *Verkannte Visionäre: 24 Schweizer Lebensgeschichten.* Zurich: NZZ Libro, 2011.

Stalder, Helmut. *Gotthard: Der Pass und sein Mythos.* Zurich: Orell Füssli, 2016.

Works by Joseph Jung

In its presentation of a number of topics, the present work draws heavily on books, studies, papers and essays that I have published over the course of many years. The relevant passages from these earlier works have been reworded, and their content has been expanded on. Such passages are indicated in the notes. The works to which I make reference in this context are the following:

Jung, Joseph. "16-Stunden-Tag, keine Ferien: Das protestantische Arbeitsethos von Alfred Escher." *NZZ Geschichte*, no. 3 (2015): 32f.

Jung, Joseph. "Vom Wehen des Zeitgeistes: Alfred Escher und die Maximen der schweizerischen Aussenpolitik." Exhibition catalogue, Galerie "le point," 62ff. Zurich, 1994.

Jung, Joseph. "'In labore virtus et vita': Ulrico Hoepli 1847–1935." In *...am literarischen Webstuhl...": Ulrico Hoepli 1847–1935; Buchhändler, Verleger, Antiquar, Mäzen*, edited by Joseph Jung, 17–73. Zurich: NZZ Verlag, 1997.

Jung, Joseph. *Das imaginäre Museum: Privates Kunstengagement und staatliche Kulturpolitik in der Schweiz; Die Gottfried Keller-Stiftung 1890–1922*. Zurich: NZZ Verlag, 1998.

Jung, Joseph. *Die Winterthur: Eine Versicherungsgeschichte*. Zurich: NZZ Verlag, 2000.

Jung, Joseph. *Von der Schweizerischen Kreditanstalt zur Credit Suisse Group: Eine Bankengeschichte*. Zurich: NZZ Verlag, 2000.

Jung, Joseph. *Der Bockenkrieg 1804: Aspekte eines Volksaufstandes*. Zurich: NZZ Verlag, 2004.

Jung, Joseph. *Alfred Escher 1819–1882: Der Aufbruch zur modernen Schweiz*. 4 vols. Zurich: NZZ Libro, 2006.

Jung, Joseph. "Das wirtschaftsliberale Zeitfenster des jungen Bundesstaates." In *Alfred Eschers Briefwechsel 1852–1866: Wirtschaftsliberales Zeitfenster, Gründungen, Aussenpolitik*, edited by Joseph Jung, 7–26. Zurich: NZZ Libro, 2013.

Jung, Joseph, ed. *Schweizer Erfolgsgeschichten: Pioniere, Unternehmen, Innovationen*, with contributions from Bruno Bohlhalter, Hans Bollmann, David Bosshart et al., vol. 100 (anniversary edition) of *Schweizer Pioniere der Wirtschaft und Technik*, edited by the Verein für wirtschaftshistorische Studien. Zurich, 2013.

Jung, Joseph. "Schweizer Revolutionär: Alfred Eschers Einfluss auf die moderne Schweiz." *Schweizer Monat*, vol. 1011 (Oktober 2013): 47–50.

Jung, Joseph. "Projekt Schweiz oder der 'Spirit of 48': Abdruck der Festrede am Festakt zum 150-Jahr-Jubiläum der Akademischen Verbindung Turicia vom 22. Mai 2010 im Kongresshaus Zürich." In *Stolzes Banner am Limmatstrand: Die Geschichte der Akademischen Verbindung Turicia 1860–2013*, edited by Alt-Turicia Zürich, 15–30. Zurich: Alt-Turicia 2014.

Jung, Joseph. "Zürichs Herrscher und der Asylant: Alfred Escher und Richard Wagner," special edition printed in honour of the Zurich "Festspielen" 2013, reprinted in *Mitteilungen der Gottfried Keller-Gesellschaft*, 38–43. Zurich: NZZ Libro, 2014.

Jung, Joseph. "'Der Prinzeps und sein Hof' oder wie die liberale Herrschaft in Zürich unterging." In *Alfred Eschers Briefwechsel 1866–1882: Private Eisenbahngesellschaften in der Krise, Gotthardbahn politische Opposition*, edited by Joseph Jung, 12–21. Zurich: NZZ Libro, 2015.

Jung, Joseph. "Die Finanzierung der Gotthardbahn: Alfred Eschers Meisterstück." In *Alfred Eschers Briefwechsel 1866–1882: Private Eisenbahngesellschaften in der Krise, Gotthardbahn, politische Opposition*, edited by Joseph Jung, 214–225. Zurich: NZZ Libro, 2015.

Jung, Joseph. "'Ein Meer von Schwierigkeiten war zu überwinden': Das Gotthardbahn-projekt in der Escher-Korrespondenz." In *Alfred Eschers Briefwechsel 1866–1882: Private Eisenbahngesellschaften in der Krise, Gotthardbahn, politische Opposition*, edited by Joseph Jung, 72–81. Zurich: NZZ Libro, 2015.

Jung, Joseph. "Friedrich Lochers Pamphlete 'Die Freiherren von Regensberg' und das liberale System Alfred Eschers." In *Alfred Eschers Briefwechsel 1866–1882: Private Eisenbahngesellschaften in der Krise, Gotthardbahn, politische Opposition*, edited by Joseph Jung, 190–213. Zurich: NZZ Libro, 2015.

Jung, Joseph. "Weltgeschichtliche Grösse in einer Zeit der grössten Konfrontation: Alfred Escher im Herbst des Lebens." In *Alfred Eschers Briefwechsel 1866–1882: Private Eisenbahngesellschaften in der Krise, Gotthardbahn, politische Opposition*, edited by Joseph Jung, 9–10. Zurich: NZZ Libro, 2015.

Jung Joseph, ed. *Im weltweiten Einsatz für Humanität: Cornelio Sommaruga, Präsident des IKRK 1987–1999: Reden und Vorträge*, with a foreword by Dick Marty and contributions from Bernhard Altermatt. Zurich: NZZ Libro, 2016.

Jung, Joseph. *Lydia Welti-Escher 1858–1891*. 5th ed. With a foreword by Hildegard Elisabeth Keller. Zurich: NZZ Libro, 2016.

Jung, Joseph. *Alfred Escher 1819–1882: Aufstieg, Macht, Tragik*. 6th ed. Zurich: NZZ Libro, 2017.

Jung, Joseph. *Hans Künzi: Operations Research und Verkehrspolitik*. Zurich: NZZ Libro 2017.

Jung, Joseph. "Der Aufstieg der Schweiz hat einen Namen." *Neue Zürcher Zeitung*, 23 February 2019.

Index of Places

Note: *Italic* page numbers refer to figures and page numbers followed by "n" denote endnotes.

Index of Persons

Note: *Italic* page numbers refer to figures and page numbers followed by "n" denote endnotes.

www.ingramcontent.com/pod-product-compliance
Ingram Content Group UK Ltd.
Pitfield, Milton Keynes, MK11 3LW, UK
UKHW020132200926
475702UK00005B/719
9781032152271